Architectural Design Portable Handbook

Architectural Design Portable Handbook

A Guide to Excellent Practices

Andy Pressman, NCARB, AIA

McGRAW-HILL

New York   Chicago   San Francisco   Lisbon
London   Madrid   Mexico City   Milan   New Delhi
San Juan   Seoul   Singapore   Sydney   Toronto

Also by Andy Pressman

- ■ *Professional Practice 101: A Compendium of Business and Management Strategies in Architecture*
- ■ *The Fountainheadache: The Politics of Architect-Client Relations*
- ■ *Architecture 101: A Guide to the Design Studio*
- ■ *Integrated Space Systems: Vocabulary for Room Language*

Cataloging-in-Publication Data is on file with the Library of Congress.

McGraw-Hill

A Division of The McGraw-Hill Companies

"Peer Review," "Competitions," and "Marginalization" courtesy of *Architectural Record* and the McGraw-Hill Companies.

1 2 3 4 5 6 7 8 9 0 • DOC/DOC 0 9 8 7 6 5 4 3 2 1
ISBN 0-07-135214-7

The sponsoring editor for this book was Wendy Lochner.
R.R. Donnelley & Sons Company was printer and binder.

This book is printed on acid-free paper.

McGraw-Hill books are available at special quantity discounts to use as premiums and sales promotions, or for use in corporate training programs. For more information, please write to the Director of Special Sales, McGraw-Hill, Two Penn Plaza, New York, NY 10121-2298. Or contact your local bookstore.

To Jacob Pressman, who is a constant reminder to view the world with fresh and positive perspective, humor, intelligence, and above all, playfulness, joy, and wonder.

Contents

The Place of People in Architectural Design: With Gerald
Weisman / 158

3 The Site 171

4 Architectural Design 243

5 Presentations 413

6 Lifelong Learning 463

7 The Future: A Manifesto 527

foreword

❏ This is a guide to the uniquely provocative and often idiosyncratic process of creating meaningful architectural form. So deep is the mystique of the architectural design process that few have had the courage or insight to write about it. A feeling persists among many in the profession that design is an almost magical pursuit that defies analysis or rational discussion. But every architect, from those whose work adorns the magazines each month to those who only read the magazines, can become better at design, and this is what Andy Pressman, through this book, sets out to help us do.

Pressman identifies and explains the core issues of design, all the while keeping an eye on the elements of delight and mystery that make the design process so fascinating to those of us who engage in it. He maintains a sharp focus on the magical aspects of design, revealing their secrets to us so that we may become better designers. He tells us how to keep our minds free and open as we work. He helps us to realize our full potential as designers.

This is a book to be read slowly, a few pages at a time, so as to absorb its lessons as completely as possible. It is a book to be read again and again, a book whose pages will gradually become dog-eared and graphite-smudged, a comforting companion for the times when a design concept refuses to emerge as well as the times when we experience the euphoria of developing a brilliant scheme. For the seasoned practitioner, it will refresh the imagination, provide outstanding new tools for design, and resharpen existing tools. For the novice, it will furnish the elements of a personal design method, extend the range of the imagination, and help to develop mental flexibility. For readers of all levels of experience, it will put temporary troubles in perspective and assist in recalling the worthy dream with which we all began, that of designing wonderful, endlessly fascinating buildings.

Wisely, Andy Pressman has not attempted this task alone. Dozens of architects and educators, through essays and interviews, have contributed valuable insights into their particular specialties and their design experience in general. Despite the diversity of their backgrounds and opinions, there is an impressive unanimity regarding the underlying principles of successful process and outcome. In this respect especially, this is an authoritative volume. You can believe what it tells you. Keep it by your side. Read it well and understand it. It will enrich your practice and contribute to your continuing professional development.

The act of architectural design is miraculous. Reviewing in my mind my own experiences as a young intern working with superb designers, as an independent architect, and as a studio teacher, I marvel at its audacity and power. The ability to design things well is a gift of inestimable value. The words on these pages celebrate this gift and enhance its worth.

Edward Allen
South Natick, Massachusetts
January 2001

preface

❏ *Architectural Design Portable Handbook* is primarily intended to assist professionals in creating excellent designs, particularly in the early phases of projects. This highly focused tool offers explicit guidance on how to view, attack, or accomplish specific tasks to facilitate optimal design solutions.

The book also promotes critical reflection about the meaning of architecture beyond function and budget—although those issues are carefully analyzed as well; theoretical and practical concerns are intertwined. This is achieved without excessive ideological narrowness or zeal, so that practitioners (and advanced students) with diverse backgrounds and degrees of experience will embrace the book and benefit more fully from its use.

As with any of the great professions, valuable continuing education in architectural design must rest upon a foundation of specialized knowledge, acquisition of focused skills, systematic development of talent, and practice. *Architectural Design Portable Handbook* should augment this foundation and at least serve to bridge the various components involved in making sense of ongoing progress in architecture.

Approaches to various aspects of the design process are illuminated in supplements contributed by nationally recognized academicians and practitioners in their respective areas of expertise. The collective effort provides capsules of wisdom and enlivens the text with energy, pragmatism, and idealism. The result is a rich and varied mixture of inspirational, provocative, and at times even contradictory statements—all geared toward infusing a creative spirit within the controversial realm of meaningful design. I have specifically solicited, linked, and interpreted the material with a single voice and perspective in what I consider a rational conception of practicing architecture.

Topic coverage is tailored to the needs of working architects. Practitioners will find the bulleted summary lists and blank sketch pages—a sort of personal sketchbook on steroids—especially helpful when thinking about projects on an airplane, in the office, or while waiting for a client.

Key elements include:

- Critical thinking in architectural design
- Influence of the vernacular
- Orchestrating client involvement
- Architecture and sustainability
- Examples of site influences on design
- Aesthetic issues, organizing elements, and brainstorming tips
- Daylighting
- Building codes and universal design
- Computing, drawing, and physical modeling
- Structures, mechanical systems, lighting, and acoustics
- Materials, tectonics, construction, and systems integration
- Conceptual design cost estimating
- Presentations and engaging the client
- Time management
- Professional development, internship, and the Architect Registration Examination (ARE)
- Demarginalizing practice, ethics, and awards

Finally, I hope *Architectural Design Portable Handbook* suggests something about the impact of our profession. Our collective professional morale and our very passion for the work of architecture have likely suffered in recent times. With ever increasing economic pressures, together with the seemingly ever present confusion about what architecture is or should be, it is clear to me that recognition and discussion of genuine architectural achievement can only be positive. At its grandest, architecture (and architects) can have enduring effects on society. At its most mundane, architecture can have an influence on the quality of a day—and, to paraphrase Thoreau, that may be the highest of arts. I trust that this book has marshaled sufficient evidence to support these assertions and remind us of the really noble possibilities intrinsic to the profession.

In sum, *Architectural Design Portable Handbook* attempts to unravel some of the mystery of creating the most beautiful, responsive, and responsible architectural design possible.

Andy Pressman
Albuquerque, New Mexico
January 2001

acknowledgments

- Wendy Lochner, Edward Allen, and Norman Rosenfeld, for recognizing the value of the undertaking.
- Amanda Miller, for unconditional support.
- Iris Slikerman, Aldo Coppelli, and Bob Deschamps, for graphic wisdom and insight.
- Marlene Stutzman, for keen editorial advice and guidance.
- Peter Pressman and Eleanor Pressman, as always.
- The many contributors to this book, who, over a long period of time or just recently, have helped shape my constantly evolving views about architectural design. I'm especially grateful to this gifted, unique, and generous group of individuals, whose expertise dramatically enriches the content herein.

chapter 1

Inspiration

"*A journey of a
thousand miles must
begin with
a single step.*"
—*Lao-tzu*

Sketches

❏ This initial chapter must begin with a general caveat regarding the presentation of material throughout the book. At first glance, the contents may seem to advocate a linear approach to the design process. My interview with Antoine Predock indicates explicitly why nothing could be further from the truth. The linearity inherent in the format of this text may be viewed as a necessary evil; it makes it possible to discuss an ambitious volume of material with some semblance of rationality, organization, and clarity. However, the very essence of this book lies in a departure from algorithms, easy solutions, and a business-centered culture. At its most idealistic, perhaps this work will help to rekindle the creative fire and the will to be excellent.

A note on the patchwork style and content of the contributions: because design is such a daunting and elusive concept, I have approached it with a shotgun and without apology. Some may say that a unitary and even dogmatic approach is the most illuminating, and I appreciate this line of reasoning. I also disagree with it. I believe that in trying to make practical sense out of such a difficult and multifaceted subject, one should examine it from as many angles and in as many varied lights as possible. Hence, I've tried to recruit as many specialists and stars who express themselves in as many different ways as I could find. I then tried to weave their input together with mine and place the result into some accessible, valuable, and I hope generally entertaining fabric. I expect you will find some collective wisdom and even synergy that may be of real value in your practice of architecture.

Kevin Lynch has written that "Design is not restricted to genius, or separate from practicality, or a sudden revelation. Fine places develop out of an intimate understanding of form possibility, which has been gained by constantly reframing the problem, by repeatedly searching for solutions." This book endeavors to cultivate understandings of form possibilities.

Architectural design is a blend of good science and genuine art. The way the blending occurs to produce a wonderful building is tempered by intelligence, experience, and sensibility. If there is an algorithm, it is based on a background of standardized knowledge, discipline, and accepted method, and then the talent kicks in. The *Architectural Design Portable Handbook* will at least shore up the background components and allude to ways in which method and data can be titrated with talent.

This chapter focuses on inspiration and how to amplify talent or that which drives creativity and innovative thinking. This includes curiosity, playfulness, spontaneity, appetite, and a capacity to see—to observe things, people, and behavior in full color and at high resolution. Going against the grain, embracing the unknown, or looking at life in a manner different than that of the majority is crucial.

Later in this chapter, I elaborate on the mechanisms of peer review and self-criticism to elevate the quality of preliminary designs. Christopher Mead discusses the role of critical thinking in architectural design. Jean Pike demonstrates how the act of drawing allows us to reconnect with the physical world and work with what is revealed in personal ways. Chris Wilson writes about how to "search for solutions" through an analysis of the vernacular. Roger Lewis talks about both the appropriate use and the pitfalls of architectural precedents. Melissa Harris's comparison of bread baking to designing is pure poetry: take pleasure in the doing and see each step along the way as a creation in and of itself. The chapter concludes with a section on time management, so that all this reflection and thinking about design quality doesn't diminish those billable hours.

What is Good Design

?

The Goose Bump Factor

A Conversation with Antoine Predock

A major component of the "magical" experience of many of Antoine Predock's buildings is derived from his rigorous and very deep understanding of site and place. Place becomes driver for determining form, materials, spatial qualities, and meaning. (Refer also to Chris Wilson's Supplement 1.3, later in this chapter, for specific ways to translate this notion to physical design. Also, Chapter 3 is dedicated to site and context issues and their influence on form making.)

Andy Pressman: *I'm asking a number of people to define good design. My hope is that the diversity of definitions and accompanying images that embody those definitions will inspire readers. Why do you think this is such a challenging question?*

Antoine Predock: I don't think of my work as purely design work. You could take a motorcycle and talk about good design, for example. But to talk about it in relation to my work is difficult since doing architecture, to me, doesn't feel like a design process. Projects coalesce both from rigorous research and pure intuition, at all stages.

Pressman: *So you can't really quantify the process. What about the outcome? What is your perception about some of your successful and beautiful buildings?*

Predock: I think the best ones embody spirit. Then we get into realms that are difficult to articulate; of not only responses by people who use or see the buildings, but in discussing it with you. There is an emanation from the best work; it's hard to analyze and say, "Hey—I like that design

What is Good Design?

because it has certain proportional relationships, or it has a compositional imperative." There is something else that's more mysterious—I'm sure you've felt it—you get goose bumps every now and then from certain buildings. This is the outcome I hope for, but can't always predict.

Pressman: *Hugh Jacobson calls that the "Jesus Christ phenomenon." When you walk into a space that knocks your socks off, you say, "Jesus Christ."*

Predock: That's exactly what I'm talking about. It's a subjective area. I think my best buildings possess that quality. For example, during a special function for Arizona State University, a woman came up to me and said, "Oh, you're the architect who designed the Nelson Fine Arts Center at ASU [see Fig. 1.1]. I just want to tell you that when I enter

FIGURE 1.1
Nelson Fine Arts Center at Arizona State University. (Courtesy of
Antoine Predock Architect.)

the place, something happens to me, but I can't quite explain it."

To me, that's the essence of architecture. When the character of space moves someone, outside the analytic discussion of design work, or sustainability, or the myriad other elements that can be articulated and quantified, that's architecture. It's a real mystery to me.

Pressman: *This mysterious quality is one that elicits emotion—would you say that's accurate?*

Predock: Yes; there is an emotional response. Concurrent with that response, however, there can also be a clinical or rational take on a building. I'm not suggesting that one precludes the other at all. For example, in much of [Louis I.] Kahn's work, there's absolutely a goose bump factor—whatever you call it—and simultaneously there's an order, a highly rational order that is operative. A mistake for students or others is that sometimes there is an assumption that the aura can be generated from order, almost by willing it. I don't think it works that way; process and outcome are much more mysterious.

Pressman: *That aligns with my feelings about teaching design—you can't. You can set forth some of the ingredients to facilitate good design, but it's impossible to really teach it. I enjoy your phrase, "the goose bump factor." It's an accurate description of the excitement of being in great architecture.*

Predock: It leaves us with a difficult discussion because the experience is in the eyes and feelings of the beholder. Some buildings move people, some don't. The discussion that is not so difficult relates to content and meaning. For me, content and meaning in architecture arise from a deep sense of belonging somewhere. Attaining that sense

What is Good Design ?

involves pinpointing the spirit of a place and empathizing with it, and then developing architectural responses to that unique spirit.

Pressman: *Much of your process, then, relies on something you said in an interview a long time ago: you've got to put your butt on the site and hang out for nine months or more.*

Predock: Either physically or metaphysically, one way or the other. It's hard to do that working all over the country as much as I do. But that is the point. It's okay for an older guy like me to talk like this. When I was younger and fishing around, credibility was an issue because this is a subjective area. I hope I've built examples of how this works. I think there are buildings that do have some of these qualities. But for a student to say, "I just put my butt on the site and kind of felt it, and here it is"—sometimes it wouldn't be appropriate.

Pressman: *From whom are you trying to elicit this emotional reaction to your buildings? Is it a typical user? Other architects?*

Predock: Anybody. Above all, the users, sure.

Pressman: *So it's accessible to everyone.*

Predock: Yes, I don't think there is a secret code; the message should be totally accessible, the way great buildings through time move the layperson. In terms of usage change through time, the Pantheon is a classic example. Who isn't moved by that building? People keep coming back for more. You can call it a church, or pagan temple, or tourist crossroads—doesn't matter. It just has that "stuff." You can perhaps dissect it compositionally and examine the oculus and the way light is admitted, the proportional relationships, and so on, but that falls short. There is another kind of aura about it.

It is the totality; how it all works together. This is precisely why I felt your motivating question, "what is good design?" is so elusive to answer, and even define. Just repeating it here doesn't do justice to its true meaning, and any attempt to respond will never approach its awesome promise.

You can say, however, that a great building not only has qualities that move you, but has the capacity to enrich by experiencing many journeys through it: rational journeys of the intellect, choreographic journeys that are very physical, journeys that have to do with the unknown—the unexpected spatial possibilities that surprise and arrest you. Then there is the realm of light as animator that shapes and conditions these journeys. So, you may begin to inventory the elements.

Pressman: *The problem with inventorying the elements is that it suggests a linear path, which of course, it's not.*

Predock: That's true, it's not. It's anything but. This point is one disturbing component of criticism and analysis. Sometimes, for the sake or convenience of rational discourse, thinking tends to become linear. It's a kind of trap and possibly misleading to the potential viewer or one who would experience the building. By establishing a linear discourse, sometimes a priority is implied because the discourse is linear—what you talk about first, and how the discourse evolves.

Pressman: *What you're saying is that it's impossible to write about buildings. Essentially, you must experience them.*

Predock: Yes, but I sure like to read about them. I'm not suggesting critics should be out of work. It's quite important to convey, critique, and analyze one's impressions, just as a poet does.

What is Good Design?

Pressman: *Do you rely on self-criticism in your own work?*

Predock: It's built into the process. I'm highly critical—applying it to myself and to my own work at all times. It's not like I just design the thing and come back and say, "Oh, okay, how is it?" There seems to be a simultaneity of critical thought along with the process of making something.

Pressman: *In terms of creating the magical qualities, all of your ideas, including a good dose of intuition, inform the process. Are you constantly aware that every move you make should have some sort of dramatic impact?*

Predock: Every move should have palpable consequences that one can sum up to make the whole building. Drama may be a by-product, but it is not the point.

Pressman: *Most architects are pretty good at solving the functional issues, so the search . . .*

Predock: Right away, I don't think you can do that and say it's good design. As you suggest, anybody ought to be able to do it—come very close to solving that stuff.

Pressman: *It's necessary but not sufficient.*

Predock: That's right.

Pressman: *So the thing to be constantly searching for in the process is something that is rather elusive to define.*

Predock: Architects must transcend the program somehow. Honor it, but at the same time transcend it.

Pressman: *And look to place for inspiration.*

Predock: Absolutely! In one area, anyway—for me, a big area.

Pressman: *What are the other areas?*

Predock: "Place" is the physicality of place—from primordial memory through today. All that to absorb. Then there is the conceptual place; there's cultural place. They all add up. I think it's the architect's, the poet's job to reinvent place, too. Not just to accept it as it is and say, "Oh yeah, I'm going to interpret it." It is our job, our responsibility to draw out unknown qualities, perhaps those that form the essence of the place that formerly may not have been understood in the most complete way.

Pressman: *That's one means to arrive at some of the special, magical qualities.*

Predock: I just watched pieces of the PBS series on New York. They kept going to Walt Whitman. And here's Walt Whitman's poetry amidst a lot of people trying to describe the place—and Walt Whitman nails it. His New York. You read it now and it's as fresh today as it was then. His understanding of its aura, and his ability to articulate it with passion and understanding, is remarkable.

Pressman: *And you do that through analysis of place and living the place. Do you feel that program is relatively insignificant in all of this discussion?*

Predock: Absolutely not. It gets everything going. It's the gasoline. It can make remarkable things happen. In some circles it's fashionable to dismiss program and say, "Okay, there's something else that we're dealing with here, and it's not program." But it is—to the extent that the program itself can be seen as inclusive of the intangible as well as the quantifiable stuff that programs normally represent.

When I work on the programming phase of a building, I'm in there. It isn't just about square footages and relationships and bubble diagrams, it's about intangibles paralleling those kinds of things. I insist that my clients fantasize and dream in the programming phase, just as much as when the evolutionary process of making a building is happening.

Pressman: *You rarely accept programs at face value, then.*

Predock: It's important to always question them and thereby extend the journey.

What Is Good Design?

❏ The following definitions and images by design stars are intended to provoke dialogue and thinking that underlies good design. While reading, see how these views align with your own—and if not, why not. Can some of them begin to suggest a rationale or framework to enhance practice?

Will Bruder

❏ Good design:

- Combines beauty and function as it balances the pragmatic and poetic

FIGURE 1.2
Courtesy of Will Bruder (© Will Bruder, 2000).

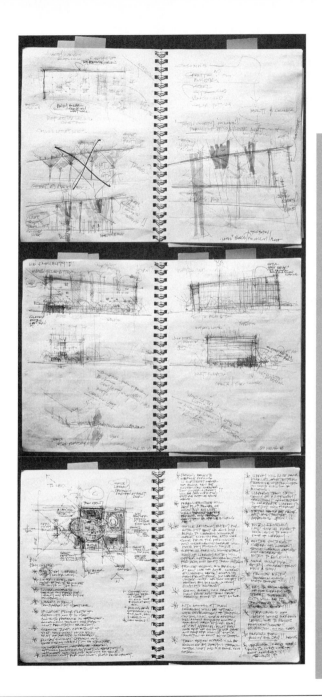

What is Good Design ?

- Makes the ordinary seem extraordinary
- Happens because of and not in spite of the problem
- Complements its context while challenging it
- Strives to be of its time while aspiring to be timeless
- Celebrates the craft of making while choreographing the magic of materials
- Seeks ideas that transcend the rules
- Embraces the sensual and the intellectual
- At its best, becomes one way a culture is measured

(See Fig. 1.2.)

Jonathan Siegel

❏ Good design is a fugue: multiple intertwined themes playing simultaneously. I am asked before we begin: is site most important? What about the client? The budget? Climate? Modernity and statement? We address ourselves wholeheartedly to each of these, first in turn, then more intuitively as the design begins to move on multiple fronts at once. The best projects, no doubt, come from an environment of trust between architect and client. Time is permitted: the first ingredient critical to a healthy relationship and process. The architect is allowed to ruminate—to risk, to wander, to dream—to fail for the moment in pursuit of an unknown end. Form is delayed in our process while the underlying forces swirl and develop from our unconscious and the client's. Goals temporarily become less articulate during the process. Space develops early; as a form is being born, I first think of the volume as much as the plan. Materials begin to speak for themselves; the goals tentatively coalesce, then are rubbed, pushed, and pulled. Basic systems are intrinsically part of the design: ducts and drains are as much a part of a wholesome design as bones and veins and organs are in a living vertebrate animal. Whimsy and humor are important ingredients in my own life, and find their places in a design as well. I hope the result looks natural and effortless: though it emerges with a groan and a great deal of thought, the whole is best when it seems authorless, obvious, just right.

Examining the design process is like seeing a mirage in the road in front of you—or looking for and naming that color behind your eyeball, beyond your cone of vision—you keep looking and it keeps vanishing in front of you; the very act of examining it makes it evaporate. The architect finally leaves; the client is left with the constructed end; the fugue dies away—the intertwining is ultimately more important than any single strand. (See Fig. 1.3.)

FIGURE 1.3
Courtesy of Jonathan Siegel.

What is Good Design?

Bart Prince

❏ For me, good design will only result from a creative and original response to the design problem. It should not be

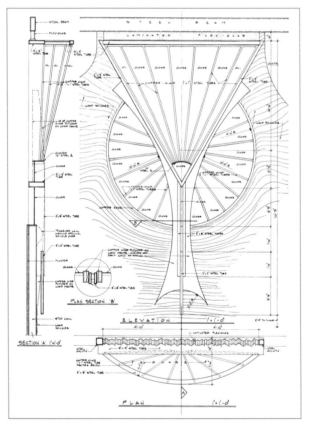

FIGURE 1.4
Courtesy of Bart Prince.

founded in precedent as a preconception applied from with-out, but should grow from an internal understanding FROM WITHIN of the essence of the problem to be solved. An infinite number of beautiful and unusual designs are thus possible. (See Fig. 1.4.)

John Klee

❑ Skillful design embodies contrasting elements, a certain spirit, mystery, and boldness. An artistic coalescence of color and form, it unfolds in such a way that it is enticing and intriguing. Then there is balance, which is related to the proportion of volume and mass, which is in turn inti-mately associated with the quality of strength. The results—

FIGURE 1.5
Courtesy of John Klee.

What is Good Design?

the final coalescence, if you will—exemplify a unified building that is both distinct as well as anchored to its site and is in genuine harmony with its surroundings. (See Fig. 1.5.)

Duo Dickinson

❏ The word *good* in good design is a loaded one. In house design (where my heart is), good design needs to do two things—and these things are frequently not done by our profession. First, since a house is a homeowner's largest set of clothes, ignoring the client is not good. Second, contrary to what is often found in magazines, houses are not sculptures; therefore, if it leaks it is not a good design.

There is another meaning to the word *good* that is seldom recognized. "Good design" can also mean "good works" in the world of design. Helping those who normally could not have access to the services of architects is a way by which the word *good* can have more than an aesthetic meaning. Ultimately, however, good design is reflected in projects that, over the course of decades, provide enrichment to those who use them or simply see them during their day-to-day lives. The proof of the pudding is in the aging, not in the temporary glorification of popular style. (See Fig. 1.6.)

Joe Bilello

❏ Good design answers architectural paraphrases of two enduring questions, one from Socrates and the ages and one from Abraham Maslow, twentieth-century psychologist. In the first case, good design brings forth architectural answers to the question, "What is the nature of a mean-

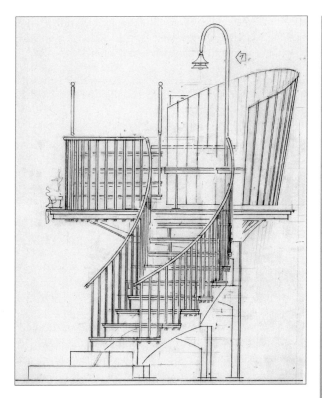

FIGURE 1.6
Courtesy of Duo Dickinson.

ingful life?" Indeed, good design answers questions of meaning. Like butterfly effects, the initially small residual perturbations experienced with good design amplify unpredictably over time. At their best, these effects produce unexpected excellence in a myriad of forms and seemingly unrelated places.

What is Good Design ?

FIGURE 1.7
Courtesy of Joe Bilello.

The second, more recent, enduring question concerns Maslow's idea of self-actualization, the pinnacle of the pyramid of human development. Good design addresses the question, "What is architecture's contribution to the possibility of achieving self-actualization?" Far beyond the capacity to shelter and protect health, safety, and welfare, excellence in design effectively addresses the question, "What is the greatest potential that can be achieved?" (See Fig. 1.7.)

Don Schlegel

❏ Architecture is a concept, an idea that captures the spirit of truth, time, and place. Architectural truth respects form and function, construction and material. Architectural time respects the epoch of its design origin. Architectural place

FIGURE 1.8
Courtesy of Don Schlegel.

respects the context of its culture, climate, and topology.
(See Fig. 1.8.)

Robert Peters

❏ Good design is:

- Appropriate form/response to the client and to the site
- Appropriate environment/response for the climate and the sun's seasons
- Appropriate perception/response of light on a surface and illuminating space
- Good design is appropriate

(See Fig. 1.9.)

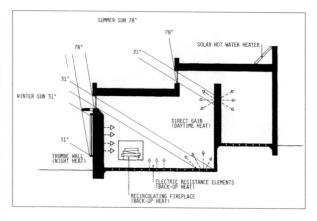

FIGURE 1.9
Courtesy of Robert Peters.

Norman Rosenfeld

❏ Good design—you know it when you see it: an Eames chair, a Brancusi sculpture, the chapel at MIT. Good architectural design is the perfect union of material, form, space, and light providing a special presence—an enclosure or environment appropriate to the charge. (See Fig. 1.10.)

George Anselevicius

❏ Thirteen commandments for searching and finding the beautiful:

1. Good design is what is done by A-plus students at school.

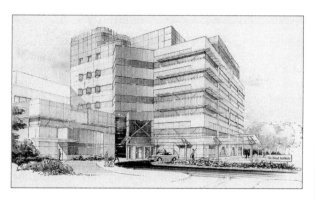

FIGURE 1.10
Courtesy of Norman Rosenfeld.

2. Good design is what is published in magazines.
3. Good design demands *firmitas, utilitas, venustas* (thank you, Vitruvius).
4. Good design is what *The New York Times* architecture critic says it is.
5. Good design is like pornography: it can't be defined, but I know it when I see it.
6. Good design demands critical text and subtexts (thank you, Heidegger, Lévi-Strauss, Derrida, et al.).
7. Good design is what makes clients happy.
8. Good design in Santa Fe is a building not to be noticed.
9. Good design in Bilbao is a building to be noticed.
10. Good design is made where employees stay for a while despite low salaries.
11. Good design need not cost any more but usually does.
12. Good design responds to the zeitgeist rather than fashion (if one can perceive the difference).
13. Good design is what hangs in architects' reception areas.

What is Good Design ?

Stefanos Polyzoides

❏ If I were a young architect, I would find it daunting to access the values supporting the practice of a contemporary architecture. It would be especially unsettling to attempt to role model leading practitioners, as their work is informed by a particularly insidious form of cynicism: knowing that it contributes to the urban and ecological unraveling of our civilization, and persisting in that direction. If I were to extract principles out of these practices, I would then confront the following points of circular thinking elevated to a credo.

Point 1. I practice a single, heroic and hermetic architecture because universal or vernacular languages are not valid today. There is no multiplicity of architectural language possible today, because I practice a heroic and hermetic architecture.

The classical and vernacular traditions have been replaced by a multitudinal order of person-based architectures. These architectures, often unintelligible, self-referential, and resistant to criticism, are confusing to the population at large. They undermine the conventional role of architecture as shared visual culture. They masquerade as art, psychology, and/or high fashion. They replace civic acceptance and popular interpretation with a combination of elitist posturing and fashionmongering.

Point 2. I undermine the received form of the city because I cannot discern its tangible order. The city is without a tangible order because I undermine it through my individual projects.

The traditional city is still suspect. It is seen as a repository of obsolete, useless buildings and inadequate infrastructure. Its complex integration of various kinds and scales of form, building, space, and infrastructure is denied in favor of a primitive and exclusive reading based on building dominance. Homogeneity of expression rejecting program, typological character, regional precedence, or site location rules. As a result, familiar urban forms are routinely violated one project at a time, and replaced with anarchic project fragments. The visual diversity, the usability, and the legibility of the traditional city are reduced to a cacophonous monoculture of monumental trash.

Point 3. I practice an architecture driven by technical innovation because traditional means and methods of construction are discredited. Traditional means and methods of construction are discredited because I practice an architecture expressive of high technology alone.

Obsessively directed by an urge to perpetual innovation, architects have paid the highest degree of attention to riding the wave of technological change. Finding ways to express the latest aspects of technological advancement is accomplished typically at the expense of exploring the building traditions of each locality. These traditions often involve time-tested, commonsense approaches to both architectural form and its technical content. Regional patterns of design are rejected at a huge cost. Cultural familiarity, human experience, and the collective memory are abandoned as a measure of assessing the fit between form and society. The rejection of historically transmitted knowledge has transformed architecture from a profession into a spectacle.

Point 4. I design buildings as isolated objects separated from nature because nature cannot be easily captured within the confines of my projects. Nature is invisible in my work because I design buildings as isolated mechanical objects.

What is Good Design ?

The understanding of architecture as the design of single buildings in a specific natural and urban setting has fallen out of fashion. Buildings consume and subjugate everything natural around them without accounting for the consequences. Incrementally constructed and divorced from nature, they slowly erase all evidence of the landscape. Gardens are dismissed as nostalgic attempts to restore psychic comfort to the top of the livability agenda. Water and air quality deteriorate as buildings increasingly do not account for the physical processes that they are subject to. The irreplaceable energy that it takes to make, maintain, and demolish temporary buildings (all buildings are now temporary) is forever lost.

Point 5. I depend on the authority of elitist institutions to promote my avant-gardist projects because there is no educated public to support and advocate my work. There is no educated public to support and advocate my work because I depend on the authority of institutions to promote my avant-gardist projects.

Contemporary architecture has been reduced to the design of a very limited number of cultural monuments, museums, university facilities, and transportation centers. These buildings are most often directly commissioned by private and/or institutional clients, generally following the corporate rather than the public process. Public patronage and the discipline of the market both demand coming to grips with popular taste. More and more, architects refuse to explain their work or subject it to public scrutiny. The result is a public divorced from the increasingly esoteric content of architecture, and architects who are enamored by abstraction of behavior and expression and, as a result, find themselves disconnected from the values of their society.

In the rush to avoid public validation of their work, architects also end up obeying and validating existing regulatory canons, such as zoning, that are both obsolete and destructive. Obsolete because they fail to take advantage of the current needs of an evolving society. Destructive because they promote sprawl in all its forms.

I am not a young architect. I am an architect in the mid-point of his practice. Based on the experience of the first half of my career, I would like to offer the following insight to colleagues who are aspiring to become part of this honorable and essential profession.

In order to break the mold of cynical and circular thinking, direct yourselves to an optimistic and constructive approach to architecture. First of all, your work is not only yours, but is also part of the construction of an architectural culture and a larger built and natural world. Every one of your projects has the ability to either contribute to or disengage and undermine the human habitat. It is your choice.

Choosing an engaged versus a cynical approach to architecture is an ethical matter. Responding to this simple choice is your civic responsibility. It will define you as it will define the long-term prospects of architecture in this society.

The terms of an engaged practice are relatively simple because they are part of a timeless way of operating as an architect in the world. By that I mean that as a code of responsible professional behavior, they were violated only very recently, essentially on our watch. They are as follows.

1. Architecture of Continuity. You are not the first and only architect. Architecture has existed before you and will exist after you. Practice in a variety of languages. There is no architecture without an audience. Your voice is most important when joined with others in an ongoing exposition of form that is comprehensible to them. Practice your ability to be multilingual by studying the vernacular, classical, and modern languages available to you in the world.

What is Good Design?

Heed the lessons of history by becoming an avid student and practitioner of architectural typology. It is the essential bridge between individual buildings and the urbanism of hamlets, villages, towns, cities, and metropolises. It is the most creative means of rooting oneself in the past while maintaining the right to self-expression.

2. Architecture of Urban Heritage. Honor the traditional city. The received city is larger, more permanent, and more complex than you are. It has an order that has evolved over 5000 years, and will defeat your attempts to undermine it or diminish its importance in isolated small parts and places. Urbanism is about designing the void between buildings, the landscape in it, and the infrastructure of mobility and services that tie all parts of the city together. It is also about regulating the incremental construction of buildings that validate all of these into a comprehensible form. It is not about the design of insular and oversized projects.

The city's course is not directed by designers. It is controlled by financial interests that demand the generation of economic value at every opportunity. Your role is to generate such value through architectural and urban projects. The key to becoming an honorable professional counsel and designer and not a faithful servant to clients is to make sure that through your work the value generated does not accrue to the first sponsor of a project alone. Instead, you must ensure that because of the quality and thoughtfulness of the Urbanism and architecture you have proposed, value builds over time, and allows others to derive benefits in the future. The people who depend on society's practice of social equity in order to survive are especially your clients too, and on every project.

3. Architecture of Appropriate Means. Be skeptical of the advantages of utilizing exclusively any one technology, high or low. The promotion and sale of materials and their assemblies is a business without a moral compass. Choose by becoming knowledgeable on the performance of all building materials utilized in your region over the last 50 years. Stop subscribing to magazines. Photography is the death of architecture. Photography promotes a view of architecture as scenography, frozen in time, isolated, and divorced from the physical erosion of the natural world. Do not photograph buildings until 10 years after their completion. Before that, they have little to reveal.

Materials arrayed in the proper form can achieve a sense of comfort in every climatic zone of the planet. Study how projects have weathered over time. Try to balance the aesthetic qualities of the materials you observe with the sense of permanence and longevity that they embody. You will discover that an appropriate use of materials and methods of construction favors the local, the inexpensive to produce, the easy to assemble and maintain, and the simple to reuse. Building knowledge derived from ongoing experience can then generate a balanced cycle of tradition informed by technical innovation. This standard of beauty linked to sustainability and permanence is the true measure of modernity.

4. Architecture of Environmental Regeneration. The centuries-old analogy of architecture as a mechanical process needs to be broken. It has led us to dangerous delusions about both human omnipotence and the prospect of survival without constant stewardship of the planet. You must now imagine architecture itself as a natural process. Added to the complicated traditional task of designing architecture in nature, you should now engage in the design of architecture as nature.

Dedicate yourself to making architecture and landscape architecture inseparable. The design of towns and cities of potent urban form adjacent to inviolate nature remains the highest design ideal of our age. The first 10 percent of build-

What is Good Design?

ing determines whether a place is urban or rural. This pattern is fundamental to our survival in nature, and your projects should help effect it. You must revitalize the millennial art of designing gardens for pleasure and for contemplation. Nature must be celebrated and, in the process, our dignity and humanity as parts of it as well.

Our biological relationship with nature should be repaired. Your projects should fully align their physical and chemical properties and processes with those of their surroundings. Consider every piece of your work to be an agent against the mindless consumption of nature. Design to produce energy, clean and recycle water and sewage, produce food, export clean air, and reuse materials. The view of architecture as the ephemeral consumption of superficial images and irreplaceable resources must reversed. The pursuit of permanent form and environmental replenishment is your next mission.

5. Architecture of Civic Engagement. After 50 years of divorce between architects and builders, you need to become re-engaged with the design of production housing for all classes of people. It is this kind of housing that, because of its enormous volume and its inflexible form, has become the principal carrier of the sprawl virus. It is this kind of project that demands engagement with the market and therefore with popular taste. It is mass housing as Urbanism that begs the reform of zoning codes and a more prudent approach to the use of land in all regions of the country.

Design public buildings that are permanent and make visible the deepest civic values of this republic. Design commercial buildings that are changeable and responsive to the unpredictable needs of the market. Make all buildings active players in the definition of a stable realm of public space that enables free and random human interaction. It is this kind of often residual, cheap space that is essential for social and civic life.

Be an architectural activist. Engage your local political process while remaining a practicing designer. Get appointed to committees and commissions. Get elected to office. Lead your fellow citizens by advocating and explaining the importance of physical design to the quality of their lives. Understand this kind of professional posture as being enabling to you and to them: providing everyone with life options while elevating architecture to an art that everyone can afford.

Discover how differently people feel about their relationship to buildings, the city, and nature. Don't assume it. Don't generalize hypothetical clients for specific projects. Don't pander to them, and don't extrapolate their wishes indefinitely into the future. Listen to them and educate them. Don't design just for yourself; design for the rest of us as well.

Conclusion. The future of architecture is not guaranteed. Every human generation needs to shape it in the image of evolving cultures, societies, and markets. After almost 80 years under the sway of Modernist ideology, architecture has veered from one end of the cultural spectrum to the other. The early ideal of a normative and authoritative single language to replace classicism has evolved into a state of debased, infinite languages—as many as there are practicing architects, good or bad. This professional relativism has diminished the status and the quality of architecture worldwide. It has reduced the natural and urban environment to a state of unprecedented barbarism and degradation.

It is now time to begin to advocate personally, academically, and professionally a different kind of architecture: clear in precedence, of form and material appropriate to the particular tasks at hand, focused in purpose on the reconstruction of the city and the regeneration of nature, and dedicated equally to the service of status and wealth and to social equity. (See Fig. 1.11.)

What is Good Design?

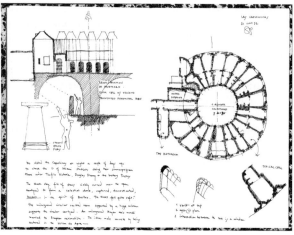

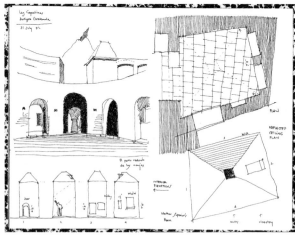

FIGURE 1.11
Las Capuchinas Convent, Antigua, Guatemala. Diego de Porres, architect,
1731–1736. (Courtesy of Stefanos Polyzoides, sketchbook #12, 1992.)

Peer Review and Self-Criticism

❏ It's not personal, it's business: peer review and self-criticism are crucial tools that elevate the quality of preliminary designs.

Most architects share the unpleasant memory of encountering a diatribe such as this: "Your project is about meaningless, multivalent form devoid of theoretical underpinning. There is little evidence of rigorous intellectual investigation or even a hint of innovation. It's a gratuitous contrivance in search of an idea. The work is so reductive, it's about nothing, and that might be vaguely eloquent if it was intentional. Can we move on?"

What can you say about a 25-year-old architecture student who was just brutally attacked in a design review? That she's quite talented, perhaps. That she listens to Massive Attack and just saw *Eyes Wide Shut*. That she loves architecture. And that she will need years to recover from the trauma of her early studio education and start to embrace pragmatic and appropriate criticism, be it from clients, peers, or public stakeholders—the kind of criticism that is essential if her projects are to be as effective and beautiful as they can be. No wonder the Boyer Report, the study of architectural education prepared by the Carnegie Foundation for the Advancement of Teaching, concluded that juries can "foster excessive egotism and an adversarial approach to clients."

Break Away from Bad Habits

❏ We're all aware that one of the developmental problems we must overcome is the systematic and often ruthless criticism presumably utilized to bring students to overarching truths or principles about architecture. Weld Coxe, Hon. AIA, founding principal of the Coxe Group, believes that the sort of destructive personal criticism alluded to in the fictitious mad professor's rant—a familiar rite of passage in schools of architecture, as we know all too well—seriously undermines the primary goal of the profession, which is simply to create excellent design.

What can we do about this problem? We must readily identify and admit to mediocrity and fraud, make every effort to avoid premature enthusiasm for trends and fads and even apparent breakthroughs, and recognize individuals for their contribution and caring.

Contribution and caring? What do these words have to do with creating better architecture? Contribution and caring are values that should be fostered in our profession and expected of all practitioners. Why? Because criticism should strengthen our colleagues and their work, rather than tear them down. Is this concept self-evident? A bit idealistic? Sure it is. But time and again history has demonstrated the value of simply reminding ourselves of who we should strive to be.

Attitude adjustments are one matter. But what specific methods can architects use to undertake positive and meaningful criticism of their work? Self-criticism and peer review—strategies that are underutilized in our field—should be a matter of course for architects in the midst of the design process.

The Art of Self-Criticism

❏ Self-criticism is an acquired skill, a subset of criticism, that can efficiently stimulate new ideas, infuse projects with special meaning, and help formulate cogent arguments in support of convictions and aspirations. I asked Christopher Mead, professor of art history and architecture at the University of New Mexico, to elaborate. (See Supplement 1.1 for more detail.)

Mead suggests that self-criticism assists the architect in "formulating a project's aesthetic and social purpose at the start, so that the project, as it develops, can constantly be measured against this original conception." Used properly as a design tool, Mead says, self-criticism "serves initially to test the strength of the original idea and then, once the value of that idea has been proven, to ensure its coherent development by editing out missteps or flaws." Every line on the paper or every pixel on the computer screen should relate to the bigger concept.

Given that we're all pretty good at design fundamentals—solving the functional equation—it follows that self-criticism must address more elusive factors. Mead suggests that this has to do with matters beyond the design's immediate utility; in other words, the question of whether an architect is creating a culturally significant work of art.

Taking an unflinching look at one's own work has tangible benefits. But outside opinions are also essential. To that end, peer review programs offer an appealing vehicle for the delivery of good criticism.

A Jury of Peers

❏ Doug McCallum, AIA, is the manager of the Works in Progress program of the Boston Society of Architects. He says that discussing design is the program's sole intent. Each month, an architect presents a project in process, and chapter members—and occasionally others from allied disciplines, such as artists, landscape architects, or planners—assemble to constructively critique the work of one of their colleagues. They do it out of the office context and away from the pressures of a business environment. McCallum says the sessions provide perceptive discourse to enrich specific projects and advance general knowledge. This program is a model of professional behavior at a high level, one that could be implemented by even a small group of local design professionals.

There is a great advantage to external reviews. Fresh eyes, unimpeded by explicit or implicit agendas, can be focused on design quality and introduce new perspectives. The more exposure there is to diversity in points of view, the more possibilities become evident. Another benefit accrues to the reviewer. Experience in evaluating the work of others will likely contribute to more objective and effective self-criticism.

Christopher Mead deftly links self-correction mechanisms with external criticism. He explains that self-criticism "provides the architect with a means to deal with the criticism offered by others, because it sets the architect's own idea of a project as the standard against which critical reactions can be judged—not defensively, but confidently." Having a solid base makes insights from external sources easier to accept.

A Communal Effort

❏ Because it is so easy to whine about the mediocrity surrounding us, we need to be especially conscientious about allocating energy toward creative and activist methods of raising the level of (or at least discussing meaning and content in) architectural design. Effective self-criticism and peer review are elements of real professionalism as well as good business.

Traditionally, criticism—whether delivered by another or self-generated—represents a dialectic. This typically means that a gulf of some type exists between that which is regarded and that which is evaluated; and as C.P. Snow has observed, the differences between the two poles often cause trouble. Misunderstanding, hostility, abject bias, and even a total absence of discriminating judgment can easily be the end result of critical effort.

The question this essay raises is how we might redefine and exercise a more effective and genuinely constructive brand of criticism. Potential answers to this question include a general rediscovery of (dare I say?) teamwork and altruistic critical thinking during the design process, as well as vigorous advancement of the art of self-criticism, which should also take place during design. Simple and accessible instruments for these solutions exist. All that is required is a commitment to utilize them.

Critical Thinking in Architectural Design
with Christopher Mead

❏ Elaborating and broadening the topic of criticism as a vehicle to raise the bar in creating and developing excellent architecture is detailed in a surgically precise manner by Christopher Mead in Supplement 1.1. Absent a specific formula, Mead is uniquely successful in suggesting how to apply and integrate criticism into an architectural design process.

Thomas Fisher has characterized two opposing camps in the realm of architectural criticism: (1) journalists who write in the popular press and who, according to Fisher, tend to confuse criticism with reporting on and description of designs and designer personalities; and (2) academic critics who write in scholarly publications including journals and limited-distribution books. These individuals bring great depth and knowledge but tend to digress into "dull recitation of fact, jargon-filled analysis, [or] highly personal effusion about architecture." Fisher identifies the rare critic who plays a part in advancing the profession: one who "addresses the underlying ideas and larger meanings of architecture and who can convey them clearly and concisely to the public and the profession." Christopher Mead does just that.

Christopher Mead

Christopher Mead is a professor of art history and of architecture at the University of New Mexico, and is currently serving as president of the Society of Architectural Historians. He is the author or editor of books on architects Charles Garnier, Robert Venturi, and Bart Prince, and is currently completing a book for the University of Chicago Press on Victor Baltard and the architecture of nineteenth-century Paris. This essay derives from an earlier essay of Mead's on the subject: "A Place for Criticism and Memory in Architectural Practice: Analyzing the 1998 AIA New Mexico Design Awards," Designer/Builder, V, no. 10 (February 1999), 5–10.

❏ While the practice of architecture may be nearly as old as humanity, the profession of architecture is itself hardly more than two centuries old. This modern discipline has from its origins, however, been threatened with obsolescence by the very conditions of modernity that brought it into existence during the eighteenth century. Whether it be the challenge to aesthetic practice posed by the scientific rationality of engineering, the shift from craft to industrial mass production, or modernity's invention of abstract and placeless systems of information that—from Diderot's Encyclopedia to the Internet—lessen the need for physically based forms of knowledge like buildings, those conditions have forced architects to survive by practicing across contradictory claims on the profession. Historically, this has engaged architects in the competing methods of art and science; between an architecture of the unique object and of the standardized commodity; between a conception of architecture as tectonic form or as merely another form of publicity. Currently, with modernity now producing the global market of a service economy for the information age, architects find themselves caught between the opposing identities of a service profession meeting a client's needs and a design profession creating culturally significant works of art.

To negotiate such differences, architects have depended since the eighteenth century upon critics—both within and outside the profession—to recognize and articulate the alternatives facing architectural practice. Evaluating stated intentions against final results, criticism fosters professional clarity by exposing the confusion of architectural aims that can result from modernity's contradictions. For this very reason, however, criticism has also been regarded with suspicion, dismissed by architects who resent its intrusion into the already complex realities of their practice. In the United States today, outside such charmed circles of critical activity as New York, Chicago, and Los Angeles, too many practitioners labor in a state of distraction, so preoccupied with doing business that they have little time to consider the cultural value of their work. All too often, what gets built betrays a critical gap between the gross facts of a building's utilitarian presence and those significant qualities of form and content that can result from a clearly identified architectural purpose.

The dangers of this inattention were recently brought home to me by the 1998 American Institute of Architects (AIA) New Mexico Design Awards, which despite the regional specificity of its subject raises topical issues of general relevance to the profession. According to the AIA, the design awards program in New Mexico has three overlapping objectives. First, it "encourages and recognizes distinguished architectural achievement by AIA New Mexico members." Second, it "serves to increase public awareness of the outstanding service provided by AIA New Mexico members." And third, rephrasing the first two objectives, it states "the importance of the architect's role in shaping the quality of the built environment through design excellence." In other words, the purpose of the AIA design awards is to foster the competitive improvement of architectural design in New Mexico by recognizing works that convince the public of the value of architecture, because those works make New Mexico a qualitatively better place in which to live.

The obvious question raised by these objectives is whether they were achieved through the 1998 awards program. But this question in turn raises another, antecedent, question: what, precisely, does the AIA mean by such terms as "distinguished architectural achievement," "outstanding service," or "design excellence"? Your design excellence, for example, is not automatically my design excellence, unless we first agree on what constitutes excellence of design. Is design excellence synonymous with outstanding service, or are those separate criteria for evaluating an architect's work? What, exactly, must the architect achieve if the result is to be judged distinguished? So long as the AIA's definitions of distinguished achievements, outstanding services, and design excellence remain unclear, it must be equally unclear what the public is supposed to make of an architect's claimed contributions to the built environment. While obviously gratifying to those receiving awards, the AIA Design Awards program risks having no real function beyond flattering its members with the illusion that what they do matters to society as a whole. If the exhibition of the winning New Mexican projects was any indication—an average of only 10 people on any day dropped in to take a look—the public didn't make much, good or bad, of the AIA and its members: instead, it ignored them.

The critical gap between the vague platitudes of the AIA's stated objectives and the actual difficulty of making architecture relevant to its contemporary public results from muddled thinking. Predictably, this led to the equally muddled outcome of the 1998 design awards. Of the 49 projects originally submitted, 9 received awards: 3 honor awards for winning projects and 6 merit awards for runners-up. In judging the projects, the jury seems to have been biased in favor of institutional buildings over residential or commercial projects: five awards went to university, research, or school facilities, while three went to houses, and one went to a frankly commercial work, a hotel addition. This suggests that a prejudice established in the nineteenth century is still vigorously in force: official commissions from the state or its equivalents are more important than other kinds of work. The jury results were roughly proportional to the 30 institutional, 12 residential, and 7 commercial projects competing for awards, though I doubt that these ratios accurately reflect the realities of contemporary architectural practice in New Mexico. Is, for example, the nearly 2-to-1 ratio of institutional to residential projects truly indicative of the balance of work in the average architectural office in this state? It would seem that, anticipating the jury's own prejudices, the competing architects gave preference whenever possible to their institutional over residential or commercial works as more likely to win an award.

The implication that all concerned—architects, AIA, and jurors—emphasized institutional buildings because of attitudes within the profession prompts another set of questions. Given this emphasis, what are the qualitative consequences for our built environment when its preponderant elements—residential and commercial buildings—are valued less as contributing factors than the more exclusive category of institutional structures? What are the presumed characteristics of institutional buildings, and to what extent are those characteristics common to or distinguished from residential and commercial work? How does "design excellence" apply to this descending hierarchy of institutional, residential, and commercial work? My point in asking such questions is not to prove either the rightness or wrongness of such a hierarchy, but rather to indicate the critical uncertainty that results when a position is adopted reflexively, without a consciously recognized and articulated understanding of that position and its consequences.

Aesthetically, the program's message was just as confused, with the jury awarding prizes to every possible design solution, from regionalist revival and postmodern kitsch to prefabricated assemblage and high-tech tectonics. One might suspect—I did—that what the AIA meant by "design excellence" was really "design democracy," in which every member of the jury got to pick his or her favorite work, trading votes with other jurors so that in the end every preference was represented. Despite the lavish use of such words of praise as "sensitive, wonderful, bold, elegant, inspired, timeless," the jury's comments in the end provided no evidence that its judgments were based on anything more consistent than individual druthers. Missing was an articulated set of criteria, framed by a coherent critical position, to explain why the services of an architect, achieved through

Sketches

design, were necessary and desirable, and hence to be preferred by clients over the alternatives offered today by engineering, contracting, and real estate development firms. Acting politically to please the interest groups and factions of its own membership, rather than advocating a program of ideas able to communicate the value of architecture to the general public, the 1998 New Mexico Design Awards failed in the AIA's stated aim of demonstrating "the importance of the architect's role in shaping the quality of the built environment."

These awards are a specific instance of the historical irrelevance confronting the architectural profession as a whole. Originating in conditions outside its control, but having immediate practical consequences for the profession, the problem can only be addressed through a greater awareness by architects of what they, uniquely, are trained to provide to the public. This requires, in New Mexico and elsewhere, a real, developed culture of architectural criticism. So long as criticism remains an exception rather than the rule within the profession—more the domain of academics than practicing architects, who argue that they have better things to do—then architecture can only continue to lose relevance in the eyes of the public; those architects who attract notoriety because of their distinctive work remain in the minority, without any effect on the invisibility of most architects. Equally an individual responsibility and a collective right, acted out in the social space between private interests and public consensus, critical thinking about our built environment might make us more attentive to architecture as the cultural practice that creates the physical context and formal circumstance in which we live our daily routines of work, play, and rest.

By critical thinking, I do not so much mean thinking negatively as I mean thinking about the difference between what a person or organization claims to be doing on the one hand and what that person or organization actually achieves on the other. For the most part, architects tend either to respond to criticism passively, ignoring the critique, or angrily, dismissing it out of hand; rarely do they accept the challenge to answer with a substantive response, which itself could alter how we think about architecture. Yet such a culture remains vitally useful, because criticism can make us see familiar things from new perspectives, shake us out of our shopworn habits, and provoke us into thinking about problems we might otherwise overlook. Criticism, in this sense, is a positive activity, even if it remains opposed to public relations, promotional advertising, and boosterism. In questioning a status quo, criticism creates possibilities for change.

Criticism is not the critic's special property. To think critically requires first of all the recognition of one's own point of view, of the assumptions that frame how one looks at and interprets the world. In this sense, criticism is a practice common to every discipline and every profession, including architecture, because it provides the perspective needed to understand not just what one does technically, but also why one does it culturally. This necessity explains why critics come from such various backgrounds: I think, for example, of the poets Charles Baudelaire and T.S. Eliot, of the social philosophers Walter Benjamin and Roland Barthes, or of the architects Robert Venturi and Peter Eisenman, all of whom have been effective critics. What criticism attempts is discourse, initially in order to identify overlooked tendencies within a particular discipline, and ultimately across disciplines to consider a culture's broader habits of thought. Throughout, criticism has as its objective what the AIA claimed to be its aim in the New Mexico design awards: the generation of public awareness of the means and ends by which we make a culture through architecture.

Admittedly, articulating a critical position on architecture is not easy to do. On the one hand, architecture is an autonomous formal discipline shaped by design criteria that are internal to the profession. On the other hand, architecture answers to a diverse audience of clients and users, which means that buildings represent the political, social, and economic conditions that bring them into being. The difficulty of reconciling these competing design and service identities, without further blurring the disciplinary limits of architecture, perhaps explains why the AIA resorts to such circumlocutions as "the architect's role in shaping the quality of the built environment." Depending upon one's agenda, this can be interpreted equally as a call to aesthetic sensitivity or to social responsiveness.

This choice, however, is a false one. Architecture results less from the split personality of such an either/or proposition than from the interdependent forces that produce a building: the forms, structures, and spaces of architecture mediate between the aesthetic objectives of a design and the political, social, and economic conditions of building. From this perspective, a work of architecture can be judged for the success with which it answers those conditions, but in terms that remain specific to the discipline. An idea about architecture is not the same as, say, a political idea, even if one can have a profound effect on the other. Ideally, the service provided by an architect consists in creating through design a new (or at least another) way of thinking about architecture and the needs it houses. Service in this sense is as much about teaching a client, or the public, about the aesthetic possibilities of architecture as it is a matter of satisfying a functional program.

The challenge comes in translating this critical understanding of architecture into the reality of practice. Absent any easy formula, some commonsense observations point the way to integrating criticism into architectural design:

- Criticism is as much the responsibility of the architect creating a design as it is something to expect from the architect's audience of colleagues, clients, and public.
- Criticism begins with self-criticism: the conscious effort by the architect to formulate a project's aesthetic and social purpose at the start, so that the project as it develops can constantly be measured against this original conception.
- Self-criticism provides the architect with a means to deal with the criticism offered by others, because it sets the architect's own idea of a project as the standard against which critical reactions can be judged, not defensively but confidently for the insights those reactions provide.
- As a qualitative rather than quantitative method of thinking about architectural design, criticism applies to every project, regardless of scale or budget: the smallest house addition is as subject to thoughtful analysis as the grandest institutional commission.
- Used properly as design tools, both self-criticism and outside criticism serve initially to test the strength of the original idea and then, once the value of that idea has been

> proven, to ensure its coherent development by editing out missteps or flaws.

■ Reviews, published or otherwise, of the built design complete the cycle of critical awareness by informing the architect's thinking in future projects.

Yielding practical benefits along with aesthetic results, such a critically based process turns each design into a self-checking system that alerts the architect to potential problems, thus making it possible to avoid difficulties in execution by anticipating and devising solutions ahead of time. This increases the design's marketability by promoting a coherently comprehensive solution to every aspect of the project, including its transformation into construction documents and its subsequent realization. But the real increase in value comes from the design's potential to have something to say beyond its immediate utility, to rise above the mass of generically anonymous building that increasingly characterizes our landscape, and capture the public's attention with a work whose aesthetic qualities make people stop, look, wonder, and think. When that happens, then the architect really has designed something critically relevant to "shaping the quality of our built environment."

Why Draw?
with Jean Pike

❏ Notwithstanding the enormous benefits of drawing and modeling on the computer, Jean Pike, in Supplement 1.2, makes a strong case for drawing as a fundamental means for inspiring designs and for personal enlightenment. Cultlike followers of this traditional mainstay of architectural practice will understand. For others, Jean Pike's brief yet powerful essay and drawings (Figs. 1.12, 1.13, and 1.14) should be a wake-up call to frequently revisit this simple tool. Refer also to Paul Laseau's "Drawing as Discovery" supplement in Chapter 4 for eloquent perspectives on this incredible medium.

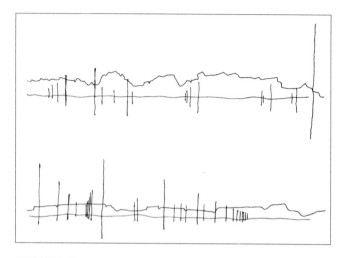

FIGURE 1.12
Changing configurations of line: The Lightning Field, Quemado, New Mexico.
(Courtesy of Jean Pike.)

Jean Pike

Jean Pike is an architect and artist who teaches drawing and architectural design at the Pratt Institute and the New Jersey Institute of Technology. She received a master of architecture degree from Yale University.

❏ While I was teaching architectural design and drawing in Rome, a colleague confided in me, "I don't have *time* to draw." My own teaching schedule and other commitments made it hard for me to find the time as well. Why spend an hour making a drawing in this city so dense with monumental works? In Rome one could easily visit and photograph a dozen in that hour, and when one's time is limited to a short stay, a frantic surge grabs hold of the aspiring architect, driving him or her to see and document as much as possible.

For Louis I. Kahn, a lover of drawing, to draw an existing structure was to work out ways of thinking about architecture. Sluggish moments in the economy, combined with being caught between a Beaux Arts education and the emergence of Modernism and the International Style in America, caused teaching

SUPPLEMENT 1.2

and drawing to become the main vehicles for Kahn's exploration of architectural notions early in his career. Later in his life, when he was able to garner commissions for substantial projects, the buildings themselves became the realization of his ideas.

Le Corbusier, on the other hand, kept a small sketchbook with him at all times, constantly recording impressions of the physical environment, both built and natural. During the design phase of a project he would keep old sketchbooks at the ready, calling up previously stored ideas. For Le Corbusier the drawing was a means not just to document, but to imprint a form or a concept on his memory.

At present, computers are utilized in the architecture profession not only as tools for design and production, but also for the storage of vast amounts of information. Can we store our own knowledge of architecture on a disk or a hard drive the way we save other files and information? As architects, we need a reservoir of knowledge to be utilized, both intuitively and intentionally, during the design process. As users and experiencers of architecture, we must have material stored in our own memories with which to make connections and associations in order for architecture to resonate with us on a meaningful level.

Visually, we live in a world dominated by two-dimensional imagery: computer, movie, and television screens, print media, and billboards.

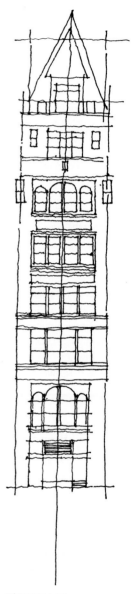

FIGURE 1.13
Façade, New York City.
(Courtesy of Jean Pike.)

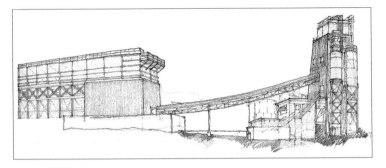

FIGURE 1.14
Materials plant, Albuquerque, New Mexico. (Courtesy of Jean Pike.)

The act of drawing allows us to reconnect with the three-dimensionality of the physical world by observing it intimately and over time. Once this intimate knowledge has been recorded in our sketchbooks, revealing what it is that we see and find compelling, we are able to pull it again to the surface and work with it as designers in a way that is truly our own.

 ## Vernacular Means
with Christopher Wilson

❏ This section presents a rich and potent subject—the vernacular—and approaches for analyzing, dissecting, and ultimately acquiring a useful understanding of the vernacular to apply to design projects. It can be an incredible source of inspiration to imbue buildings with special content and meaning beyond superficial regional style.

Charles Linn, for example, in *Architectural Record* (04/00, p. 109), critiques the Howard House in Nova Scotia, Canada, by architect Brian MacKay-Lyons. This is a wonderful demonstration of how Architecture (with a capital "A") is derived, thoughtfully, from a place. The architect's "deep knowledge of the local material culture—an understanding of what materials are used to build, and why and how they are put together" informs the work. MacKay-Lyons creatively employs boat-builders and ironworkers to construct his projects. It is the antithesis of a "vernacular pastiche." The house is unconventional—it's not the traditional clapboard frame—but very much appreciated by the neighbors, the fishermen, the builders: a true measure of its success.

In Supplement 1.3, Chris Wilson explains the historical perspective, and pragmatically, what to look for, extract, and interpret that may be significant in enhancing designs of routine projects.

Chris Wilson

Jackson Professor of Cultural Landscape Studies at the University of New Mexico School of Architecture and Planning, Wilson is author of Facing Southwest: The Life and Houses of John Gaw Meem *(W.W. Norton, 2001), and is currently working with Stefanos Polyzoides on a study of the historic plazas of New Mexico. (© Christopher Wilson)*

SUPPLEMENT 1.3

First Quiz

❑ Check all that apply.
Vernacular means:

☐ The common language of a country or locality
☐ From the Latin, *vernacula*—domestic, native
☐ Someone chosen or elected to the nobility
☐ The customary architecture of a region, culture, or period
☐ Everyday, ordinary, popular
☐ Universal, international, global
☐ Orally transmitted, illiterate, unschooled
☐ Indigenous, local, regional

As you have undoubtedly concluded, most of these are examples of vernacular, although "universal, international, global" mean the opposite, while "someone elected to the nobility" is the original meaning of *elite*. The sense of the vernacular as something common, everyday, and unschooled is sometimes summed up in the negative formulation "not designed by an architect." This definition precludes you as an architect from working in the vernacular. So for this discussion of the relationship between architects and the vernacular, it is more useful to adopt the sense of vernacular as design that is linked to a particular region, that is adapted to its climate, and that builds on its particular history, cultural values, and natural material resources.

Because people were once limited to local materials, to ideas learned face-to-face, and to customary, low-tech methods of construction, heating, and cooling, almost everything built was once vernacular out of necessity. But with the beginning of the Industrial Revolution and mass communication and transportation about 200 years ago, technological innovations, building materials, and architectural fashions began to cross regional and national boundaries with growing frequency. Now almost everything constructed—whether designed by an architect or an owner-builder—is affected by global forces and widely circulated ideas.

Second Quiz

❑ Check those that in some important sense are vernacular designs.

☐ Le Corbusier's Villa Savoye
☐ Mizner's Mediterranean-style mansions in Palm Beach
☐ Philip Johnson's glass house, New Canaan
☐ Moore and Lyndon's Sea Ranch north of San Francisco
☐ Rogers and Piano's Pompidou Center
☐ Predock's La Luz, a solar adobe community
☐ Gehry's Guggenheim Museum in Bilbao
☐ Duany Plater-Zyberk's hipped cottages with screened porches at Seaside

The Villa Savoye, the New Canaan glass house, the Pompidou Center, and the Guggenheim—Bilbao are each consciously divorced from the vernacular, emphasize modern technology, and would be equally at home almost anywhere. The other examples, by contrast, build on the vernacular of their locales in their varying mixtures of climate-sensitive layouts, locally produced materials, conventional building types, regional forms, and popular symbolism.

Architects have found a variety of ways to balance contemporary social conditions and technological innovations with still-important local design considerations. Those trained in the Beaux Arts approach during the nineteenth and early twentieth centuries studied the best high-style and vernacular designs to absorb time-honored design conventions. In the U.S., particularly during the 1920s and 1930s, many architects specialized in adapting regional vernaculars for contemporary needs. Modernist architects disparaged this approach as inappropriate to the machine age, although they found inspiration of their own in select vernacular examples, typically those with bold geometric forms, little ornament, and exposed materials and structure. The Neotraditionalist strain of Postmodernism—recast in the early 1990s as the New Urbanism—revitalizes the earlier interest in classical and regional design conventions. Its proponents study historic typologies of house plan, civic space, and street section to understand deeper levels of regional cultural variety, climatic adaptation, and pedestrian environments that foster face-to-face community.

Today, tight budgets and pressing schedules limit the amount of contextual research that a firm can devote to a single project. So, to make local and regional considerations central to your design practice requires a long-term commitment to the study of vernacular traditions. Delving deeply into the interrelations among architectural form, cultural pattern, local materials, and climate in one region prepares you to more quickly identify pertinent issues in a new setting.

Four Means for Engaging the Vernacular

1. Travel, Question, Look, Sketch. Whether in the region where you most often work, or a new area where you have received a commission, take field trips and interrogate the cultural landscape about its history and contemporary developments. Sketching is an essential way to see and analyze buildings. It permits you to absorb on a subconscious level vernacular forms that then intuitively inform your schematic design sketches. However visually attractive vernacular forms may be, remember to also engage deeper spatial issues by noting plans and sections of buildings and public spaces, and by diagramming climatic and cultural patterns. Although the full impact of the computer remains to be seen, I have yet to observe anyone making CAD sketches on a laptop in the field, and suspect that the hand sketch will remain a basic means for designers to connect with the vernacular. (See Fig. 1.15.)

2. Lay Your Hands on Materials. A time-honored, arts-and-crafts approach to mastering the characteristics and potentials of everyday materials is to build things with your own hands. Volunteer for Habitat for Humanity and historic building work days, design a piece of furniture, or build an addition on your house. It can be difficult, however, to bridge the gulf between working with wood, brick, and adobe and designing for industrial materials. Architect Will Bruder, for instance, began and continues to work as a sculptor, served a hands-on apprenticeship with Paolo Soleri, thereby mastering bronze and concrete casting, and regularly seeks out old lumberyards, hardware stores, brickyards, stone quarries, and junkyard welders—all the while cultivating his nonelitist love for materials and particular affinity for the mundane and utilitarian. Most brilliantly deployed in the Phoenix Central Library, his modern vernacular palette includes clear, tinted, and translucent glass; standard industrial joints and fasteners; corrugated copper

FIGURE 1.15
This mid-1980s conceptual design sketch for an Albuquerque branch library by George Clayton Pearl, FAIA, draws inspiration from semisubterranean Anasazi pit houses, sheltered Spanish courtyards, the clerestory windows of mission churches, and the forms of nearby volcanic mesas. (© George Clayton Pearl.)

sheets and stainless steel; irregular cast concrete panels and structural grids; and chain-link fencing, crane rigging cables, and sail fittings with a PVC-coated polyester fabric mesh.

3. Cultivate Personal Contacts. The quickest route into the history and culture of an area is talking with knowledgeable individuals ranging from established scholars and historic preservationists to local community historians and fellow architects who share your interest in the vernacular. They will provide leads on important publications, out-of-the-way historic collections, and quintessential buildings and neighborhoods. State preservation offices and city planning departments maintain particularly useful files on historic buildings and districts. Participating in the conferences of national groups such as the Vernacular Architecture Forum, the Society of Architectural Historians, and the Congress for the New Urbanism, or in local preservation groups or AIA chapters, is essential to expanding your contacts and knowledge. On your field trips, also stop at construction sites, cafes, libraries, and public squares to meet people and ask them about the history and current developments in the area. Since vernacular culture is an everyday undertaking, your contribution comes not merely through your designs, but also through your ongoing participation in the local web of human interactions.

4. Build Your Library and Knowledge. Through personal contacts and trips to libraries and bookstores, identify, collect, read, and digest the best publications on the architecture and social history of the region or regions where you work. Newspapers, business and real estate journals—even ephemeral tourist publications—provide invaluable windows on current developments. The books noted in the references that follow also present a variety of approaches to the vernacular, and provide overviews of American regional design traditions.

Toward Modern Vernaculars

❏ I am equally enthusiastic about two seemingly contradictory approaches for integrating the vernacular in contemporary design. On the one hand is the exuberant materiality of modern technology and locally available materials found in the work of some avant-garde designers such as Bruder—enriched in his public buildings by iconic form—making links to narratives of local history, building craft, and environment. On the other hand is the increasing attention of New Urbanists to regional building types, their insistence that buildings contribute to the definition of streets and public squares hospitable to community life, and their willingness to engage popular taste through historicist vernaculars.

But one-of-a-kind, icon buildings, floating free in seas of parking and green lawn, contribute less than they should to coherent urban fabrics. Meanwhile, New Urbanist communities frequently embrace a literal historicism that risks an easy escape into nostalgia. I await the day when New Urbanists encourage architects such as Bruder to employ contemporary aesthetics and everyday materials in their communities—in Hueco, near El Paso, or Civano, near Tucson, say, communities master-planned by Moule and Polyzoides. In return, latter-day modernists such as Bruder would work within the prescribed urban patterns of plaza, street wall, and courtyard building type. Such a meeting of creative approaches could go a long way toward reconciling these competing tendencies, and, in the process, would bring new vigor to the vernacular by leavening it with the modern, and to the avant-garde by tempering it with the vernacular.

Best Books on Vernacular Architecture

Alexander, Christopher, et al. *A Pattern Language*. New York: Oxford University Press, 1977.

Brand, Stewart. *How Buildings Learn: What Happens After They're Built*. New York: Viking, 1994.

Carter, Thomas (ed.). *Images of an American Land: Vernacular Architecture in the Western United States*. Albuquerque, NM: University of New Mexico Press, 1997.

Congress for the New Urbanism. *Charter of the New Urbanism*. New York: McGraw-Hill, 1999.

Davis, Howard. *The Culture of Buildings*. New York: Oxford University Press, 2000.

Jackson, John Brinkerhoff. *Landscape in Sight: Looking at America*. New Haven, CT: Yale University Press, 1997.

Kelbaugh, Douglas. *Common Place: Toward Neighborhood and Regional Design*. Seattle, WA: University of Washington Press, 1997.

Liebs, Chester. *Main Street to Miracle Mile: American Roadside Architecture*. Boston: Little, Brown, 1985.

McAlester, Virginia, and McAlester, Lee. *A Field Guide to American Houses*. New York: Knopf, 1990.

Polyzoides, Stefanos, Sherwood, Roger, and Tice, James. *Courtyard Housing in Los Angeles* reprinted. New York: Princeton Architectural Press, 1992.

Society of Architectural Historians, various authors. *Buildings of the United States*. New York: Oxford University Press. [State-by-state architectural guide series; begun in 1993.]

Upton, Dell and Vlach, John (eds.). *Common Place: Readings in American Vernacular Architecture*. Athens, GA: University of Georgia Press, 1986. [East of the Mississippi only.]

Venturi, Robert, Scott Brown, Denise, and Izenor, Steven. *Learning from Las Vegas*. Cambridge, MA: MIT Press, 1972.

Vernacular Architecture Forum, various editors. *Perspectives in Vernacular Architecture*. Columbia, MO: University of Missouri Press (Vol. I, 1982; Vol. II, 1986; Vol. III, 1989; Vol. IV, 1991); Knoxville, TN: University of Tennessee Press (Vol. V, 1995; Vol. VI, 1997; Vol. VIII, 1997). [Each with 15 to 20 articles.]

Walker, Lester. *American Shelter* (revised ed.). New York: Overlook Press, 1997.

Wilson, Chris. *The Myth of Santa Fe: Creating a Modern Regional Tradition*. Albuquerque, NM: University of New Mexico Press, 1997.

Setting Precedents for Using Precedents

with Roger K. Lewis

❏ Using precedents in architecture can be a dangerous thing! Emerson claimed, "The imitator dooms himself to hopeless mediocrity." As Roger Lewis admonishes in Supplement 1.4, it is all too easy to extract the wrong lessons—for example, strictly visual without rigorous analytic underpinnings. Be wary of accepting prototypes, stereotypes, or fashion out of context. Eduard Sekler believed in the importance of analyzing form and the creative process to fully appreciate a design idea. He then considered how that idea could be purposefully applied to support the development of a current project.

Roger Lewis offers guidance on how to look at buildings with a critical eye, without a formula—even examining details seemingly unrelated to current work—for inspiration. The underlying principles may have great value in the discovery process.

Roger K. Lewis

Roger K. Lewis, FAIA, is a professor at the University of Maryland School of Architecture and a practicing architect in Washington, DC. His weekly column, "Shaping the City," appears in The Washington Post. *Professor Lewis authored* Architect? A Candid Guide to the Profession *(MIT Press, 1998), now in its second edition. His projects have received many AIA design awards and have been cited in both the popular and trade press.*

SUPPLEMENT 1.4

What Are Architectural Precedents?

❏ A precedent, by dictionary definition, is "any act that serves as a guide or justification for subsequent situations." To be a meaningful architectural precedent, such an act must be subject to documentation and analysis and must provide useful information, design lessons, and aesthetic principles applicable to a current project. Precedents can enlighten us about formal typology and composition; functional patterns and spatial organization; materials and details of assembly; technical systems; scale and proportion; color and texture; sensory perception; cultural meaning; and even construction costs. In architecture, a precedent can be a space, structure, landscape, or building; a part of a building; a collection of buildings; a campus, village, neighborhood, town, or city; or, equally important, an idea for the design of such built artifacts and environments.

How Have Precedents Been Used from Ancient Times to the Present?

❏ Throughout recorded history and in virtually all of the world's cultures, builders and architects have relied on local precedents, embodied both in specific buildings and building traditions, as the primary source of spatial and structural concepts, technical methods, stylistic motifs, architectural character, and spiritual inspiration. At the same time, profound understanding of historical precedents, whether near at hand or far away, often has led imaginative, inventive designers to create new directions in architecture often considered unprecedented. However, designs are rarely so original as to be wholly without precedent. Even the aesthetically innovative buildings of Frank Lloyd Wright, Le Corbusier, Antonio Gaudi, Frank Gehry, or Rem Koolhaas can be linked to previously conceived works of architecture.

The most commonly used precedents are typologically and functionally specific, as well as specific to a culture. In his *Ten Books on Architecture,* the first-century B.C.E. Roman architect Vitruvius, acknowledged generally as Western civilization's first architectural theoretician, codified Roman architectural and engineering traditions based on practical, well-established precedents—for structures ranging from temples and military forts to markets and aqueducts—with which he and his colleagues were familiar. Vitruvius asserted that these proven, traditional design templates were immutable, subject only to minor interpretation, refinement, and compositional leeway. Moreover, he considered them universal and exportable, applicable anywhere in the known world if suitably adapted to local site conditions. In effect, Vitruvius set the precedent for the use of precedent.

Over the past two millennia, significant historical periods in architecture have been repeatedly marked either by the rediscovery and reinterpretation of traditional precedents or by the conscious, proactive rejection of contemporaneous, traditional precedents. The invention of genuinely innovative Gothic architecture in northern Europe during the Middle Ages represents one of history's most radical breaks with precedent. Subsequently, the humanistic Renaissance in southern Europe during the fifteenth and sixteenth centuries was both a reaction to the deeply spiritual Gothic and a willful, intellectually motivated revival of classical Greek and Roman precedents. During the nineteenth century, architects again found romantic inspiration in picturesque Gothic architecture, only to turn yet again to more rational neoclassicism. Thus the history of architecture can be understood in part as recurring cycles of revivalism. And every generation in every culture continually faces the same architectural question: are yesterday's precedents appropriate for tomorrow's design challenges?

Using Precedents Appropriately

❑ In today's world of instantaneous global communication, localized demographic diversity, and rapid dissemination of increasingly vast quantities of information and ideas, the quantity of accessible precedents is staggering. How, then, can an architect intelligently and efficiently choose and use precedents?

Precedents are encountered in two ways. One way is not linked to a specific project, but rather stems from the architect's motivation and ability to observe and analyze precedents anywhere while traveling or reading. Any interesting building or environment can be a source of ideas and information. This simply requires remaining alert and attentive; exploring and thinking about the places and structures encountered; and documenting observations with notes, sketches, photos, and analytical diagrams. This generates an experiential inventory of precedents, a repertoire always available to the architect for future reference when the need arises.

The other way to engage precedents is project-specific, and it requires, above all, that the architect understand profoundly the

FIGURE 1.16
Courtesy of Roger K. Lewis.

nature of the project and all it entails: the client and users, site and context, functional program, building typology, construction and operating budgets, and applicable regulations. Then, in selecting and studying precedents, the designer must decide what is truly relevant. Precedents can be categorized based on the special lessons they impart and the comparative relevance of those lessons to the project at hand. The most common lessons and areas of relevant comparison include:

- Function: similarity in purpose, program, and user population
- Architectural typology: traditional building types (e.g., courtyard buildings or row housing) linked to function and form

- Architectural symbolism: buildings that deliver messages metaphorically
- Relation to context: site, climatic, and other environmental conditions
- Massing (size and scale) and volumetric geometry
- Plan and section configuration: spatial composition and proportions
- Circulation patterns and modes of movement
- Interior spatial character: light, color, texture, ornament
- Façade composition and character
- Construction materials, finishes, and details of assembly
- Structural systems and details
- Mechanical systems and other environmental control strategies
- Energy conservation and sustainability
- Landscape composition
- Construction cost

A single precedent usually encompasses several of these areas of comparison. Most important, a useful precedent for a current project does not have to be a structure or space whose function is the same as that of the project. For example, the plan configuration and circulation pattern of a seventeenth-century palace might inspire and inform the layout of a twenty-first-century school or corporate headquarters.

The Pitfalls of Precedents

❑ Probably the greatest sin in applying precedents is drawing the wrong lessons from the precedent selected and therefore using the precedent inappropriately. Architecture students very often choose precedents for design studio projects based less on rigorous, comparative analysis than on personal taste and image infatuation. Consequently, they sometimes produce designs whose only real connection to the precedent cited is superficial, visual resemblance. Rather than seeking to understand the fundamental design principles that gave form to the precedent structure, they merely replicate its external appearance.

Practicing architects are susceptible to doing likewise. This can lead to adopting a form or specifying materials visually or technically inappropriate to a site, culture, or climate. Lack of critical analysis of a chosen precedent can result in creating a precedent-derived design that, in paying homage to an obsolete model, fails to satisfy the real, functional demands of a contemporary program and contemporary users. Borrowing some precedent's compositional grammar and vocabulary purely for expressionistic purposes in executing a new building, perhaps in a less-than-faithful manner using expedient building techniques, can produce architecture that looks ersatz, artificial, or even constructionally insubstantial. This was a common pitfall trapping many architects in the 1980s who too indiscriminately embraced Postmodernism's taste for historical allusion and illusion.

Ultimately the purpose of studying precedents is not merely to find something to copy, but rather to gain greater insight, through design analysis, into how architects in the past have approached and creatively solved particular design problems. Conversely, using precedents does not stifle design creativity or innovation, contrary to what some architects believe. Indeed, only by knowing what is possible, what has been tried and accomplished previously, can a talented architect both understand a design challenge and perhaps discover a new way of meeting that challenge.

Daily Bread
with Melissa Harris

❏ Here is a real treat: a lyrical, brilliant, and passionate story by Melissa Harris that compares bread baking to designing. (See Supplement 1.5.) It is a plea for the integration of aesthetic experience into daily life. Melissa's simple yet profound thesis is indeed inspirational: take pleasure in the doing and see each step along the way as a creation in and of itself. The story concludes with some great architecture as well. Enjoy.

A. Melissa Harris

A. Melissa Harris is the associate dean of academic affairs and an associate professor at the Taubman College of Architecture and Urban Planning at the University of Michigan. A licensed architect, Harris was educated at North Carolina State University and the University of California, Berkeley. She teaches building design and graphic communication. Her professional experience includes five years as a designer at Esherick, Homsey, Dodge and Davis in San Francisco, shorter stints in the offices of Edward Larrabee Barnes in New York and Helmer Stenros in Helsinki, and archeological work with Brigham Young University on the Seila Pyramid in Egypt. Recognized for both her architectural and artistic work, Harris has received an Interiors Design Award and a Jurors Award from the American Society of Architectural Perspectivists. Interests in the social aspects of architecture inspired Harris to create the first Girl Scout badge in architecture.

❏ Baking bread is like designing buildings. Bread fills our stomachs and buildings keep us warm and dry. Both may also transport the mind or elevate the soul. Baking and architecture are essentially defined through transformation of material. When inert materials or ingredients such as wood, metal, and cement—or flour, salt, and water—coalesce, a building or a loaf of bread is born. But, of even more value to me as an architectural educator, the discipline required to bake good bread and the aesthetic considerations essential to its success translate directly to teaching students the basics of drawing and designing buildings.

I have noticed a pattern during my bread baking. The more aesthetic pleasure I take in the actual making, the better my bread is. By aesthetic pleasure I mean visual and sensual, cerebral and corporal—observing each step as a uniquely creative process within itself. Kneading dough and solving quadratic equations for building dimensions weave together seemingly unrelated activities, but the roles of craft, economy, and proportion are critical to the process going on both in the kitchen and in the architect's studio. All involve discipline.

I bake bread every week. The ingredients of great bread are elementary: water, flour, and salt added to a sourdough culture. But from these basic ingredients a process evolves that demands precision, sensitivity, and the discipline of constant involvement. A myriad of variables affects the outcome of bread—temperature, humidity, timing, how to stir and for how long, how to knead the dough and for how long, the selection of flour, the water, regular salt or sea salt . . . the possibilities go on and on. The interaction among the variables boggles a casual attempt to correlate cause and effect. Every experience informs my next baking.

The culture I use is a living organism with a history that predates anyone reading this. Supposedly, it is originally from Russia. It came to me through my stepfather, Professor Harold Hopfenberg, via another professor in North Carolina, David Auerbach, who got it from Sourdough International, an organization that nurtures, catalogues, and distributes sourdough cultures. The two professors taught me the basics of making this bread.

Maintaining the culture is a responsibility not dissimilar to caring for any other living being like a dog. It languishes if neglected, dies if abandoned, and flourishes vigorously with frequent use. The more you bake, the better the bread, because the starter is extremely active. There is no added yeast; the bread is leavened by wild yeast complemented by symbiotic bacteria in the mother culture. These are living organisms that demand food.

Making the bread is a two-day process. The first day requires three periods of "feeding" or doubling the starter to generate a basis for the actual bread dough and, of course, recycling a small reserve for the next baking. The second day involves kneading and shaping the dough, waiting for the rise, and then baking. Professional bakers use a wood-fired oven; I use a standard kitchen oven, with more than acceptable results.

FIGURE 1.17
Courtesy of A. Melissa Harris.

Why do I bake this particular labor-intensive bread when I could pop into any food market and buy bread for a few dollars? Or when a bread machine could do it for me? Because no bread I have eaten in traveling around the world (with the exception of Rohe-limpuu in Helsinki) rivals the taste. The process satisfies two basic urges—to eat well and to make things with my hands. It also stimulates my scientific curiosity and my inclination to record, to measure. Because the general steps are consistent—adding, mixing, shaping—the impact of each finely tuned nuance is pronounced.

FIGURE 1.18
Courtesy of A. Melissa Harris.

Baking Bread

❏ The series of procedural steps spaced over a 36-hour period are all gerunds: feeding, waiting, mixing, kneading, stretching, shaping, proofing, and baking. For me, sequence matters—from which ingredient touches the bowl first to where the others land when added. At each step there are goals of proportion and balancing of forces—how aggressively to stir, in what shape or motion, and when it is stirred enough. Unfortunately or fortunately, depending upon your personality and point of view, everything matters.

Feeding. Feeding the starter means doubling it by weight with equal parts water and high-gluten flour. The flour and water are mixed into a refrigerated culture held over from the last baking. The consistency of a one-week-old starter hovers between liquid and solid. Even in its embryonic condition, the bread seduces you with a mysterious inner nature defying classification. If the characteristics of both liquid and solid are maintained, the bread is better.

Mix is an ambiguous verb—sort of like my grandmother's final instruction in a recipe: "Cook until done." I've been into mixing since I could see over the top of the stove. During this "feeding" stage, I try to preserve the textural integrity of the starter. I create a pyramid of ingredients—first the dry flour as a base, then the stretchy starter, and last the water—a gradation from dry to wet.

Machine Mixing. Spread the flour up the side of the bowl to facilitate the integration of flour and water. The angle of repose of flour is steep, characteristic of small particles. How far up the side of the bowl the flour can reach before collapsing is an ongoing challenge, a personal competition from week to week. I take it to the point of collapse and begin again.

I choose the same tool over and over—my great-grandmother's old spoon. It is almost spherical in section, and when I drag it against the flour, the shape of its trail is graceful. One groove segues into another with intergenerational ease—an inverted flower.

Kneading. Kneading follows the initial, tougher work of the machine mixer. The machine step is optional, but hand kneading is not. The aim is to stimulate the development of gluten, indispensable to the dough's elasticity. The best bread results from a very loose, wet dough. This is both counterintuitive and physically difficult to achieve. Wet dough sticks to your hands and to your kneading surface. And when it sticks, the glutinous strands you've worked to achieve and want to preserve tend to tear both themselves and your nerves apart. It may be the origin of our Southern idiom, "It tore me all to pieces."

Neatness, craftsmanship, or economy may all seem outside the concern for taste or quality of the loaf. But a kneading surface that is overly floured or floured haphazardly results in a dry dough, or worse, small clumps that survive during baking.

Equipoise is a term I first heard used with reference to baseball. Now I use it often in my drawing class to encourage thoughtful, fluid lines. The term combines two apparent opposites—relaxation and concentration—both essential to effective kneading. Movements must be flowing and continuous, yet powerful and assertive. The choreography of this step requires a pas de deux between sprinkling flour and keeping the dough in motion. Even the slightest hesitation results in a stick. And that could lead to a tear. Hand jive.

Rising. The dough rises initially for four to five hours depending on the temperature and the humidity. After the hand kneading, the dough, like a newborn calf, is wobbly and barely able to stand alone. Moving my hands back and forth in a scissors-like motion enables me to form the most spherical shape, one I believe is conducive to a high rise—a figure ground of dough and air.

Stretching. A quick respite from the long rise: the dough is stretched, not torn, into a rectangle. This organic liquid/solid resists the precision of an orthogonal shape, yet this visual goal probably increases the likelihood of an even rise, with no air hole disproportionate to the rest. Even folds, and back into the rising bowl.

Shaping. For the final rise, or the proofing step, the dough is formed into loaves. These can take many shapes, but my current favorite is the batard—a larger, baguette-shaped loaf. The boule, yet another shape, may be the most beautiful, resembling a large, dark mountain stone. Again, my lesson of shaping this loaf is passed from Paris through David Auerbach, philosopher and an organizer of the Slow Food movement in America. David learned his baking from Michel Cousin, master baker of L'Autre Boulange in the eleventh arrondissement. Folding, rolling, and pinching into a smooth and consistent form—while the visual image may motivate this, clarity of form is crucial. The crumb (the part inside the crust) should be coarse and resistant to the tooth but absent of huge blowouts where air bubbles distort like a human goiter.

Proofing. The batards are now placed in long, flowered bannetons (linen-lined baskets), which allow air circulation and also wick moisture from the dough's surface. They rest covered for two hours.

Baking. The actual baking of bread is a complex procedure. Chemical transformations (mostly of water inside the dough) exceed the limits of my knowledge (for beautifully written descriptions of all aspects, see *The Bread Builders* by Daniel Wing and Alan Scott [Chelsea Green, 1999]). High heat (over 500°F) and moisture in the oven are key.

The transition from the banneton to the baking sheet or stone demands great finesse. Though I do not use a stone or peel, I treat the loaves like fragile newborns. Any trauma adversely affects the height of the loaf. Sometimes my best loaves happen when failure seems certain. The other day I forgot to turn the oven temperature down for the last 20 minutes and I discovered a multilayered crust that I had never before achieved.

Considerations move deeper into the subconscious the more I bake. They are part of the experience that informs my hands. Every time is different, because no two-day period is the same. Each loaf is a temporary record of its making. Last week, movie times coincided with starter preparation.

The ticket-taker stopped me at the door of the Michigan Theater.

FIGURE 1.19
Courtesy of A. Melissa Harris.

"Excuse me, what's in your paper bag?"

"It's my bread ingredients. I have to feed my bread the day before I bake it," I responded.

Inside the bag was my tall plastic bowl, a plastic bag full of premeasured flour, an old olive jar filled with 10 ounces of water, and a wooden spoon for stirring. After a quick survey, the ticket taker remained perplexed, but let me in. I saw the movie and added the final mix by the light of the screen. That night the culture stayed out of the refrigerator longer and the resulting bread was flat due to over-extension.

My bread reinforces the need to revel in the process of making, and my buildings are beginning to reflect a cross-fertilization of designing and baking. At no point in creation can a vision of the end product diminish the significance of each step or divert the urge to ride the wave of a tangent, even if momentary. Applying the golden mean to a garden structure may, at first glance, tread on the dangerous ground of formulaic formalism. A proportioning system might offer the designer relief from the need to be continually present, engaged. But understanding the mathematics of the golden mean is as elegant and sensual as shaping a round loaf of soft dough, and may be the necessary aesthetic immersion for a better structure.

A Shade Structure

❏ Sometime around November and February each year I explain the golden mean to my basic drawing students by way of a graphic demonstration. I discuss the golden mean as a specific proportion whose usefulness and beauty lay within the larger arena of relationships. The challenge is to distinguish for the students a means from an end, taking care not to cast visual and formal decisions as mere formulas.

This concern stems from past experience teaching beginning design students and witnessing the explosion of proportioning rationale seeking to justify design decisions. In such rhetoric I miss what I consider larger ideas, goals with tentacles to reach both broadly and deeply into issues of form, structure, and experience. Beginning design students always look first for rational answers to design questions.

I have always felt prepared for the class on the golden mean, armed with colored chalks and a steady hand. First a square, divide that in half, rotate the diagonal of one of those halves, extend the base. But this summer I received a design request that shook my confidence and changed the way I teach. The client, my mother, wanted a shade structure roughly 10 by 16 feet.

Last winter a cherry tree marking the middle of my mother's and stepfather's garden blew over in an ice storm—roots and all. They had always eaten meals under that old tree in the good weather. Sheltered and shaded under limbs of white blossoms, the table rested on a bed of dark mulch and fallen petals. Practically speaking, the cherry tree with its wide, protective embrace enabled summer use of the backyard. A young replacement would not mature until my parents were well into their eighties. That seemed too long to wait.

Ten by 16 feet is so close to the golden mean ratio that I bit. But I did not realize what I would relearn about the beauty of mathematics. There is, of course, an irreconcilable dilemma when applying a proportioning system of an irrational root onto lumber and posts limited by whole numbers—two-by-twos, two-by-fours, and four-by-sixes. Because of its irrationality, there is no end to sizing or dimensioning. One must "cheat" or approximate dimensions since the tools of most contractors do not recognize decimals. I began to discover the significance of the Fibonacci series and to rediscover the elegant algebra and calculus I left behind years ago.

To actually solve for the golden mean, one could ask what length would be added to a square to create a rectangle whose sides are both arithmetically and geometrically related. In other words, what rectangle whose one side is shared by a square will, when added to the original square, form a larger rectangle proportional to the first?

If the two rectangles are similar (in a geometric sense), then

$$1/x = (1 + x)/1$$

which rearranges to

$$x^2 + x - 1 = 0$$

Since any quadratic equation of the form $ax^2 + bx + c = 0$ can be solved by the quadratic equation

$$x = \frac{-b \pm \sqrt{b^2 - 4ac}}{2a}$$

and the equation describing the golden mean is

$$x^2 + x - 1 = 0,$$

$$\text{where } a = 1$$

$$b = 1$$

$$c = -1$$

then, when we substitute these values for a, b, and c into the quadratic equation, the equation solves for x with two values

$$x = -1$$

$$x = 0.6180339$$

Of course, only the positive value, $x = 0.6180339$, is relevant to the real-world problem of rectangles. The ratio corresponding to the golden mean is, therefore, 1.0 plus 0.6180339 or 1.6180339. This unique result reveals that the only ratio of rectangular dimensions that satisfies the similarity criterion is 1.6180339.

From a seemingly completely different point of view, the Fibonacci series is an arithmetic series wherein each progressive number is the sum of the two previous numbers, e.g., 0, 1, 1, 2, 3, 5, 8, 13, 21, 34, etc. This is deceptively related to the golden mean because as the series progresses, the ratio of one number divided by its predecessor approaches 1.6180339. As the numbers being divided increase, the value of the ratio begins to move above and then below the value of the golden mean, oscillating with diminishing amplitude, coming ever so close, but never reaching the limit of 1.6180339, the exact number of the golden mean.

FIGURE 1.20
Courtesy of A. Melissa Harris.

The arbor was shaped by other desires as well. The view through the structure needed to frame a "captured landscape" as in a Japanese garden, with a clear view of the distant, white Carrara marble sculpture in front of weeping Japanese maples. It had to be structurally strong enough to support annual shade vines. And I wanted a feeling of two spaces inside—one more private or service-oriented and the other more open. I chose the natural divide between the infinitely repeating square and the golden rectangle to distinguish these two functions. It is marked both in plan (by a smaller-grain floor decking), in elevation (by horizontal slats increasing in interval spacing according to the Fibonacci series), and in a more dense spacing of overhead members. In plan, the square rotates into the section to become a golden rectangle and the golden rectangle becomes a square in elevation.

I have recorded most of the past 20 years of my life in sketchbooks (now almost 40 of them) filled with daily drawings. A friend recently dubbed this addiction to visual recording "note-itis." I see in drawings the creation of relationships. All of my work—teaching, designing, baking, writing—is influenced by my drawing, which demands daily refinement of one's awareness, visual acuity, and skilled hand-eye coordination, as in kneading bread. On each page of my sketchbooks are conscious and subconscious decisions—where text goes in relation to image, what medium I use and why, what type projection. This is surely the path to my life as a teacher. And it is, again, where bread baking and building converge.

Training in the visual and applied arts has far-reaching implications when one weaves the experience it provides into all disciplined production. The aesthetic concerns of a building's proportion or the shape of the dough that forms a loaf of bread become almost second nature to someone involved in routine baking and drawing. The product is nothing if you have not enjoyed the fragile beauty of a mountain of flour, the flow of ink on smooth toothed paper, or the disciplined struggle to calculate a set of dimensions.

Designing Your Time

with Nancy Greiff

❏ Typically in architecture school, bad work habits become ingrained. The macho stay-up-all-night mentality is valued by students and actually viewed as a badge of honor. This habit may lead to terrible time-management practices in the real world.

There is no question that it takes a long time to design a building thoughtfully. For many of us, the creative process is stimulating, boring, energizing, tortured, filled with self-doubts, and satisfying in varying degrees and sequences, depending on the particular project and frame of mind. Because creativity is so idiosyncratic and often quirky, it may be very difficult to manipulate all the variables and forces toward planned inspiration. But plan you must to promote, to the extent possible, balanced, healthy, stress-free, and productive professional and personal experiences.

John Lyons, PhD, proposes how to think about the relevance of what one does, and this has implications for prioritizing time. He says, "The process I invoke has to do with defining the impact of the work. I ask: 'What are the specific effects, and what is the maximum potential?' Of course you have to prioritize—order the dimensions you want to impact most. Try to define these as specifically as possible. When you decide exactly what you want to achieve, it is much easier to go out and fulfill the prophecy."

Consider time management as a design problem, as management expert Nancy Greiff explains in Supplement 1.6. Baby steps! If at first things seem overwhelming, just chip away one small step at a time. (And don't forget to take a running jump at that first step.)

Nancy Greiff

Nancy Greiff, PhD, owns Positive Resolutions, an Albuquerque-based training and consulting business specializing in people skills for the workplace. She enjoys helping client organizations with negotiation, win-win conflict resolution, customer service, and time management. Formerly a professor at Cornell University, Dr. Greiff now leads events and training programs nationwide. Participants in Dr. Greiff's training programs have come from over 100 of the Fortune 500 companies, as well as from small and mid-size businesses, government agencies, and nonprofit organizations. © 2000 Nancy Greiff.

SUPPLEMENT 1.6

❏ One of the greatest ironies of professional training is that we are taught a vast array of complex skills, but not how to manage our time so that we can use these skills effectively! This short essay provides tips for some of the most common time challenges at work and at home.

The Difference Between Efficiency and Effectiveness

❏ You can be very efficient at completing tasks before you, but if these tasks do not contribute to the career and the life you want, then you are not using your time *effectively*. It is possible to be very good at doing the wrong things! Here is a wonderful story that highlights the difference between efficiency and effectiveness.

> *A team of managers was supervising a crew building a road through a jungle. The crew was working steadily, clearing trees and brush, grading the road, installing drainage—doing all the tasks necessary to build a good road. The road looked to be a great success.*
>
> *Then, the project leader arrived and climbed up a tree in order to get an overview. After surveying the activity below, he called down to the managers, "Wrong jungle!"*
>
> *The managers, undaunted, called back to the leader, "Shut up; we're making progress!"* (Adapted from First Things First, *by Stephen R. Covey, A. Roger Merrill, and Rebecca R. Merrill [Simon & Schuster, 1994].*)

Sometimes we are so caught up in the heady feeling of getting things done efficiently that we do not ask ourselves if these things are leading us in the right direction. *Efficiency* is about building a road with a minimum of wasted resources, such as time, effort, and materials. *Effectiveness* is about building a road through the right jungle!

To be effective, figure out—and write down—your long-term goals. This may require some careful soul-searching, as well as discussion with partners in your plans (your spouse or significant other, your boss). Then make sure that each day includes actions directly relevant to these goals. Study that state-of-the-art building material you would like to be using in your designs. Play with your kids. "Now" is the only time you have. "Later" never comes.

A good way to head in the right direction is to ask yourself: "What are three things I could do today (or this week, month, or year) that would most benefit my organization (or career, work group, or project)?" This will help you set priorities and act on them.

Ask yourself frequently, "What is the best use of my time right now?" If the answer is something other than what you find yourself doing, consider switching to the more important task.

Create Goals That Are Specific and Meaningful

❑ To use time more effectively, set specific, measurable goals and create an action plan to achieve those goals. Vague and ill-defined New Year's resolutions, for example, tend to fade away into the haze of good intentions. "Get in shape this year," is not specific and measurable. Even, "Go to the gym three times a week" is too vague. Go to the gym and do what? "Swim a half-mile three times a week," is an example of a specific and measurable goal.

Once you have set specific and measurable goals, you can identify the tasks necessary to accomplish them. Then, decide the order in which these tasks should be done and what resources are needed. Set reasonable deadlines. For example, if you want to build your family vacation home in the mountains, first set a time frame; otherwise, dreams remain in the future, and fail to become present realities. Then, determine how much money you must save, where you want to build, and so on.

Keep your action plan in a visible place, not tucked away. Believe it or not, in the daily crush of small tasks, you can forget to move toward your most important goals.

At the end of each day, take a few minutes to organize your desk and lay out your top-priority task for the next day. This will give you a "jump start" in the morning and will encourage you to do important things first. Starting the day with the most important task will give you a feeling of success and progress, and eliminate that feeling of something unfinished hanging over your head.

Resist the Path of Least Resistance

❏ Sometimes the really important things seem too overwhelming, so we take the path of least resistance. We spend time doing things we know are not very important, but that give us the illusion that we are in control.

It *is* satisfying to cross items off the list. The trick is to divide important tasks into small blocks and use those as the easy-to-handle items. That way, you make progress on the big tasks. It is so much easier to get started if the task before you does not seem huge and daunting.

Interrupt the Vicious Cycle of Interruptions!

❏ When asked to name their most frustrating time management problems at work, most people mention interruptions. Even coworkers who make their desks their "second home" probably feel that interruptions are a big problem for them too.

People are right in feeling that interruptions often waste time. On average, you can finish three times as much work in a stretch of uninterrupted time as you can in the same period of time with interruptions. In other words, a half-hour of uninterrupted time is equivalent to an hour and a half of stop-and-start work.

The trick to controlling interruptions is to understand that everyone at work feels the day gets too chopped up to make a concentrated effort. Enlist your coworkers' help, even your boss's help, in implementing the following suggestions:

■ Schedule "closed-door" time, where you can only be disturbed for genuine emergencies. If you have a door, close it and put a sign on the door with some message such as, "Back at 10 A.M." Even if your workspace does not literally have a door, you can do this simply by letting others know that this is your uninterrupted time and you will be available both before and after this time.

■ Determine what your peak energy time is, and make this your closed-door time. Do high-priority work during your most alert times.

■ During closed-door time, let voice mail pick up the telephone. If your job depends heavily on telephone contact, it will help if you change your voice mail message during closed-door time to let people know when you will be returning calls. "Hello, this is John Smith. I will be in a meeting between 9 and 10 A.M. today, and will be returning voice messages from 10:15 to 11:30. I would like to speak with you, so please leave a message . . ." Most people care more about knowing when they will speak with you than they care about doing so now.

■ Encourage others to treat themselves to closed-door time as well, and respect their time. This gives them a great incentive to leave you alone during *your* no-interruptions time. With bosses, it helps to cite the "3-to-1" rule—"I know it is difficult not to have access to me for that hour in the morning, but it means I can finish the project you gave me three times faster!"

■ Understand that you may be the chief interrupter of your own work. Perhaps you are scheduling your most important projects in "residual time" when you do not have a meeting or some other activity scheduled. Instead, make appointments with yourself to work on big projects. Write these in your calendar and treat them as you would treat an appointment with an important client or with your boss. Schedule other things that come up around them, just as you would with any other important commitment.

■ Set time limits on less important work that interrupts progress toward your major goals. Defer or shorten low-priority or low-value tasks. For example, do not read your junk mail.

■ Minimize self-interrupting by scheduling similar tasks at the same time. Switching mental gears takes time. So, return telephone calls all at once, write memos in a chunk of time devoted to that, and so on.

"Tickle" Your Papers

❏ "If we're moving toward the paperless office, how come I still cannot see the top of my desk?"

Along with interruptions, most people name organizing paperwork as a large time robber. Many people create piles of paper, little by little. You might think, "If I don't leave this memo about submitting my budget request where I can see it, I'll forget to do it before the deadline." The trouble with this approach is that each reminder is soon covered by the next must-see item, again and again, until you find yourself in a maze of paper.

The solution is a tickler file. A tickler file is a series of 43 folders, the first 31 of which are labeled 1 through 31, and the last twelve of which are labeled with the names of the months. Paper that needs to be saved because some action will be required on your part goes into the tickler file. So, if you receive an item on April 10 that you will not use until April 20 (directions to an April 20 meeting, for example), put it in the folder labeled "20." If you receive an item on April 10 that only becomes important in June, place it in the June folder. At the end of May, take out the June folder and arrange the accumulated items into the appropriate 1 through 30 folders.

If today is April 10, then at the end of the day take the 11 folder out of the filing cabinet and place it front and center on your pile-free desk. All the pieces of mail and other papers you'll need for the next day will then be waiting when you arrive at work the next morning.

Here are a few other simple tips:

■ Always refile what you take out and create new files for new items.
■ Process mail on a daily basis. Incoming paper goes into one of three places:

    1. Your filing cabinet, if it is important enough to keep but does not require action.
    2. Your tickler file, if it is an action item.
    3. The trash. The trash is a great place to put paper. Be honest with yourself about all those things you save because you'll get to them "someday."

■ Clean out files as you use them. Cull outdated items while you're using the file. Then you won't have to clean your files because they no longer fit in your cabinet! And your mind will be working much more effectively and efficiently than it would if you had to do many files at once.

■ To vanquish existing piles of paper, just process 5 to 10 pieces a day. Before long, your backlog will be gone.

Defeat Defeatism

❏ If you use even a few of these tips, life really will become easier. But we all fight against years of habit, and we fear that we will not have the energy or discipline to change. A natural tendency is to conjure up all the reasons why a new strategy will not work (others will not cooperate, and so on). Remember that even if a new strategy does not solve the problem completely, any improvement *is* improvement. You may reduce unwanted interruptions by only one-third at first, but even one-third means that life is better. You now have one-third more time to concentrate on major projects—or even play with the kids.

Finally, be sure to congratulate yourself for changing your use of time! And enjoy the results!

chapter 2

The Program

"The genes of a building
are determined before
a sketch is made."
—Bill Caudill

Sketches

❏ In evaluating a retrospective on the architecture of Louis Kahn at the Philadelphia Museum of Art in 1991, Herbert Muschamp observed something incredibly profound specifically about Kahn, and generally about the program in architectural design. Muschamp states, "He [Kahn] was no mere formalist in love with powerful shapes. He was obsessed with powerful ideas he could shape into forms. His frequent allusion to 'silence and light' meant just this: that forms should emerge into the light of physical reality only after long reflection on the metaphysical aspects of a building program . . . for Kahn, a library was not a place for storage and circulation . . . it was a shrine to the human act of learning." Muschamp continues by asserting that Kahn's "reverence" for the program is what distinguished his work from the "empty monumentality" of some of his colleagues.

Kahn himself wrote, regarding his design for Mikveh Israel, "I must be in tune with the spirit that created the first synagogue. I must rediscover that sense of beginnings through beliefs."

Wow. This is energizing stuff. A deep understanding of the cultural, social, and historical contexts that begin to define the underpinnings of the program (as exemplified by Kahn's immersion) is quite a compelling way to launch the design process.

Norman Foster has a slightly different viewpoint. In a discussion about program, he says, "If there is one aspect that unifies all our buildings, it is the suitability of the building to the requirements. We do an unusual amount of research, not only into the technological systems that we eventually use, but also to develop the program, before we ever develop a physical image of the structure."

Simply stated, *the program is the design problem*. It usually includes project goals; functional requirements, activities, and organizational relationships; client and/or user preferences; a mandate for budget, construction quality, and schedule; future expansion, conversion, and phasing capabilities; utilization and scheduling of spaces; and any other criteria to facilitate the user's activities. Clients' wish lists and the architects' personal expectations for the project may all have an effect at this stage. It is easy to see why the program is the single most important element in shaping successful buildings: it is the foundation for many design decisions. The program is what makes architecture one of the great professions, distinguishing it from pure art.

Meaningful discussions with the client and with typical building users are invaluable in eliciting information that helps define the problem. Because the client often has difficulty in voicing needs and problems, the architect has an early opportunity to be a creative diagnostician. Continuing dialogues and diagnoses through all design phases fine-tune (or in some cases redefine) the program to ensure an optimal design response. In fact, since programming and design are so interdependent, it may be helpful to view programming as the initial stage of design.

FIGURE 2.1
Even though the building user may be large and shaggy and have a limited vocabulary, the architect is still obliged to try to understand his or her point of view and needs. (Courtesy of Andy Pressman.)

The program can assume many forms. As a function of project scale and circumstance, a verbal command from client to designer may be sufficient ("I want a new Las Vegas–style bathroom with a hot tub and a skylight"), or something more comprehensive may be necessary (a five-pound document describing the special needs of inmates of a large urban correctional facility). The program can be the tool that empowers the client and users in helping shape physical design. For complex projects, programming may be enhanced or performed by specialists, consultants who conduct sophisticated social, behavioral, and market research. A client's demands for specific building "components and systems" to minimize energy use, for example, may also be elicited and will have an impact on design. Good rapport and trust with client and/or building users will ensure ongoing, effective communication. It is this communication that shapes the program. And it is the program, in turn, that very significantly drives the design.

As a complement to the metaphysical approach just described, programming phases may be organized pragmatically as follows (I have invoked much of the scheme by David Haviland, writing about "Predesign Services" in *The Architect's Handbook of Professional Practice*, 11th ed. [AIA, 1987]).

■ *Information gathering.* This phase encompasses two types of research: collecting primary data (personal contact with all the players) and accumulating secondary data (looking at precedents—familiarization with what has been done before; identification of applicable codes and regulations; awareness of construction budget; observation of typical activity patterns in similar buildings; and study of existing condition surveys if the project is a renovation).

■ *Analysis and interpretation of information.* This phase involves laying out all material in order to define and inventory all problems, needs, and other program elements comprehensively and with the highest possible degree of resolution. Patterns of circulation are determined, and organizational requirements that may diverge from the norm are carefully documented and diagrammed. This exercise, in turn, helps the designer conceive of spatial qualities that represent the unique character and scale of the program elements.

■ *Concept development.* The "soul" of the project may emerge at this point. Suddenly there is a light in the designer's eye, stimulated by just about anything that might have evolved during the previous work, or even the architect's own evolving agenda (see my conversation with Thom Mayne of Morphosis in Chapter 7 for more on this subject). That the "functional" aspect of a solution arises in this final phase of programming makes it potentially as exciting as the first design sketches.

This chapter generally describes what is included and how to execute the three broad phases of the programming process as just outlined. The process is likely to become very personalized; the following strategies are suggested only as an example of a rational basis upon which to develop what works best for you.

The chapter begins with interesting views about how clients look and think about buildings—perhaps intuitive, but quite enlightening as a basic reminder. Programming expert Edie Cherry writes about orchestrating client involvement to address client objectives of function, cost, and schedule. A related supplement by Min Kantrowitz focuses on interactions between client and architect and good communication. Kantrowitz offers an innovative "decision pyramid approach to design excellence." Information gathering, including facilitating client interviews and finding useful information quickly, extends the discourse on effective programming. Conceptual design cost estimating, value engineering, and building codes and regulations (including universal design), while seemingly not as seductive as searching for the big idea, are all an integral part of doing design, and can be exciting (really!), as will be evident in the discussions that follow. The chapter ends with a truly rare application of environment-behavior principles to architecture in a provocative essay by Jerry Weisman.

Ten Ways of Looking at a Building
with Ralph Caplan

❏ I met Bob Hillier, chairman of the board and chief executive officer of the Hillier Group, during final thesis reviews at the University of Maryland. His comments struck me as razor sharp with a light touch, constructive, and perfectly suited to the students' projects. He then told me about a booklet that he and his wife created and commissioned, *Ten Ways of Looking at a Building*, designed for prospective clients. It is clear that Bob is very much in tune with understanding the views of others, be they students presenting their work or clients trying to figure out the meaning of architecture. This understanding of people is a decided advantage in building a successful client relationship. Supplement 2.1 contains Bob's introduction followed by the text of the booklet, by Ralph Caplan.

Ralph Caplan

Ralph Caplan, author of Ten Ways of Looking at a Building: A Guide to the Rights of Clients, *has also written* By Design: Why There Are No Locks on the Bathroom Doors in the Hotel Louis XIV, and Other Object Lessons *(St. Martin's Press, 1982).*

"At the Hillier Group architecture is serious business, but it is useful occasionally to approach it from a perspective that doesn't take it, or us, too seriously. With that in mind the Hillier Group commissioned this small book that looks lightly but insightfully at what buildings mean to clients and other people who use them."

Bob Hillier

❑ We all look at buildings (it is the best thing to do with some of them), but we don't all look at them in the same way. We don't talk about them in the same way either. Clients talk about space and rooms. Architects talk about programming and formatting. Clients talk about privacy. Architects talk about footprints. Clients talk about image and corporate culture. Architects talk about design statements and historical resonance. Clients talk about windows. Architects talk about fenestration. Clients talk about color. Architects talk about color. People talk about buildings. Architects talk about architecture.

Most people don't think like architects. And architects too often don't think like people. If they did, they might begin by asking the kinds of questions people ask: how big? How much? How soon? What for? Will it pay off? What will it be like to work in? To drive up to? Will the students feel proud of this campus? What are the various roles in getting it built, and who plays them?

People look at buildings in hundreds of ways. Here are 10 of the ways most common to the commissioned environment.

- ■ *The building as an investment.* A building represents an investment to owners, developers, management, and—in the case of public corporations—to shareholders, who may never actually visit it or need to. They have a right to a reasonable return.
- ■ *The building as a neighbor.* Buildings don't exist in isolation. They go where something else already is or used to be. Long

before environmental impact statements were mandated, environmental impact was a fact of life. Clients have a right to a building that gets along with the rest of the neighborhood. And so does the neighborhood.

■ *The building as a tool.* Le Corbusier said that a house was a machine for living—a provocative image, evoking one way of looking at building. From that point of view, an office building is a machine for working, a college campus a machine for learning, a hotel a machine for staying in when you have to be away from the machine for living. Whether or not buildings are machines, they certainly can be seen as tools, facilities that people use for office work, sales, education, and other purposes. All users see them in this way and so do the people who have to take care of them. A client has the right to a tool that works.

■ *The building as an invitation.* Some buildings invite people in. Others look prohibitive. There are stores people don't like even if they want the merchandise in them, and there are stores that create traffic even among people who never intended to shop. Administrative buildings can be imposing, forbidding, indifferent, or welcoming. Every vice president of human resources knows the importance of an inviting workplace. A building's users, whether employees or the public, have a right to feel welcome.

■ *The building as an adventure.* Murphy's Law must have been written by a contractor. A building can be seen as a traumatic experience, or at least as a series of crises. The human urge to build seems to be countered at every turn by a superhuman resistance to getting something built. Until it's built, a building is a project. No one has a right to a project free of problems, but every client has a right to a satisfying adventure.

■ *The building as an image.* "The ancient Greeks used buildings not for shelter but to communicate," James Ackerman writes. So do we. All buildings say something, so they may as well say something about what they are and for whom. Both the owners and the public perceive each building as part of the organization whose name it bears and whose activities it houses. Buildings stand for the institutions that built or occupy them. Companies have a right to buildings that stand up for them.

■ *The building as home*. Home is where you hang your hat, where you hang out, where your pictures hang. Any building may be home to people who spend most of their time in it. In that sense office is home. School is home. Factory is home. As an increasing variety of buildings take on some of the functions of home, they need also to provide some of the comforts of home.

■ *The building as a collaboration*. Clients require buildings, which in turn require architects. Architects, on the other hand, cannot usually design without clients. So architects and clients need each other. At best they deserve each other. Clients have the right to an understanding collaborator.

■ *The building as an interior*. The meaning of most buildings depends upon what goes on inside them, so interior architecture matters at least as much as the outside does. That's why people who work in a building tend to look at it inside out. They have a right to a building that makes sense when someone looks at it that way.

■ *The building as architectural statement*. Although a building stands for the client, it invariably stands as well for the architect who designed it. Some buildings make architectural statements that enhance their value, and therefore their client's contribution, to society. Clients have a right to the very best design they can get, and also to the assurance that no statement in form is made at the expense of the building's purpose.

Afterword

❑ Those 10 ways of looking at a building are not *the* 10 ways; neither are they mutually exclusive. They overlap. Buildings, like everything else important in our lives, are usually seen in several ways simultaneously. But, although hardly anyone sees a building in only one way, each of the 10 perceptions shown may be of primary concern to someone. The building as a tool is likely to be the highest priority to facility managers. The building as an interior may be the most important view from the standpoint of the people who work in it. The building as an image may be most important to large numbers of people who never actually see or use it, which is why business letterheads used to be topped with engravings of offices and factories that made the company tangible, and why television shows use buildings to represent San Francisco, Miami, Paris, and New York. The building as architectural statement is usually not the primary point of view. (If it is the architect's first priority, you may need a second opinion or another architect.)

Although people see buildings in any of a variety of ways, there are two people who have to look at a building in all these ways and more—the client and the architect. But the building belongs to more than the client and the architect. It belongs to the developer, to the public, to the city where it's located, and to the individuals and groups who use it or merely encounter it. Whose building is it anyway?

Institutional language, which has the effect of flattening perceptions in general, tends to pluralize individuals. "We are going to need more work surface for the Sally Jordans," a facility manager will say. "The Mike Carters are not going to appreciate this façade," the vice president of marketing may say. Actually there is only one Sally Jordan and one Mike Carter, but there are thousands who are like them in some ways and unlike them in others.

Buildings have to work and they have to please people. No building can please everybody, but every building ought to work for everybody who uses it. In looking at a building it is essential to keep Sally Jordan and Mike Carter in mind. When architects think like people, they do.

Orchestrating Client Involvement

with Edie Cherry

❑ Chicago architect Carol Ross Barney, FAIA, neatly characterizes the spirit of this section: "Ownership is really bad. It *prevents* an open mind. Now, if someone at my company starts talking about 'my design,' we put them on a different project." In Supplement 2.2, Edie Cherry specifically details how to maintain an open mind during the programming process, elicit and manage appropriate input from a range of stakeholders, and develop truly reciprocal communication between architect and client.

One overlooked aspect of architectural practice is the satisfaction inherent in serving people. Responding both creatively and with maximum appreciation of human needs ultimately yields perhaps the greatest reward: the manifest pleasure and improved quality of life of building inhabitants.

SUPPLEMENT 2.2

Edie Cherry

Edie Cherry, FAIA, is the author of Programming for Design: From Theory to Practice *(Wiley, 1999). Her professional experience includes 7 years at Caudill Rowlett Scott (CRS) (now Hellmuth, Obata & Kassabaum, Inc. [HOK]) and over 20 years as a partner in the award-winning firm Cherry/See Architects. She is also a former professor and director of architecture at the University of New Mexico.*

❑ Clients! Sometimes, we can't live with 'em. Always, we can't live without 'em.

How can we work more effectively with clients? How can we get them to do things our way? This essay seeks to answer the former question, and suggests that the reader reconsider the latter question altogether. Why? Because it lacks an attitude of reciprocity, and such an attitude is necessary for any valued enterprise, from trading grain for shells 3000 years ago to designing a project for the twenty-first-century client. Architects who believe reciprocity is important have happy clients that return to build again. Who wants to do business with someone who is only interested in his or her own agenda?

Who Are Our Clients?

❑ We begin by defining clients in a very broad way. We should think of clients as all of the people who will be affected by our design efforts. Some of these people are the actual owners of the project. They have the legal authority to alter the built environment under their jurisdiction. Some clients are tenants of the environment to be changed, meaning they have a right to be there, remain there. This type of client includes the users of the facility to be designed. They come and go every day, and their lives are enriched or diminished by the quality of the designed environment. We can also include the general public in this broad definition of clients because they also are affected by the presence of this design in their midst.

There is a notion—a democratic, perhaps even an ethical notion—that those who are affected by design should have a say in that design. If we accept that notion, we have to realize it by developing appropriate methods for including clients in the design process. Clients should be included at a time in the process when their expertise can be incorporated in a meaningful way. The best time for that involvement is during the architectural programming phase. At this point a wide range of solutions is possible, and client input can be accommodated in a variety of ways. Clients know how they work and operate. They often know what they need to be effective at their endeavors. In the cases when they do not know what they need, they are often in the best position to provide the information that can lead to the provision of an environment that accommodates them most effectively.

Usually clients do not speak "architectese." They often do not know how to articulate their needs in a way that is readily translated into information for designers to use. It is the architect's responsibility to make the translations. In a situation where the client numbers are small, for example a custom single-family residential project in the country, the owner and users may be the same people, and there are few members of the general public to consider. Informal conversations take place and eye contact can be made. An architect who wishes to communicate well with the client must listen carefully, speak carefully, and watch the eyes and facial expressions of the client. Understanding, or lack of it, is often signaled by the expressions in eyes and on faces.

If the client group is large, there is the need for someone to organize the information-gathering process and translate that information into a package that can guide design. This translator is often an architectural programmer, or a designer acting in a programming mode. It is to this translator that the remainder of this essay is directed. We will look at techniques for organizing and facilitating the involvement of clients in the architectural programming process.

Owner's Approval

❏ The first step in involving the users of a project is to get the permission of the owner to do so. The architectural programmer should meet with the owner and be prepared with a draft proposal of the process for involving the other clients. It is generally in the owner's best interest that users of the facility and the general public be consulted regarding a facility to be developed in their midst. In the case of a project built with public funds, community involvement is, in many places, required by law. We will assume for the sake of the following presentation that the owner approves wholeheartedly of wide participation.

Organizing Group Participation

❏ When the identifiable client group is large, a representative type of participation is in order; that is, a committee representing the major types of clients should be selected to represent the greater whole. The size can vary from 3 to 20 or so, but beyond a group of 20, it is difficult to have the entire group participating in the same discussion. When representative groups need to be larger than 20 or so, they can be broken down into smaller groups.

With a representative committee, perhaps called the building or project committee, it is important to arrange periodic presentations to the larger group that is represented. Regarding either the project committee meetings or the more widely attended public meeting, there are some basic preparatory items to keep in mind. One is the selection of meeting time and place. The needs of the constituents, not the needs of the programmer, are paramount here. If the meeting is for workers, their employer should help decide the place and time—preferably during working hours, since the meeting is a matter of business. If the meeting is intended to attract the public, it should be held in a place that is familiar and at a time that is not during working hours. Announcement of the meeting must be widely disseminated as well, including information about why the meeting is important to the constituency it hopes to attract.

Meetings of both small and large attendance should begin with introductions of the people doing the presenting. Ideally, the person making the introductions will be someone who is widely known to the attendees. The president of the neighborhood association or the owner of the business makes a good introducer. The purpose here is to give some credibility to the programmer. The audience members should feel that this new person in their midst is the one who is supposed to be there, who is recommended by people they know.

If the audience is small enough, and time allows, each member can introduce him- or herself and describe his or her interest in the project. Often programmers assume that members of a group such as a neighborhood association or a small business already know each other. But, of course, new neighbors or employees may be in attendance and may appreciate the opportunity to introduce themselves to their new colleagues. If the group is too large for individual introductions, the programmer, who is by now acting as a facilitator, can ask for the members of the audience who belong to various constituencies to raise their hands. For example, the facilitator may say, "How many of you are members of the Silver Hills Neighborhood Association?" or "How many of you work in the shipping and receiving department?" When the majority of the groups have been identified, then the question can be asked, "Have we missed anyone? Please tell us about your interest in the project." There is another purpose in making the introductions beyond the obvious one of knowing who is in attendance, and that is that it is important for members of the audience to know who else is interested in the project. This knowledge delivers the message that one's own interest is not likely to be the only viewpoint.

If this meeting is not the first, it is important to ask if anyone was not able to attend the last meeting. This should be done in a way that is not reproachful, but welcoming. A bit of review of the previous meeting is desirable under any circumstances, since people lead busy lives and may not have been able to stay for the entire length of the previous meeting. Depending on the response, the facilitator can go over the results of the previous meeting or meetings lightly or in more depth.

Decision Making

❏ It is important to any group to understand what its role is in the bigger picture. Is this group an advisory one? Will it be making recommendations to a higher authority—a city council, perhaps, or a board of directors? It is not wise to let members of a group believe that they have more decision-making authority than they really have, because if their decision is overridden at a higher level, they may feel betrayed by the facilitator.

Once a group understands its role, the next step is to decide how the group will make its decisions. In a way, any group is a small society, and societies have a political aspect in that they make decisions. Some use anarchy ("without rule"); some use democracy ("people rule"); some use oligarchy ("a few rule"); some use monarchy ("one rules"); and some use consensus, meaning everyone must come to the same decision, or at least not be opposed to the decision. Many small committees decide to try to use consensus, but if it takes too long, they will revert to majority rule. Sometimes, as with a neighborhood association, there are already bylaws established that spell out how the group makes decisions.

There is an important reason that the decision-making process should be selected before discussion of the project begins. Once an issue arises that requires a decision, the very act of selecting a decision-making process can be seen as partisan. For example, if the discussion begins and a difference of opinion is evident, majority rule may be proposed by those who estimate that they are in the majority. Those in the minority may propose consensus. The discussion that follows is likely not to be fruitful regarding the project itself, and may be quite the opposite.

One of the most common and difficult decisions that clients have to make is the ordering of priorities. Single clients and large groups of clients often have to choose (or recommend choices to decision makers at a higher level) between aspects of a project that are very valuable to them. The programming architect or facilitator can orchestrate this decision by helping the client identify all of the choices, and then by proposing a method of setting priorities. With a small group it is possible to then look at the list, discuss the merits of each item, assign some sort of value to each, and discuss adding other items at a later date. With a larger group, the "wish list" can be developed and then passed out with instructions to rank the items based upon personal priorities. It is imperative that a consistent ranking system be used making it clear whether item 1 is of high priority or low priority. The results can be collected and tabulated to determine the overall ranking of the group. Here, as with a smaller group, adding other items at a later date can be discussed. Clients seem to relax somewhat if they feel that items that receive a lower ranking may be considered for a later building phase.

Managing Larger Groups

❏ When dealing with larger groups, it is still possible to involve individuals in a meaningful way. In these cases, the meeting can be divided into three parts: introduction, breaking into smaller groups, and reuniting to describe the work of the smaller groups. In this type of structure, it is important to tend to logistical issues: (1) there must be sufficient space and furniture to divide the larger group into small, working units of perhaps 5 to 12 people; (2) there should be assignments given to each group; and (3) there should be a group leader or at least a group recorder appointed to document the work of each group. After the breakout session, each small group can present its results to the larger group. Determining the membership of the small groups can be done by random assignment, or by announcing the topics each small group will discuss and allowing people to join the group of their choosing.

Documenting Participatory Group Meetings

❏ It is often important to have a record of who is in attendance. Having a sign-in sheet at the door, or passing around a sheet for that purpose, can produce this record. Attendees should be reminded to sign at the beginning of the meeting and again at the end. The facilitator should make arrangements for someone to keep notes on the meeting, including any decisions that the group makes. If ideas are to be solicited from the audience, there should be a way to write them down and display them to the group as a whole. Flip charts, 5×7 cards, butcher paper, or other media can be used. The ideas are written down and posted on the wall. They can be arranged by predetermined topics or by topics that arise out of the discussion. After the meeting, this display can be collated and typed up and then reviewed at the next meeting or by the project committee.

In any large group meetings, it is recommended that the facilitator be freed of the documentation tasks in order to focus on the content of the discussion. This recommendation means that there should be at least two people involved in running the meeting. Keeping the conversation on the target of the project and allowing for a broad range of ideas is often very difficult. It is important to allow participation, but sometimes certain members of the audience have their own agenda, or simply like to hear themselves talk. The facilitator has to be able to discourage someone who wishes to monopolize the discussion without antagonizing him or her. One way to do this is to call on people who have not spoken and ask for their opinion. The facilitator can say, "Let's get as many different opinions as we can. Let's hear from someone who hasn't had a chance to speak yet."

Closing a meeting properly is as important as a good introduction. Meetings should be announced to last for a certain amount of time, and should begin and end on time. Prior to the announced closing time, a brief review of what has transpired should be given. The time and place for the next meeting, if there is to be one, should be announced. The major intentions of the next meeting should also be announced. If the group is not to meet again, the next step in the project should be described, so that people know what to look for regarding the project.

Becoming a Good Listener

❏ Throughout this discussion we have assumed that the architect and the client are communicating well. The notion of reciprocity—a fair exchange—is inherent in any good communication. We assume that the burden of communication is on the architect because he or she is the one that speaks architectese. We must also assume that the client offers ideas in his or her language, and that the architect reciprocates by listening. If clients do not understand what we say, we must alter our delivery to accommodate them; we cannot expect them to alter their delivery to accommodate us. If we do not understand the client, we must ask precise questions that get at his or her meaning.

In a sense, we have to become the teacher; we have to listen to clients, diagnose their thoughts, and then respond in a way that brings us closer together intellectually. This type of listening is called *active listening*. We are concentrating on what clients say, how they say it, and most importantly, why they say it. Active listening can be exhausting because it is much like simultaneous translation. One is listening, analyzing, synthesizing, and sympathizing all at the same time. Active listening requires exceptional effort, and, as with most exceptional efforts, it can glean exceptional results. When the architect and client are involved in a truly reciprocal communication, exciting things can happen. It takes good listeners, and to quote the essayist Sven Birkerts, ". . . to listen . . . is to admit a stance, a vantage, a world other than our own."

Communication with Your Client: A Decision Pyramid Approach to Design Excellence

with Min Kantrowitz

❑ Renzo Piano, in his Pritzker Architecture Prize speech of 1998, described a challenging line to straddle between one's own ideas and those of others: "Listening to people is important. And this is especially difficult for an architect. Because there is always the temptation to impose one's own design, one's own way of thinking, or, even worse, one's own style. I believe, instead, that a light approach is needed. Light, but without abandoning the stubbornness that enables you to put forward your own ideas whilst being permeable to the ideas of others."

In Supplement 2.3, Min Kantrowitz extends the discussion of communicating well with clients, and presents a fascinating approach to decision making in this realm.

Min Kantrowitz

Min Kantrowitz, AICP, is President of MKA, Inc., an Albuquerque, New Mexico, design research and consulting firm. The recipient of numerous national awards for applied design research, Kantrowitz holds graduate degrees in architecture and psychology, and is a member of the American Institute of Certified Planners. She is also a half-time associate professor at the University of New Mexico, with a joint appointment in the architecture and community and regional planning programs.

❑ One of the most challenging aspects of the design process is the often frustrating interaction between architect and client. Architects seek an opportunity to create an innovative and elegant design solution. Client expectations focus on a built solution to their problems. However, clients often have difficulty articulating their design ideas. As a result, architects spend a lot of time developing design concepts that clients then reject. While necessary to some extent, a protracted, iterative process of design, rejection, and redesign can dilute the design concept and damage the client-architect relationship, as well as endanger the project budget and decrease the opportunity for profit.

While most architectural projects start with mutual hopes for a high level of design quality, this cyclical process often wears down both parties. Under time pressure, clients compromise their ideas, hoping that, perhaps in the next redesign, an approximation of what they were originally thinking (and what they can afford) will be forthcoming within their time constraints. Architects compromise their design concepts, often becoming less enthusiastic about the final design and becoming more reluctant to explore new design solutions, recognizing that each iteration decreases their net fee. Design solutions based on a long series of compromises, while occasionally surprisingly successful, are more often a source of the kind of buildings that architects may be reluctant to claim proudly as examples of design excellence. This scenario also can harm the profession, as potential clients see mediocre designs as the product of what is often depicted as a difficult client-architect interaction.

With increasing consolidation of organizations in the private and nonprofit sectors, an awkward building, a frustrated client, or a lost opportunity for design excellence can multiply the impact of these flawed relationships. Perhaps what is needed is a new way to communicate about design, an approach to developing a more effective client-architect interaction, which should lead to more exciting and responsive design solutions.

The approach presented here assumes that the source of ineffective design communication between architect and client is often based in a particular kind of misunderstanding. Design is based on a series of interrelated decisions; the issue is whether the architect understands where in the decision process the client is at any point. If not, miscommunication will be assured; time will be wasted; good designs will be rejected; and it is more likely that mutual frustration will result in mediocre compromise solutions. With better understanding of the client decision process, the architect can better know:

- What information to present (and what to leave out)
- When the client is ready to move to the next step of a decision
- How to recognize a mismatch between architect and client about a particular decision

Figure 2.2 refers to the process most people use when making a decision. Here, it is most useful to think about this process as one your client will be using when considering an innovative design you will present.

The decision pyramid has five steps. For each decision, all five steps must be taken in order. The bottom of the pyramid is widest because it represents a larger number of people. Some people will not make the transition to the next stage. A narrowing of the pyramid represents each successive stage. Your goal as the architect is to assist the client in moving up the decision pyramid, step by step, until he or she reaches the Action

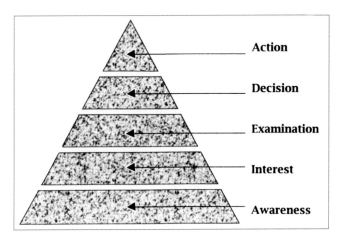

FIGURE 2.2
The Decision Pyramid. (Courtesy of Min Kantrowitz.)

step, where he or she enthusiastically supports your implementing the specific design idea. If you misinterpret where the client is on the decision pyramid, you risk delivering information inappropriate for the client's level of understanding. If a client stays stuck somewhere on the pyramid, you will waste time, energy, and design ideas.

The bottom step on the pyramid is called Awareness. This is where all clients begin. At this point, the architect must assume that the client knows nothing about the design idea. Your major tasks are introducing the concept, anticipating initial questions and concerns, and providing examples of successful and relevant applications of similar design concepts. Clients sometimes reject wonderful design ideas because they seem strange or unfamiliar. The Awareness stage builds exposure. The goal is to move the client to the next step of the pyramid, Interest. The key questions to ask your client are these: do you know about X? can I tell you about it?

At the Interest stage, the client has become curious, but is not yet ready to seriously consider the idea. Clients at this stage are ready for inspiration, but not yet ready to make any commitment. Your goal at this stage is to build your clients' curiosity by expanding their understanding of the potential of the design idea. For some clients, the most powerful way to increase curiosity is based on profit potential; for others it is organizational efficiency; for others, a memorable design statement, and for others, low construction cost. If client curiosity is not cultivated at this point, new design ideas are often abandoned. Understanding the motivation of the client is the key to helping that client move through the Interest stage to the next one, Examination. The key question to ask your client is this: can I show you some examples of X?

At the Examination stage, the goal is exploration. Here, you can explore applications of the new design idea to the clients' problem. This stage is an active one that can involve both client and architect in examining the implications of using the new design idea. By providing the client with detailed examples, supported by appropriate data on cost and performance, the architect can propel the client toward the next level, Decision. The key question to ask your client is this: can we explore how this idea might work for you?

The Decision stage is delicate. At this stage, the client is convinced, in theory, that the approach is a good one. However, some clients may stop at this point, hesitant about risks involved with taking action. Clients have many types of risks in mind at this point: financial, aesthetic, logistical, administrative, and political concerns can each contribute to a client's being reluctant to commit to take action. By understanding the sources of client concerns, you can anticipate client uncertainties and provide support and information to alleviate them. The key question to ask your client is this: what information could I give you that would address your concerns?

Once the Action stage has been reached, the client and architect share a mutual understanding, a situation that promotes design excellence in a context of positive client-architect interactions and that enhances the architect, the profession, and the public.

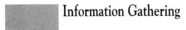 **Information Gathering**

❏ This chapter focuses on the qualitative rather than the quantitative aspects of programming. A basic knowledge of required spaces with their respective square footages (net assignable area), for example, is assumed. As well, gross area, including space for mechanical equipment, wall thicknesses, circulation, and other servant spaces, or tare—to determine the final size—is also assumed. (The gross square footage, then, equals net plus tare. Tare is hard to precisely define early on because it is a function of the specific design. But there are standard percentages for various building types, based on precedent, that can be used at this stage to facilitate planning.)

Now is a crucial time to launch yourself into a full understanding of the client, the client's business, how and why the project came into being, what the building is truly about, how it functions, and its relationship to the community. Some of this, however, may already have been accomplished to secure the commission. The following material provides guidance on obtaining high-quality information.

Primary Data

❏ Arrange interviews with clients and stakeholders. There is simply no substitute for getting out in the field and observing firsthand similar buildings and the people who use (or commission) them. Make time to do this—it is a small investment that can yield enormous benefit. (It's even a good strategy for marketing preparation, before you have secured the job!) For example, at a fire station, visit the fire chief and firefighters. Ask questions about special needs and preferences; ask for a wish list for a new facility. Review the standard program and ask about functional clarifications and equipment uses, and suggestions for improvement. Sit, sip a mug of coffee, share some of what you are about, and you are bound to get a great deal in return. Try to appreciate the client's and user's special points of view.

Effective assessment requires personal contact and connection. Discover the value of what is being said between the lines, then check it out. Test any hypotheses you may form simply by asking, "Does this make sense?" Try to take notes privately; reflect *after* you've left the site. Writing while someone is taking the time to talk with you may be experienced as distancing or even rude. You will surprise yourself at the level of detail you can recall and meaningfully recreate from memory.

Apart from client/user issues, broader concerns should not be neglected. Uncovering this data is especially important if you are unfamiliar with the community. What social factors may influence or shape the project? Talk to influential people in the neighborhood (see Chapter 7 to help identify these people). If appropriate or possible, solicit opinions in the local park or grocery store. Elicit reactions to the possibility of a prospective project. Ask what might be done to mobilize community support. Ask about the pressing problems and the political exigencies in the area. Observe what is happening during the day and night, and note what seems positive together with what seems negative. Record your thoughts.

It is conventional wisdom that sensitivity to community input will not only promote the ultimate success of a project, but will likely enhance the probability of approvals from any design review boards, public agencies, associations, or planning boards that have authority to approve designs.

One note of caution: much tangential information is bound to result from your discussions. Try to avoid preoccupation with irrelevant factors, however colorful they may be. Keep the big picture in clear focus. In addition to obtaining answers to your standard or designed questions, remain alert to valuable bits of information that may emerge spontaneously from conversations with clients and/or users.

Obviously, the good interview is one in which stated problems are clarified, and unstated problems are discovered and given voice. A level of understanding is achieved, and this points the way toward optimal design. The good interview is one in which a trusting alliance is established with the client; little if anything of value will ensue without trust. If there is such a thing as the standard condition for engaging people, it is rapport. To have rapport with another, be yourself; you should neither affect

Sketches

some wooden formality you may believe is "professional" nor be excessively casual and familiar.

In Supplement 2.4, Peter Pressman, MD, offers a valuable multidisciplinary perspective for engaging clients during interviews, including essential dos and don'ts.

Peter Pressman

Peter Pressman, MD, is a physician who also holds graduate degrees in social sciences and clinical psychology. He has trained at the University of Wisconsin, Northwestern University, and Rush-Presbyterian-St. Luke's Medical Center. He has had considerable experience teaching interviewing to both medical students and graduate students.

SUPPLEMENT 2.4

Examination of the Client: Clinical Guidelines for Facilitating the Client Interview

❏ The term *clinical* relates to direct observation and treatment of patients. This medical model of interviewing or history taking is powerful and applicable to the interchange that ought to occur between any professional and the individual receiving services. The reasons for this are fairly self-evident but deserve review. (1) There is both a "scientific" and problem-oriented emphasis to the acquisition and evaluation of information. The scientific theme underscores a systematic and thorough approach, while the problem orientation calls for sustained focus on a particular issue or puzzle to be probed or solved. (2) An implicit goal is to provide care or help; this is a reminder that the ultimate result of the exercise is to improve quality of life, not to deliver a product, create art, or make profit—which may or may not be components of professional services. The client's perception that at some level he or she is being cared for will likely enhance participation and quality of information offered and wishes voiced.

Apart from surveys or inventories that serve to collect data and may in fact prove to be quite useful, the client interview has the potential for shedding light on just who the client is. What are some of the strengths, struggles, and lifestyle issues that make this individual distinctive and that will, in turn, help make the resulting architecture more effective and distinctive?

In order to guide the diagnostic encounter with the client toward maximizing efficiency, take some time before the initial meeting to form some specific hypotheses about what the current clients/building users want and need. Utilize these notions to shape probing and questioning either to confirm or reject your ideas. Confirmation of hypotheses allows you the luxury of eliciting valuable details, and rejection of expectations immediately sets up questioning designed to discover new facts that will in turn support alternative and accurate information and concepts.

In general, there are a few dos and don'ts in regard to the technique or style of the interview. Again, these recommendations are self-evident, but in the interest of staying sharp, it seems useful to review the basics on occasion.

Do:

- Employ a warm, appropriate greeting. Be certain to introduce yourself, summarize the purpose of the meeting, and indicate your expectations for translating data into a design schema.
- Maintain eye contact; use gestures, smiles, and nods to support and appreciate the client's self-revelation, spontaneous comments, and meaningful detail in conversation and responses to questions.
- Paraphrase the client's responses to invite clarification, correction, and additional data.
- Ask general questions to encourage elaboration; for example, "More space?" or "How do you mean?"
- Use some open-ended questions, but provide gentle direction to help keep the client focused on the issue at hand, i.e., "I'd like to hear more about that, but I was particularly intrigued by what you started to say about. . . ."

Don't:

- Make comments that may threaten the client's self-esteem or that may be construed as confrontational, devaluing, or challenging.
- Pose questions that result in yes or no responses.
- Ask leading questions that may consciously or unconsciously elicit your desired response; try not to manipulate the client.

■ Use jargon or technical/artistic vocabulary.
■ Make premature promises about design solutions and performance of possible features.

To caricature the benefits of architect-client dialogue, here is a simplistic example. Consider an office project. If the architect invests the time to make him- or herself visible and well known as a good and responsive listener, he or she is likely to be seen as a kind of employee advocate. This situation has the tendency to enhance employee morale and even productivity: not only are employee needs given voice, but there is personal investment in the design process. Another less obvious question to explore is: how do clients perceive and engage the office? Meet with representative clients. This may not only reveal another point of view and stimulate new concepts, but may serve to deepen existing relationships and add to the firm's service reputation. Maximize the participatory element; enlist people connected with the project as collaborators. This will often yield a richer and more responsive architecture.

Secondary Data

❏ At the start of any project, it is useful to become fully informed about similar projects, details, precedents, the history of the region in which the project is located, "cookbook" solutions (to quickly ascertain typical spatial relationships and sizes), and so on. Moreover, materials and special equipment research, for example, all become helpful in building a project-specific knowledge base. We all get the major professional journals, and they are indexed—a good beginning (many firms subscribe to the *Architectural Index*).

The following two supplements explain how to obtain information fast. Supplement 2.5 serves as an introduction to the Internet for those of us over 40. It is written by a member of the Generation X crowd, one who has literally grown up along with the Internet, and who also possesses the innate quality of being at one with electronic media. Supplement 2.6 is written by an expert in reference and instruction related to architectural and fine arts materials.

SUPPLEMENT 2.5

Joseph Moschella

Joseph Moschella will graduate with a degree in political science from the University of Wisconsin in spring 2001. He plans to attend law school and specialize in issues dealing with the Internet, technology, and its relevance in the international arena. Moschella has been an avid user of the Internet from the time it existed without the modern-day World Wide Web.

❏ The Internet isn't as young as it used to be, and that's a good and bad thing. As time passes and more people become a part of this massive online community, it becomes much more likely that someone will have placed relevant information online about a topic you might be interested in. But the surge in the volume of information coming from increased usage raises the problem of being able to find what you're looking for among literally billions of Web pages. So search engines were born to help Internet users find what they needed, and you can't get along in today's Information Age without having a vague notion of how to use them.

First things first: you can't be afraid of the Internet, and you can't be easily discouraged or you'll hardly ever find what you're looking for. The World Wide Web is still hugely disjointed, and it grows every day with no set framework. Its lack of internal structure means that there's nothing to guide the growth of information and very little to guide you to exactly what you need.

But there's little to be afraid of when you're looking for something on the Internet. Except under rare circumstances, you can't get a virus and you won't crash your computer. The worst that may happen is you'll be mistakenly directed to a pornography site just as a coworker or client drops by to say hello, and be terribly embarrassed for the rest of the day. To find exactly what you need requires some time and a little bit of hard work, but as the Internet grows, the chances increase that what you need is out there.

For the beginner, the best place to start is with a *Web portal*, a type of search engine. You've most likely heard of portals before, as some of the largest include Yahoo!, Excite, and Lycos. [These are detailed in Supplement 2.6.] The purpose of these sites is to present a starting point for what you're looking for. They take Web sites and categorize them to give the Web some kind of hierarchical structure.

Portals are a great place to start if you're looking for an established corporation or organization and don't know the Web address. Typing in "Ford Motor Company" at a Web portal will likely present you with a link to Ford's site. For many people, portals are all they'll ever use. Most give excellent responses to queries and provide a host of other services such as stock portfolio tracking and free e-mail service. However, this is the purpose of the Web portal—once you're in, the company doesn't want you to leave and provides you with an abundance of other services.

But in many cases, the Web portal won't do the trick. Sometimes searching for a phrase in a document will get you nowhere on a portal, but searching on a basic search engine will provide you thousands of results. Three great basic search engines I use often are Google, FAST, and AltaVista (www.google.com, www.alltheweb.com, and www.altavista.com). These sites search millions of pages in less than a second to find the exact words you're looking for, and while they're a little more difficult to use, they can be the most useful.

Don't be surprised if thousands of possible Web pages are returned when you are searching for a topic. The ones that most closely match your search are listed first, and because most Web search engines generate simple text results, it takes little time to page through the results. It's not unheard of to review 5 to 10 pages of results before you find exactly what you need.

But to narrow down huge numbers of results, don't be afraid to do an advanced search. Most search engines give you this option, and it allows you to very precisely tune the results you receive. For example, you can search for "flying buttresses," but can have the search *not* include any Web pages that also contain the words *Paris* or *Notre-Dame*. You can understand how much this might narrow your results. The search engines that include these advanced features all implement them a little differently, so it's best to consult that individual search engine's instructions on how to use them.

Search engines, which often have very basic-looking search pages, actually use some of the largest and most complex servers on the Web. Imagine a computer that has cataloged 1 billion Web pages it can search for you in less than a second. The servers don't really "know" what you're searching for, so if one search doesn't produce the result you're after, try a similar one and don't let yourself become frustrated.

Remember, it could take 10 different searches until the search engine finds an acceptable result. You might even end up with search results in foreign languages. (Yes, English is the most often used language on the Web, but as Internet access sweeps across the globe, foreign-language Web sites continue to grow.) The modern-day problem of a Web site in another language has borne a modern-day solution.

The AltaVista search engine has devised a way of translating Web pages from select foreign languages into broken, but many times understandable, English. You can also translate in the reverse fashion, and could easily have an essay in English translated into a basic Italian. The Web address for this feature is babel.altavista.com, and it can also be used by prospective international clients. As the translation gets better and operates more seamlessly, you can see the possibility not just for your personal searches, but for the trading of information among professionals in separate nations otherwise barred by lack of a common language.

As you can imagine, I've hardly scratched the surface with this essay. As the Internet becomes a larger part of everyone's daily lives, you'll learn more on your own than I or any book can ever teach you. But you'll only learn more if you're not afraid of using the technology. It takes a great deal to get started and to get a feel of how the Internet really operates, but the more you use it, the easier it will become. In many cases, the Internet operates very logically, and people whose professional careers or studies are based on method and logic already have a head start on the Zen of the Internet. This phenomenal new tool for communication looks like it's here to stay, so there's no use in waiting to get acquainted with it.

Carroll L. Botts

SUPPLEMENT 2.6

Carroll Botts began her academic career in the architectural design program at California Polytechnic State University, San Luis Obispo, where she discovered her real interest was in art and architectural history. She is currently the coordinator of reference and instruction at the University of New Mexico Fine Arts Library.

How Can an Architect Find Information?

❑ We are living in the Information Age. More information is produced than any other commodity on earth. With all of this information in existence, the most significant questions are: where is it? How do I get to it?

The Internet. No matter where you have your practice, one of the most important information-finding tools you can have in your office is a good computer with a fast modem and an Internet connection. More and more good-quality information is being put on the Internet and it's getting easier to find than ever. There are many free and efficient search engines available to help you locate information on the Internet. A couple of good ones are:

■ Yahoo! (www.yahoo.com)
■ AltaVista (www.altavista.com)

With these search engines you can easily learn how to access quite literally a world of information. Hint: if you have a series of words that go together, enclose them in quotes in your search so that your results will only include those terms in the proper sequence; for example, "American Institute of Architects." This will save a lot of time.

Beware—not all of the information you might find on the Internet will be good information. One of the easiest ways to evaluate this information is by looking at the URL (Internet address) of the site where you find it. Addresses usually read www.something.org. The last three letters can tell you much about the site. Here are just a few examples:

■ *.com.* This is a commercial site. Information found on these sites is as reputable as the companies the sites represent.

- *.edu.* This is the site of an educational institution; it probably contains good information.
- *.gov.* This is the site of a government agency. Its information should be valid.
- *.org.* This is the site of a nonprofit organization. If you agree with the views of that organization, you will probably feel comfortable with any information provided.

What information on the Internet can be of use to the architect? The answer to this question is easy: more than you could possibly imagine!

- *Professional associations*, such as the American Institute of Architects (www.aiaonline.com), have very useful Web sites.
- *Product and online order information* is available. Many individual manufacturers and building suppliers have their own Web sites. The Pierpoint Products link on the American Institute of Architects (AIA) site (www.e-architect.com/products/pierpoint) has many useful links. Sweets Online (www.sweets.com) is also very good.
- *Architectural firms* can have information about their practices, projects, philosophies, and recruitment online. Foster and Partners (www.fosterandpartners.com) is a good example.
- *City and regional information* provided by city governments can furnish the architect with data about place, history, climate, and so on. For example: San Luis Obispo, California has a site at www.ci.san-luis-obispo.ca.us.
- *City planning department information* is available online for most major cities in the U.S. Here you can find information on planned development, demographics, employment, per capita income, housing, land use, and more (for example, the Planning Department of Austin, Texas, at www.ci.austin.texas.us/planning).
- *The U.S. government* is the largest publisher of information in the world. Government publications can provide useful background information on architectural projects. Here are just a few agencies and their addresses:
  - The Census Department (www.census.gov) site contains population, housing, and income statistics, busi-

ness profiles, and the latest economic indicators by state, city, and, in some cases, specific neighborhood.

- The National Climatic Data Center (www.ncdc.noaa .gov/ol/ncdc.html) has current weather information and annual climatological summaries for recent years, searchable by state or city.
- The U.S. Geological Survey (USGS) site at www.usgs .gov basically describes the planet, including mineral, water, and biological resources, and earthquake information. The USGS also has printed information on soil studies.
- The Federal Bureau of Investigation (FBI) site at www.fbi.gov has uniform crime reports that contain crime statistics from around the country, by state and city.

Non-Internet Resources. Even in our electronic times, there remain the standard journals and texts that still must be consulted and relied upon for what is in effect quality control. *The Avery Index to Architectural Periodicals* is the best and most comprehensive index to journals in the field. If your practice does not have a subscription to this index, you should contact the library of your local college or university to see if it has one you can use in the library.

You may find it necessary to investigate a particular building type, but not find enough information on the Internet or in journals. Books at either your local public library or academic library may prove useful. Fortunately, most of these libraries have their online catalogs available on the Internet and you can explore their holdings from your office or home.

- Simple keyword searches (i.e., "shopping malls") will usually get you started in finding the information you need. Hint: using the plural of the term searched usually produces better results.
- When you find a book in the catalog that looks useful, try searches using the terms in the subject area of the record and you may find more related information.
- In the library, the most valuable tool for finding information is often the person at the information desk. Don't hes-

itate to ask for assistance. These people are paid to help you and most of them actually enjoy doing it!

■ Find out if your library offers electronic mail reference service. This can often save a lot of time.

Conclusion

❏ There is more information available now than at any time in history. By mastering a few simple information-seeking skills, today's architect can have access to more resources than ever before. Public and academic libraries are usually open to all; be sure to take advantage of them. More importantly, because of the Internet, now even the smallest practices have access to the same information as the world's largest architectural firms.

Conceptual Design Cost Estimating
with Brian Bowen

❏ Cost is almost always the one big issue for all projects; therefore, budget is central to the design problem. From the first doodles on napkins and the first conversations with the client, there should be a growing awareness of priorities for allocating money available for the project, both initially and for the life of the building. This awareness will, of course, set you free to maximize design possibilities.

In some instances, it may be important to set forth clearly the savings of investing in superior materials or systems from the very beginning of a project. Although initial expenses may be higher, savings in reduced maintenance and operating costs over the long run will be significant.

Inaccurate budgeting in the conceptual design stages has two major negative consequences, always worth reviewing: (1) if underestimated, schemes will need to be modified, or worse, completely redesigned, resulting in less profit for the architect, less time to complete the work, and perhaps an undermining of confidence in the architect's abilities. (2) If overestimated (or if filled with inflated contingencies to reduce perceived risk), the exaggerated costs could wipe out some potentially exciting design moves.

So, be cognizant of cost constraints early, and throughout the course of the project, but do not allow the idea of budget limitations to in any way inhibit creativity or innovative ideas. Ray Novitske, a Washington, DC, architect, resolves the apparent conflict intrinsic in the preceding statement. He believes that restrictions in budget may actually improve an architect's work. A large budget implies more freedom of choice, and thus reduced pressure to innovate. "Some architects' best work was produced on shoestring budgets because they were forced to be resourceful with what was available or affordable." Novitske continues, "It is fine to think that the high-tech aesthetic came from cerebral designers wanting to strip away the bourgeois, but it is more realistic to believe it was developed by imaginative designers who could not afford finishes."

In Supplement 2.7, Brian Bowen, Fellow of the Royal Institute of Chartered Surveyors (FRICS), discusses conceptual cost estimating in terms of the significance of project budgets, the characteristics of a sound budget, budgeting techniques, a cost plan, ongoing cost control, accuracy, and strategies for dealing with clients on costing issues.

SUPPLEMENT 2.7

Brian Bowen

Brian Bowen, FRICS, now retired, was a principal of Hanscomb Associates, Inc., cost consultants and construction managers. He was based in the firm's Atlanta office. He has written on this subject in The Architect's Handbook of Professional Practice, *12th ed. (AIA, 1994).*

❏ The battle to control costs in planning, designing, procuring, and constructing a new building is won or lost at the very early stages of the architect's involvement in the project. The key battle tactics are, first, the establishment of and agreement on a realistic budget for the project, and second, the production of a design concept that respects that budget and has every chance of being designed and constructed within the ceiling established.

Generally there are two points of entry to a project:

1. The architect is hired by the client to help determine the client's requirements and establish a building program prior to design.
2. A program has been established by the client or others, and a design in response is to begin immediately.

In the first case, it is unlikely that a budget will have been established, but one may well be included in the final building program. In the second case, it is probable that a budget will already have been set.

Project Budgets

❏ Many projects come to grief from a cost standpoint because of unrealistic or misunderstood budgets. The problem with budgets for most projects is that they are usually established with incomplete information on the key factors that affect cost magnitudes. While it is unusual for budgets to be set before a building program is developed, it is not unheard of, especially in the public sector, where a politically acceptable figure for a project is often produced before the scope is fully defined.

The sensible approach to developing a budget is:

- Determine a rough order-of-magnitude figure based on the building program using single-rate estimating methods. Alternatively, if the budget has been prepared by the owner or a consultant, the architect should first test the validity of the budget against the building program and, if there does not appear to be a serious mismatch, proceed to interpret the building program into a conceptual design.
- Based on the conceptual design, an elemental cost estimate is produced and reconciled to the budget. If adjustments to the building scope and/or program are necessary to match the budget, these are made.
- We now have a building program and a budget that are in balance, and the budget can be confirmed.

Unfortunately, many owners expect architects to commit to a construction cost budget before they have had the opportunity to produce a conceptual design, or even to test the budget against the building program. Commitments of this kind are to be completely avoided. Any comments on budget acceptability must be qualified to allow for a period of checking and the proper balancing of scope, quality, and cost.

Characteristics of a Sound Budget

"Setting a budget too low is like sky diving without a parachute— everything is fine at the start of the trip, but it doesn't end up too well."

—Attributed to Chuck Thompson, president, 3DI

- A good budget should be achievable and accepted by all key project participants as being reasonable.
- A good budget should reflect adequately the full scope of work required to deliver the client's requirements.
- A good budget should include everything it is supposed to include and state clearly what is excluded. The budget for the work for which the architect will be responsible will only be part of the story. Unless addressed, this leaves plenty of opportunity for misunderstandings over whose pocket funds will come from to complete the facility.
- A good budget should reflect the quality/performance expectations of the client. Perhaps this is the most difficult factor to determine, but a point of reference to another project or an abbreviated outline specification can be useful.
- A good budget should reflect the client's value objectives. First, cost is only part of the story for a client who intends to continue owning and/or occupying the building, when total life cycle costs become more critical.
- A good budget should contain adequate reserves to reflect estimating uncertainty at this early stage, to provide for the inevitable changes that will occur, and to cover inflation over the period of implementation.

❑ Items usually excluded from the architect's Scope of Work:

■ Loose and movable furniture
■ Movable equipment
■ Telecommunications installation
■ All "soft" costs—for example, design and management fees, financing, leasing and occupancy, and marketing
■ Furnishings (drapes, rugs, etc.)
■ Tenant work (partitions, finishes, etc.)
■ Demolition
■ Site acquisition costs

■ Finally, a good budget should be structured in such a way as to be a bridge to ongoing cost control. This can be achieved by framing the budget for transition into a cost plan, as described later.

Things to be avoided are:

■ Socially acceptable budgets—that is, telling people what they want to hear. It is better to get over the bad news early, rather than later.
■ Playing it safe by fattening up the budget to protect against an overrun. This will lead to waste, poor value, or a budget underrun, which can often be as embarrassing as an overrun.

Budgeting Techniques

❑ Due to time constraints and lack of information, most budgets are established using single-rate estimating techniques. This will mostly involve the calculation of a gross built floor area and the selection of a unit price rate, which are multiplied together to arrive at a budget figure. Occasionally, accommodation units are used instead—for example, parking spaces, hospital beds, or hotel rooms.

Both of these techniques appear on the surface to be fairly simple, but can be highly hazardous. There is a maxim in estimating that the simpler the measurement, the more difficult the pricing. In this case even the measurement may not be so simple. Building programs usually reflect space in net usable or programmable area. To this must be added nonusable area in circulation, access, toilets, storage, service spaces, etc. It is easy to make a mistake or a misjudgment and arrive at a gross built area that is either too small, or conceivably too large.

Selecting the correct single-unit rate is the most difficult part of the process. The traditional approach is to refer back to one or more projects of similar character that have been recently completed. The use of historical price data is a perfectly rational and sound approach if used properly. Here are some of the problems:

■ Even under the same building type classification, the functional content of buildings can be very dissimilar between high-cost components like laboratories and toilet and bathroom spaces, and between high-quality finished areas like lobbies and unfinished areas. This imbalance can create distortions between buildings and their unit costs.

■ The building floor area represents the horizontal dimensions of the facility and not its vertical ones, thus ignoring issues such as story heights, high bay spaces, etc. As the vertical components of a building probably account for about one-third of the costs, distortions can occur between unit costs of buildings with different volumetric ratios.

■ Historical project data is often from a different place and time frame and needs adjustment to the new location and current date.

■ Building qualities vary in many respects, and it is often difficult to find a true match from a historical database.

■ Sitework costs are highly variable from project to project and need to be factored out or separated in historical data.

■ Each building has a different configuration, or plan shape, that will affect a single square foot unit rate.

One variation on the single-unit rate approach is to estimate the functional areas of a facility separately and aggregate them into a total estimate. This is easier said than done, as little historical or published cost data exists in this form. The answer, therefore, is to only use previous project costs where one has a knowledge of the project and an adequate breakdown of costs, to enable adjustments to be made for use for the subject project.

A Cost Plan

❑ The next step is to take the budget for construction and begin to set up some targets for each key system or element of the building and its sitework. An illustration of a cost plan is given in Table 2.1. Its features are:

■ The UNIFORMAT classification system (described in the following text)
■ Contingency reserves that are separated out
■ A reasonable sitework target
■ Distribution of the balance to the key functional elements of the proposed building based on judgment, past experience, and cost data records

UNIFORMAT

❑ The UNIFORMAT classification system has been around since the mid-1970s and has slowly gained currency as *the* framework to use for design cost estimating and control. The original UNIFORMAT was revised and updated in the early 1990s and retitled UNIFORMAT II. It has been adopted by the Construction Specifications Institute (CSI) and has become an American Society for Testing and Materials (ASTM) national standard.

Its advantages over the 16-division MASTERFORMAT are that it is functionally not materially based:

Table 2.1
SAMPLE PROJECT COST PLAN

Project: Elementary School
Location: Middletown, VA

Project number:
Estimated by:

Construction Cost	Cost Plan	Schematic Estimate	Design Development	Prebid Estimate	Bid Analysis
	Date: 4/00	Date:	Date:	Date:	Date:
A10 Foundation	$460,000				
A20 Basement construction	—				
B10 Superstructure	560,000				
B20 Exterior enclosure	560,000				
B30 Roofing	330,000				
C10 Interior construction	590,000				
C20 Stairs	—				
C30 Interior finishes	425,000				
D10 Conveying systems	10,000				
D20 Plumbing	470,000				
D30 HVAC	1,100,000				
D40 Fire protection	160,000				
D50 Electrical	860,000				

E Equipment and furnishings	250,000
F Special construction and demolition	—
G Sitework	880,000
Z General conditions and profit	680,000
Subtotal	$7,375,000
Design contingency	360,000
Construction contingency	230,000
Escalation reserve	200,000
Target construction cost	$7,765,000
Difference from target cost	0
Gross floor area (in SF)	78,300
Cost per SF gross floor area	$99.17

Source: Hanscomb Inc., Atlanta, GA
This cost plan lists the amount available for each part of the project to provide guidance during design.
The UNIFORMAT II (level 2) is used in this example.

Table 2.2
UNIFORMAT FRAMEWORK

UNIFORMAT II Classification for Building Elements and Related Sitework

Level 1		Level 2		Level 3
A Substructure	A10	Foundations	A1010	Standard foundations
			A1020	Other foundations
			A1030	Slab on grade
	A20	Basement construction	A2010	Basement excavation
			A2020	Basement walls
B Shell	B10	Superstructure	B1010	Floor construction
			B1020	Roof construction
	B20	Exterior enclosure	B2010	Exterior walls
			B2020	Exterior windows
			B2030	Exterior doors
	B30	Roofing	B3010	Roof coverings
			B3020	Roof openings
C Interiors	C10	Interior construction	C1010	Partitions
			C1020	Interior doors
			C1030	Specialties
	C20	Stairs	C2010	Stair construction
			C2020	Stair finishes
	C30	Interior finishes	C3010	Wall finishes
			C3020	Floor finishes
			C3030	Ceiling finishes
D Services	D10	Conveying systems	D1010	Elevators and lifts
			D1020	Escalators and moving walks
			D1090	Other conveying systems
	D20	Plumbing	D2010	Plumbing fixtures
			D2020	Domestic water distribution
			D2030	Sanitary waste
			D2040	Rainwater drainage
			D2090	Other plumbing systems

Table 2.2
UNIFORMAT FRAMEWORK (Continued)

UNIFORMAT II Classification for Building Elements and Related Sitework

Level 1		Level 2		Level 3
	D30	HVAC	D3010	Energy supply
			D3020	Heat-generating systems
			D3030	Cooling-generating systems
			D3040	Distribution systems
			D3050	Terminal and package units
			D3060	Controls and instrumentation
			D3070	Special HVAC systems
			D3080	Systems testing and balancing
	D40	Fire protection	D4010	Sprinklers
			D4020	Standpipes
			D4030	Fire protection specialties
			D4090	Other fire protection systems
	D50	Electrical	D5010	Electrical service and distribution
			D5020	Lighting and branch wiring
			D5030	Communications and security
			D5040	Other electrical systems
E Equipment and furnishings	E10	Equipment	E1010	Commercial equipment
			E1020	Institutional equipment
			E1030	Vehicular equipment
			E1040	Other equipment

Table 2.2
UNIFORMAT FRAMEWORK (Continued)

UNIFORMAT II Classification for Building Elements and Related Sitework

Level 1		Level 2		Level 3
	E20	Furnishings	E2010	Fixed furnishings
			E2020	Movable furnishings
F Special construction and demolition	F10	Special construction	F1010	Special structures
			F1020	Integrated construction
			F1030	Special construction systems
			F1040	Special facilities
			F1050	Special controls and instrumentation
	F20	Selective building demolition	F2010	Building element demolition
			F2020	Hazardous component abatement
G Building sitework	G10	Site preparation	G1010	Site clearing
			G1020	Site demolition and relocation
			G1030	Site earthwork
			G1040	Hazardous waste remediation
	G20	Site improvements	G2010	Roadways
			G2020	Parking lots
			G2030	Pedestrian paving
			G2040	Site development
			G2050	Landscaping
	G30	Site mechanical utilities	G3010	Water supply
			G3020	Sanitary sewer
			G3030	Storm sewer
			G3040	Heating distribution
			G3050	Cooling distribution
			G3060	Fuel distribution
			G3070	Other site mechanical systems

Table 2.2
UNIFORMAT FRAMEWORK (*Continued*)

UNIFORMAT II Classification for Building Elements and Related Sitework

Level 1	Level 2	Level 3
	G40 Site electrical utilities	G4010 Electrical distribution utilities
		G4020 Site lighting
		G4030 Site communication and security
		G4040 Other site electrical utilities
	G50 Other site construction	G5010 Tunnels
		G5020 Other site systems

Source: ASTM Standard E1557-97

- It breaks a building down into the language of design.
- It enables a fair and direct comparison between different systems.
- It forms an excellent checklist for the estimator.

Table 2.2 contains UNIFORMAT II from Levels 1 to 3.

Conceptual Cost Estimating

❏ This is the stage where the power of UNIFORMAT becomes evident. With a concept design that configures and masses a proposed building and shows the interrelationship of its spaces, an amazingly detailed estimate can be prepared using the UNIFORMAT system. This involves the following steps:

- Mini-estimates are prepared for each key UNIFORMAT element, selecting the appropriate level of detail for the purpose.
- For each element, an appropriate measurement factor is selected (e.g., B-20, exterior enclosure—square feet of enclosure, B-30, roofing—area of roof in square feet [SF], etc.). Quantities are measured from the concept design, or

simulated, e.g., it is unlikely that the full-length partitions can be measured from a concept design, but they can be simulated by factoring from similar buildings or by using a rule-of-thumb formula.

- At concept stage, mechanical and electrical elements are frequently estimated on a square foot of building floor area basis.
- Allowances are included for equipment and special construction, based on experience and judgment.
- Sitework can be conceptually measured and priced if there is sufficient detail; otherwise, an allowance is included.
- A percentage estimate is included to cover general conditions, overheads, and profit.
- Finally, contingencies are provided for unforeseen elements and changes during design and construction and for escalation (anticipated price increases from date of estimate to bid date).

Each of the individual elemental mini-estimates is aggregated to a total and unit cost per square foot and percentages of each component are calculated. The whole is then carefully reviewed against the cost plan; discrepancies are examined, alternatives are considered, and a final cost report is prepared.

Ongoing Design Cost Control

❏ It is critical that the concept design estimate be reconciled to the cost plan budget and that unresolved issues are not ignored or deferred. If the concept design has been balanced against the budget, then cost control during the remainder of design should be relatively easy, with periodic checking to make sure everything is on track.

However, changes do occur for a wide variety of reasons as designs are developed and construction documents prepared. The cost implications of these changes need to be assessed and reported, with appropriate adjustments to the cost plan if necessary. The design contingency should take care of most of these.

It is usually wise during preparation of construction documents to have another estimate prepared, especially if the changes have been significant. Such an estimate also provides a good background for controlling costs during the procurement and construction periods.

Creation of Cost Databases to Support Improved Conceptual Cost Estimating

❏ Most publishers of construction cost manuals produce system, assembly, or elemental pricing information. However, for the architectural practice, the best potential source of cost data is the projects completed by the firm over the years. These need to be recycled in a form that can be used quickly and accurately in the conceptual cost estimating process.

These costs should be recycled into a shared database with descriptive, statistical, and unit costs structured into UNIFOR-MAT categories. Translating contractors' schedules of values, which are usually in a trade format, into elements may require some assistance and some approximation, but the effort is worth it, especially when the number of projects recorded in the database begins to increase. Not only does this give some statistical relevance to the data, it also enables information on different systems to be used creatively. For example, a roof system on an existing building can be applied to a new design even though the functions of the buildings may be quite different.

Estimating Accuracy

❏ Any construction cost estimate represents the architect's best judgment of the price that will be bid by a group of contractors for the subject project. These prices are heavily influenced by supply and demand and can fluctuate quite rapidly from place to place and over time. Various statistical studies have come to broadly similar conclusions that there is only a 50-50 chance of an estimate being within a 5 percent range of accuracy, and the probability is that one estimate out of every six will show a 10 percent variance or more.

How can you best deal with such odds? Here are a few suggestions:

- ■ Make sure that the client is aware that your estimate is just that, and not a guaranteed price.
- ■ Include alternates in the bidding documents, which can be used to accommodate any difference between estimate and bid.
- ■ Consider hiring a professional specialist cost consultant to prepare the estimates. This is a good idea in situations where you are not familiar with market conditions at the project location, or for a project of some complexity. There is also nothing wrong with taking opinions from local contractors—just be careful not to be seen to be favoring any one of them.
- ■ Prior to completion of the final prebid estimate, carry out a thorough market survey to ascertain probable bidding conditions for your project.
- ■ "Sell" your project to the local contractor community prior to bid in order to create as much competition as you can—one way to ensure lower bidding prices.

Dealing with Clients on Costing Issues

❑ The first thing to establish is the level of your client's knowledge of the construction industry in general and how cost estimates are put together in particular. "Professional" clients, who build frequently, usually but not always have a better grasp than "lay" clients, who will need some education.

Perhaps the two most important subjects to be tackled with owners of all stripes are:

- ■ *Client changes*. It is essential to be firm with clients and inform them of the cost and time implications of changes at the time such changes are requested. Do not assume that when a client asks for a change he or she automatically knows that this is going to have a cost effect, especially if you do not tell him or her.

■ *Contingencies*. Establish from the outset that creation of contingency reserves is a prudent and essential component of good cost control. Many clients are suspicious of contingencies and see them as a hidden way of increasing their costs. Design and construction are full of unforeseen elements and changes do occur. One approach to ameliorate clients' concerns is to give them responsibility for controlling and managing the contingency.

Costs can be used creatively during design to ensure an economically satisfying project for both client and architect.

The Value of Value Engineering

with Glenn Fellows

❏ Where's the beef? Where's the value in value engineering (VE)? Why is it a subject in a book about design? Why should VE not automatically inspire terror when the prospect of doing it is mentioned to an architect?

An effective VE analysis involves a rigorous procedure for optimizing cost, quality, performance, schedule, and so on. Targeting specific areas for potential savings and defining alternative strategies to address those areas without diminishing the spirit of the design are the main objectives. It makes sense, therefore, to conduct VE analyses early in the design phase.

It is also important to precisely define value beyond the negative connotation of simply a cost-cutting, architecture-destroying device—hence the bad reputation. It is critical to be cognizant of VE issues in preliminary design—where the substantive ideas can be appropriately assessed and well integrated into the design—rather than slicing and dicing pieces of the project in later phases.

The overarching message is to keep an open mind if a VE analysis becomes an early part of the process; consider embracing it in a way that speaks to economy of means in the architectural outcome. Chicago area architect David Hovey does not view VE as compromise or selling out. Rather, he says, "There's more than one way to do things"—very much an architectural stance. And the late Charles Moore would always jump at another opportunity to design. Mark Simon has characterized Moore's attitude: "How can we make the project *more* interesting, not *as* interesting, when we edit it down?"

In Supplement 2.8, Glenn Fellows, AIA, talks about his firm's experience with value engineering and cites some specific examples of its benefits.

Glenn Fellows

Glenn H. Fellows, AIA, is the current AIA New Mexico President. He is a senior principal at SMPC Architects, an Albuquerque architecture, planning, and interior design firm, where he has worked since 1978. SMPC Architects specializes in technologically complex projects in the health care, education, and emerging high-tech fields.

❏ Value engineering (VE) is synonymous with value analysis, a process developed during World War II, primarily by General Electric, to help deal with labor and material shortages and the inevitable substitution issue. The process is used throughout industry and in the construction field. The subject has been well documented, perhaps best by Alphonse J. Dell'Isola, PE, in his book *Value Engineering: Practical Applications for Design, Construction, Maintenance & Operations* (Means, 1997). VE is taught at most engineering schools and should be offered, if not mandatory, as a part of architectural school curricula.

Our firm has been involved in some extremely worthwhile VE sessions. VE that occurs during the concept or schematic design phase proves most valuable for all parties, including owner, architect, and engineers. The educated architect/engineer will insist that this is the time to do serious value analysis. VE that is forced on the design process during the contract document phase or after bidding should be done as an additional service. This understanding between the client and the design professional is critical to the success of the project and the continued relationship with the client.

Case Examples

❑ We worked on a large office building a few years back with CRS Architects (now HOK), Morrison Knudsen, construction managers, and the client, Mountain Bell (now US West). With the schematic design drawings in hand, everyone on the VE team submitted a list of items to be considered for VE. We spent two days (10 of us—engineers, client reps, designers, and contractors) discussing alternates for almost every system in the building, and eventually considered six systems that had the most potential for short-term and life cycle cost savings. The daylighting system analysis for the east and north elevations (all of the open office spaces) was the most intriguing to me. We went full circle considering glass types, ceiling heights, light shelves, curtain wall components, blinds and shutters, artificial lighting, heat gain and loss, and light reflectance of the materials. In the end, the solution was simple and straightforward; put as much clear glass as high as possible on the north façade, and forget about the light shelf. The benefit of the natural light (and views) to the occupants is immeasurable, but the reality was, and still is, that it is less expensive to heat the space in Albuquerque's climate than it is to artificially light the space. We found that when the ceiling was raised to 12 feet (tight to the structure) at the building's perimeter, natural light would penetrate at least 30 feet into the interior. We didn't need the lights on for half of the building! On the east façade we used tinted glass at the clerestory section to control the morning heat gain.

Another example that demonstrates the need to stay flexible and well informed happened in our recent project with the University of New Mexico. The program for research labs in the Center for High Technology Materials defined critical vibration sensitivities in the range of 0.03 m. Train movements 1000 yards away produced such vibrations, and the building design needed to accommodate these constraints. Vibration-isolation lab tables were considered, but were cost prohibitive. The VE solution included isolated connections at the column/footing joints and a waffle slab on grade. The low-frequency condition was difficult to control given the soil conditions. This solution was constantly questioned and refined, and it required extensive detailing throughout all building systems. When the university was ready to bid the project, it made the wise choice to hire a construction manager, Kitchell Construction, that was experienced with the outfitting of clean rooms. Further investigation into vibration isolation was suggested, and during the course of that study (some 18 months after the initial study) the price of vibration-isolated lab tables had come down so much that it was less costly to buy tables than to isolate the structure.

Building Codes and Standards

with Marvin Cantor

❏ True or False:

■ An egress is a big white bird from northern New England
■ Building codes are mazelike, elliptical, and convoluted—a twisted labyrinth with no beginning or end

Some jurisdictions are notorious for being inconsistent and picky. One of my colleagues once had a code official classify a whirlpool bathtub as a swimming pool. As such, there could be no electric lights within 10 feet of it. Fortunately the code official did not require a chain link fence around the bathroom. My friend gave his clients flashlights. And you thought the topic of codes was humorless!

Codes (and their interpretation) can be quite complicated and vary between jurisdictions. An excellent reference that facilitates incorporating building code information simply and quickly into schematic designs is *The Architect's Studio Companion*, 2nd ed. (Wiley, 1995), by Edward Allen and Joseph Iano.

This section begins with a primer and reminder that summarizes the basic intent and application of codes and standards. (See Supplement 2.9.) Barry Yatt then discusses the impact of codes on achieving design excellence—the primary mission of the book. (See Supplement 2.10.) Michael Crosbie concludes the section with the latest on universal design, and how to capture its spirit rather than just the letter of the applicable laws and accessibility guidelines. (See Supplement 2.11.)

Marvin Cantor

SUPPLEMENT 2.9

Marvin J. Cantor, FAIA, of Fairfax, Virginia, is former chair of the American Institute of Architects' Building Codes and Standards Professional Interest Area, and has written frequently and conducted national seminars on this topic.

❏ Building codes have historically evolved in conjunction with responses to disasters in the built environment. Their primary charge has been to define the minimum standards to which construction must adhere, below which there would be a significant detrimental impact on the public's health, welfare, and safety. More recently, the rights of the physically disabled have also been incorporated into the regulations governing the built environment.

In the process of preliminary design for a structure, one must balance the size of the structure with its type of construction and its primary use. Building codes establish a rational process for doing this. When more than one type of use exists in a structure, one must determine whether it is more cost efficient to treat the entire structure under the regulations governing the most critical use involved, or whether the building can effectively be "compartmented" with fire separation structural elements for each use (virtually treating each such building use as a separate structure).

The steps outlined briefly in the following text illustrate consideration of the building code (and other complementary regulatory steps) as the preliminary design evolves.

1. Determine if covenants pertaining to the site involved limit the size and uses of any structure erected on that site.
2. Determine the maximum envelope (length, width, height, and gross area above grade) of structures permitted by zoning regulations.
3. Evaluate the particular topography of the site and of surrounding adjacent site areas to see if such an envelope can in fact be accommodated.

4. Evaluate the client's needs in terms of area required. This summary step (encompassing steps 1, 2, and 3) establishes the desired maximum building envelope for the design.

5. Classify the building by its use (B, business; M, mercantile; I, industrial; A, assembly; S, storage; etc.).

6. Using the code's *height and area* table, determine the maximum size of building permitted as it relates to the structural type being used. Here, alternate types of structure (1, fire resistant; 2, incombustible; 3, combustible protected; 4, mill; 5, wood frame) will be considered to arrive at the optimum structure/building area to be designed.

7. Moving next to the structural elements table, determine the fire resistivity required for the particular structure involved with respect to the major elements in the building (exterior walls, columns, floors, ceilings, shafts, stairways, etc.). This is measured in hours that a particular element can resist a fire before failing (according to testing established by the American Society for Testing and Materials [ASTM] and carried out by testing laboratories such as Underwriters' Laboratories, Factory Mutual, etc.).

Having established the maximum permitted size, the type of structure that will be used, and the basic structural elements' fire-resistive requirements, one can address the other significant items in the code as the preliminary design progresses:

1. *Egress.* Normally, two remote means of appropriate egress (exit) are required for the typical structure (remoteness is defined in the code). Keep in mind that one of the required means of egress should be usable by the physically disabled (which means having an "area of refuge" near one of the required stairs unless an approved acceptable elevator for egress has been incorporated; at this time, no such elevator construction has been certified to my knowledge as meeting the code's requirements for an acceptable emergency egress).

2. *Accessibility.* All parts of the structure's primary use areas must be accessible to the physically disabled (this includes those with impairments in mobility, sensory function, and cognitive development). Accessibility should be achieved without extraordinary auxiliary aids. In particular, one

should look at the building's primary entrance, corridor routes to various parts of the structure, the primary use areas, toilets, drinking fountains, and egress.

3. *Miscellaneous code requirements.* These cover a broad range of elements, including:
   A. Stair construction
   B. Minimum room heights and areas
   C. Railing (guard and stair) requirements
   D. Roofing and general building waterproofing requirements
   E. Sprinklers and other requirements for fire-resistive items
   F. Structural, seismic, wind, and snow load requirements
   G. Building occupancy design factors
   H. Energy conservation factors

Finally, if a project involves the adaptive reuse of an existing structure, one should become familiar with the code chapter that deals with this item; certain trade-offs are permitted. For example, where it is economically impractical to install certain code-required items, they may sometimes be omitted if in other areas additional protective measures are incorporated (i.e., compartmenting a structure may permit longer egress corridors than otherwise mandated in new construction).

Keeping the code in mind as the preliminary design evolves makes it much easier to ensure the resulting structure's compliance with legal building regulations, and reduces the probability of embarrassing moments between the designer, client, and building official at a point when the design has been largely finalized.

The Carrot in the Codes

with Barry Yatt

Barry Yatt

Barry D. Yatt, AIA, CSI, CDT, is a practicing architect, an associate professor of practice management and construction technology at The Catholic University of America's School of Architecture and Planning, Director of the Architectural Practice Research Project (worth a visit at http://archprac.cua.edu), author of Cracking the Codes: An Architect's Guide to Building Regulations (Wiley, 1998), and a member of the AIA Documents Committee.

SUPPLEMENT 2.10

Impact on Design Excellence

❏ The thought of dealing with codes may be enough to strike terror—or at least resentment and boredom—into the hearts of many a developer, architect, or builder. Building, zoning, historic preservation, and accessibility rules are usually seen as the stick that prods them, grudgingly, to design and build things that weren't on their agendas. Rarely are these rules understood as either the societal assurance or as the designers' resource that they are.

What's the point? Using regulations to get a leg up on design can benefit in two ways. First, it reduces the amount of knowledge you will need for producing workable designs, since you can leverage the knowledge and experience embodied in codes. Second, by introducing a level of detail in a conceptual way, using codes reduces the possibility of needing major changes in a project after schematic design work is complete.

Building regulations and standards help the industry establish and maintain a standard of care, a baseline that sets minimum acceptable levels of quality. In a profession and an industry that are compelled to constant invention (since every project introduces a new site, new goals, and new user issues), where products often do not have the luxury of being refined in successive production runs, and where feedback after completion rarely makes it back to those who create the projects, rules can rightly be viewed as providing a relatively stable and sorely needed knowledge base. The more designers understand each project's formative influences, the more responsive and appropriate (and therefore successful) their building designs can be. This is a major factor in design excellence.

This is the carrot in the codes, the upside of rules that intimately affect the way the building industry works. The public is willing to allow greater design freedoms to projects that are inherently more safe, and greater concessions to developers of projects that provide public benefits. Practitioners and industry leaders who recognize the value of this carrot find ways to take advantage of the incentives, exceptions, and bonuses that rules allow for responsive projects.

Great design work requires a thorough understanding of the issues that regulators worry about. Why? Because one can't be cutting-edge without knowing where the edge is. For example, without understanding the difference between such building code terms as *project, building,* and *fire area,* project teams would likely be forced, through misinterpretation, to design with unnecessarily reduced floor areas. If designers do not understand the differences between fire walls and fire area separations, partitions that might otherwise be opened with windows and railings might remain walled off.

Getting a Handle on Code Requirements

❏ So there's the situation. How does an architect respond? Is there a "Cliff Notes," a weekend seminar, or perhaps a consultant or software program that will help translate the architect's design intent into a final design by way of these codes? Time constraints may not allow many architects to achieve extensive familiarity with a constantly changing field of regulations. Setting priorities is key in these days of lean, efficient business practice.

It may well be that the best way to spend time at the start of a design effort is in finding out which rules apply. This way, the full scope of requirements, and their implications, can be identified before design work starts.

FIGURE 2.3
Courtesy of Iris Slikerman.

The obvious ones—zoning ordinances and building codes—are well known and can be identified with a call to the local building department or a visit to a public library. But project teams also need to establish which other rules are mandated and which rules might simply make good business and design sense to follow. Examples of mandated but not necessarily obvious rules include local amendments to model regulations, private covenants, federal regulations such as those administered by the Occupational Safety and Health Administration (OSHA) or the Environmental Protection Agency (EPA), and preservation guidelines that apply to properties designated as historic. Examples of rules that one might opt to follow include those contained in materials and workmanship standards (as written by the American National Standards Institute [ANSI], ASTM, and many other organizations), standards suggested by insurance carriers, and regulations that bring tax incentives to owners of projects that comply.

Once the applicable rules are identified, architects need to review them and make some decisions. Regulations are all about choosing among possibilities. They tend to preclude design alternatives that are demonstrably unsafe or undesirable to the community. They rarely, however, limit possibilities to one alternative. Architects are well advised to read codes with an eye toward options. Architects can compare the design implications of each exception, premium, or alternate formula, and choose the combination that best supports the design intent of a project.

Here is a common example: codes do not dictate construction classification—the minimum degree of fire resistance required of a building. Rather, they specify a broad mixture of conditions including floor area, building height, inclusion of sprinkler systems, and relative amount of street exposure, that can be combined in various ways to arrive at the construction classification for a project. When construction classification is determined first due to budgetary or other considerations, the whole process can be reversed, so that a specific combination of these variables determines the need for sprinklers. The American Institute of Architects will soon be publishing a new series of analysis forms and worksheets, tentatively designated G808 and G808A, intended to help architects with this type of analysis.

For more detailed explorations of these issues, there are several excellent resources. Each of the model code organizations and some private publishers produce illustrated handbooks that comment, paragraph by paragraph, on the model codes. My own book, *Cracking the Codes: An Architect's Guide to Building Regulations*, deals with regulatory issues in a broader way, putting the universe of regulations in cross-referenced perspective. And several Web sites contain links to codes and excellent commentaries and forums, including The Building Code Library (www. buildingsite.com/bcl1.htm) and Delphi's Code Forum (http:// forums.delphi.com/preview/main.asp?sigdir=buildingcode).

Impact of the International Building Code

❑ For some practitioners, the situation will be simplified with the year 2000 publication of the International Building Code (IBC) and the consequent retirement of the three twentieth-century model codes, the Building Officials and Code Administrators (BOCA) code, Southern Building Code (SBC), and Uniform Building Code (UBC). Instead of being concerned with three model building codes, design professionals will only have to work with one. Although the IBC is a product of American organizations, it may eventually establish some degree of standardization around the world through adoption or reference by foreign governments.

While this unification may sound like a welcome relief, design professionals whose projects are within a single region of the country have always had to deal with only one model building code. Further, all practitioners will still have multiple codes to juggle, for two reasons: there will still be local amendments to the IBC in most places that adopt it, and other codes will remain in force for design issues that are not sufficiently addressed by the IBC and its family of mechanical, private sewage disposal, and other related codes. The latter category includes the National Fire Protection Association (NFPA) Life Safety Code, regulations such as the EPA's environmental assessment requirements, and historic preservation guidelines. And of course, there will always be local zoning ordinances and covenants. The primary beneficiaries of the change to the IBC will be those practitioners whose projects are scattered around the country, foreign design professionals interested in doing projects in the United States, and perhaps, if other countries adopt parts or all of the IBC, American firms involved in international practice.

Finally, the advent of the IBC isn't likely to affect many design professionals for quite some time, since model codes have no power until adopted by local governments. In many jurisdictions, such adoptions may still be many years away. Still, the change is coming. Practitioners will need to learn the IBC's new ways, even though much of its content will be familiar to them from previous model codes, and the order of its chapters will follow the pattern that has been used in the model codes since 1993.

Conclusion

❏ Regulatory familiarity is necessary to achieving design excellence. Design professionals are well served by a level of regulatory familiarity appropriate for their projects. The better informed they are, the more design control they retain. To the extent that they can't do it all themselves, design professionals should make sure they have good consultants or employees who will sort through regulatory issues with their project priorities in mind. Design regulations and standards aren't going away anytime soon. Although design professionals sometimes resist them and complain about the difficulties regulations and standards pose, their jobs would be that much more difficult were such guidelines not available.

Universal Design
with Michael Crosbie

Michael Crosbie

Michael J. Crosbie is an architect, educator, and author of several books on architecture. He is an associate with Steven Winter Associates, Inc., an architectural research and consulting firm in Norwalk, Connecticut, that specializes in disability research and design. He can be reached at mcrosbie@ swinter.com.

❏ Universal design is a simple concept with very important implications. The concept is that the built environment should

SUPPLEMENT 2.11

be designed and constructed to accommodate anyone, no matter what their physical abilities. This is not quite the same as "handicapped design," which differentiates an environment for those with disabilities apart from one that is less than accommodating. For example, "handicapped design" might place a nasty ramp around the side of a building's main entrance in a half-hearted effort to satisfy the letter of the Americans with Disabilities Act Accessibility Guidelines (ADAAG) or the Fair Housing Act Accessibility Guidelines. In contrast, universal design attempts to capture the spirit of the law. The spirit is that the built environment should be designed and constructed for use by anyone, both disabled and able-bodied, without differentiation of accommodation. This would mean, in the preceding example, that the ramp to the front entrance is an integral part of the entry design, or, better yet, that the finished grade at all entrances meets the threshold to allow anyone access, wheelchair or not. Universally designed buildings have accessible elements integrated into the overall architectural concept, not tacked on at the last minute. Universal design is an attitude about the built environment that sees people as equals, not as "normal" or "handicapped." Universal design is universally usable, and makes no distinction between those who are able-bodied and those who are differently abled.

The Center for Universal Design at North Carolina State University, perhaps the best resource for information on the subject, notes that good universal design has the following attributes: equitable use (useful and marketable to people with diverse abilities); flexibility in use (accommodates a wide range of individual preferences and abilities); simple and intuitive use (easy to understand, regardless of the user's experience, knowledge, language skills, or current concentration level); perceptible information (communicates necessary information effectively to the user, regardless of ambient conditions or the user's sensory abilities); tolerance for error (minimizes hazards and adverse consequences of accidental or unintended actions); low physical effort (can be used efficiently and comfortably and with a minimum of fatigue); size and space for approach and use (appropriate size and space provided for approach, reach, manipulation, and use regardless of user's body size, posture, or mobility).

The Center for Universal Design also has simple design guidelines, which should be incorporated into every building:

Entrances

- Provide an accessible route to the entrance from vehicle drop-off area or parking.
- Maximum slope to the entry door should be 1:20.
- Provide a covered entryway, if possible, for shelter from the weather.
- Provide a 5-foot-square maneuvering space.
- Provide a package shelf or bench to hold parcels or groceries.
- Provide a full-length sidelight at the entry door (allows occupants to see who is at the door before opening it, and also increases natural light in foyer).
- Use a movement sensor light control to turn lights on and off.
- Provide ambient and focused lighting at the lockset to aid in operation.
- Use high-visibility address numbers on the façade that faces the road.

General Interior Design

- Use lever-type door handles throughout.
- A force of no more than 5 pounds should be needed to operate and open doors.
- Use 32-inch minimum clear door opening widths throughout.
- Provide an 18-inch minimum space at the latch side of doors.
- Provide adjustable-height closet rods and shelves (also increases storage space).

- Accessible routes throughout the home should be at least 42 inches wide.
- Light switches should be no more than 44 to 48 inches above the floor (also makes them accessible to children).
- Electrical outlets should be no more than 18 inches above the floor.
- Windows for views should have sills no higher than 36 inches above the floor (permits views for those seated and increases natural lighting).
- Crank-operated casement windows are a preferable style.
- Use loop handle pulls on all drawers and cabinets.
- Floors should have high-contrast, glare-free surfaces and trim.
- Provide a 5-foot-square maneuvering space in all rooms.

Kitchen Design

- Use lever-type faucets for ease in adjusting temperature and volume.
- Provide knee space under the sink and near the cooktop.
- Provide variable-height work surfaces between 28 and 45 inches above the floor (permits everyone in household to help with meal preparation).
- Use a contrasting color for border treatments at the edges of countertops.
- Provide stretches of continuous counter space for sliding heavy objects.
- Pull-out drawers should extend fully to allow easy access.
- Provide pull-out shelves in base cabinets (makes it easier to maneuver large items in and out).
- Use adjustable-height shelves in wall cabinets.
- Provide full-height pantry cabinets with storage from top to bottom (permits access from all heights, and maximizes storage).
- Provide a 30-by-48-inch area of approach in front of all appliances.
- Use appliances with front-mounted controls.

■ Cooktops with staggered burners to eliminate dangerous reaching are preferable.
■ Provide glare-free task lighting.

Bathroom Design

■ Use lever-type faucets for ease in adjusting temperature and volume.
■ Provide knee space under the lavatory.
■ Lavatory counter height should be a minimum of 32 inches above the floor.
■ Extend mirror to lavatory backsplash to make it low enough for wheelchair users and people of diminutive stature.
■ Offset controls in tub or shower so that they can be operated from outside the fixture.
■ Provide an integral transfer seat in the tub or shower.
■ Use an adjustable-height shower head.
■ Provide grab bar blocking and bars in the tub or shower (can also be used for hanging towels).
■ Use a mixer valve with pressure balancing and a hot water governor (prevents scalding and conserves hot water).
■ Allow 18 inches of maneuvering space at both ends of the tub or shower.
■ Center toilets at least 18 inches from sidewalls.
■ Provide grab bar blocking and bars around toilets (can also be used for hanging towels).
■ Provide a 30-by-48-inch area of approach in front of all fixtures.

Further Information

❏ The Center for Universal Design, North Carolina State University, School of Design, Box 8613, 219 Oberlin Road, Raleigh, North Carolina, 27695-8613; telephone/TTY: 919-515-3082; fax: 919-515-3023; InfoLine: 800-647-6777; e-mail: cud@ncsu.edu; Web site: www.design.ncsu.edu/cud.

Analysis and Interpretation of Information

❏ Converting raw program, code, cost, and other data into forms that are analytically illuminating can be quite useful. Analysis is a meaningful prerequisite for designing; it results in a clear and fine-grained view of the problem, and may even provoke the designer's creativity. For example, following discussions with management and employees for an office project, desired conference rooms are projected as underutilized. The architect is in a position to suggest a dual function: meeting room and employee lounge/library. With careful scheduling, multipurpose utilization can save space and improve overall efficiency. Note that this is an administrative action, with the only formal result being the potential reduction of space required and concomitant reduction in construction cost.

Diagramming Program Data and Initial Concepts

❏ Visual depiction of data invariably helps us, and perhaps clients, to understand problems more precisely (even within the context of an idea, if there is one at this stage). Graphic techniques allow designers to organize efficiently and perceive relationships between program elements; assess ideal patterns of use; suggest zoning or grouping of like functions with respective adjacency and access requirements; and develop and reveal a sense of scale, area, and volume or mass (particularly with three-dimensional diagrams). Figure 2.4 shows a 3-D diagram example that was used in a client meeting.

Bubble diagrams are abstract graphic representations of the program spaces and their layout (see Fig. 2.5 for an example). Bubble diagrams can also be scary things! Exercise extreme caution in using them beyond acquiring a fundamental understanding of the program. They can be addictive! And, if bubble diagrams are taken too literally or relied upon too extensively to drive the process, a diagrammatic building will result—a building that is an extrusion of the plan. The danger is that bubble dia-

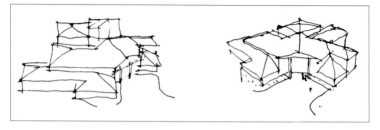

FIGURE 2.4
Two sketches of the exterior of a house help to give a sense of its massing. The aerial views assist in visualizing the entire form at a glance. (Courtesy of Andy Pressman.)

grams will allow the architect to present a quick fix that is supported by the client, without taking time to investigate more sophisticated underlying ideas or conceptual strategies. On the other hand, they can facilitate a necessary immersion in pragmatic issues of program.

Bubble diagrams are quickly drawn and lend themselves to a variety of arrangements simply by ease of manipulation. It may be useful to imagine yourself as each type of building user who "walks through" the bubbles to explore the validity of proposed relationships. The paths that are traced become circulation diagrams, and represent a good way to start thinking about arranging bubbles. Remember to treat all exterior program elements (i.e., parking, service access, playgrounds, courtyards, and so on) similarly.

It is often helpful to draw bubbles in relative scale to each other. Connect related bubbles with lines (use dotted or dashed lines to represent a specific type of relationship [i.e., public versus private]); move them close together to show proximity; use heavy lines to show heavy or frequent traffic flow. If there are too many bubbles, collapse those that are closely associated. For example, bedroom, bathroom, and closets may comprise the single bubble representing a master bedroom. Moreover, you may want to annotate the diagrams to clarify or convey additional information (see Fig. 2.6). Note that this sort of documentation, while intuitive or obvious for the experienced

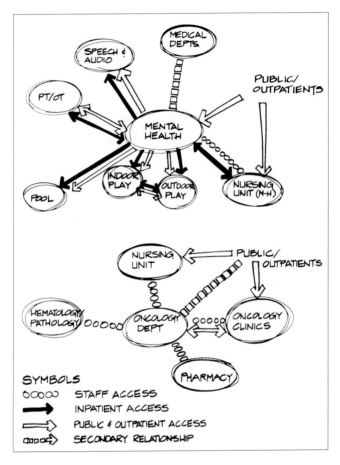

FIGURE 2.5
In these bubble diagrams, note how the symbols connecting the bubbles indicate different types of circulation, or different types of relationships between program spaces. The diagram is from the development plan for the Children's Hospital of Denver. (Courtesy of Kaplan/McLaughlin/Diaz Architects/Planners, San Francisco, California.)

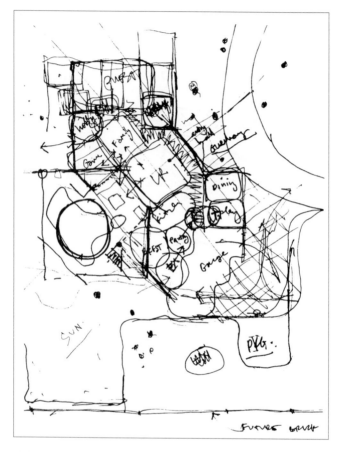

FIGURE 2.6
In this condensed version of a bubble diagram for a large residence in Florida, the bubbles are drawn at relative scale and pushed together to emphasize the importance of spatial adjacencies. (Courtesy of Andy Pressman.)

practitioner, can be a great tool for explaining design decisions to clients.

There are multitudes of other diagrams that may help in study of the problem (see Figs. 2.7 and 2.8). Some demonstrate circulation, showing vehicular, pedestrian, and service movement;

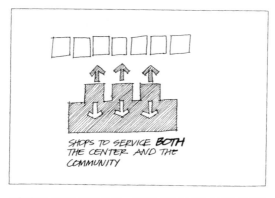

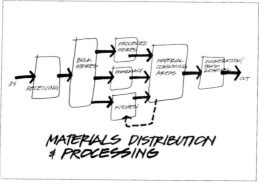

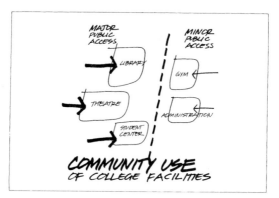

FIGURE 2.7

More examples of programming graphics: a diagram of relationship of building and community; flowchart; and illustration of public access to a private institution. (Source: Pena, William, Parshall, Steven, and Kelly, Kevin. Problem Seeking: An Architectural Programming Primer. AIA Press, 1987.)

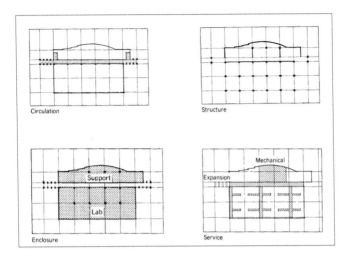

FIGURE 2.8
This series of diagrams forms a study of basic issues of circulation, enclosure, structure, and mechanical systems of Fluke Hall at the University of Washington. Integration of these issues is resolved to form a basis of functional integrity. (© NBBJ, David C. Hoedemaker, Rick Buckley, designers.)

others, such as adjacency matrixes, catalog all spaces and categorize the relationships between spaces (i.e., direct, indirect, unrelated). For complex programs there are more sophisticated bookkeeping methods for collecting and analyzing data, which are frequently employed by programming consultants.

Save all your diagrams! Sign and date them. Your biographer may want them for that monograph on your firm's work! They are also an important part of the record of design decisions. You may want to refer to them when designing to test new strategies. They can be incorporated in some form (perhaps reduced) in the final presentation. In any case, as alluded to previously, they help to demonstrate graphically to clients the logic behind key decisions and thus provide evidence of genuine accountability.

Concept Clues. As in "get a life," it's fairly important to "get a concept." Clues for arriving at a big idea can arise from bits of the data collected specific to the project's circumstance; or perhaps part of

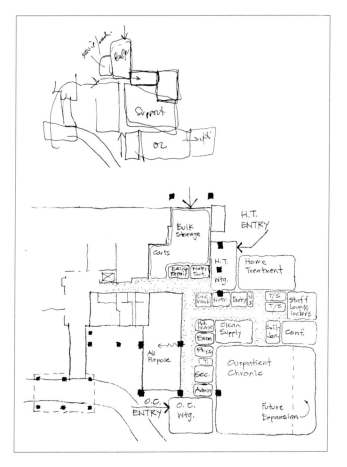

FIGURE 2.9

These two diagrams illustrate the evolutionary sequence from the roughest initial concept sketch of large chunks of space to a more detailed clustering of common services and major components of a proposed new renal dialysis facility for a hospital. (Courtesy of Andy Pressman.)

FIGURE 2.10
Space analysis for a classroom and public meeting facility drawn with the client during a presentation. (Courtesy of Andy Pressman.)

a broader worldview or a personal, evolving agenda; or a combination of all of the above. In any case, the concept is surely an avenue to the project's soul. In a sense, design begins with how the program is framed or conceptualized—an enormously creative act. One or all of the objective program elements, the site and context, the community, or anything that may be associated with the project may inspire a concept. A personal mandate from the client, a seemingly unimportant comment from a typical user, a particularly uplifting view, and a relevant philosophical or political position—all these factors may contribute to the nascent concept. There is an entire spectrum of examples in this book, from my conversation with Antoine Predock and the definitions of good design in Chapter 1, to those cited in the chapters on site and architectural design, to my interview with Thom Mayne in Chapter 7.

A strong design concept facilitates decision making at all scales, from building footprint to door hardware (or lack thereof). When decisions, then, are less arbitrary, the architecture truly becomes greater. Moreover, if the client introduces changes over the course of design development and construction documentation, or when changes occur during construction due to an unexpected field condition, the design intent is usually not significantly diminished when there are powerful, bold initial ideas.

Here is an example of creating a concept for a low-budget retail build-out. A concept can begin with the particular product. From psychological research, we know that the more a product is associated with meaning, the more readily it will be remembered. If a customer is interested in a product over and above his or her immediate need for that product, he or she is very likely to remember it and look for it again. Architecture can create a context or framework that reinforces themes that are both related to a product and promote any intrinsic interest and meaning for the customer. For Prime Time, a store in Charleston, South Carolina, specializing in products for entertainment and leisure time, the concept developed was that of stage sets. Each set corresponds to a different department. In contrast to the more conventional dedication of every square inch to product display, the use of some space for creating context yields returns in customer behavior. (See Fig. 2.11.)

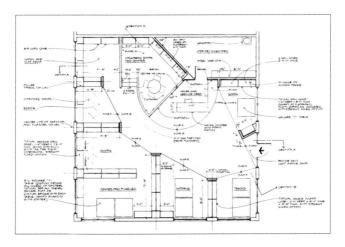

FIGURE 2.11
Translation of concept to floor plan for Prime Time: stage sets correspond to different departments within the store. (Courtesy of Andy Pressman.)

Scheduling Note. Programming is such an essential part of the design process that adequate time must be allotted to do it comprehensively and successfully. Perhaps extra time spent up front in understanding client needs and requirements will actually reduce time in later phases due to fewer questions and changes requested. As always, build in time for contingencies, and note that there will, of course, be some overlapping tasks.

Program-Related Obligations. "Design excellence and social responsibility are inextricably connected." This quote from James Stewart Polshek, FAIA, appeared in *AIA Memo,* February 1992, in response to Polshek's winning that year's AIA Architecture Firm Award.

As design professionals, architects (including students) have an obligation to serve the personal interests of clients, and equally important, have a transcendent social responsibility. Automatically challenge what you judge as less than noble and ambitious programmatic goals. Do not necessarily accept a list of functions at face value; identify and exploit hidden opportunities to make more socially responsive environments. Clients may be somewhat nearsighted; they may not be aware of greater possibilities. And this does not necessarily translate to inflation of the construction budget or increasing the scope of work. Be prepared to sell unconventional ideas to clients; back them up with facts and observations from your research. Being persuasive often simply amounts to illuminating a well-studied idea.

Here is a brief examination of the generic challenge to achieve a degree of social awareness and community responsibility among projects of modest scale.

Educational and social activities not only constitute a direct community service but also potentially give valuable exposure to businesses. For example, a computer store in a suburban setting now offers evening classes and demonstrations for beginning users. A specialty bookstore invites local authors to address small groups and book clubs. And a camera store offers instruction on basic photography and darkroom techniques. The attitude of service not only provides a public resource, but it intensifies product interest and broadens the potential market. While there may not be direct financial return on the time invested, real service is never wasted.

These creative programming suggestions did not increase costs, but did have some design implications. Accommodation of small gatherings may be facilitated by using mobile fixtures and by oversizing circulation space that is normally occupied by lightweight seasonal displays. Flexibility or multiple use also is achieved with platforms; these can help zone a store and are ideal for casual seating. So, creative, after-hours use of retail space can expose and effectively promote goods while educating and enriching those present. Thus we can attempt to elevate retail settings as loci for positive cultural events; and design professionals should strive for that ideal wherever possible.

A Client's View of the Design Process
A Conversation with Scott Gordon

My interview with a "typical" client—Scott Gordon, MD—reveals the importance of the personal relationship between architect and client—a refrain that underlies much of what we do in terms of design.

Andy Pressman: *What do you really want from an architect?*

Scott Gordon: I want the architect to be able to read my mind—to get to know me so well that he or she could make consistent field decisions without consulting me, and try to keep personal taste to him- or herself.

Pressman: *How do you react when an architect suggests ideas that are contrary to your own?*

Gordon: I'm open to suggestions, and similarly I would hope my architect is open to my ideas—be thoughtful, don't make snap judgments. Not all of us clients are airheads! I'm interested in seeing how my ideas could be made even better. If there's no common ground, then you will have to end the relationship. The architect should get to know his or her clients very well. In-depth interviews will help to determine exactly what the needs are, because sometimes clients don't even know what the needs are.

Pressman: *Describe your image of the architect in general.*

Gordon: The architect is like a private investigator—a fact-finder—and must be inspiring within constraints. I have an interesting story about my project. I went through design and construction documents (about 25 architectural drawings) for a larger building, and then determined it was going to be too expensive. For me, it wasn't too hard to let the initial design go, it was harder to break it to my architect that we couldn't get this built!

Pressman: *That's amusing, but it is an interesting point. Perhaps it is a failing of the architect to keep the big picture in sight: if the design doesn't work for whatever reason, the architect has a responsibility to work with the client to realize a successful project—that's why he or she was hired.*

Gordon: The client, too, has a responsibility to get personally involved through all phases of design and construction—so he or she is not just a name on a contract. Architecture is a team endeavor.

The Place of People in Architectural Design
with Gerald Weisman

❏ Social and behavioral forces have influenced a significant body of modern architecture. Demands for better affordable housing, a humane workplace, and high-quality design across the entire spectrum of public spaces have catalyzed architects' awareness of contributions from the environment/behavior field. This broad field represented by environmental psychology, sociology, and cultural anthropology has in turn been stimulated to investigate current architectural issues.

Gerald Weisman, PhD, an expert in environment/behavior research, points out in Supplement 2.12 that understanding something of the patterns of human use and need in general can be of central importance to all architectural design.

Gerald Weisman

Gerald D. Weisman, PhD, is a professor of architecture and codirector of the Institute on Aging and Environment, School of Architecture and Urban Planning, University of Wisconsin-Milwaukee. An architect and environmental psychologist, Jerry Weisman has for the past 20 years been actively engaged in teaching, research, and service directed toward the design of better environments for older and cognitively impaired persons. He coauthored (with Uriel Cohen) Holding on to Home: Designing Environments for People with Dementia *(Johns Hopkins University Press, 1991), which received a citation from the* Progressive Architecture *awards program and an award from the AIA International Design Book Fair competition.*

❏ What is the place of people in architecture? At one level we recognize that people—as clients, colleagues, consultants, critics, and most especially as consumers—are central to what we do, but exactly where and how do they fit within the architectural design process? How can we address issues of human needs and human use of the environment without becoming enmeshed in arcane social/behavioral science jargon and data analyses that—as demonstrated in Dana Cuff's (Cuff, 1989) interviews with seven well-known New York designers—are unlikely to stir the architect's soul?

The relationship between architecture and the social/behavioral sciences is seemingly cyclical, as well as occasionally conflictual. There was much excitement and enthusiasm for the topic through the 1970s, as reflected in a dozen or more books on environment-behavior studies and programming methods, with one of the latter produced and published by the AIA (Palmer, 1981). Concern with the "people" side of architecture, however, was to a great extent swept away in the subsequent tide of Postmodernism in the 1980s (see Dean, 1989). Now, there

SUPPLEMENT 2.12

once again seems to be interest in more effectively integrating people into the architectural design process, and three new books on programming, authored by Cherry (1999), Duerk (1993), and Hershberger (1999) are presently on the market.

This essay endeavors to build upon this reawakening of interest in the "people side" of architecture as well as my own observations and professional experience over the past 25 years. Past obstacles to integration of issues of human needs and use are identified and a set of basic propositions is presented. While these five propositions do not completely define excellent practices within this arena, taken together—and they must be considered collectively—they begin to sketch a conceptual and process model that can contribute to the creation of a more central place for people in architectural design.

■ *Proposition 1: broadening our focus from buildings to places.* Most fundamentally, we must recognize that for clients and consumers the ultimate goal of the architectural design process goes beyond the building we design.

We typically consider our professional responsibilities to terminate with the construction of a building. However, for our clients and users, this is not the true culmination of the planning, programming, and design process. For them, the ultimate goal is the living, breathing place that hopefully comes to life within the building we provide. Schools, hospitals, or hotels certainly include one or more buildings, but they are more than that. To fulfill its purpose, each of these buildings must be peopled: a school must have pupils and teachers, much as a hospital requires patients and medical staff, and a hotel is created to house guests. People and buildings, in turn, are linked by a program. The program describes a set of essential features and characteristics specific to the proposed project. It typically also includes a second set of expectations—sometimes explicit but more often implicit—regarding the purpose(s), participants, and patterns of use of a building. Thus building, program, and people collectively define a place. (See Fig. 2.12.)

■ *Proposition 2: conceptualizing the components of place.* The components of place—building, people, and program—

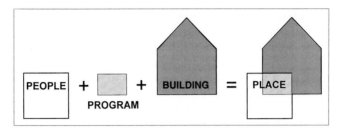

FIGURE 2.12
People plus program plus building creates place. (Courtesy of Gerald Weisman.)

must each be conceptualized in a manner that allows us to effectively link them in the planning, programming, and design process.

We typically conceptualize buildings in two complementary but quite distinct ways, each focusing on particular components or characteristics. Most commonly we think of buildings in bricks-and-mortar terms: their actual physical setting, including structural shell, enclosure system, mechanical systems, finishes, and furnishings. The second approach—while not tangible in the same way as the physical setting—is in fact equally objective and measurable with tape measure, light level meter, or thermometer. This approach focuses on the spatial and sensory properties that the physical setting creates. Size, proportion, and location of spaces relative to one another are key spatial properties, while light and sound levels, temperature, odors, and textures are typically the most salient sensory properties. (See Fig. 2.13.)

This distinction between physical setting on the one hand and sensory and spatial properties on the other is perhaps clearest in the domain of architectural specifications; traditional prescriptive specs focus on bricks and mortar, while performance specs define required areas, distances, light levels, etc.

Dana Cuff's interviews with seven well-known practitioners suggest that architects—to the extent they focus on the people who will use that which they design—tend to image them as individuals. While it is essential to recognize and respect the unique nature of each individual, we must also recognize that groups—teachers, nursing aides, business travelers—as well as organizations—school boards, hospital corporations, park districts—are essential components of places. People may thus be conceptualized at three levels of social aggregation. (See Fig. 2.14.)

It is worth remembering that it is most often organizations that initiate projects and that the formulation of a project program is the result of often intense negotiation among organizations, groups, and individuals (e.g., school board, teachers' union, and pupils' parents).

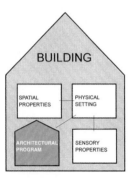

FIGURE 2.13
Desired sensory and spatial properties as well as elements of the physical setting— structure, enclosure, mechanical systems, finishes, and furnishings—may all be specified in the architectural program. (Courtesy of Gerald Weisman.)

It is the program that ultimately links people and buildings. We may conceptualize the program in two non-overlapping ways. The most common categorization—that between functional and architectural programs—will be detailed in proposition 4. Here we will draw an even more fundamental distinction, that between the explicit program document—the written program prepared by client and/or architect for a specific project—and what architects Murray Silverstein and Max Jacobson have characterized as the "hidden program" (see Silverstein and Jacobson, 1978). Within any given era or culture, Silverstein and Jacobson argue, there is a consensual understanding of the nature of specific place types. It is assumed— taken for granted—that schools, hospitals, or hotels ought to take a given form, architecturally as well as organizationally. Only when an innovative place type appears—the open plan school, the Planetree hospital, the first "destination hotels" with dramatic atria at their center—do we recognize that the forms these places take are in fact what sociologists call social constructions; the hidden program—that bundle of unexamined assumptions that underlies these constructions—becomes clear.

The hidden program typically encompasses a socially agreed-upon set of expectations regarding purpose, participants, and what constitutes acceptable and unacceptable behavior within a place. The hidden program defines whether schools are places for socialization as well as education, hospitals places for preventative as well as acute care, prisons places for punishment or rehabilitation. The hidden program plays a significant role in shaping group and individual action. To the extent we share society's definition of "gourmet restaurant," "corner bar," and "fast food joint," we know what to expect, and even what to order in each, and are able to behave in a manner deemed socially appropriate. With due credit to the early English economist Adam Smith, we must recognize that the invisible hand of the hidden program plays a role in shaping every place we design.

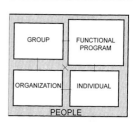

FIGURE 2.14
People may be conceptualized at three levels of social aggregation: individual, group, and organization. The functional program is often the result of intense negotiation across these levels. (Courtesy of Gerald Weisman.)

■ *Proposition 3: behavior in places vs. place experience.* Traditional ways of defining the environmental experience of individuals are of limited value in the architectural planning, programming, and design process.

There is a tradition within psychology of defining people's experience in terms of what we might call modalities: perception, cognition, behavior, emotion, and meaning. A sequential ordering of these modalities is assumed—perception followed by cognition, etc.—and particular emphasis is typically placed on behavior as the most overt and measurable facet of experience. While this conceptualization has had great heuristic value for the behavioral sciences, there is little to suggest that such modalities of place experience in general, or behavior in particular, are the most productive ways in which to link human concerns to architectural decision making (see Weisman, Chaudhury, and Diaz Moore, 2000).

A different, and potentially more productive, approach considers attributes rather than modalities of place experience. The focus of this approach is on those qualities that we attribute to places in the context of our interactions with them. Much of environmental design research, user need studies, and environmental psychology—as well as the layperson's reactions to places—addresses such attributes. The following set of attributes emerges as common across a broad range of place types.

- *Stimulation:* the quality and quantity of stimulation as experienced by the various sensory modalities (visual, thermal, auditory, etc.)
- *Accessibility:* the ease of locomotion through and use of an environment; also referred to as universal design
- *Crowdedness:* the perceived (as opposed to actual) density level within an environment
- *Privacy:* the ability to control the flow of visual and auditory information to and from others
- *Control:* the extent to which an environment facilitates personalization and territorial claims to space
- *Legibility:* the ease with which people can conceptualize key spatial relationships and effectively find their way within an environment
- *Comfort:* the extent to which an environment provides sensory and anthropometric fit and facilitates task performance
- *Adaptability:* the ease with which an environment and its components can be reorganized to accommodate different patterns of use
- *Sociality:* the degree to which an environment facilitates or inhibits social contact among people
- *Meaning:* the extent to which an environment holds individual or collective significance for people (e.g., attachment, challenge, beauty)

It is essential to recognize that these terms do not represent qualities inherent in buildings themselves, but rather qualities we attribute to places as a consequence of our interactions with them. We should also think of these attributes as not antithetical but rather complementary to the modalities of place experience previously described. To say that we attribute the quality of legibility to a complex hospital implies a great deal about what we perceive (are there signs?), how we organize that information (is the building a rectangle in plan?), what actions we may or may not take (should I ask for directions?), our emotional state (feeling disoriented is quite distressing), and meaning (this is not a user-friendly place). As addressed in the following two propositions, conceptualizing place experience in terms of such attributes, rather than the more traditional formulation of modalities, may be substantially more effective in the integration of people issues in architectural design.

■ *Proposition 4: from functional to architectural program: experience as the bridge.* Moving from the functional to the architectural program can be a difficult and frustrating exercise. Consideration of attributes supportive of the function(s) of a place can assist in effecting the transition to the architectural program.

Development of the program for a project is commonly subdivided into two phases: functional programming and architectural programming. The functional program, traditionally developed by the client, details the who, what, when, and why of a project. What activities comprise the typical day of a student and teacher in a school or a patient, visitor, or nurse in a hospital? How do these activities relate to and hopefully reinforce the mission of the organization and the purpose for which the building is being designed? The architectural or space program, by contrast, is typically made up of a listing of room titles (spaces) coupled with square footage allocations, perhaps locational criteria (spatial properties), and, less commonly, requirements for lighting levels, luminous and thermal conditions (sensory properties), and perhaps furniture and equipment (physical setting). (See Fig. 2.15.)

Moving from the functional to the architectural program, and from the architectural program to design, is often a challenge if not a frustration for the architect. Little of the functional program

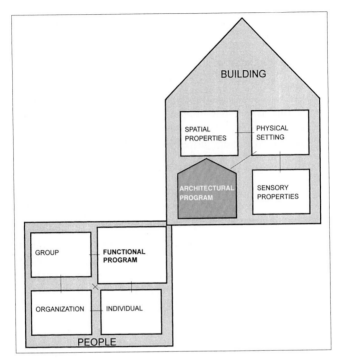

FIGURE 2.15
It is often difficult to move from functional to architectural program. The two are barely connected to one another. (Courtesy of Gerald Weisman.)

is directly suggestive or evocative of the built environment. Simply knowing that a social worker will interview three clients per hour tells us precious little about the nature of the interchange between the two; will the client be ill at ease? Is it essential that the conversation be confidential? Similarly, knowing that an interview room is to be 100 square feet with a desk, computer, and phone jack provides very little guidance for the myriad design decisions required in even such a simple space. How can one link the world of human use and the world of bricks and mortar?

One effective answer to this question is what we might call *experiential programming*. Experiential programming occurs between—and serves to link—traditional functional and architectural phases. Once we learn from the functional program that a social worker will be conducting intake interviews, our next questions—rather than being about the size of his or her desk or the color of the walls—should concern those attributes of place experience that can best support his or her activities. Is privacy important? Will the interchange be casual or formal? What level of stimulation should the interview space provide? Once we understand the answers to these questions, we can far more readily translate such requirements into the performance terms of sensory and spatial properties. Walls must have a specific sound attenuation value to ensure privacy; seating arranged at right angles will be more congenial and less confrontational than sitting across a table. Liberal use of color and personal artifacts will also assist in putting the prospective client at ease. To complete the design cycle, performance specs provide the basis for more prescriptive specifications, and then for the traditional design of the physical setting.

Figure 2.16 illustrates the process whereby we move from functional program (the result of negotiation among organization, group, and individuals) to experiential program (framed in terms of attributes of place experience) to architectural program (which defines required sensory and spatial properties as well as specifics of the physical setting). We can thus view the complete program (functional, experiential, architectural) as a simulation, or miniature, of the place to be designed.

■ *Proposition 5: research and application: pragmatism and patterns.* Structuring knowledge as practitioners do—in terms of what works—enhances the likelihood of that knowledge being integrated into design decision making.

Finally, we should recognize and perhaps take comfort in the fact that the estrangement of research from application is in no way unique to architecture. To the contrary, it is a common problem across a broad range of professions and disciplines. At least part of the reason for this problem appears to be the philosophical assumptions of logical positivism that underlie most forms of scientific research—including behavioral science research—to this day. These positivist assumptions hold that research data

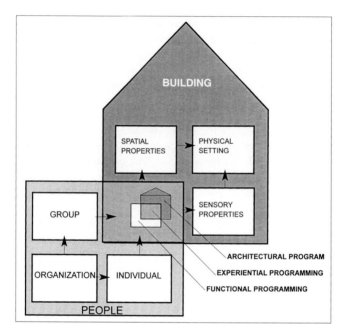

FIGURE 2.16
Functional, experiential, and architectural programs provide a bridge from people to building. (Courtesy of Gerald Weisman.)

must be applied in a very literal way and that the making of decisions that go beyond the specifics of these data is not acceptable.

Study of decision making by practitioners, however, whether they are psychotherapists, social workers, or architects, tells a story very different from the orthodoxy of positivism, and presents a very different model for research utilization. Rather than literal utilization of discrete research findings, practitioners build up through their work much less formal theories regarding what works. Such theories will be an amalgam of personal experience and informal professional folk wisdom, as well as some formal research findings (see Polkinghorne, 1992). In the architectural world we are most familiar with such informal, pragmatic theories as design guidelines, excellent practices (such as those in this book), or patterns. Beginning with the work of Christopher Alexander and his colleagues, the pattern approach has been employed for the understanding and design of place types as diverse as children's health facilities, assisted living for the elderly, New Urbanist communities, and the natural landscape. Though typically limited to specific spaces or issues, individual patterns can be seen as including and integrating the kinds of information included in functional, experiential, and architectural programming. Patterns have proven to be a powerful tool for effective integration of research and decision making.

Summary

❑ Expanding our vision from buildings to places makes people—as individuals, groups, and organizations—an integral component of our professional focus rather than an ancillary matter. Shifting our attention from the behaviors in which people engage to their environmental experiences—current and desired—allows us to build a bridge from functional to architectural program and then from architectural program to design. Finally, we can look to patterns as a natural and effective device for communication and guidance regarding how best to meet people's needs, desires, and aspirations in the places where they spend their lives.

References

Cherry, E. *Programming for Design: From Theory to Practice*. New York: Wiley, 1999.

Cuff, D. "Through the Looking Glass: Seven New York Architects and Their People." In Ellis, R., and Cuff, D. (eds.), *Architects' People*. New York: Oxford University Press, 1989.

Dean, A. "The Architect and Society." *Architecture*, July, 78:7, 1989.

Duerk, D. *Architectural Programming: Information Management for Design*. New York: Van Nostrand Reinhold, 1993.

Hershberger, R. *Architectural Programming and Predesign Manager*. New York: McGraw-Hill, 1999.

Palmer, M. *The Architect's Guide to Facility Programming*. New York: American Institute of Architects and Architectural Record Books, 1981.

Polkinghorne, D. "Postmodern Epistemology of Practice." In Kvale, S. (ed.), *Psychology and Postmodernism*. London: Sage, 1992.

Silverstein, M., and Jacobson, M. "Restructuring the Hidden Program: Toward an Architecture of Social Change." In Preiser, W. (ed.), *Facility Programming*. Stroudsburg, PA: Dowden, Hutchinson & Ross, 1978.

Weisman, G., Chaudhury, H., and Diaz Moore, K. "Theory and Practice of Place: Toward an Integrative Model." In Rubenstein, R., Moss, M., and Kleban, M. (eds.), *The Many Dimensions of Aging*. New York: Springer, 2000.

chapter 3

The Site

*"Like voting in Chicago,
go early and often."*
—William P. Miles

Sketches

❏ Architect Yoshio Taniguchi said in a recent *New York Times Magazine* interview that "The site is the point of departure, the most basic issue in architecture." He continued, talking about his design process: "I visit the site to assure that I do not succumb to abstract theories and a vision of style that applies only to the work's surface, so that I arrive at architecture in its true and full form."

Incorporation of site issues into design is so fundamental to achieving excellence—should be so ingrained in the process—that the "environmental movement" is somewhat moot and a bit baffling. Good architecture has always been defined by an active engagement with, and response to, a constellation of site factors: topography, solar path, wind, vegetation, climate, views, context, preservation of natural site amenities, and on and on.

■ Palm trees swaying in cool breezes, powder-blue skies, warm sunny days, white sand beaches, turquoise ocean water filled with smiling dolphins, dazzling orange sunsets, lush green foliage, fragrant flowers and berries, chirping exotic birds with big beaks, all just beyond the cabana: it's another day in paradise.

FIGURE 3.1
Courtesy of Andy Pressman.

FIGURE 3.2
Courtesy of Andy Pressman.

■ Barren desert, dry wind, and tumbleweed. Every few minutes a prairie dog's head pops up and then disappears. Soaring snow-capped mountains to one side. In the flat
distance, a huge tractor-trailer rumbles by at very high
speed—only a few miles from the elite Southwest artists'
colony.

■ Steel, glass, and concrete, tall and angular. Shimmering surfaces, dark canyons, sidewalks teeming with well-groomed
pedestrians, and a palpable intensity, excitement, and
power. Amid all this urban density lies an asphalt oasis:
"Quick-Park."

Location, location, and location: as the preceding scenes
indicate, any given site and its surrounding context are made up
of unique attributes and powerful environmental forces. The
spectacular, the mundane, and even the grim characteristics of a
proposed site must be observed, inventoried, analyzed (much like
program elements), and considered as factors that influence the
architecture. This is where the *place* of place making originates.
Integration, optimal fit, and harmony of building and site are

FIGURE 3.3
Courtesy of Andy Pressman.

extremely important in attaining design excellence. Both Malcolm Wells and Cesar Pelli—representing fairly diverse theoretical positions—share a similar sentiment. (Wells: "Improve the land when you build, or don't build there." Pelli: "We should not judge a building by how beautiful it is in isolation, but instead by how much better or worse that particular place has become by its addition.")

This chapter begins with discussions of landscape architecture by luminaries Lawrence Halprin and Paul Friedberg. Then comes a primer on current thinking about environmentally sensitive design, followed by a state-of-the-art case study by Croxton Collaborative Architects (building sections with lots of squiggly arrows not included). Specific examples of site influences on design, together with a site inventory checklist, are intended to assist with site analyses. A supplement on daylighting by specialist Ginger Cartwright sheds new light on the subject. What to do with parking—a fact of life regarding larger site issues—is handled in an erudite essay by reluctant parking guru Mark Childs. The chapter comes full circle and ends with a provocative discussion by Baker Morrow, another landscape architect.

Appreciating the Environment

❏ In the introduction to *Design with Nature* (Doubleday/Natural History Press, 1969), the classic text by Ian McHarg, Lewis Mumford succinctly restates the wisdom of Hippocrates: "Man's life, in sickness and in health, is bound up with the forces of nature, and that nature, so far from being opposed and conquered, must rather be treated as an ally and friend, whose ways must be understood, and whose counsel must be respected." In light of the urgency associated with sustainability and environmental protection, the application to architecture could not be more salient today no matter what one's philosophical, moral, or cultural stance. Thoughtful responses to the environment not only help tie a building to its site, but may have real impact in preservation of vital ecologies.

Landscape Architecture
with Lawrence Halprin and Paul Friedberg

❏ Landscape design and our responses to the manipulation of land form, water, and vegetation constitute what may well be the least appreciated and most underrated architectural specialty. As Supplements 3.1 and 3.2 demonstrate, there is often a large measure of overlap between priorities of landscape design and those of building design. Thus, it is critical that architects be conversant with the vocabulary and the values of landscape design.

Lawrence Halprin

Landscape architect Lawrence Halprin pens this overview. His writing, lectures, exhibits, and projects have been on the cutting edge of the discipline for over 40 years. Halprin's brilliance lies in a vision that promotes global awareness while maintaining sensitivity to the microscale. Some of his best-known projects include Sea Ranch Master Plan in Northern California, San Francisco's Ghirardelli Square, and Seattle's Freeway Park.

❏ Landscape architecture as a design profession deals with the total environment. It works, however, at many different scales, from whole regions that cross political boundaries and ecological zones (like a national park) to small personal house and garden designs.

Some people think that landscape architecture deals only with open spaces left over after buildings are designed. In fact, the opposite is true. On a conceptual level, it is vital to think first about the whole configuration of human life on the planet and then develop an overview about how a particular composition will work at appropriate scale. This conception includes transportation networks, open space systems, and functional requirements for food-growing facilities, workplaces, recreational areas, and so on. Landscape architecture should focus attention on how the whole integrates.

The basic tool for landscape architecture is the land itself and its configuration. We need contour maps to establish grades, elevation changes, drainage, vegetative cover, soil types, and wind patterns. We need to understand where wetlands are located and what animals are present. This ecological background and knowledge forms a preamble to the beginning of design studies. This is our fundamental resource. After that comes knowledge and information about the human ecology—the demographics, archeology, and history of the area; the language and living patterns that currently exist; and the part that art plays in the value system of the community. Landscape design should be holistic in its approach!

After gathering all these factual resources as a foundation, the next part of the process is still conceptual. You ask yourself, on a design level, how to use the previous information to develop a sense of community. The word *community*, in this case, refers back to its original Latin meaning of home and environment. In other words, how can a house, a garden, a street, a plaza, or a neighborhood fit together to form a living pattern that enhances life? At this stage you start to evolve a plan in space—a plan that locates things in relation to each other.

Then you come to the specific design issue. At this point, design usually shifts into specialty areas, but with a full overview of how the whole project fits together. Architects, structural engineers, and civil engineers focus on their areas of expertise.

At this point, open space design becomes vital as the matrix of the living pattern. It details the way overall design links into and utilizes existing landscape configurations, the way existing land uses fit, the way grading works with existing contours. It takes care not to destroy existing vegetation, scar hillsides, or mangle existing drainage patterns in streams. Conservation of existing natural resources is a major concern and influences the amount and configuration of structures and the way they are sited on the landforms. Questions of density, height, skylines, and view corridors all need to be studied and protected on a macroscale.

On the microscale, where people are walking, the choreography of human scale needs thoughtful study. How do we interact on streets and paths, in gardens and plazas? How do we interact in the life of the street, in sidewalk cafes, or in festivals?

Finally, the quality and character of the design is developed through sketches and three-dimensional models. Spaces must be designed not only through two-dimensional plans, but also with great emphasis on the sensory experience people will have there—the kinetic feel of movement, the mix of sound and smell, the variety of opportunities for creativity, enjoyment, and human interaction. Constantly remember that the purpose of these designs is to make places for the full range of human experiences.

❑ How can you begin to operationalize the study methods referred to by Halprin? The act of spending a few hours at a site at different intervals throughout the day, over a period of time, will expose you to the dynamic events occurring at the site—both natural and human-made. Ideally, one would camp out for a year to get a sense of the inherent rhythms, cycles, and patterns there. Alas, in traditional practice, that is a bit impractical (though not for some designers). Antoine Predock, the Albuquerque-based architect (see Chapter 1), is a champion of this direct approach. He has stressed the importance of understanding the natural context over time. He says architects must "sit on a site, put their butts on the ground, feeling and sensing the spirit of the place." Predock elaborates by suggesting that his sensitivity to site is due in part to living in New Mexico, a place where "the geological presence is palpable. Your feet feel time. You can sense the land moving through your body."

An intimate knowledge of the site can electrify design concepts. How does one become intimate with the site? Start with a simple walk-through; plan on as many trips as possible during the course of the project, as your design develops. Go before breakfast; have dinner at the coffee shop across the street. Walk your dog on the site! The goal is to log some quality time there and in the neighborhood, and constantly test design ideas.

Paul Friedberg

Award-winning and noted landscape architect Paul Friedberg, of M. Paul Friedberg & Partners Landscape Architecture & Urban Design, has offices in New York and Tel Aviv. He discusses a variety of topics, including achieving success in design, working with architects, and encountering the site.

How to Achieve Success

❏ There are no formulas. The design world is fluid. To use a platitude, change is a constant and we provide new ideas to respond. There is no way to teach anyone how to formulate an idea. We only speculate where ideas come from. What we can communicate is a way to think. To discriminate, so that ideas may have relevance.

It's also been curious to me that designers, who have an effect on the environment and people, are not typically exposed to philosophy and ethics in their curriculum. These disciplines provide us with values, an understanding of who we are, our aspirations, hopes, and capabilities. Armed with this knowledge, talented form makers can provide meanings for forms. That's success.

What's My Experience Working with Architects?

❏ Ironically, some of my best work has been accomplished with the least talented architects. For they have given me free reign. I have always found it difficult to work with designers who do not feel, understand, or respect the nature of other sensibilities. The world is systemic. Integration and cooperation are essential to any successful enterprise. Recently, I have discovered that working with artists expands my perspective. The artist's sensibility tends to be complementary to that of the landscape architect. It's a mutually reinforcing relationship, one that could and should work with architects.

How to Encounter and Understand the Site

❏ The site is an attitude as well as a physical presence. Most designers relate to the site from the property line in, and to the most immediate context. I see the site as a complex of interwoven observations and experiences. Any relationship to site starts at where I come from, what I go through, and where and when I arrive. Once there, I ask whether I am to be confronted or presented. Is the site to be one or a sequence of experiences? Is the site volume or a space? Then there are questions that arise when a site has not been urbanized—when the transformation alters the larger context. This is an issue that relates back to one's own philosophy and ethics. I've always found it easier to confront transformation of a site that has already been urbanized.

How Should a Designer Deal with Environmental Conservation?

❏ Conservation is a matter of personal values. My work is primarily urban. I endeavor to accommodate human conservation, biological rather than botanical. My work is focused on accommodating need, to provide an expanded vision, to broaden one's outlook. It's a triangulated relationship between you, me, and a place.

Who Are We and Should We Be Who We Are?

❏ I've watched the times change from the 1960s, 1970s, and 1980s, where we as professionals have developed oversized egos with misplaced values. We now seek meaning and pleasure in

FIGURE 3.4
Pershing Park, Washington, DC. The design is animated when people make themselves an integral part of the composition. The design challenge is to facilitate this possibility. (Courtesy of M. Paul Friedberg & Partners.)

ourselves. The dialogue is intraprofessional, intellectual, and exclusive of people. It's always curious to me why people are not present in the articles in architectural magazines. Are they considered intrusive, irrelevant? Is this omission an indictment? We are not designing objects and environment. We are designing how people live—lifestyles. We can provide meaning or create obstacles. We have the option to ignore or to follow, or the power to lead. The choice starts with social values, our perspective of society, and our relationship to it.

Well-Grounded Design, or It's Not Easy Being Green

❑ Does your building have green performance anxiety? Do your diagrams lack lots of squiggly arrows? Any definition of excellent design practices must include a range of green/sustainable/ environmental attributes. Overall building and site performance strategies are discussed in a succinct yet detailed manner by expert Stephen Dent in Supplement 3.3, followed by a glimpse of a state-of-the-art new project by Croxton Collaborative Architects, PC, in Supplement 3.4.

Steve Dent's piece examines the issue from a variety of scales and perspectives that have immediate applicability to whatever you're working on in the office. Take full advantage of these insights, and incorporate them into preliminary design thinking. Andrew St. John, AIA, has proclaimed in his book, *The Sourcebook for Sustainable Design* (Architects for Social Responsibility, 1992), "The environment is not an issue or set of issues. It is the context in which all issues occur."

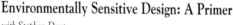

Environmentally Sensitive Design: A Primer

with Stephen Dent

Stephen Dent

Stephen Dent is an associate professor of architecture at the University of New Mexico School of Architecture and Planning. He has been teaching design studios, passive environmental controls, and lighting for over 20 years. He is also a partner in Dent & Nordhaus, Architects, specializing, of course, in environmentally sensitive designs.

❏ It is part of our professional responsibility to design, to the best of our abilities, buildings and communities that are sensitive to the larger environment.

This is not a law, but an ethic. It is easily espoused, but usually not followed. As a profession, architecture has significant impact on the use of resources, and that impact is way beyond "paper or plastic?"—it is for the life of the building. U.S. architects are part of a society that constitutes about 5 percent of the world's population and uses about 40 percent of the world's resources. This profligate consumption is not a right. We can live well *and* use less. We can live softly on the land *and* create stimulating environments. We can be highly efficient in our use of resources while slowing global warming *and* have a more productive economy.

SUPPLEMENT 3.3

FIGURE 3.5
Winter view of Dent residence, Cedar Crest, New Mexico. (Stephen Dent, architect. Photo: Stephen Dent.)

I know that *sustainable* is the current catchphrase, but I feel that, because sustainability is so extraordinarily difficult to fully achieve in a strict sense, *environmentally sensitive* is a better description for now. For a designer this is not an onerous proposition. As a matter of fact, it is an opening to a more dynamic and richer architectural aesthetic. Understanding natural forces will allow the creative designer to develop innovative formal responses in the same way that a designer who is conversant with structural principles and systems has more tools at his or her disposal for solving architectural problems (see Fig. 3.6). The forces of nature are ever changing, and an architecture that responds to these forces with intelligence will exhibit "purposeful differentiation." The resulting forms and surfaces will not be the same on

FIGURE 3.6
Desolation wilderness, California. Natural systems exhibit a "purposeful differentiation" that varies with orientation, solar and wind exposure, and altitude. Design conditions will vary dramatically depending on one's exact position in such a setting, thus requiring a detailed and thoughtful site analysis. (Photo: Stephen Dent.)

all orientations and will usually have the property of variation over time built into them. This may be as simple as an adjustable sunshade or louver or as intriguing as a material that changes its properties over time in response to heat, radiation, or air pressure.

Some architects have expressed the opinion that sustainable or green architecture inherently results in a recognizable style or aesthetic and either limits or contradicts their personal expressive tendencies. However, many basic environmentally sensitive design decisions, such as building orientation and massing, are independent of style. Many others, such as shading, can be dealt with expressively through exterior features or subtly through glazing technology. Even the selection of products for their environmental characteristics has become much easier and less limiting over time. I do believe, though, that there is a tendency for environmentally sensitive design to be a design of layers. Designs will be layered because there are multiple issues to be resolved in responding to and using to maximum advantage the environmental forces of solar radiation, air motion, temperature, humidity, precipitation, and light. No single material or detail can heat and insulate a passive solar building, generate power, collect and recycle water, and provide natural ventilation as needed. Responding to variable climatic forces almost invariably leads to solutions that are not singular and are not fixed.

Understanding the Problem

❏ The best way to start designs that are environmentally sensitive is to investigate and understand three issues at the very beginning of the process:

■ Site climate
■ Site physiography and context
■ Environmental building program

Site Climate. A designer needs to know the climatic forces on the building site, i.e., the site climate. The analysis of these factors goes beyond recording available weather data and a sun path diagram. The essence of the problem of climate is knowing how the forces of solar radiation, temperature, humidity, wind, and rain or snow come together on your site. Where is the wind coming from when it is very cold and should be avoided? Does the temperature drop during summer nights to a level that is useful for night ventilation cooling? When can a combination of shading and cross-ventilation create thermal comfort in your building? In other words, to use or avoid climatic forces, you need to see them in combinations—not individually. Perhaps the best approach to doing this is plotting your climatic data on a psychrometric chart. Unless you are designing at an airport or post office where weather data is usually collected, your site will exhibit some variations from the data. The amount of cloud cover and solar radiation will be driven by the larger climate regime, but wind and shadowing from hills or buildings can vary dramatically in a short distance and temperature will vary with altitude and urbanization. On-site observation over a full year is desirable in order to understand site climate nuances.

Site Physiography and Context. Architects are always taught to record and respond to the surrounding built context. The response may be deferential or it might be aggressive, but there are factors such as roads, buildings, easements, and zoning to respond to. A deeper analysis will also include larger social and community issues. In environmentally responsive design, the nature of the land and its essential natural features is critical. Topography and underlying geology have always been of immediate concern for the designer, but we should also be fully aware of critical habitats for endangered plants and animals, storm runoff and control, stream quality, importance of a particular site in the larger ecological context, viewsheds, and impact on air quality. This is just a partial list of the factors that might be considered in a comprehensive site analysis. There seem to be no simple sites anymore. Whether a site is urban or rural, there is a multitude of issues for which the analytical skills of a conscientious designer are needed.

Environmental Building Program. The architect may be given a detailed program for a building project or may be required to develop one. In addition to the traditional issues of function, adjacencies, and areas, an environmental building program would include such information as occupancy, hours of use, lighting and equipment requirements, specific environmental issues or problems, and any goals for environmental performance. This refinement of the traditional programming process is needed in order to define the nature and severity of the comfort, resource, and energy use problems to be solved. The architect should have a basic understanding of these issues in order to begin conceptualizing a design solution. For example, a high-occupancy office building, even in a cold climate, will typically have an energy use pattern in which lighting and cooling—not heating—are the dominate energy cost issues.

Smaller-Scale Buildings

❏ The thermal performance of smaller buildings, such as houses or commercial structures under about 5000 square feet, is usually dominated by the nature of exterior building surfaces. The heating, cooling, and ventilation requirements are largely determined by the orientation and massing of the structure; the amount of insulation; the size, type, and orientation of glazing; shading provisions; amount of thermal storage mass; and potential for natural ventilation. Except in unusual cases, the internal heat gain due to lighting or electrical equipment demands or from occupancy densities is relatively unimportant. These skin load–dominated (SLD) buildings are ideal candidates for passive climatic design approaches. After years of research and application in numerous designs throughout the world, we can say unequivocally that this climatic design approach works! With simple design efforts you can economically reduce heating demand by 30 percent in Chicago or 80 percent in Los Angeles. With more aggressive design and construction measures, these levels of performance can be exceeded. It is also easy to greatly reduce cooling demands. Conceptually, the architect should make the building resistant to the negative climatic forces and welcoming to the positive climatic forces. This is where an understanding of the site climate and the thermal requirements of the occupants and the building over time comes into play.

What have we learned about SLD buildings where the dominant energy and comfort concern is with heating?

■ *Build well.* Well-insulated buildings with low infiltration levels are a great start. In extreme climates, the use of special framing techniques to allow for thick insulation may be required, and air-to-air heat exchangers are a good idea if infiltration rates are below half an air change per hour. Vapor-permeable infiltration barriers are highly recommended.
■ *Collect the sun's warmth.* Orient solar apertures within 30 degrees of south, and try to get solar radiation into all major spaces (while designing shading systems for variable control of direct glare and overheating). You can use 7 to 10 per-

FIGURE 3.7
(a) *Dent residence, Cedar Crest, New Mexico. Compact form for minimal surface-to-volume ratio and efficient construction. High levels of insulation, low-E windows, and partial earth sheltering for energy conservation. Trombe walls and direct solar gain for heating. Removable sunshades and venting stair tower for summer cooling. (Photo: Madeleine Dent-Coleman.)*

cent of your floor area in south-facing windows if your small building uses light frame construction with no appreciable thermal mass in the construction. (A concrete slab covered with carpet doesn't count!) If the building is frame with significant areas of thermal mass, such as brick floors or masonry partitions, then 13 to 18 percent of floor area in south windows is recommended. And if you build an adobe or masonry home with the insulation on the outside, you may use 20 to 25 percent of the floor area in south glass. These rough guidelines help to prevent serious overheating of the interior on mild days during the heating season. The amount of recommended solar aperture is generally less in warm climates and more in colder climates.

■ *Use thermal mass to collect and store the solar heat.* Try to get 5 to 6 square feet of massive materials of no more than 4 inches of thickness for each square foot of south-facing

FIGURE 3.7
(b) *Interior of Dent residence. Open plan for efficient air and heat distribution. Exposed Trombe wall and brick floor for thermal storage of passive solar heat. (Stephen Dent, Architect. Photo: Madeleine Dent-Coleman.)*

glass. Mass exposed directly to the sunlight is significantly more efficient than that in the shade.

■ *Thermal walls and sunspaces.* Thermal storage walls or Trombe walls behind glass areas can provide the necessary collection and storage of solar heat while providing structure and enclosure. Sunspaces such as greenhouses provide for solar collection, usable rooms, and a buffer space between the inside and the harsher exterior environment—besides offering great expressive possibilities for the architecture.

■ *Shading.* Know the periods when you *must* have full shading of your windows and when you *may* need shading. The climate is never fully predictable, so there is a strong argument for adjustable or flexible shading systems, which can also be significant architectural elements in the façade. The biggest complaint from owners of passive solar homes is overheating, so don't overdo it. Besides, electricity for cooling is much more expensive than heating fuels.

■ *Natural ventilation.* Allow for plenty of cross-ventilation through operable windows, skylights, or vents. If calm periods are a problem in the summer, remember that the ideal situation for inducing ventilation is a low, cool inlet and a high, warm outlet.

■ *Glazing.* Use clear double-glazing for maximum solar collection in climates up to 6000 Heating Degree Days (HDD) and consider triple glazing or double-glazed windows with night insulation for climates over 6000 HDD. I recommend low-E windows (with low-emittance coatings) on east, west, or north exposures. For most good-quality windows, low-E glass is now standard or available at low cost. These coatings reflect radiated heat from interior surfaces back into the interior and make double glazing perform like triple glazing. This is good news from the viewpoint of building well and for the thermal comfort of anyone near a window on a cold night or hot day.

These are some "quick and dirty" guidelines. For greater detail and explanation, see the listed references.

Larger-Scale Buildings

❏ As buildings get larger, their energy cost problems become dominated by lighting and cooling demands, not by heating. The internal thermal loads caused by the electric lighting, the computers and other electrical equipment, and the occupants themselves often outweigh the thermal loads due to heat gain or loss at the skin of the building. For this reason such buildings are often called internal load–dominated (ILD) buildings. Even in cold climates, the areas away from the window walls will need to be cooled all year due to the excess internal loads. When poorly controlled solar radiation is added to the mix, overheating is guaranteed and cooling costs skyrocket. To further complicate the matter, electric utilities typically impose a demand charge on large commercial buildings. This pays for the extra power plant needed to supply electricity for that July afternoon when the temperature is 102°F and employees are at their computers with all the lights on while the copier is humming and the coffee is on! The demand charge can easily double the basic electric bill. There are all sorts of HVAC and control fixes that can help reduce costs in this situation. But, doing this for a building that does not respond to its climate can be likened to rearranging the deck chairs on the Titanic—it won't avoid the energy use and financial disaster to come.

However, a building that shades itself from unwanted solar radiation, but is designed in plan and section to admit controlled daylight to replace electric light where possible, can be highly energy efficient, cheap to operate, and a more productive place to work. More and more recent research is leading to the conclu-

FIGURE 3.8
Dresdner Bank, Stuttgart, Germany. (a) Multiple shading strategies include both interior and exterior, fixed and operable strategies in a layered system including high-performance glass.

FIGURE 3.8
Dresdner Bank, Stuttgart, Germany. (b) Close-up reveals the full range of shading strategies in a rich and variable façade. (Photos: Stephen Dent.)

sion that employees, not surprisingly, like daylit buildings more than those without access to daylight. But even more importantly for the owners, the employees are more productive in buildings with access to daylight. In a world where technology and productivity are driving the economic engine, this is an important input for designers. (Note that the overall costs of operating a large office building are more than 90 percent in people costs and less than 10 percent in building and operating the facility.)

Following are some rough design guidelines for larger buildings:

■ *Think daylighting.* Sunlight is free and should be used wherever possible for the ambient lighting in schools,

FIGURE 3.9
Johnson Controls, Milwaukee, Wisconsin. Interior with daylighting, high-efficiency ambient lighting, provision for individual task lighting, and desktop diffuser for individually controlled heating/cooling/ventilation system. (Architect: HOK. Photo: Stephen Dent.)

offices, warehouses, and many other building types. This can reduce electrical lighting usage and costs and, if windows are properly sized, will reduce air conditioning loads. The designer must be thinking about daylight utilization from the earliest schematics so that such issues as building orientation, massing, sections, and fenestration are coordinated. A thorough understanding of the available sunlight or skylight at your site is needed in order to size openings and design the critical control and distribution components. Daylit buildings tend to have thin sections to maximize the floor area next to exterior windows or atria and higher ceilings to maximize the depth to which the light will penetrate. In general, useful levels of daylight will penetrate into a space a horizontal distance about twice the height of the window head. Light shelves are useful in reducing the illumination intensity next to a window and provide a more even distribution of light in a space. In climates dominated by clear skies, sun control is critical. Your first inclination as a designer will be to use too much glazing. But with the sophisticated glass technology available today and the potential for exterior and interior sun control devices, you can create design responses that are both exciting and effective. In most interiors it is best to bring daylight into a space, but not the direct beam of sunlight—so bounce the light and diffuse it. Due to the use of computers in many, if not all, larger buildings, the designer must reduce brightness levels that are "seen" by the monitor. This, in turn, has led to requirements for lower ambient light levels. Bringing in low levels of glare-free daylight often means the use of tinted glazing and reduced window areas, but more inventive design solutions are possible. More than half of all commercial and school buildings in the U.S. are single story. Consequently, the openings in the roof surface are ideal for daylighting. It is easier and more natural to distribute light from above, but it will cause overheating if the openings are oversized and there are few control strategies. A great design tool is the daylight model. A replication of the basic room geometry and surface reflectance will yield highly accurate information on daylight levels. In general, with daylight you should bounce it, control it, not overdo it, use it to achieve both ambient light and special effects, and enjoy it!

■ *Shading*. This is absolutely critical! You must not allow your designs to overheat because you haven't understood solar geometry and intensity. Besides, responding to the dynamics of the sun's movement can lead to a purposeful differentiation in responses on different building orientations that will bring a unique vitality to your designs. There are a number of exciting design possibilities in new glass coatings, electrically switched glass that alters its transparency, double curtain walls with integral shading louvers, and new materials like Cloud Gel, which can turn a skylight from clear to translucent at a particular temperature to prevent overheating.

■ *Efficient electrical lighting.* Use highly efficient electrical lighting systems that have been designed to be coordinated with the daylighting concept through continuous dimming, step switching, and the use of occupancy sensors. The newest T8 and T5 fluorescent lighting systems with their electronic ballasts offer flicker-free light, good color rendition, and continuous dimming to maintain a constant light level while maximizing the use of daylight—all at greatly reduced power levels. As a matter of fact, complete replacement of an older fluorescent system that uses T12 lamps and magnetic ballasts with the new systems is often paid for in less than three years from the energy cost savings.

■ *Natural ventilation.* This is often seen by the mechanical engineer as an obscene phrase, but operable windows and the use of natural ventilation are desirable for the users and can be a major energy-saving feature when properly integrated in the building design.

Indoor Air Quality, Embodied Energy, and Environmentally Sensitive Production

❏ These are three issues that are of great environmental importance in both small and large buildings that may not have a big impact on building form. Ideally, you would design with products that don't adversely effect the quality of the air inside a building, that use the least amounts of energy in their production, and that are harvested or manufactured with minimal environmental impact. To do this, you must be committed to the effort and willing to do your research. The available product guides are extremely useful but are still limited in their application due to the immense number of products in the marketplace and, in many cases, a lack of agreement on standards for environmental performance and labeling. Persist and you will reap the rewards of creating a more environmentally sensitive and healthy building.

FIGURE 3.10
Solar Triplex, Stuttgart, Germany. High-density housing with greenhouses for passive solar heating and semitransparent photovoltaic modules for shading and sun control. (Photo: Stephen Dent.)

Community Scale Issues

❑ The advent of the car completely overwhelmed the compact pedestrian scale of the historic city. Auto-based cities are voracious consumers of raw land and resources. They require extensive and continually expanding infrastructure to serve the inefficient little separate buildings that constitute our suburban housing stock. At this scale, the relevant environmental issues are too numerous and complicated to adequately address even in summary format. However, I will make an appeal for community design that fosters the ability of many of its residents to live, work, shop, go to school, and play without using a vehicle to perform the most ordinary of daily tasks. I didn't say that *all* of the residents must function on foot or commute via mass transit. Personal mobility is so ingrained in this society and its economy that we aren't going to eliminate cars or return to some imaginary bucolic auto-free way of life in the near future. However, there are some design principles we can incorporate now.

FIGURE 3.11
Mixed-use building in Russelsheim, Germany. Retail, office, housing, and parking in a single, community-scaled project. (Photo: Stephen Dent.)

■ *Create neighborhood and community nodes of integrated activities.* Attractive and functional mixes of activities that are integrated with higher-density housing and public transportation can make a start toward more environmentally sensitive cities. If we can eliminate one vehicle per family for those living in these neighborhood centers, we will have achieved much. We need to be thinking and designing in mixed-use mode. Almost all current land development is for a single use or function. Shopping centers and supermarkets have no connections, let alone design relationship, to surrounding housing. Office parks have no housing or shopping included and are surrounded by such large seas of cars and lack of pedestrian amenities that no office worker dares walk to lunch. A new overlay of neighborhood centers on the faceless suburbs would create a more comprehensible visual order, accumulate the necessary concentrations of riders for transit to function, and achieve the population density for new and efficient shared support systems.

■ *Pursue the design possibilities in the new city form.* Most of the design paradigms for the new, environmentally sensitive city are really from an earlier era or from different social and cultural settings. Responding to the new Information Age and its resultant economic and social changes creates the potential for truly original built responses that could give new meaning and forms to environmentally sensitive design. We must think as urban ecologists and design for both complex environmental systems and their interrelationships with our human activities and aspirations.

References (A Brief List)

Balcomb, J. D., and Wray, W. O. *Passive Solar Heating Analysis: A Design Manual.* Atlanta, GA: American Society of Heating, Refrigerating, and Air-Conditioning Engineers, 1984.

Calthorpe, Peter. *The Next American Metropolis.* New York: Princeton Architectural Press, 1993.

Knowles, Ralph. *Energy and Form.* Cambridge, MA: MIT Press, 1974.

Stein, Benjamin, and Reynolds, John S. *Mechanical and Electrical Equipment for Buildings.* New York: Wiley, 2000.

Watson, Donald, and Labs, Kenneth. *Climatic Design.* New York: McGraw-Hill, 1983.

Software

■ Energy design tools including Solar-5 (interactive thermal simulation program) and Climate Consultant can be downloaded at no cost from UCLA's Web site at www.aud.ucla.edu/energy-design-tools.

■ Energy-10, an energy simulation program, and its excellent manual are available from the Sustainable Buildings Industries Council, Washington, DC. (e-mail: sbicouncil@aol.com)

Several Good Web Sites (Look for Links!)

- ■ Alliance to Save Energy (www.ase.org)
- ■ Department of Energy (www.eren.doe.gov/cleanenergy)
- ■ A Web-based course on building science principles (www. openet.ola.bc.ca/arct501/)

Architecture and Sustainability Case Study
with Randolph Croxton

❏ How can a building be considered beautiful if it damages the environment or compromises the health of its inhabitants? On the other hand, Antoine Predock makes an excellent point about not becoming too infatuated with technology. For example, he cites the 1960s and 1970s as a time when an exclusive focus on passive solar design became an excuse not to do architecture. Predock says, "To trot out new devices, new stealth diagrams—as beautiful as they may be—will be soulless unless an artist is doing it."

The following proposed new building by Croxton Collaborative Architects demonstrates how beautiful architecture and sustainability can be when an artist is doing it.

Randy Croxton

Randolph R. Croxton, FAIA, founding principal of Croxton Collaborative Architects, PC, is internationally recognized as a pioneer and innovator in the achievement of environmental and sustainable architectural design, best exemplified in Audubon House, New York City. His firm has received the AIA National Honor Award for design excellence.

Sustainability Compendium: A Dozen Nuggets

❏ Site planning in an environmental/sustainable context seeks to go beyond code and zoning requirements to create an optimum connection between the project and the natural and community

SUPPLEMENT 3.4

context based on a deep understanding of these key issues. Using the Chattanooga Resource Development Center as a case study (see Fig. 3.12), the following characteristics emerge as central:

- *Solar orientation.* Always exploit solar orientation in order to reach full potentials of daylighting, thermal advantage, and future photovoltaic/renewable options.
- *Climate.* Analyze profiles for optimum 100 percent outside air potentials and identification of high-potential system strategies.
- *Air quality and wind patterns.* For optimum operational interface, never make systems dependent on a prevailing wind direction.

FIGURE 3.12
Daylighting component cross section, Chattanooga Development Resource Center. Skylight above stairs and circulation zone provides natural light; splayed surfaces reduce glare; offices straddling this central feature use furnishings to block direct light or bounce it deeper into the office space. Daylight reaches just about every square inch of the area, with light penetrating from the exterior window wall in combination with the skylight. (Rendering by AP Digital Studio, © Croxton Collaborative Architects.)

- *Rainfall.* Assess harvest/storage/utilization for landscape and/or gray water.
- *Soil and soil hydrology.* Make use of soil characteristics in order to reach productive landscape potentials for bioremediation, water retention, cooling, flood (risk reduction), and so on.
- *Indigenous flora/fauna.* Utilize endangered species as indicators of regionally threatened habitat; also, select the most restorative palette of the landscape.
- *Natural history/evolution of the site.* This is critical knowledge to inform optimum design of a productive landscape.
- *Community context (cultural/social).* This knowledge is critical to establishing positive, enduring connections.
- *Urban design (physical fabric).* This is critical to establishing identity, clarity of access, and function (way finding).
- *Acoustical context.* This informs massing strategies, materials, and orientation.
- *Storm/sewer systems.* These are critical to restorative potentials of connection to natural waterways and rivers.
- *Electrical/gas/fuel profiles.* Obtain a full description of direct/indirect environmental impact and cost profiles for economic optimization and long-term viability of design.

Client missions and objectives are informed by rigorous testing of a design solution against these criteria. All opportunities to incorporate natural systems, creating a powerful blend of nature-driven and energy-driven systems, result in solutions that perform exponentially better than the code-compliant minimum building.

Basic Examples of Site Influences on Design

Vegetation

❏ Proximity to a wooded area may suggest a particular architectural expression. Pinecote, the Crosby Arboretum Interpretive Center by Fay Jones, FAIA, takes full advantage of the surrounding Mississippi pine savannah. Says Jones: "The time of day and the seasonal changes modify the shadows that frame the light. The edges of the roof are not crisp at all. Like the pine straw and pine limbs, they progressively thin out from something that's close and dense to something open and fragile." Design concepts can indeed be derived from the natural qualities of the site. Pinecote is a fine example.

Climate

Sun. Orient building and outdoor spaces to coordinate heating/cooling characteristics with seasonal, regional, and programmatic factors—for example, design fenestration, overhangs, and other devices to allow penetration of low winter sun and block high summer sun; consider thermal characteristics when selecting cladding materials; promote and control the quality of daylighting; consider using deciduous trees that can help filter sun in summer and allow penetration of sunlight in winter. Evergreens, of course, provide a year-round barrier. In tropical latitudes, tall palms provide shade without blocking cool breezes at window level.

Wind. Protect/shelter entries from cold winter winds; capture summer breezes for good ventilation and outdoor areas. Moreover, the force of wind produces a variety of stresses and strains, which can lift the roof off a house or cause skyscrapers to sway. These potential stresses, obviously, should be considered for a particular location and factored into the design.

Rain. Avoid siting the building in low areas subject to flooding (without some sort of control system); address water runoff from paved and built areas.

Arthur Erickson's Fire Island house is a good example of a building very much attuned to the exigencies of a climate influenced by salt air and intense beachfront light. The house is finished in cedar boards, which resist corrosion, and two mechanical features control lighting and views. Hinged fences, which are attached to the deck, can be raised or lowered. When the beach is empty and the light is low, the fences can be lowered. When they are upright, the bright reflected light is at least partially blocked, and a degree of privacy is ensured. The living-room roof is also mobile, with the capacity to slide open and reveal the summer night sky.

Slope

❑ A steep slope may suggest a multilevel scheme and zoning of functions by level with interesting three-dimensional potential. With a steep slope, there will be accessibility issues. Design slender forms that align with contours to minimize cutting and filling and disruption to the site. For a flat slope, the maximum potential for the plan is based on regular arrays of identical units; construction is more economical than on steep sites.

A notable example of how a design responds to slope is The Portland, Maine, Museum of Art by architect Henry Cobb of Pei Cobb Freed & Partners. Behind its oversized but thin front façade, the building visually steps down a long, sloping site through a series of distinct masses. This scheme underscores the natural dynamics of the slope while helping the new building to relate more easily to the smaller scale of two historic museum buildings that sit at the base of the site. The discrete masses of the new museum serve to house a unique sequence of galleries designed from cubelike modules. The articulation of the roof and elevation as the museum drops down the slope seems to amplify the perception of natural light; a series of octagonal lantern skylights yield illumination likened by critics to that achieved in Kahn's late museums.

Actually exploiting a sloping site in direct support of programmatic objectives may also result in an effective design. The public library in Great Neck, New York, by Gibbons and Heidtmann (now Gibbons, Heidtmann, and Salvador) is just such a design. A basement level facing a large pond can be entered only from the lowest part of the site. This effectively separates the main public library (at the top of the slope) from the basement level, which is used as a youth center. A special advantage of this scheme is that it allows use of the youth center when the library is closed. Thus, the site is incorporated as a natural zoning device.

Noise, Smells, and Bad Views

❏ Oh well, sometimes it's *not* another day in paradise. Provide buffer zones (and distance, if possible) to dissipate the problem; pay attention to materials selections (i.e., a translucent material such as glass block, to let in daylight and blur the view). Special construction detailing can help a lot toward acoustical separation.

Barker, Rinker, Seacat & Partners were commissioned to design a recreation center in Commerce City, on Denver's industrial fringe. While the region is known for its beauty, dominant local features such as a strip development, oil refineries, warehousing, and a dog track presented decidedly negative site characteristics. The architects responded by designing an inwardly focused building with exterior sweeps of translucent glass block. This "glass masonry" allows penetration of sunlight while effectively muting the frankly bad views. Interior window walls, skylights, and a hub atrium/lobby help make the recreation center an interior oasis.

Good Views

❏ Consider sight lines both to and from the site; study what is appropriate relative to your concept. Frame views from the site to heighten drama, or configure building elements to mediate views to specific areas.

Josh Schweitzer's weekend retreat is sited in the dramatic (and sometimes seismic) landscape of Joshua Tree, California. It is a spare structure from which one can seemingly become immersed in the beauty and rawness of the desert. The essence of the retreat lies in its windows: meticulously placed, eccentrically cut, and breathtakingly effective at framing views of mountains and desert from the site.

Shepley Bulfinch Richardson and Abbott's Center for African, Near Eastern and Asian Culture provides a good example of the control of views to a building. In response to pressures to conserve open space at the Smithsonian, 96 percent of the new cultural center was located underground. Three entry pavilions represent the only aboveground structure. The effect is not only to preserve an expansive quadrangle, but also to maintain views to the very essence of the Smithsonian—the original "castle" designed by James Renwick in 1849.

Context

❑ Acknowledgment or some kind of response to surroundings—obviously very circumstance specific—may include massing, materials, orchestrating regulating lines (i.e., fenestration, cornice), siting of the building, extension of existing circulation patterns into the site and building, and so on. Herbert Muschamp has an appealing sentiment regarding context: "Architecture should contribute to, rather than fit in with, its surroundings."

Kohn Pedersen Fox Associates' 125 Summer Street, a 300-foot-tall office tower in Boston, is a fine example of contextual responsiveness. The new office building was set back on an irregularly shaped site, behind two nineteenth-century granite-clad five-story structures. The principal entrance was inserted in the gap that existed between the two older buildings, matching their height, maintaining the building line, and echoing the classically inspired façade elements.

Traffic

❑ Locate access to parking away from busy streets and intersections. Minimize the number of curb cuts and vehicular and pedestrian conflict (i.e., prevent people and automobile routes from crossing). (See "The Art of Parking" later in this chapter.)

Thinking about traffic may seem mundane and self-evident, but this is decidedly not the case. A most celebrated and infamous example of how easy it is *not* to address pedestrian circulation is Tysons Corner, Virginia, near Washington, D.C. A relatively recent and genuinely huge mosaic of commercial, retail, office, and residential space, Tysons Corner is an archetypal edge city: a high-density, mixed-use development that is not a municipality, although it is sufficiently large and populated to qualify as one.

A score of studies and journalistic accounts have documented that walking is virtually impossible. Tysons Corner sits in a network of two major expressways, two cross-county arteries, vast parking lots and garages, and innumerable on/off ramps. The speed and sound of the cars, trucks, buses, and tractor-trailers alone is intimidating to anyone even considering crossing the street from an office building to a shopping mall. The reality is that to cross the street, one has to have a car.

Sociocultural Context

❏ This factor may have implications for modifying the building program to meet community need. Think about the conditions of a particular group in a particular place and time. Consider the group's resources, struggles, and future.

Charles Harrison Pawley's Caribbean Marketplace in Miami, Florida, epitomizes response to sociocultural factors. Located in the Little Haiti section of the city, the Marketplace represents two events: the revival of a very poor neighborhood, and the new life being established in the United States by Haitian immigrants.

In a former warehouse, the Marketplace sports new gables, garden lattice, pretreated lumber, corrugated metal, and tropical colors. A system of booths offer a combination of everyday and exotic items and produce. The feeling of the place captures the unique tradition and flavor of the Caribbean market, with the fresh prospects of reestablishing that tradition in mainstream American society.

Site Inventory Checklist

❏ This section can be used as a guide and checklist for recording site data and deriving the most from frequent visits. In general, the mission is to identify the inherent makeup of the project area both objectively and impressionistically (what are the possibilities and problems, and what is the karma of the site?). Use the following outline as appropriate; not all items may apply to a given case.

Start with the Big Picture

Maps. Buy a good map at the local bookstore or check the library for maps, including the applicable U.S. Geological Survey or Sanborn maps for urban contexts (these may be available at the local city planner's or zoning office). This is a way to begin assessing regional issues—land use (zoning, adjacent building types), access (the nature of traffic: roads, highways, sidewalks), topography, open space, public transportation, and any other features that are important in the area. Attempt to gain a sense of the sociocultural context.

History. Do some research about the history of the jurisdiction and the site. What are the building traditions, i.e., materials, typologies, etc., and why are they traditions? What are they responding to? (See Chris Wilson's essay, "Vernacular Means," in Chapter 1.) All this may have an influence on design. Document community services (i.e., religious, shopping, health care). Good architecture is comprehensive and compulsive.

Site Impressions. Pound the pavement; take photos and sketch typical scenes and details *after* you've walked through undistracted. Try to get an overall feeling—the "unique spirit of the place" (in Kevin Lynch's terms; his book, *Site Planning*, 3rd ed. [MIT Press, 1984], written with Gary Hack, is a fine resource). Make personal judgments as to the value of aesthetic, social, and other visible elements. Know where you are: always be able to relate or key your position (and any photos/sketches) to the maps. If you're not comfortable making notes in the field, try talking into a pocket tape recorder.

Other Factors. Be aware of anything close to your site that may strongly influence design decisions. Pay particular attention to the immediate context: buildings and open space, views, smells, sounds, pedestrian traffic, vehicular traffic. (When is the area most congested? Which roads bounding the site have less traffic?) There is little question that these environmental factors are, collectively, all intrinsic to the site. The gestalt also includes buildings in the neighborhood that can provide valuable cues for the architect in terms of massing, detailing, and material selections.

Zero In on Your Site: Preparation

Documents. Obtain all available documentation about the site—a scaled site plan, survey, and/or aerial photographs showing boundaries, topography, north (you may need to bring a compass), easements, and so on.

Site Plan. Make multiple copies of the site plan (perhaps at a reduced scale) in preparation for your field visits. Observations and notes can then be recorded directly and accurately on the plans (see Fig. 3.13).

Equipment. Bring a camera (a wide-angle lens is preferable) and sketching equipment. Bring a ruler or tape measure; you may want to take and/or confirm specific dimensions and relative locations of various site elements.

Record Site Data

Views. Photograph the site. And sketch. Awareness of detail is heightened when you actually draw it. In his wonderful book, *Landscape Architecture* 3rd ed. (McGraw-Hill, 1998), John Simonds instructs: "Get the feel of the land . . . look, listen, sense." Capture views approaching the site (by foot and/or car) and looking from the site. And study details (whatever may be useful, i.e., existing structures, rock formations). Remember (mentally or on paper) to key all snapshots and sketches to the site plan.

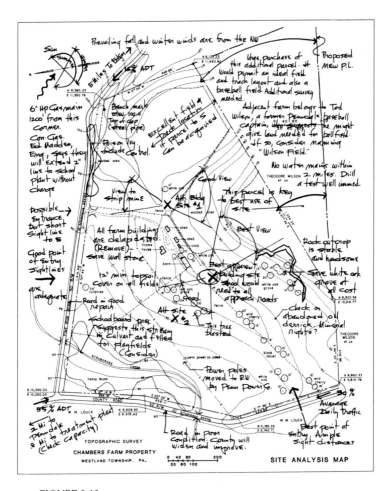

FIGURE 3.13

A superb example of a site analysis diagram, including inventory information together with supporting commentary written in the field on a copy of the site survey. (Simonds, John. Landscape Architecture, 3d ed., 1998, reproduced with permission of The McGraw-Hill Companies.)

Microclimate. Investigate solar path; determine sun angles at various times of the day, and how they change throughout the year. There are many readily available resources, including *Architectural Graphic Standards* 10th ed. (Wiley, 2000), which graphically depict how sun angles vary with time and geographical location (latitude). Get a sense of the altitude (angle above the horizon) and azimuth (surface angle measured from the south-north line).

Observe shadows and shade patterns from nearby buildings, trees, and other features. Also note potential glare problems from reflections from nearby water or shiny façades of existing buildings.

Determine direction (and velocity) of prevailing summer and winter winds. Document any changes to typical wind patterns due to hills, buildings, or dense vegetation.

Note any other pertinent climatological and meteorological data, such as patterns of temperature variation, humidity, precipitation (including monsoons, snowfall, or drought), and hurricanes. The national AIA is a good source if local references or the National Weather Service are not accessible.

Slopes. Field-verify that the topography indicated on the survey is accurate. Show where the land varies from steep to flat, and note the orientation of any slopes. (A quick reminder: contours are lines of equal elevation, and usually occur at intervals of 1 to 10 feet, depending on the scale of the plan; see "Contour Refresher" later in this chapter.)

Determine how water runoff relates to the slopes. Try to visit the site during a rainstorm. Document drainage features of all types.

Back in the office, draw a few key cross sections through the site.

Vegetation and Wildlife. Note species of trees—evergreen or deciduous—as well as the density, height, and width of the canopy. Identify all types of ground cover.

Are there moose, koalas, spotted owls, or other creatures great and small living on the site? Describe their habitats.

Existing Objects, Materials, and Public Works. Inventory and describe the condition and approximate sizes of existing items, and confirm this on the plan. Much of this is usually indicated on the survey. Include furniture (i.e., benches, picnic tables); lighting; retaining walls; paving; utilities (electricity, gas, water, sanitary sewers, storm drainage, phone lines); curbs, steps, ramps, handrails, and fences; and fire and police protection. If there are any structures on the site, they need to be evaluated carefully for possible relationship to the proposed new project.

Noise and Smells. Listen for anything potentially disturbing (i.e., an interstate highway bisects your site, your neighbor is an international jetport).

Are there signs of pollution (i.e., is the site downwind of a baked bean factory or a paper mill)?

Subsurface Conditions. Information on subsoil and groundwater conditions and data from percolation tests and borings (investigated and analyzed by geotechnical engineers) determine such things as bearing capacity, suitability for septic tank drainage systems, water runoff characteristics, permeability, and risk of erosion. Note the presence of topsoil and its influences on potential planting. These studies are fairly routine and are usually commissioned by the client, in accordance with typical owner-architect agreements.

Depending on site location, seismic factors may be extremely relevant to the design. Check local codes.

Zoning. Zoning is the legal process by which local government specifies and regulates land use and building type, size, and context. Some items you may need to consider include setbacks, yards, maximum lot coverage and building height, off-street parking, floor area ratio (FAR [ratio of total floor area to site area]), sky exposure plane, and of course, permitted uses.

There may be other restrictive covenants; for example, a homeowners' association may require a 60-foot setback, whereas zoning requires only 20 feet. Diagram those regulations that have an effect on your site and design.

Renovation of an Existing Building. This provides a somewhat different set of cataloging and documentation duties, although many of those mentioned in the preceding text may still be applicable, especially if an addition or outdoor space is programmed.

If not available, scaled (and most important, dimensioned) "as-built" floor plans and elevations must be developed (or if available, verified). Note floor-to-ceiling heights, fenestration dimensions, sill heights, door sizes, and so on. Getting on your hands and knees to measure a building may be a dirty job, but it has its rewards: you are forced to really *see* detail, and in some cases to uncover the building's "soul." Photography here is critical—missed dimensions (there always are a few) can usually be determined by counting bricks, planks, and the like, from a snapshot. Any element with a known modular size can be used to achieve a close estimation of an overall dimension. Also, take snapshots with a ruler attached to building components. Existing systems (and all associated components)—mechanical and structural—must be recorded. Check the roof and basement; these may be sites of future development. All this information might be available from the original architects or the building department.

Be aware of special architectural detailing—craftsmanship and design features worth preserving or responding to—both inside and out.

Miscellaneous. This includes anything else specific to your site and immediate vicinity not mentioned in the preceding text (i.e., proximity to bodies of water, floodplains, mud slides, grazing cows, final approach to an airport, or how the garbage is removed). Attempt to determine if there are plans for future development in the area.

Diagramming Site Data

❏ With all the inventorying of site data complete, the implications can now be investigated in the office. Use copies of the site plan, perhaps in a reduced form, to overlay information collected in the field. Try one diagram for each inventory category, or combine several categories. Employ symbols to convert the data graphically to make it easy to understand at a glance (i.e., show steep grades in dark gray and flat areas in white, with light gray for variations in between). Annotate where necessary. Another example is the figure-ground (plan) diagram: looking at neighborhoods in urban districts, building masses are black and open spaces are white. As with the programmatic diagrams, save all drawings (sign and date them). They are an integral part of the design process, help to form a rationale for design decisions, and can be used artfully and persuasively in the final presentation. (See Fig. 3.14.)

The inventory and subsequent analysis give coherence to development of the site. Start generally (with a small-scale site plan) by identifying and justifying logical areas to build and to circulate (with cars, people, service, and emergency vehicles). Begin to define areas that must be preserved in their natural state, and determine how the integrity of that state may be assured or accentuated by an architectural presence. Conversely,

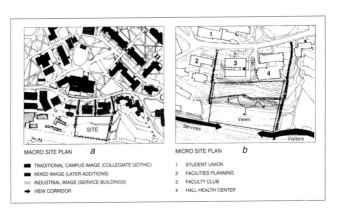

MACRO SITE PLAN *a*

- ■ TRADITIONAL CAMPUS IMAGE (COLLEGIATE GOTHIC)
- ■ MIXED IMAGE (LATER ADDITIONS)
- ▨ INDUSTRIAL IMAGE (SERVICE BUILDINGS)
- ➡ VIEW CORRIDOR

MICRO SITE PLAN *b*

1   STUDENT UNION
2   FACILITIES PLANNING
3   FACULTY CLUB
4   HALL HEALTH CENTER

FIGURE 3.14
These diagrams were used to study some of the site influences on Fluke Hall, a technology center of offices and laboratories at the University of Washington. Site selection was part of the challenge for the architects. (a) A variation of the figure-ground diagram. (b) Diagram conveying access, slope, and view information. (© NBBJ, David C. Hoedemaker and Rick Buckley, designers.)

what areas scream (or whisper) for development? In other words, zone the site; judge how existing patterns (pedestrian, vehicular, open spaces, etc.) should be extended to and through the site. Is there a natural focus of some sort? If so, should it be left alone, framed, or developed? Your observations from spending time at the site will almost automatically address these issues and raise others that are crucial. It is the site elements that may give clues and have the greatest impact on shaping and orienting the building and supporting circulation. John Simonds, in *Landscape Architecture*, makes the point eloquently: "To preserve or create a pleasing site or landscape character for an area . . . ranging from completely natural to completely man-made . . . a harmony of all the various elements or parts must be retained or developed."

Experiment with many alternatives in the interpretation of the data. Location and orientation have such an influence on the architecture that, given the same program, a building on one side of a site would have a very different expression than if it were located on a different side. It is interesting and useful to predict the differences in design responses as a function of differences in siting.

Like program analysis, site analysis varies greatly with the scope, substance, and context of the project. Above all, use common sense to weigh the importance of site factors! (See Figs. 3.13 and 3.15.)

Marrying Program and Site

❏ Determining how the program and site fit together might be likened to leading a talk show on dating and marriage. You, as the host, will ask: "Do the program and site constantly fight?" and "Does one try to change the other to make the relationship work? Is there simply an initial infatuation stemming from a blind date, or are there long-term implications? Does a mutual support (of setting and function, as Kevin Lynch might say) bring out the best qualities in each? Can there be some sort of ongoing chemistry?" Or, as *The Architect's Handbook of Profes-*

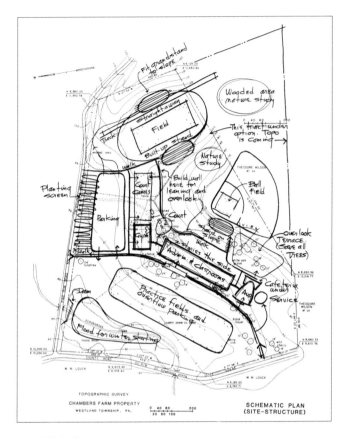

FIGURE 3.15
This drawing begins to relate the site data (from Fig. 3.13) to program elements—a logical next step in the design process. (Simonds, John. Landscape Architecture, *3d ed., 1998, reproduced with permission of The McGraw-Hill Companies.)*

sional Practice, 11th ed. (AIA, 1987), asks, are site and program "right for each other?"

Gordon Cullen, in his classic book *The Concise Townscape* (Van Nostrand Reinhold, 1961), suggests: "There is an *art of relationship* just as there is an art of architecture. Its purpose is to take all the elements that go to create the environment: buildings, trees, nature, water, traffic, advertisements and so on, and weave them together in such a way that drama is released."

Now is the time to start testing the goodness of the relationship: the fit of program requirements (perhaps as defined in bubble diagrams) and site potentials (as defined in site analysis diagrams). Begin to arrange the bubbles as an overlay on the site plan (Fig. 3.15 is a model for this kind of diagramming). Consider the spatial needs together with the physical realities of the site. Also keep in mind the concept for the project. There will no doubt be some conflicts. The design process is getting more exciting and challenging! Attempt a rough blocking-out of many alternatives and possibilities (see Fig. 3.16). Even at this early stage, this will help in optimizing both program and site relationships. Keep these beginning explorations very loose—use soft pencils, thick markers, cheap trace. Make a note to always be

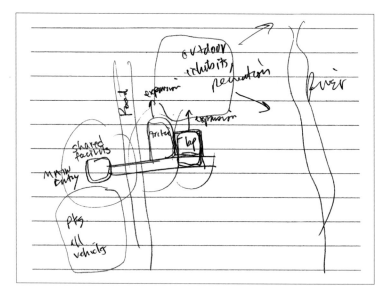

FIGURE 3.16

An example of a primitive "napkin" sketch—diagrammatic layout of a museum complex in Finland informed by a few essential program and site factors. (Courtesy of Andy Pressman.)

aware of and show the site context in the medium in which you are working, no matter what the scale. Usually, if it is out of sight, it is out of mind.

Entry Sequence

❏ The idea of procession—designing the approach to the site via car (drive-in, drop-off, parking, walking from car to building) or on foot (pedestrian ways from sidewalk to building)—can be a delightful extension of design themes of the building to the larger site context. Or the entry sequence can function as a contrast to, say, the building lobby, where experience is then heightened and accentuated. In any event, strive for control over the design of these outdoor areas; look for opportunities in the program to charge them with energy and activity or serenity. This can have lasting impact on the total architectural experience and have much to do with place making.

By itself, the entry sequence can be a rich, eventful experience. It doesn't necessarily have to be the shortest distance between site boundary and entry. There may be an intentionally circuitous path that allows for surprise and discovery. Or, one may catch a glimpse of the building to come around one turn, and a panoramic vista may be revealed around another. I'll never forget the experience of traveling to Baxter State Park in north central Maine. After about 30 minutes on a seemingly unending monotonous, meandering dirt road surrounded on both sides by walls of pine and birch, the road curved sharply, the woods cleared, and the snow-covered peak of Mt. Katahdin loomed in our windshield, then suddenly, disappeared into a new stand of trees. What theater!

As effective as dramatic punch and soaring emotional response may be, I would like to reiterate Simonds' notion of harmony. In particular, I want to stress the importance of harmonizing site elements that form an entry sequence. If the specific design approach engages or grows from the site, the architecture of building entries can be very intimate with the larger site issues. If the specific design approach is one of theater (to highlight the best features of both site and building), a more inwardly focused or object-oriented architectural response may be appropriate.

Design decisions become less arbitrary when considering the significance of entering the proposed structure in a context beyond the boundaries of the building itself.

Indoor/Outdoor Transitions

❏ The quality of the relationship of building and site may have a lot to do with just how they are physically engaged. Blurring the distinction between these realms can elevate functioning over the entire site. Identify program spaces that would benefit from a flowing of activity or a special dialogue with the outside environment. Consider anything that filters or shelters, such as arcades, pergolas, overhangs, and exposed framing. Again, harmony of building design theme and site characteristics helps in form development. Materials can be used to great advantage. Here is a simple example: a lobby opens to a small courtyard; brick pavers used in the lobby extend through the court, serving to unify and reinforce the connection. Moreover, expression of access (physical or visual) to outside space can animate an elevation. For example, Frank Lloyd Wright's Taliesin West in Scottsdale, Arizona, is frequently recognized as a building so resonant with its site that the two entities are almost as one. The apparent contradiction lies in Wright's selection of materials and forms, which remain distinct and assertive, yet are perfectly consistent with the desert landscape.

Alternatively, indoor/outdoor transition may be defined by a dramatic and abrupt difference between building and site. This approach may serve to focus attention on a particular attribute. Building form and/or materials can support this idea, which in turn should support programmatic goals. For example, Richard Meier's Giovannitti House in Pittsburgh, with its white porcelain enamel panels and bold forms, contrasts sharply with its suburban setting and appears offset as a unique architectural jewel.

Contour Refresher

❏ Many clients and a few inexperienced designers find it difficult at first to understand the representation of land forms or topography by contour lines on site plans, surveys, or maps. It takes only a little time to comfortably recognize a contour pattern (i.e., for valleys, ridges, uniform slopes, etc.) and relate it to actual field conditions. Contour lines trace points of equal elevation (usually measured as altitude above sea level) and represent a vertical separation or interval. Cultivate the habit of checking the scale relative to the contour interval shown on the site plan or survey; you may find that sketching cross sections through the site is very helpful and revealing in fully understanding site conditions. Contour lines do not cross (except at vertical planes); spaced evenly, they signal a constant slope; close together, a steep slope; far apart, a flat or gentle slope. Visit the site and compare it with contours depicted on the site plan so that there is no ambiguity about understanding the shape of the land. (See Figs. 3.17 and 3.18.)

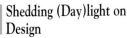

Shedding (Day)light on Design

with Virginia Cartwright

❏ Use of natural light and views can be a major form determinant in making architecture. Caren M. Connolly, visiting professor at the University of Wisconsin-Milwaukee, talks about her personal approach regarding landscape architecture: "I consider daylighting part of landscape architecture and envi-

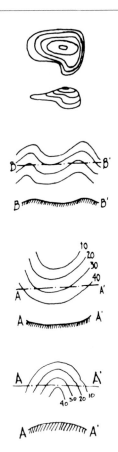

FIGURE 3.17
Graphic depictions of contours—in plan—which are then translated to elevation (a) and cross sections (b–d). (Lynch, Kevin and Hack, Gary. Site Planning, 3d ed., 1984, reproduced with permission of the MIT Press.)

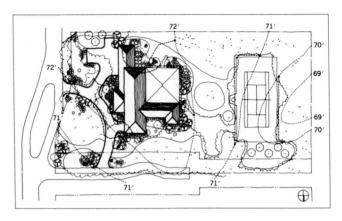

FIGURE 3.18
Some amount of grading or modification to contours will probably be required around new structures. In a simple example, note how the contours (represented by dotted lines) were manipulated on this site plan around the tennis court, house, and driveway for a project in Florida. (Courtesy of Andy Pressman.)

ronmental concerns. The thing I try to use most often is not plant material, but light and shadows. When you have a window and at certain times of the day, the leaf pattern goes across your wall, I consider that a landscape element. I borrowed this idea from Lutyens! If you don't have a budget for landscape, but there's one in view, make sure the windows in your building look right out on it. There are often nice things on other parcels, or conversely, if something's really ugly, make sure you don't put a window there! I'd like to add that landscape architects traditionally have been collaborative and integrative, and the best landscape architecture programs really stress the word *multidisciplinary*. Architects, engineers, and landscape architects have to work together; mutual respect is critical."

Jeff Harner, a Santa Fe architect, comments on the special qualities of light in the southwestern desert: "Here, natural light is almost like a building material." This idea crystallizes the important role that daylighting can play in designing buildings.

Daylight and outside views are precious resources. Every effort must be made to facilitate penetration of natural light (even to

FIGURE 3.19
*In this modestly scaled residential addition in Princeton, New Jersey, a trellis
above a cantilevered deck allows sun to illuminate white clapboard siding and
create a glow that can be seen from a distance. The shadow in the foreground
neatly describes the configuration of wood trellis members. (Andy Pressman,
architect. Photo © Norman McGrath.)*

belowgrade spaces) and promote direct lines of sight to windows
for areas inhabited for big blocks of time.

Two master manipulators of light and shadow are Louis Kahn
and Tadao Ando. Monographs of their work are filled with extraordinary demonstrations. Kahn once described a building as a
"natural lighting fixture." Awe-inspiring words!

The capture of natural light in a building is an incredible
source for sculpting architectural form and also for optimizing

energy performance. The resulting luminous environments created within buildings can be delightful and dramatic, particularly in spaces where task lighting is not important to the functions, such as lobbies and circulation areas. Daylighting, or more precisely sunlighting, as lighting designer William Lam suggests, is the positive control and utilization of direct light.

Virginia "Ginger" Cartwright sets forth in Supplement 3.5 a concise and informative summary of the nature and impact of daylighting in buildings. Her views are very much rooted in aspects of the site—climate, latitude, and local weather are seen as motivating a range of design decisions.

SUPPLEMENT 3.5

Virginia Cartwright

Ginger Cartwright is an associate professor of architecture at the University of Oregon, and a daylighting consultant. Her writing on the subject has appeared in Architectural Record *and other journals and books.*

"We may define the ideal goals of architecture by saying that the purpose of a building is to act as an instrument that collects all the positive influences in nature for man's benefit, while also sheltering him from all the unfavorable influences that appear in nature and the building's specific surroundings. If we accept this as a valid generalization on the purpose of architecture—and I really cannot think of a better one—we must also understand that a building cannot fulfill its purpose if it does not possess itself of a wealth of nuances equal to that of the natural environment to which it will belong as a permanent element."

—**Alvar Aalto (from a speech, "The Reconstruction of Europe Is the Key Problem for the Architecture of Our Time," given in 1941. Published in *Alvar Aalto In His Own Words*, Schildt, Goran [ed.], New York: Rizzoli, 1998, p. 153)**

❏ Daylighting is the use of light from the sun and sky to provide illumination within buildings. Daylight enriches architecture with character, changing from morning to afternoon, day to night, and summer to winter. Each day brings a different light. As the light changes, subtly or dramatically, the nature of built form and space changes. To create architecture that fulfills its purpose, as suggested by Aalto, and enriches people's experiences and retains its meaning over time, architects must design with daylight.

The light from the sun has been the primary source of lighting in buildings until fairly recently, and even now it is the most common source of light in many parts of the world. The sun's light comes directly from the sun, and indirectly, through diffusion through the earth's atmosphere, from the sky and from clouds. At night it reaches the earth indirectly by reflection from the moon. In addition, sunlight may be reflected from the ground and from surrounding buildings. It has only been since the development of the fluorescent light in the early part of the twentieth century that architects have designed buildings without considering the use of daylight. Today architects have a choice of designing with daylight or without it. However, as people become more conscious of the benefits of energy conservation in building design and of the experiential richness of the connections to the exterior environment, they expect their buildings to be daylit.

Once the decision has been made to incorporate daylight as a means of providing light in a building, two issues must be considered: the climate and site conditions of the proposed building, and the nature of the activities to be housed. Museums, libraries, schools, hospitals, homes, and offices each have different lighting requirements. It is important to evaluate lighting requirements based not only on the major programmatic activity of a building type, but also, on a finer scale, the various activities within each building. Almost all buildings can use daylighting for some portion of their rooms. A part of good daylighting is assessing the lighting requirements for each of the activities to be accommodated and including daylight where appropriate.

Climate and latitude affect the quantity and quality of daylight. When the sun is high in the sky, its light has less atmosphere to pass through, and thus is much more intense. This is the situation during the middle of the day at lower latitudes. Moisture in the air, such as clouds or humidity, changes the light. In places with clear, cloudless skies, the light is intense and dynamic. In these places the light creates both strong highlights and deep shadows. Forms are clearly articulated. The light is directional and dynamic, changing with the movement of the sun. In addition to the light from the sun, the light from the clear sky is three times brighter at the horizon than directly overhead at the zenith. Other regions, characterized by overcast skies and rainy days, have a softer light. The overcast sky provides a lower level of light, and one that is almost uniform in all directions. The light from a completely overcast sky is three times brighter at the zenith than at the horizon. In this light, forms have soft shadows, making it more difficult to discern their three-dimensional character. Though the light levels will change during the course of the day, orientation makes little difference in the amount of daylight. It is important to note the predominant characteristics of daylight determined by the climate. Regional climate patterns may be modified by local conditions; pollution and other conditions may affect the quantity and quality of daylight.

Other site conditions should also be considered. Surrounding trees, buildings, and topography will affect the availability of daylight at a site. An adjacent building to the east may block access to daylight in the morning, yet reflect sunlight into interior spaces in the afternoon. Trees, both on the site and immediately adjacent, block the sun as well as light from parts of the sky during certain times of the day. The position of a site on top of a hill may increase the opportunities of occupants of a building to see the sky, while a site at the foot of a hill lessens the amount of daylight available. Ground surfaces influence the amount of daylight as well. Light-colored paving materials can increase the daylight in lower floors of a building—though too much light reflected from the ground can be a source of glare.

Massing and orientation of the building are the first considerations in the design of a daylit building. As illustrated in Fig. 3.20, wide buildings have large interior zones that have little access to daylight. Buildings that are thin in section provide more opportunities for daylight to reach interior spaces. Orienting thin buildings with their long elevations facing north and south decreases problems of shading the windows from low-angled morning and afternoon sun. Thin buildings can be straight or bent, creating "alphabet buildings" as shown in Fig. 3.21. Buildings with central courtyards or atria are another variation on the thin building section. Various windows and sky-lights can be used to bring light into the interiors. Windows are the most common type of aperture. Multistory buildings require the use of windows for daylighting. Windows with a high head height allow more daylight to reach the inner zones of a building. A rule of thumb is that daylight is sufficient at the back of the room when the depth is 2½ times the window height. As day-lighting devices, windows can produce an imbalance of light in a room, from overly bright at the window zone to relatively dark at the innermost zone. Multiple windows provide a better distribu-tion of light within a room than does a single window. Windows on two sides of a room correct the imbalance between the light-est and darkest parts of a room. Skylights can be used in one-story buildings and the top floors of multistoried buildings. The light provided by skylights is less impacted by partitions and fur-nishings than that provided by windows. However, it is difficult to keep the direct sun out of skylights, which could lead to exces-sive heat gain and overly bright spots within the room. While this can be controlled with external shading devices, these can be more costly and require greater maintenance.

The design of shading devices is another essential part of day-lighting. Exterior shading devices include fixed devices such as overhangs, light shelves, and louvers, and operable devices such as awnings (see Fig. 3.22). Interior operable devices such as lou-vers, shutters, and blinds are also usually incorporated. The

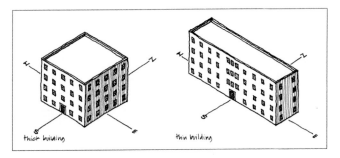

FIGURE 3.20
Courtesy of Virginia Cartwright.

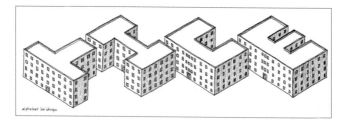

FIGURE 3.21
Courtesy of Virginia Cartwright.

thickness of the wall or ceiling in which the aperture is located is a significant factor in daylight control and distribution. The jambs and sills of windows, and the wells of skylights, can both block the direct sun and provide a secondary source of reflected light that increases the distribution of light in the interior. The windows in the original library at the University of Virginia, designed by Thomas Jefferson, have splayed jambs that help to distribute the daylight within the room, as well as serving as small niches. (See Fig. 3.23.)

In daylighting architecture, the design of the interiors is just as important as the design of the exterior. The size and proportion of rooms, and their relationship to the windows or skylights, are critical to good daylighting design. Interior surfaces, walls, ceilings, and floors are other factors to be considered. The color, and most important, the reflectance (whether light in value or dark), affect the amount of light in the interior. Given the same

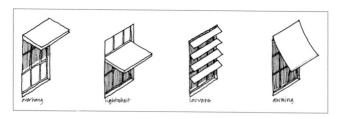

FIGURE 3.22
Courtesy of Virginia Cartwright.

University of Virginia Library, T. Jefferson   vcartwright '00

FIGURE 3.23
Courtesy of Virginia Cartwright.

size window, rooms with high-reflectance surfaces white or light in value will be much brighter than rooms with low-reflectance surfaces. In general, ceilings should be the lightest surfaces and floors the darkest. High-reflectance surfaces reflect much of the light that they receive, improving the overall level and distribution of light. For some programs, such as museums, lower surface reflectance on walls may be appropriate to lower the overall light levels.

The organization of activities and the choice of furniture and its layout are another set of critical design decisions for daylighting buildings. It is important to design the appropriate lighting for each activity. When windows are the primary source of light, consideration must be given to potential obstruction of the light by partitions and furniture. The orientation of activities should be considered so that people do not cast shadows on their tasks and are not subjected to uncomfortable contrast in their cone vision.

The easiest means of designing with daylight is using models. Computer modeling can also be used to evaluate daylighting, but is somewhat more difficult to use. Physical scale models provide a true analog of real lighting conditions. The more carefully made and the more detailed the model, the more closely it will represent the patterns of light within the building. Care must be taken to model the interior surfaces and the apertures accurately. The joints should be sealed to avoid light leaks. If the modeling material is translucent, then cover the exterior of the model with dark paper. It is typically not critical to model exterior surfaces except when they reflect light into the interior. Transparent glazing is not important to model. Models can be taken outside to be studied and photographed under real sky and sunlight conditions. Not only is a daylighting model an effective tool for making design decisions, but it is also an excellent means of presenting design ideas to critics and clients. Most architectural offices have the tools to make daylight models that can be used to visually assess the quantity and quality of daylight. To get a detailed evaluation of the light levels in a daylighting model requires light meters and, perhaps, the use of an artificial sky. There are a number of these located in lighting labs across the country. (See Chapter 5 for more on daylighting models.)

Daylit buildings that are beautiful environments and conserve energy are a result of thoughtful consideration of all these issues. To achieve this, the decision to include daylight should be made at the beginning of the design process and developed through to the selection of finishes and furniture placement.

The Art of Parking
with Mark Childs

❏ Following my somewhat brief, formulaic, and engineering-oriented treatment of parking, Mark Childs, celebrated author of *Parking Spaces* (McGraw-Hill, 1999), writes an engaging complement on the art of parking in Supplement 3.6. He details how parking can become an important strategic feature of urban design, among other inspiring ways of addressing how best to pave paradise and put up a parking lot.

Like it or not, the automobile is a fact of American life, and parking it may not be pretty. View the accommodation of parking on your site as another design opportunity. Always be on the lookout for any special design tasks that may seem to be ordinary or adjuncts to the program (i.e., parking)—they can be turned into real assets that add much to the architectural identity of the project. Consider it part of the challenge to design an unforgettable, or at least pleasant, part of the entry sequence to the building.

In general, once an area has been identified as reasonable for parking, design goals include (1) reducing the visual impact from almost everywhere, (2) close proximity to building entries (this may be negotiable depending on the project and typical duration of parking), (3) keeping people traffic and car traffic separated, (4) providing universally accessible spaces very close to entries, and (5) simplicity of layout (minimize turns and number of entrances and exits; in small lots, one outlet for both ingress and egress is sufficient). We've all found ourselves at one time or another trapped in some mazelike parking lot that should have been in a Hitchcock film—so, strive for simplicity! And avoid dead ends! Reference books such as *Architectural Graphic Standards* describe specific parking layouts, rules of thumb, dimensions, turning radii, number of spaces for a given use (usually mandated by city ordinances), and drop-off design criteria. This is a good starting point from which to understand the basic functional and space requirements, but remember that these are strictly "cookbook" and imply no innovation.

To summarize and simplify the gross conventions: allow about 400 square feet per car (includes stall and circulation). The "standard" car stall is 9 feet wide by 19 feet long (Americans with Disabilities Act [ADA] universal parking space design for two adjacent 90° spaces recommends a total of 27 feet—an 11-foot-wide space, a 5-foot-wide access lane, then another 11-foot-wide space, and so on, to accommodate cars or vans). Aisle or lane widths are a function of stall angle—the selection of which depends on total space allotted for parking and design intent. Angles vary from 90° (perpendicular parking, which accommodates two-way lanes and is most space efficient) to 60° (employed most often, promotes ease of maneuvering with one- or two-way lanes as well as efficient use of space) to 45° and 30° (affords best maneuverability, but less efficient use of space; also suggests one-way lanes). Minimum lane widths are 20 feet for two-way lanes, 12 feet for one-way lanes. Parallel parking, the bane of novice drivers, may be another option in some instances.

Achieving a balance between packing in as many cars as possible (in terms of space efficiency) and creating a character and quality consistent with the overall design is vital. These are not necessarily mutually exclusive goals. Consider walkway design, orientation of traffic aisles in relation to the building (if pedestrians are indeed utilizing them, you don't want to force people to slalom between rows of parked cars), landscaping, space for plowed snow, and accommodation of service and/or emergency vehicles. Is there a way of breaking down the scale of the lot so that there's not just one big sea of asphalt? Are there logical separations in the program to accomplish this (i.e., staff, public, service)?

Some examples of reducing the unpleasant aesthetic impact of parking lots include designing earth berms around the periphery, lowering the lot level or proposing a terraced scheme (this strategy tends to preserve sight lines to the building and may depend on topography), constructing walls or other screening devices (which may further give unity to, or hide, the site and building), and changing the shape of the lot itself. Choose appropriately durable materials of contrasting texture and color for walkways in the lot—relate these to materials of other pedestrian paths in the area.

Dave Barry talks about finding a parking space at the mall during the Christmas season. He describes the patented strategy of driving around the lot until a shopper emerges, then following him or her until you are led to a space. The rule of thumb, according to Barry, is to stay about 4 inches from the shopper's legs so that other circling cars know that the shopper belongs to you. This also has the benefit of persuading the shopper not to just drop off packages and return to shopping, but to fully commit to leaving the parking space. On that note, Mark Childs takes a more serious look at the whole issue of parking in Supplement 3.6.

Mark Childs

Mark C. Childs is the author of Parking Spaces: A Design, Implementation, and Use Manual for Architects, Planners, and Engineers *(McGraw-Hill, 1999) and coauthor of* Never Say Good-bye: The Albuquerque Rephotography Project *(Albuquerque Museum Press, 2000). He is an assistant professor of architecture and planning at the University of New Mexico. His work focuses on the design of civic places.*

SUPPLEMENT 3.6

❏ The craft of architecture goes beyond simple utility. If this is an unimpeachable axiom, then why have we paved the world with acres of parking lots that do not aspire beyond a very narrow utility?

The standard layout of the parking lot is nothing more than the application of engineering formula. Yet, parking lots are built spaces, inhabited by people. In addition to housing cars, they must be safe for drivers and pedestrians. People using a lot should feel secure in person and property. Moreover, parking lots are social places—places of the ceremonies of arrival and departure. Street hockey players, lovers, and girl scouts selling cookies have staked out uses of the parking lot, and farmers' markets, swap meets, and car rallies regularly claim the territory. The parking lot is a significant part of the public realm.

Parking is also a strategic feature of urban design. The amount of land devoted to parking, the location of parking relative to the sidewalk, and the character of parking lots are all critical to the fabric of the city. Newman and Kenworthy, in *Cities and Automobile Dependence* (Newman and Kenworthy, 1987), propose an inverse relationship between the attractiveness of a central city and the amount of parking. San Francisco, for example, has fewer parking spaces per person and a higher attractiveness rating than Houston.

There are approximately seven parking spaces per automobile in the U.S., and more cars than registered drivers. Clearly, we have devoted a large portion of our urban resources to the car. The Federal Highway Administration notes, "In cities such as Chicago, Philadelphia, and New York, from 70 to 80 percent of all intra-downtown trips are walking trips. In addition, a significant percentage of the total trip length of all trips [involving a] car also [involve a significant amount of] walking. Yet, approximately 50 to 70 percent of the downtown is devoted to vehicles" (Federal Highway Administration, 1978, p. 2). Careful thought about how, when, and where we provide parking is clearly in order.

Parking is not an end in itself (that is, of course, unless we are discussing the slang use of the term, which may be a good in itself). Parking lots should be designed to support, not overwhelm, the places they serve. Thoughtful design (or redesign) of the parking lot can provide a judicious supply of parking, support multiple alternative uses, increase the safety and security of people and their vehicles, reduce environmental harms caused by the parking lot, and help make vital cities. The environmental movement's mantra, "reduce, reuse, recycle," can guide this design.

We can reduce the amount of land, money, and other resources we spend on parking in a number of ways. Regulatory and administrative changes such as the California "cash out" law can have a significant effect. The cash out law requires certain employers who provide free parking to give employees the option of free parking or the cash equivalent. Other approaches include demand management programs, removing minimum parking requirements from zoning codes, and increasing on-street parking. Architects and urban designers should be actively involved in these policy changes. As individuals we can talk to our city representatives, write op-ed pieces for the newspaper, and volunteer to sit on city policy committees. As members of local professional organizations, we can draft and propose changes to city ordinances, sponsor talks by experts, or adopt practice guidelines.

More directly architectural approaches focus on creating a viable pedestrian environment. The main doors to buildings should open directly onto the sidewalk, and parking should be moved to the rear, to the side, or onto the street. These back or side parking lots should not have back entrances to buildings; rather, pedestrians should enter and exit from the sidewalks. The edges of lots and garages should help create pleasant and active sidewalks by providing places for stores or vendors, benches and shade, waterfalls or artwork, and other amenities.

Many parking facilities are sized to provide sufficient spaces for the "design hour," typically the 20th busiest hour of the year.

FIGURE 3.24
Food vendors line the edge of this Portland, Oregon, sidewalk, providing an income to the lot owner and making for an active, pleasant sidewalk. (© Mark C. Childs.)

This means that 99 percent of the time there are unused spaces, and at least half the spaces are vacant 40 percent of the time (Urban Land Institute, 1982, p. 12). This represents a tremendous wasted resource waiting to be tapped. Two design methods can help reuse the parking lot. First, buildings that have different peak demand times may share a lot. The joint use of a lot by a church and a school is a typical example. The church occupies the lot on weekends and evenings, and the school during weekdays. An overlooked shared use is to provide facilities to support truckers parking at night. There is a dangerous undersupply of safe, convenient, and pleasant resting places for long-haul truckers (Federal Highway Administration, 1996). The second method is to design districts so that people may park once and easily walk to many different destinations. This requires the development of a compact, functionally diverse place with pleasant walkways, such as pre-World War II downtowns.

On-street parking is inherently shared parking. It is also usually the most land- and time-efficient type of parking, and provides a barrier between moving vehicles and pedestrians. Traffic engineers have frequently encouraged removing parking from arterials because it slows traffic and may increase accidents. There are three approaches to balancing on-street parking and arterial traffic flow. Side streets may be designed as parking rows similar to a bay of parking in a parking lot, or as "U" streets enclosing a neighborhood park (see Fig. 3.25). Boulevards with "contra-allees" or side streets for parking have been shown to provide both more parking and a more pleasant environment than arterials (Bosselmann, Macdonald, and Kronemeyer, 1999). Finally, we may question if traffic speed is the highest priority for a particular street. In some commercial areas, it may be appropriate to construct "streetplazas" in which pedestrians have right-of-way and cars are "guests" (see Fig. 3.26). The concept of sharing streets began with residential streets in Europe and has since been applied to commercial streets throughout the world.

Perhaps, the most "architectural" approach to rethinking the parking lot is to "recycle" it by expanding its program, that is, to design parking lots not simply as spaces to store vehicles, but also as courtyards, plazas, gardens, art galleries, farmers' markets, and sports courts. This is not simply a matter of spending more money

FIGURE 3.25
This "U" street in New York City's Battery Park provides both parking and a park. (© Mark C. Childs.)

FIGURE 3.26
Although not designed specifically as a streetplaza, the street along Seattle's Pike Place market is controlled by pedestrians. The brick pavement provides a visual and auditory signal to drivers that this is a different type of street, angled parking slows down traffic, and the overflow of vendors and customers into the street enforces the automobiles' status as "guests." (© Mark C. Childs.)

to decorate the parking lot, but rather finding uses and designs that add value (e.g., through increased safety, additional rentable area, or improved public acceptance of the development). The anthropologist of shopping, Paco Underhill, suggests that retailers could be well served by making parking lots an active part of their stores. "Pushing the store outside also begins to address an interesting situation in America—the fact that so much of the country has been turned into parking lots" (Underhill, 1999, pp. 49–50).

To transform our seas of asphalt into pleasant multiuse courtyards requires that we (1) treat them as positive space—outdoor rooms with walls, floors, and, perhaps, even ceilings implied by tree canopies, lighting levels, cornices or tents; (2) understand the vital ingredients of public space.

The research literature on public places (Gehl, 1987; Joardar and Neill, 1978; Marcus and Francis, 1990; Whyte, 1980, 1988) suggests four critical components. Public spaces must:

- *Be integrated with the city.* There should as few physical and psychological barriers between the space and the sidewalk as possible. It should be and appear open and inviting, and be placed so as to have a high concentration of potential users within 900 feet.

- *Be great places to hang out—to sit, watch people and activities, eat, read, or shop.* People hang out along the edges of spaces and thus need seats, places to lean, and subspaces that they can temporarily occupy as their territory. Seating, William Whyte suggests, should be designed as a prop for a variety of interpersonal interactions. "Ideally, sitting should be physically comfortable . . . it's most important, however, that it be socially comfortable."

- *Have active, engaging environments.* A view of children playing, the smell of food cooking, an afternoon concert, the mist of a fountain in the sunlight are some of the joys of being out in public. People like to have a complex sensory environment in which to hang out. Bare, monotonous plazas are poorly used. As any high school parking lot shows, the comings and goings inherent in parking can be a part of the active sensory environment.

- *Have comfortable microclimates.* The inside temperature of an automobile left in the sun can reach nearly 200°F. Our open black tar expanses of parking are often colder during the evenings of Christmas shopping and hotter in the summer than the surrounding environment. These terrible microclimates not only destroy the chance of creating public spaces, but increase the heating and cooling bills of adjacent buildings and contribute to the formation of smog (both from the increased air temperature and the emission of hydrocarbons from hot cars). Shade, windbreaks, fountains, and light-colored pavements can all be used to temper the environment.

Once we structure our design with these four components in mind, we may then create a pleasant parking lot garden that the local rose society tends and where the public comes to stroll in the evenings after the office workers have emptied the parking lot. We may be able to transform the school parking lot into a weekend playground, or a church's lot into an outdoor wedding chapel.

The craft of architecture goes beyond simple utility. The typical grid of white lines on black asphalt is poor architecture. Early on a Saturday morning, the delight of a farmers' market may bring customers to the shopping mall in whose parking lot it is held. A thick canopy of trees over a visitors' parking lot may provide a delightful entrance court and reduce the cooling bill for the adjacent buildings. It is our professional commission to add value to built places, whether they are palaces or parking lots or both.

References

Bosselmann, Peter, Macdonald, Elizabeth, and Kronemeyer, Thomas. "Livable Streets Revisited." *Journal of the American Planning Association,* Spring, 65(2):168–180, 1999.

Federal Highway Administration. "A Pedestrian Planning Procedures Manual." Report No. FHWA-RD-79-45 and No. FHWA-RD-79-47, 1978.

Federal Highway Administration. "Commercial Driver Rest and Parking Requirements." Report No. FHWA-MC-96-0010, 1996.

Gehl, Jan. *Life Between Buildings: Using Public Spaces.* New York: Van Nostrand Reinhold, 1987.

Joardar, S.D., and Neill, J.W. "The Subtle Differences in Configuration of Small Public Spaces." *Landscape Architecture*, 68(11):487–491, 1978.

Marcus, Clare Cooper, and Francis, Carolyn. *People Places: Design Guidelines for Urban Open Space*. New York: Van Nostrand Reinhold, 1990.

Newman, Peter, and Kenworthy, Jeffrey R. *Cities and Automobile Dependence*. Aldershot, UK: Grower Technical, 1989.

Underhill, Paco. *Why We Buy: The Science of Shopping*. New York: Simon & Schuster, 1999.

Urban Land Institute. *Parking Requirements for Shopping Centers*. Washington DC, 1982.

Whyte, William H. *The Social Life of Small Urban Spaces*. Washington, DC: The Conservation Foundation, 1980.

Whyte, William H. *City: Rediscovering the Center*. New York: Doubleday, 1988.

Design Value and the Modern Machine

with Baker Morrow

❑ Landscape architect Baker Morrow completes this chapter on the site. He implores us to pay attention to the site as the primary driver of design—one that is timeless, and that has absolutely nothing to do with Web sites or virtual simulations!

Baker Morrow

Baker H. Morrow, ASLA, is a principal of Morrow and Reardon, Ltd., Landscape Architects in Albuquerque, New Mexico. His firm has won over 48 design awards or citations for excellence in landscape architectural design, research, and consultation. He is founding director and adjunct professor of the program in landscape architecture at the University of New Mexico. Morrow is the author or editor of numerous publications, including Anasazi Architecture and American Design *(UNM Press, 1997; with V. B. Price).*

SUPPLEMENT 3.7

❏ I wonder how people go about designing landscapes and buildings without trying to puzzle out the history of a place—or *histories*, better put.

Every site was something else once, and often it retains traces or even a strong direct impression of what it has been. Landscape success is measured in generations. An old landscape has worked well for a lot of people, and probably for plant and animal communities as well, over a long period of time. A good designer will want to know why.

But a great deal of site planning and landscape architecture gets done these days without the designer ever visiting the site. It's often just a clean slate with bothersome grading and drainage problems in the designer's mind. This is simply reprehensible and stupid, and it usually happens for the most pedestrian reasons: *everything* is sacrificed to speed. Most landscape architects and architects with whom I work labor through nights, lunches, and weekends in a turbulent effort to keep up with project schedules. The engineers do much the same. And our quick computers with their endless new releases of drafting software and pulsating memory capacity have subverted our inherent need to make sound and inspired design decisions. These customarily take time, a commodity much in demand but low in supply, and they are based on a kind of deference to the land itself.

However, designers simply tend to focus on the wrong thing out of necessity. We have a horrendous series of production schedules to meet, and we cannot let romantic or quaint notions of what we should do interfere with the compelling work of the mice and keyboards in front of us.

It's a silly trap, and we've all walked into it. We find ourselves inside the gray bars looking out at the distant green hills. But we can easily improve what we do by considering a couple of notions. (See Fig. 3.27.)

■ We need to think of the technical production of design as a secondary concern. We do not practice landscape architecture or engineering or architecture to toss more billions of dollars onto the piles already accumulated by Microsoft, Intel, and America Online. We design what and as we do to create more harmony, beauty, and utility in human life, and

FIGURE 3.27
*Journal Center Business Park, Albuquerque, New Mexico. (Courtesy of
Langdon & Wilson, architects; Morrow and Reardon, Ltd., landscape
architects.)*

perhaps to encourage people to act a little more responsibly
in their dealings with the natural world. That's our focus.

We can bank the time we save by not paying immediate
attention to every self-promoting virtual nuance of technical advancement that comes our way. Then we can, if we
wish, put our time savings into a more thoughtful review of
site meaning and opportunity. Save a tree, or a special grove
of trees. Don't put creeks in culverts. Convert an old building, or façade or wing of an old building, into an integral
part of a new complex. Don't shove half a mountain into a
valley just to make a new access road to Paradise Pointe.
Use similar materials and suggestive form as new buildings
meet old in established neighborhoods. Make friends with
the site, and everyone will reap the benefits of friendship.

We can approach these salutary goals if we just put a little thought and a simple extra day or two into the process.

As developers, city fathers, city mothers, federal agencies,
tycoons, neighbors, and large land-guzzling corporations

ask us to develop an "image" for them out there in the designed environment, we should remember that our formidable means of materials transport at the turn of the new century have made it possible to ship anything anywhere. You can build an igloo in Orlando if you want to, and keep it cold, or an adobe palace in Paris.

This makes regionalism and local character, which are the sure anchors of social nostalgia (often a desirable thing) difficult to achieve. If we are able, with our technology, to build what we wish anywhere we want, the temptation is mighty strong to simply do so.

But regional styles and building materials and plants are keys to ongoing local site integrity. So as we set to work on our project concepts, we must identify them, understand their import, avoid their deconstruction, and encourage their integrity. Regional design, which often includes the use of genuinely local materials and traditional landscape forms, can give the users of our design the satisfaction of a comfortably developing sense of place for the future. And I think that landscape architects, engineers, and architects should serve as safe bridges to that future, not demolition squads in an advancing army of goons.

Paying attention to our sites as a primary—not a secondary—goal ties us to a rather timeless ethic of what our responsibility to society should be. It places a useful tool in our hands and sharpens our judgment as we face the next wave of data, sales pitches, Internet connections, and clamorous background news spilling into our lives over the transom and across the wires in endless, mind-numbing, thoroughly modern profusion.

Sketches

chapter 4

Architectural Design

*How to avoid having
your work seen as
"artificially inseminated
rather than passionately conceived."*

—Coy Howard

Sketches

"Well, well, I . . . to me—I . . . I mean, it's—it's—it's all instinctive, you know. I mean, I just try to uh, feel it, you know? I try to get a sense of it and not think about it so much."

—Annie Hall (from the screenplay by Woody Allen and Marshall Brickman)

❏ For most practitioners, there is indeed an "instinctive" element to design. That instinct, talent, or intuition, informed by the program, site, and concept, will likely lead to the creation of architecture. Most of us broadly define design not as something that is tacked on after analysis, or after solving the space-planning puzzle; nor do we see it as purely aesthetic. The consensus seems to lie in a way of looking at and addressing problems that starts from day one of the project and extends into the final stages of building and beyond (until after the photographer is hired and the film is in the can). Intuition or instinct alone, however, is clearly no substitute for rigorous research, analysis, and sweat.

Facilitating Design

❏ The purpose of this chapter is to facilitate the design process with a compendium of key ingredients. These include a series of brainstorming notes together with a listing of common mistakes to be recognized and avoided. A section on tools—advanced and primitive media (and their mixing), including drawing, models, and computers—follows. There are supplements by Paul Laseau and Glenn Goldman, with an intriguing case study on computing in preliminary design from the New York City office of Resolution: 4 Architecture.

Construction technology, use of materials, and color, often overlooked in the beginning phases of design, are placed up front and center. Professors and award-winning practitioners Geoffrey Adams and John Brittingham celebrate craft: connections, the detail, materials, and their extraordinary importance in making architecture. Additional supplements by Chris Jofeh, Director of Arup's Cardiff Bay office, Terry Patterson, and Deborah Sussman round out this discussion.

Let's move on to the nitty-gritty. Building systems, including structural, mechanical, lighting, and acoustical systems, and their integration are stressed. Systems integration must be considered central to the development of preliminary schemes. The chapter ends with a departure of sorts: an application of design method in the community domain.

This chapter might be entitled, "Design Development," but not in the traditional American Institute of Architects (AIA) B141 Owner-Architect Agreement sense. It is obvious that the so-called predesign program and site analysis tasks discussed in previous chapters comprise far more than mere analysis and associated diagramming. Design starts with the way in which you read the program; how the problem is interpreted, how you engage the client, and even how you conduct research and collect information. Assessing a site, visualizing possibilities, arranging bubbles of spaces on a site plan or in your mind, conceiving of concepts—this is all very creative stuff that comprises the first stages of design. Synthesis, yes; magical, no. If there is magic, it is the spirit and the soul that arise from a passionate, perhaps instinctive, and almost systematic involvement and excitement with the project at every phase.

Brainstorming Tips

❏ There is no conscious intent in this book to advocate any one theoretical approach to architectural design. The issues raised here (and in all other chapters) are meant to introduce and demonstrate some general and specific principles that can be applied to myriad projects in the search for creating built form and establishing meaningful concepts.

Aspects of designing are individual and often very personal. The process and results can be as varied as the projects undertaken. James Stewart Polshek, whose practice received an AIA Firm Award, believes that the approach to and the style of his projects are a function of the particular circumstance. What unifies the work of his office is an "openness to many different forms—contemporary and traditional, Western and non-

Western—and a willingness to assimilate and incorporate those forms when appropriate" (from Helen Searing, *James Stewart Polshek: Context and Responsibility*, Rizzoli, 1988).

Standardized methods for designing, blanketly applied across all projects, are clearly inadequate. They may be effective at demonstrating minimal competence (i.e., at protecting the safety and welfare of occupants, and helping one to pass the state licensing exam), but they also may limit possibilities—or worse, rigid methodology may inhibit brilliance. All factors affecting design (programmatic, site, technical, and aesthetic, and all that these imply) must be weighed and brought together in a mutually reinforcing poetic balance. Therefore, the following sections continue to lay out key ingredients for facilitating design rather than prescribing specific formulas.

A Brief Review of Standard Organizing Elements

❏ Development of a circulation system—that is, moving through the building—is a powerful means of ordering and linking the programmed spaces on the site. The program and site analyses will give strong clues about the formal nature of the circulation patterns. For example, a linear scheme may offer a real richness for serial development, clarity, and hierarchy in accessing spaces, and allow for easy future expansion. There are many ways of conceptualizing the linear idea, including the spine, axis, indoor street, and sequential path (i.e., one that is curved or angled)—with alternatives and permutations (i.e., parallel, perpendicular, and secondary routes). All of the aforementioned may accommodate a number of special events and contribute quite a bit of variation along the way. Relating functions to the path can establish focal points, or areas of real importance. An axis terminating in a distinctive way can have tremendous impact. An example is the stair in the Sainsbury Wing, the addition to London's National Gallery (by Venturi, Scott Brown & Associates). Critic Paul Goldberger describes its function beyond just circulation: "The stair widens as it rises, as if opening up to the art to be found at its top, and as we climb there is a real sense of mounting toward a goal, of aspiring. The stair is not merely a part of the mechanical process of circulation but a potent symbol of pilgrimage toward art."

In any case, easily perceived circulation is essential to orient the user (especially for very large-scale projects such as hospitals or shopping malls) and to provide information about how the building functions. There should be natural cues built into the architecture; a good test I invoke is whether lots of signage is required to identify the building from the outside and to know how to proceed on the inside. If the answer is, "Yes, I need all sorts of arrows and direction," there may be a fundamental problem with the essential images and the order of the building. Be judicious in optimizing area and concept: the most efficient buildings are those with the minimum amount of area dedicated to circulation, or those that incorporate segments of circulation into the functional program.

Integration of all building systems should be a logical outgrowth and reinforcement of the basic concept and organizing elements. This adds real power, meaning, and effectiveness to the architectural concept. Returning to our linear circulation example, the structural system could align on both sides of the circulation, and mechanical and electrical systems could have major distribution trunks following the circulation as well. These strategies are potentially very buildable, efficient, and self-evident. Further, as a high-use and high-visibility element, circulation would be an ideal place to focus design attention and budget, a place to revel in the purpose of the project. Be creative here! Use all site factors to full advantage (i.e., daylighting, views); be opportunistic about programming issues (i.e., what functions can spill, mix, or take advantage of this amenity in some way?). Some of the early work of Kallmann and McKinnell, specifically the Physical Education Facilities at Phillips Exeter Academy, highlights movement systems as the essence of building organization.

Another form of linear circulation, the grid, can also be a helpful planning and organizing element. There is much precedent for the use of this time-honored basis for the layout of numerous cities and villages. The work of Mies van der Rohe is infused with reverence for the grid in three dimensions. (See Fig. 4.1.)

The tradition of utilizing a major central space, the core

FIGURE 4.1
Pennzoil Place, in Houston, Texas, elevates the simple grid to dynamic sheets of sculptural mosaics. (Johnson/Burgee Architects; Courtesy of Andy Pressman.)

around which other spaces are organized, is another long-standing approach to ordering the program. When surrounded by functions or circulation on all sides, obviously it becomes an inwardly focused element. Natural light and air can pour into the space, greatly affecting those around it. Examples include atria, lobbies, and courtyards. Application of the central space idea along with other forms of circulation is common. A stunning contemporary example is the Ford Foundation in New York by Kevin Roche John Dinkeloo & Associates.

Other common organizational devices include radial patterns, dispersion schemes (where program elements are separated across a site), doughnut- or racetrack-shaped schemes, and the idea of hierarchy (where most spaces are assigned a hierarchical priority or weight, i.e., convenient location and/or special form for heavy public use, higher floor and/or more regular pattern for private use).

Experiment with refinement of space diagrams on the site plan. Clustering areas of comparable scale and like function may present a most efficient and buildable scheme. At the very least,

FIGURE 4.2

Here is an example of a great central space (the family room) that serves as the focal point of the design for this 6500-square-foot house. The skylit, double-height volume is ringed by a second-story bridge connecting the master bedroom suite in one wing to the childrens' bedrooms in another. (Andy Pressman, AIA, architect; Photo © Dan Forer.)

structural and mechanical system integration will be greatly facilitated. In some instances the fact that massing reflects this special pattern of internal functions and systems may result in an interesting visual manifestation of the program, as in a three-dimensional diagram. This strategy may be used to spur full investigation of three-dimensional potentials.

These may be helpful starting points for initial planning, again perhaps to be mixed, matched, and otherwise messed with. The key is to be in constant touch with the collection of program and site data as identified in Chapters 2 and 3. Design is not necessarily simply a question of finding one big formal idea (although sometimes it might be), superimposing it on the site, and squeezing in the functions. Creating order, delight, and a sense of place out of a great deal of important information and resolving a myriad of conflicts is the big challenge.

Three-Dimensional Considerations

❑ Architecture is experienced in full color and in many dimensions. As a result, starting with the first doodles on napkins (or yellow trace), there should be a keen awareness of three-dimensional qualities related to general space organization. Dynamic three-dimensional sculptural spaces (consistent, of course, with project mandates) are part of what makes the whole of architecture something greater than the sum of its parts. There is a magnetism, a unique force of attraction to engage buildings with this kind of inherent volumetric spatial interest. Often, these spaces serve as the focus for the project. Moreover, three-dimensional solutions may be the optimal means of achieving certain functional relationships. (See Fig. 4.3.)

In considering the program and site, always look for opportunities to develop three-dimensional relationships. Examples include lobbies with visual access to mezzanine functions; light scoops for bringing daylight deep into interiors; monumental spaces for special civic impact; and bridges and overlooks traversing double-height (or greater) volumes. At the smaller, room scale, the same thinking applies: should there be differences in ceiling heights (perhaps reinforced by artificial lighting, i.e.,

FIGURE 4.3

This is an example of a low-budget, small-scale project where some three-dimensional quality was sought out and developed. The lobby and mezzanine/ conference core of this factory for a sailmaker in Falmouth, Maine, bisects large work bays and received the most design attention. The mass of a scissors truss was expressed above the mezzanine, where the conference area was set back to create a deck overlooking the lobby below. The concept was to create a focus for the lobby and to enhance perception of a discrete volume and special place above the first floor. (Courtesy of Andy Pressman.)

lower over workstations for more direct light and intimacy, and higher over circulation for diffuse light and more public scale), or changes in floor height (i.e., raised or sunken levels to help zone activities, etc.)? All the answers to these questions regarding interior volumes and exterior massing are likely to give further direction and meaning to the appearance of elevations and perhaps contribute to their composition.

In developing designs (and this is somewhat personal and idiosyncratic), it is important to think in cross section as well as in plan. Sometimes there is a tendency to get fixated on the plan and extrude the diagram in three dimensions. Opportunities might be missed with this diagrammatic focus. It is worth reiterating the value of amplifying the experience of soaring space, with the qualification that this tactic must be relevant to the project aims. For example, an intentionally constricting, dim corridor leading to an airy open space will generate more emotion than a progression with less contrast.

The idea of enclosure to capture space is relevant here. It serves to define an area—both outdoors and indoors, up and down. It can be achieved by a minimum of means, from a simple beam to a solid wall. Degrees of openness, flowing space, or tight, confined space are all within control of the designer.

History

❑ Refer to Supplement 1.4 on precedents by Roger K. Lewis. In a column on an exhibit of the work of McKim, Mead & White, the famed and prolific turn-of-the-century New York architectural firm, Paul Goldberger has written: "These architects looked to history not for something to copy, but for inspiration; to spark creativity." Analyzing, understanding, interpreting, and finally invoking ideas from the past can facilitate arriving at design solutions in the present. For example, as Roger Kimball illustrates (*Architectural Record,* October 1991), Louis Kahn mapped history to contemporary needs. The galleries of the Kimbell Art Museum are traditional in concept but contemporary in execution and feeling. Kahn's design of the Yale Center for British Art is arrayed about "courtyards with commercial rental space on the ground floor, and is reminiscent of traditional Italian Renaissance townhouses." Kimball goes on to proclaim that "nothing could be more contemporary in its use of materials, disposition of light, and ambiance than that elegant urban museum."

"Architects must gain control over the history of architecture—its inevitable influence—and use it," says Lydia Soo, PhD, associate professor at the Taubman College of Architecture and Urban Planning, University of Michigan. "Knowledge of the history of architecture promotes the kind of broad-mindedness and sensitivity essential to the creation of buildings that end up in history books."

Aesthetic Issues

"I believe in an 'emotional architecture.' It is very important for humankind that architecture should move by its beauty; if there are many equally valid technical solutions to a problem, the one which offers the user a message of beauty and emotion, that one is architecture."

—Luis Barragan

"Architects need to see the building as part of a complex society. But a building is not socially responsible unless it is very beautiful."

—James Stewart Polshek

❑ In a discussion of aesthetics, William Strunk and E.B. White, in their famous little book *The Elements of Style* (Allyn & Bacon, 2000), describe some universals that can be applied to visual qualities of buildings: "Here we leave solid ground. Who can confidently say what ignites a certain combination of [forms], causing them to explode in the mind? Who knows why certain notes in music are capable of stirring the listener deeply, though the same notes slightly rearranged are impotent? These are high mysteries." Indeed, there are no rules for creating beauty (and be wary of those who compulsively claim otherwise).

We all know that much of aesthetic expression, including

massing and basic form making, materials selection, and elevation development, cannot be thought about independently; it may result from a wide range of issues already integrated into the design process from the program and site analyses. For example, adjacent buildings may have a huge impact in an urban context on specific elevation detailing. A concept related to technological or structural systems may dictate an aesthetic direction. Or, if there is a rationale for historical allusion, certainly aesthetic criteria will be derived from that viewpoint. Usually, basic form has (at least) something to do with the programmed activity within.

Following is an elementary/partial list of factors (in no particular order) that can be considered and manipulated in support of design concepts. Note also that the way in which they are manipulated (as Strunk and White point out) reveals something of the spirit, the expression of the self.

To introduce the list, let me restate that facts of site and program will suggest design features. Some clarifying examples: overhangs, light shelves, or other shading devices to control sunlight are very visible parts of the design that can impart richness and beauty to an elevation while simultaneously solving a problem. A projecting bay window might be selected to provide views up and down a street in order to maximize observation of children at play; hence, a potentially dynamic three-dimensional aesthetic feature results from a programmatic requirement.

■ Scale is an important factor in imagining and designing interior space and exterior massing. It is generally defined as size in relationship to human proportion. Scale can be controlled to reinforce concepts (i.e., grand, to express power or monumentality; small, to encourage intimacy).

There are various techniques for breaking down the scale of huge spaces that may be dictated by the program. Articulation of building components or materials—even changes in color, for example—can give human scale to a big blank wall. Conversely, overscaling may be a desirable tactic: larger-than-ordinary windows for a fire station in a residential neighborhood can serve to reduce perception of overall building size and thus make the building relate better to adjacent housing.

A subcategory of scale may be considered as anthropometrics/ergonomics, or the relationship of human body measurements and performance capabilities to the environments in which specific tasks must be accomplished. This field documents norms or the typical case but becomes crucial when studying how well varied groups or individuals with exceptional characteristics function in a particular space. Young children, the elderly, those who use wheelchairs, or even persons of different ethnic origin may exhibit anthropometric/ergonomic variations that will have an impact on configuration and sizing of architectural elements. (See the segment on universal design in Chapter 2.)

■ Proportion is an index of the concordance of various parts to each other. Leonardo da Vinci, Vitruvius, and Le Corbusier, among others, have devised theories of proportion based on the human form that could be applied to buildings to create beauty. And there are other mathematical approaches, including the "golden section." Be sure to consider beauty and harmony of the building components as a part of the greater surroundings.

I think it is quite salient to quote from John Dixon's July 1976 editorial in *Progressive Architecture* on the work of Alvar Aalto: "Above all, Aalto demonstrated in all of his buildings design determined by human experience rather than mere abstraction: the changes in ceiling height that signaled degrees of privacy, the windows placed for the view rather than the formal pattern . . . the handrail shaped for a satisfying grip."

■ Light and shadow can be used to articulate or amplify forms (i.e., projecting window jambs on elevations produce shadows, creating a sense of depth and emphasis on verticality).

■ Perspective conveys depth and distance (i.e., angled walls in two and/or three dimensions can seemingly elongate or foreshorten distances).

■ Ornament suggests a beautifying accessory that can also be part of an intentionally expressed building system (celebrating the inherent aesthetic of a construction technology), or perhaps some applied decoration (i.e., a stage set to evoke whimsical imagery).

Sketches

- Focus is a quality that is important in virtually all design disciplines: it crystallizes and draws attention to the most important aspect(s) of a scheme. The focus of a building could be a major public entry, or a main central space—the specific concept will clarify its application and expression. Special massing, scale, materials, lighting, orientation, and so on might be used by the designer to reinforce the focus as an important node in the building.

- Visual coherence of all building forms or materials has to do with achieving a sense of harmony. Some unifying thread weaving together disparate parts (if indeed there are disparate parts) should be considered. Forms that appear tacked on, almost as an afterthought, or three-dimensionally unresolved, discordant pieces of the program are usually symptoms of too much emphasis on plan.

- The terms symmetry/asymmetry describe arrangements on either side of an axis or center. Symmetry implies a very formal order, whereas asymmetry is less formal and potentially more dynamic. Subtle manipulations in an asymmetric framework can produce interesting results. For example, the Barcelona Pavilion, designed by Mies van der Rohe, epitomizes the beauty of an asymmetric balance in forms and materials. Look to the program and concept for applicability. (The investigation of symmetry/asymmetry from several viewpoints—perception/physiological psychology, cultural anthropology and semiology, and traditional analysis of visual art—can be a fascinating and worthwhile study.)

- Contrast and blending are ideas that have been discussed in Chapter 3 in relation to emphasizing the best characteristics of both the site and the structure. The principles apply at the building scale as well. For example, consider blending in a dense urban site where buildings are tight on either side; the front faces a major street, the back is open to a court. One response might be to pick up the hard edges and solid forms along the street, while the back façade loosens up with softer and more open forms. H.H. Richardson's Glessner House in Chicago exemplifies this strategy, at least in the sense that a fortresslike front façade gives way to an open, almost delicately articulated rear courtyard. In contrast, the entry pyramid at the Louvre in Paris, designed by I.M. Pei, employs the converse strategy with its glazed skin in sharp opposition to surrounding classical forms and textures.

■ Rhythm is the cadence of some kind of design theme at a building or detail scale (i.e., fenestration, exposed structure, or material) in some kind of regular pattern or modulation. Varying the pattern of a particular rhythmic scheme may reinforce a concept or highlight a feature. Expanding or contracting the space between recurring elements can add novelty while preserving the rhythmic scheme.

■ Variety is the spice of life; avoid boring, arbitrary themes. This is not to say that more neutral or "background" buildings do not represent good architecture given certain conditions. But even if this type of building is appropriate, there must be something very special about it: perhaps in its craft or detailing, or in some aspect that imbues it with the forces of magic and spirit.

Brainstorming Tips, Part 2

■ Assume that your project will be built. This kind of mindset will ensure your personal investment, which is so important in designing.

In his seminal text on environmental planning, John Simonds implores us to bring drawings alive—imagine yourself as not just one typical building user, but each type, from a maintenance person to a manager to a CEO to the public. Imagine how each actor would specifically do his or her job or experience the project. In this fashion, your sketches and design come to life.

■ Remain open to new ideas (i.e., sketch freely and copiously). Generate as many rough, unbridled, unconventional (and conventional) ideas as possible. Fight against the natural tendency to erase. Use overlays—you may want to retrieve an idea later.

■ "Trial, error, and refinement" is an old dictum that constitutes a fine strategy for stimulating creativity. Sometimes design decisions end up being arbitrary, and you need a starting point from which to jump in. (For the most part, all design decisions should be accountable, certainly, at least, to facilitate educating the client.) So just put marker on trace and record all ideas. They're a basis for further exploration and discussion.

■ Resolve conflicts in all dimensions. In a *New York Times* piece, Wendy Steiner writes: "The essence of the architectural task is switching back and forth between two- and three-dimensional conception." Modify an element in plan, then see what happens in section and model (or perspective), and vice versa.

■ Embrace failure and mistakes! Ideas that don't work can provide some of the most useful information and motivation to innovate. View revision as an opportunity to make the work more potent. "Alas, you just didn't capture JoAnne's imagination," was the stated reason I was fired by one client's husband. Turn it into a positive experience; "design" an appropriate response. I'm still getting publicity today for JoAnne's unbuilt project. "Can you learn from the mistakes?" is not the question; the question is, "How much can you learn?" There are few temperamental artists who are effective architects.

■ Frugality can come at later stages of design. It is not necessary to employ every design feature ever learned simultaneously—but now is the time to try something if the urge is upon you. Edit later.

■ View specific problems as unique assets. For example, in a renovation there is an existing structural column in the middle of an important space that seemingly disrupts the space. Attempt to highlight it—put glow-in-the-dark pink tiles on it; add another (nonstructural) matching column to create a gateway, set up a circulation path, or create a focus or support core.

■ There are always going to be conflicting needs; it takes time and experimentation to test possible outcomes for spatial relationships to evolve in accordance with the design concept or theme. If, however, it appears that too much revision is required, be prepared (and willing) to start anew. The time has not been wasted; the exercise usually results in a deeper knowledge and understanding of the project.

- If frozen, work on an unrelated task; come back to the problem at a later time from a different perspective. Isolate the problem; do more research, become more informed about it; return to the site; visit or read about a related and architecturally significant work. Try changing drawing scales or media (if drawing, build a quick-and-dirty model, and vice versa). Engage in a dialogue with colleagues.

- Most important, develop the habit of being confident, assume success, and enjoy the process.

Common Mistakes

- Sometimes a designer believes that he or she has such an incredibly good singular idea that it must be carried through to the final scheme. Infatuation should not get in the way of larger goals, and openness to alternatives (perhaps equally infatuating but very different) is the mark of experience. Explore alternatives! Revise! Clients often change their minds midway through a project, or have different design ideas, or simply might not like what you've done for no apparent or logical reason. You must learn to be enthusiastic about developing other schemes and responding to new input. Or become a better educator.

- Avoid the tail wagging the dog syndrome. No one feature should be that precious; do not let an impressive detail dominate decision making.

- Projects are developed where there are lots of terrific ideas and concepts. This can be problematic: when too many things are happening simultaneously, there is no one strong point of view. Do not dilute a good, solid concept.

- Obscure references and concepts that are too personal or that can only be perceived by an elite few are not in the public interest and bring into question the role of the professional. But this must be qualified: sometimes, depending on the circumstances, there may be a good reason for being less than totally clear or explicit. One cannot script or predict personal reactions to art—this certainly encompasses the artful aspects of any architectural work. Do make sure that any intentional allusions in the architecture have significant objective meaning. Moreover, ideas must be understood in three-dimensional reality—buildings are not experienced in eighth scale, in plan, on the computer.

■ Some less experienced designers feel that whatever is drawn must be perfect. This couldn't be a more inhibiting and destructive belief in the first stages of design. Loosen up!

■ Some designers, not to mention students, feel insecure during the creative process. This is natural; there is always the question of whether you'll come through with the brilliant final product as expected. If you share these feelings, acknowledge and accept that this is the way you operate, and with a systematic approach, perseverance, and experience you will gradually learn that there is really little question about the outcome.

■ Remind yourself that architecture supports or ideally facilitates activity; it is not the end in itself. With a focus on building form rather than the bigger picture of place making, it is easy to lose sight of the goal.

■ Clients may ask, "Why did you make that particular design move?" I cannot overemphasize the value of a thoughtful reason behind important design decisions, even those involving more subjective issues of taste.

■ Outdoor spaces that are residual from the building mass are another common occurrence. (See Supplement 3.1, by Lawrence Halprin, in Chapter 3.)

Tools

❏ The overarching message is: use the tools in the beginning stages of a design project that help you focus best on three-dimensional imagination and abstract thinking.

The following discussion of tools (drawings, physical models, and computers) identifies some options for facilitating the design process. Like the process itself, the choice of what to use is quite personal. There are advantages and disadvantages of each tool, and it is often productive to employ a combination of tools at different stages of design or simultaneously—as in going back and forth from two to three dimensions. Architect Steven Cantor says, "The best approach is to use whatever tool is best suited for each part of the job."

There are simply no rules; initially, use what's comfortable. It is also important to experiment and develop expertise in a variety of modes. As language is central to thinking and communicating verbally, so too are graphic and visual tools central to thinking and communicating three-dimensional form.

Drawings

❑ Just as the smell of sawdust from freshly cut wood and exposed steel, conduit, and ducts at a construction site holds a raw sensual appeal, the feeling of soft pencil or marker or fountain pen on canary trace is almost an end in itself. There should be an inherent pleasure—a melange of tactile, visual, and auditory stimuli that invite you to continue drawing or pursuing your medium of choice.

The instruments are simple and inexpensive: pens, markers, pencils, and paper—from sketchbooks to trace—and of course napkins on airplanes (for architects such as Antoine Predock) or napkins on Greyhound buses (for sole proprietors or students), where some of the best ideas are drawn.

To me, there's a certain consistency to freehand sketches in early designs—there's an appropriate ambiguity to the lines; things aren't resolved to a high degree conceptually, so why should they be graphically? Hard line drawings imply a precision that may not be intended by the designer. However, some people find the use of straight edges liberating, and that kind of assertion cannot be disputed. Choice may even be a function of the design concept.

FIGURE 4.4
This is a precise interior perspective, used to both analyze the appearance of the "floating" ceiling and convey the feeling of experiencing the space for the client. The drawing attempts to approximate a photographic view, although the emphasis is on forms rather than detail. (Courtesy of Andy Pressman.)

Kirby Lockard, in his exceptional book, *Drawing as a Means to Architecture* (Van Nostrand Reinhold, 1977), states: "Perspective is the most natural way of drawing space, since it is how we see space. . . . The experience of a building is an infinite number of perspectives." Lockard strongly believes that designs should be

FIGURE 4.5
The ambiguous, conceptual, freehand perspective sketch; here, a proposed 20,000-square-foot classroom facility in Eliot, Maine. (Courtesy of Andy Pressman.)

studied in perspective, not just in plan, section, and elevation. Kirby goes on to say that the best drawings are never those final presentation masterpieces hanging on the wall, but the ones that showed you the opportunities for improving your ideas, and are now crumpled in the wastebasket.

Drawing as Discovery
With Paul Laseau

❏ Paul Laseau writes passionately in Supplement 4.1 about freehand drawing as (1) continuing one's education about architecture and (2) developing skills to represent qualities of the environment in discussions with clients. He talks openly about his own sketches of existing environments, what he has learned from them, and how they have influenced his design thinking.

Paul Laseau

SUPPLEMENT 4.1

Paul Laseau is a registered architect and professor of architecture at Ball State University in Muncie, Indiana. He is a critically acclaimed author of numerous books on drawing and architecture, including Graphic Thinking for Architects and Designers, *3d ed. (Wiley, 2001) and* Graphic Problem Solving for Architects and Designers, *2d ed. (Van Nostrand Reinhold, 1986). He has worked with architectural firms in New York and Paris.*

❏ Beyond the debate of the positive or negative impacts of digital illustration is the simple observation that all images are as useful as whatever human perception or imagination finds in them.

The potential of drawing to nurture the richness of our imagination is based on three realizations: the oneness of seeing, drawing, and thinking, the value of variety in drawing subjects, and a reinforcing relationship between drawing and living.

■ Like many people who sketch extensively, I am aware that drawing has affected the way I see things and that the way I see is an important factor in the effectiveness and quality of my drawings. Similarly, what I see critically affects the way I think. It is these relationships that provide each of us with unique ways of drawing and thinking creatively. For these

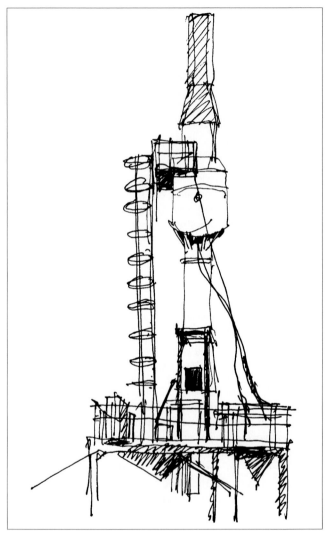

FIGURE 4.6
Sketches of Poole, UK. (Courtesy of Paul Laseau.)

FIGURE 4.6 (Continued)

reasons seeing and thinking should be considered an integral part of drawing.

■ To take full advantage of the versatility of drawing, we must stretch our exercises to cover a variety of subject matter. Just as exercises in composition and perspective are mutually reinforcing, the drawing of both people and architecture or flowers and machinery brings new perceptions and increased sensitivity to each subject.

■ Among those studying human potential and the quality of life, there is a growing affirmation of the importance of the reintegration of our lives. This means the dissolving of artificial barriers between work and leisure, productivity and creativity, or physical and mental activity. In this light, drawing is not just a means to an end but also a healthy part of daily living. A relaxed state often accompanies deep concentration in drawing; many authors have described this as similar to meditation, which is widely advocated as a benefit to physical and mental as well as spiritual health.

For many, the prime reason to take up sketching is to produce admirable drawings that give us a sense of accomplishment. Although such motivation is important, narrow concern about results not only inhibits learning but also hides an even greater

FIGURE 4.7
Sketch of a Paris street. (Courtesy of Paul Laseau.)

source of motivation, the wealth of other experiences that sketching brings. If we look carefully at the subjects we sketch, a new, exciting world of awareness and delight opens to us.

I sketched a Paris street in Fig. 4.7 while sitting on a public bench. As the sketch developed, I became aware of how the regular patterns of similar buildings became animated by:

- The influence of the unusual pattern of Paris streets
- The play of light and shadow
- The contrasts between the cool darkness under the cafe awning and the dazzling glare of the sun rebounding from the buildings in the background
- The important role of people in making a view stimulating

Sketching is also a means of escaping from the world around us. The level of concentration is such that one can become completely absorbed in the process, losing all sense of or concern for time.

FIGURE 4.8
Sketch of Meigi Mora, a historic preservation park in central Japan that contains a collection of preserved buildings from the Meigi period of Japanese history. (Courtesy of Paul Laseau.)

FIGURE 4.9
Sketch of Vicksburg, Mississippi. (Courtesy of Paul Laseau.)

Finally, sketching is an enjoyable physical experience; the feel of the paper and the movement of the pen across the surface become part of the stimulation and reward of sketching. Accomplished sketchers know that ultimately the quality of their drawings is derived from these experiences of awareness, concentration, and touch. If we fully participate in these experiences, we need not worry about the results.

The sketch of the gatehouse at Montecute in Fig. 4.10 was done in 10 minutes. I cannot tell you how it was done; the result was a complete surprise to me. What I can say is that I was completely absorbed in what I was doing and that I thoroughly enjoyed myself; and I think that is reflected in the drawing. If you enjoy looking at drawings, sketches, or paintings, you will almost surely enjoy sketching. Remember that you are sketching for your own enjoyment and not for someone else or for some other goal.

We are often hard on ourselves, feeling that we cannot afford the time to indulge in something that does not have immediate practical, even financial, rewards. To see ourselves as purely functional or economic beings is to cut ourselves off from much

FIGURE 4.10
Sketch of gatehouse at Montecute, UK. (Courtesy of Paul Laseau.)

FIGURE 4.11
Sketch of small shrines at Sensoji Temple, Tokyo, Japan. (Courtesy of Paul Laseau.)

FIGURE 4.12
Sketch of Olympic Park, Seoul, Korea. (Courtesy of Paul Laseau.)

FIGURE 4.13
Sketch of South Gate, Nara, Japan. (Courtesy of Paul Laseau.)

FIGURE 4.14
Sketch of Santa Maria de la Salute, Venice, Italy. (Courtesy of Paul Laseau.)

of life. If you open yourself to it, sketching can be an immensely rewarding pursuit, an enriching view not only of the world and people around you, but also an insight into your own perceptions of that world. It is this discovery that reveals the power of drawing to uncover unique human contributions to architecture.

The impact of sketching experiences on the subsequent design process is the bonus for architects. The sketch of the Cemetery of Père Lachaise in Fig. 4.15 was made a few years ago. I had occasion to study it as I was exploring ideas for an atrium

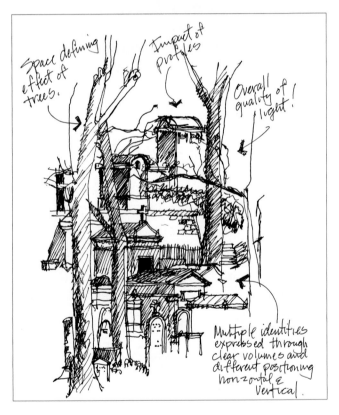

FIGURE 4.15
Sketch of Père Lachaise Cemetery, Paris. (Courtesy of Paul Laseau.)

FIGURE 4.16
Sketch of design study: student center. (Courtesy of Paul Laseau.)

for a student center. (See Fig. 4.16.) I noticed qualities of the cemetery that paralleled needs for the student center, including diversity of identities within a sense of unified space and the overall quality of light. Although the design sketches are the first of many needed to arrive at an appropriate level of refinement for the student center, they represent an important first step by establishing a design approach.

Physical Models

❏ Study models, those that are quick (i.e., not a lot of billable time required) and dirty and can be ripped apart with ease, are invaluable tools in developing and testing three-dimensional ideas. The models I admire the most look like they've been targeted by smart bombs, they have so many rips, tears, and changes. William Lam, the lighting designer who has taught at MIT and Harvard, offers some commonsense advice to designers: "Build a model, hold it up to the window, then clients don't have to speculate about the lighting effects for 20 minutes!" Study models used in development of preliminary designs are valuable on many dimensions, including efficiently presenting multiple schemes to clients. Models are great props for clients who can use them to demystify two-dimensional drawings (they can be touched and are interactive).

One Way to Build Them

❏ My preference is chipboard, white glue, and Spray Mount. Chipboard or illustration board can be cut easily with a mat knife or scissors, and the white glue sets very quickly. A useful technique follows:

- ■ Copy the preliminary design—floor plans and elevations.
- ■ Roughly cut out the copies with scissors.
- ■ Apply Spray Mount on the back of the copies and set them on the chipboard.
- ■ Cut the chipboard following the lines on the copies, and voilà, you have the major pieces of the model.

Now the real fun begins. After assembling the parts, or some of the parts—you may want to leave one side open or have the capa-

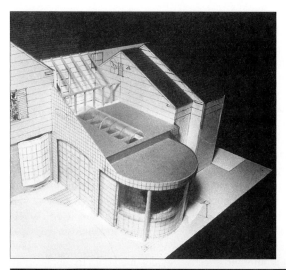

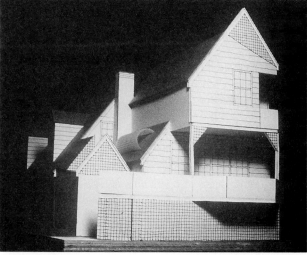

FIGURE 4.17
These massing models have been pulled apart and put back together on numerous occasions during design, and still function as essential parts of client presentations. (Courtesy of Andy Pressman.)

bility to lift off the roof or floors to see what's happening inside on larger-scale models—experimenting is unbelievably easy. Use scraps of cardboard to test, develop, and manipulate new forms and sculpt three-dimensional space; cut away part of a floor, and perhaps glue only a small piece of it back. Get some pieces of balsa wood or cut cardboard strips to simulate beams or columns, or build structural components (i.e., trusses). Buy empty plastic bottles from a drugstore in cylindrical or square shapes, and cut them in half to create a vaulted skylight or bay window; do the same with a table tennis ball and you have a small dome—there are many ways to create your own rough model kit of parts!

Return to the floor plan or section, make an adjustment, and see what the implications are in the model (and vice versa). Cut and paste freely—the glue (or tape) makes it simple and quick. Remember to keep the context in mind and build its edges, at least, even at the large building scale.

Clay is another effective model material. Its application, though, is limited to studying exterior massing in small scale. The material is so plastic that the advantages in molding things are obvious. Children's modular building blocks are also good for the study of massing and give you an excuse to regress in service of the ego (i.e., have fun).

Another added benefit of building a model is that many perspectives can be generated through photography. Photos of study models can be enlarged to block out an infinite number of views (at any size), from flybys to worm's-eye to the most important— eye level. Detail can then be added efficiently by drawing rather than building it into the model.

- ■ *Tip 1*: Add some scaled grid lines on or in the model prior to photographing; this will help in sketching more accurately.
- ■ *Tip 2*: Place the model on the site plan (at the same scale, of course); this helps in drawing in part of the context (i.e., roads, sidewalks, curbs, etc.).

Use a fast film and the smallest aperture setting to maximize depth of field (so that most of the model is in focus). If photographing a model interior, minimum scale is about ¼ inch; ½ inch is best, so you can fit the lens inside. Exterior views can be

FIGURE 4.18

Quick study models of interior spaces, even though quite crude (with a few light leaks), are very effective at simulating the impact of daylighting. Scale was ½ inch = 1 foot. The use of scale elements, such as people and furniture, adds considerably to the overall perception, particularly by nonarchitects. (Courtesy of Andy Pressman.)

FIGURE 4.18 (Continued)

shot easily at smaller scales as well. (See Chapter 5 for Supplement 5.5, by photographer Norman McGrath, on photographing presentation models.)

Computers
With Glenn Goldman

❏ William J. Mitchell, dean of MIT's School of Architecture and Planning, states the obvious: "We will be radically rethinking the role of digital technology in architectural practice, teaching, and research; those who cling too long to old ideas will be left struggling."

Glenn Goldman, AIA, author of Supplement 4.2, tells us how not to be left struggling. He covers everything from the impact of e-mail—"the only phone calls I get anymore are people calling to see if I got their e-mail"—to new opportunities for design exploration. He addresses three-dimensional modeling and the potentials for innovative synthesis that can be generated by crossing media.

Glenn Goldman

SUPPLEMENT 4.2

Glenn Goldman, AIA, is professor and director of the Imaging Laboratory at the School of Architecture at the New Jersey Institute of Technology, where he has been teaching architectural design studios with digital media continually since 1985. A former president of the Association for Computer-Aided Design in Architecture (ACADIA), he is the author of Architectural Graphics: Traditional and Digital Communication *(Prentice Hall, 1997) and numerous articles about computing and architecture. A co-recipient of an honorable mention in the AIA Education Honors Program (1989), he also received a Citation for Applied Research in the 1991* Progressive Architecture *Awards Program. He earned his BA from Columbia and his Master of Architecture from Harvard.*

❏ The computer is proving itself to be one of the most important design tools an architect has. At the end of the twentieth century, "drawing" with a computer is commonplace in the profession. Digital media have transformed the way architecture and most design fields are practiced. From automotive and airplane design to the design of advertising brochures to the entire building delivery process, computers are ubiquitous.

Drawing, as has been commonly said, is a way of communicating. In architecture, we communicate to ourselves, colleagues, clients, contractors, regulatory agencies, and the general public. At each step, the computer assists us in creating the graphics that aid in this communication. For better or worse, we can now illustrate virtually anything we can imagine. If we can visualize it in our minds, we have the tools to create the image—and we have therefore expanded our design opportunities.

Computers in the Design and Representation Processes

❏ For decades now the computer has been looked upon as the "magic tool" that will design buildings for society. The Association of Computing Machinery's Special Interest Group in Graphics (SIGGRAPH), founded in 1969, is now more than 30 years old. Years ago, Nicolas Negroponte's "architecture machine" and Ivan Sutherland's "Sketchpad" interactive graphics software, developed at MIT, focused popular attention on research as to how ones and zeros could be turned into useful design information for engineers, artists, and architects. Shading algorithms and texture mapping were developed in the 1970s, and the first paint program, Super-Paint, was developed by Dick Shoup and Alvy Ray Smith in 1974. In 1982 computer graphics first played a major role in a feature film, *TRON*. And personal computer–based CAD software was commercially introduced in 1983. By the beginning of the 1990s, entire "digital backlots" were being created by architects for motion picture studios. At the beginning of a new millennium, the rapid expansion of the role of digital media in society in general, and in the design fields in particular, has been enormous. Today, there are many ways the computer can assist architects in the design process.

Nongraphic Computer-Assisted Design Tools

❏ While it is not (necessarily) graphical in nature, one should not underestimate the impact that simple e-mail has had. If one accepts the idea that the design process involves more than one person, then e-mail—which has facilitated interaction—has facilitated the design process. A client or a consultant can respond or send information at whatever time is convenient. A client can respond to an in-person progress presentation by an architect while the architect is on his or her way back to the office (or home). Drawings as attachments can be digitally whisked from one place to another for review and comment. Time is compressed. The fax machine and e-mail (as well as the cellular phone) have put architects in a position to get more information and feedback more often—whether they like it or not. Unfortunately, this does not give the architect any more time to digest this information and respond. On the contrary, the immediacy of the medium almost screams for instant response. If an e-mail is not responded to quickly enough to satisfy the sender, phone calls come to the office just to check if the architect has received the message(s). This is not a problem with the medium. Rather, it is a management problem if the architect responds in too much haste or sends out drawings without proper review. The speed of the medium can be used to the architect's advantage if the process is controlled. E-mail is a wonderful way to get quick responses to specific questions from consultants and clients. Furthermore, it leaves a written record of decisions in a way that unrecorded telephone conversations cannot. E-mail can reduce much of the unproductive time spent waiting for information in the presentation, response, and redesign cycle of a project. Architects must simply remember not to make decisions before they can be thoughtfully considered and checked (if necessary). Any architect who uses e-mail to correspond with clients or consultants during the initial phase of a project is, in fact, using the computer to assist in design.

The design phase of the project often includes great numbers of preliminary calculations that assist in the determination of form. Evaluation of solar data and thermal transfer can affect a building's orientation on a site, the nature and frequency of windows, and the materials/mass (thermal lag) of the building envelope. In all cases, using relatively simple software, the computer can process very preliminary design information to give the architect guidance in making decisions. While reserving final decisions for the architect, this extra analysis can save redesign time later on in the project. Similarly, structural information and the preliminary sizing of structural members can be made in house with a greater degree of accuracy and with greater speed. (Note that the computer does not replace the role of the structural engineer.) Furthermore, a greater number of alternatives can be evaluated earlier in the design process.

New Types of Representation Provide New Opportunities for Design Exploration

❏ While e-mail and analysis are important components of architectural design and practice management, they are clearly not the only areas in which the computer has an impact. Perhaps the most influential portion of architectural design exploration is tied to graphics. Styles of representation have long influenced the nature of architectural design. During the design process, architects respond to their sketches and imagery, which, in turn, affect the final outcome. The list of architectural works and the influence/interchangeability of representation and product is long. The balanced asymmetry of a number of Henry Hobson Richardson's great works reflects the nature of the perspective sketches he created during the design process. Among the (speculative) examples are Michelangelo's design of the Capitoline Hill in Rome and the visual focal point in the Belvedere Exedra (one-point perspective), the geometric forms of I.M. Pei and ink axonometric drawings (a favorite representation type of Modernist architects), Rietveld's Schroder House and "colored" renderings and De Stijl paintings, and so on.

Three-dimensional modeling on the computer has created a new set of image types that can be used as visual stimuli during the design process. Most notably, the "wireframe" model is a new type of image made popular by the computer. Also, wireframes create a new type of ambiguity that is very important in the early stages of design. This type of image allows architects to see through a building and study the relationship of elements across space. A typical surface model forces the viewer to observe the relationship of elements based on adjacencies. By starting with a wireframe image, and selectively filling in various planes, one can study proportions and alignments in an entirely new way. The types of relationships Le Corbusier wrote about and demonstrated in two-dimensional diagrams are now made manifest three-dimensionally with wireframe images and simple overlays. These relationships across space may be emphasized in the final building at the discretion of the architect. They may be "hidden" and remain as a subtle organizing principle behind the building, or they may be exposed. Most literally, these linear elements may be physically built in a somewhat deconstructivist idiom. Or, varying degrees of transparency/opacity may be used to selectively emphasize some of the design relationships.

The use of near and far clipping planes effectively turns on and off how much of a building can be seen. Slicing a building allows the designer to look at selected sections or pieces of a project. Furthermore, the thickness and angle of the slice may be varied to expose new pieces for exploration. By looking at these slices in sequence (much like a computerized tomography [CT] scan), the designer can explore relationships between interior and exterior, solid and void, parts and whole, and so on. The spatial experience of a person in a building may be studied conceptually and perceptually—and dynamically—as one sees the thin three-dimensional models of building transform from mass into volume.

Perhaps of equal significance to the new types of images is the ability to interactively and in real time change aspects of images to see the immediate impacts of alternatives. Just as the immediacy of e-mail brings information and comments to the designer, so too does the instant modification of an on-screen image.

The Fourth Dimension: Movement Through Time

❏ Short of tediously creating traditionally drawn flip books, architects must rely on computer graphics to study dynamic changes or movement through the spaces they propose to create. Animated walk-throughs are now a staple in almost every three-dimensional modeling program used by architects.

In general, computer animation may be created by either moving or animating a character or object, or by moving a camera and setting up key frames. Because architecture only occasionally moves, most of the time it is easiest for designers to select a few critical camera and target locations and then decide on the number of frames between them so that the computer automatically generates the animated sequence. Because this task is integrated within the design modeling program, architects can easily simulate the perceptual characteristics of moving around in a building from the earliest simple three-dimensional sketches as a design tool, not worrying about finished textures, graphics, slick transitions, and so on. With the addition of lighting in the model, designers can visually evaluate the impacts of changing time of day or night as well as seasons of the year. The solar effects on a building rotated on the site can be seen.

Because the computer facilitates the building of architectural three-dimensional models with primitives (predetermined blocks or components), there is another opportunity for animation in the design and design development phases of a project. The primitives may be abstract geometric elements (such as those found in software applications that are not specifically designed for the building-related industries) or architectural elements (doors, windows, walls, etc.). Architectural elements may be built from geometric ones. Regardless of the type of objects used to create a model, once the model is constructed, various elements may be turned on or off and moved about to simulate a construction process and/or to facilitate design analysis of discrete components of a proposed project.

In addition to walking through one's proposal, sound may be tested as well. Jacques Tati's film *Playtime* hilariously depicts the impact sound has on many of the spaces designed by architects. While acoustic modeling programs are not as common as those used for animation, they do exist. Even if "quick-and-dirty" approximations using sound effects are employed, they can give an architect more information about the nature of a space than simply adding inexpensive royalty-free "clip music" purchased from a catalog to liven up animations. As multimedia applications are developed, as well as the cross-media applications of film, video, and scientific visualization, the ability to integrate objective (and nonobjective) sound into animated design studies will be facilitated.

Conceptual Collage—The Beginning Stages of Design

❏ Analogous to music sampling, in which sounds from the environment are recorded, distorted, and used in unique ways to create music, image sampling is the visual equivalent of a sound bite used to create new visual forms, textures, patterns, and types of architecture. The use of video and image processing capabilities together with three-dimensional modeling permits the architect to create new design proposals that can be modified, saved, and applied.

How does an architect evaluate the initial design concept in context? Sketches, site models, preliminary designs, and the like are all tried-and-true—and labor-intensive—methods used by architects to start design projects. With image sampling, there is a time-saving way to visually explore design approaches. Using a scanned photo of the site, a designer using an image-processing program can create a "conceptual collage" in a matter of minutes. Buildings or objects that represent metaphors or approaches to scale may be superimposed on the site. Photorealism is not required, as these images are not meant for presentation—they are notes to oneself (and maybe a colleague or two). All one needs is to be able to test a variety of approaches quickly in order to select a path for pursuit. This path can, of course, be changed along the way. But in less than one hour, a designer can actually test different parti alternatives in context! It is also important to note that architects may sketch directly on the scanned images and/or may sketch with traditional media, scan the sketches into digital format, and then manipulate them with all of the tools the computer has to offer (including autotrace commands that convert the traditional sketch to editable vector diagrams).

With image sampling, architects can create two-dimensional illustrations of three-dimensional objects without creating the model itself (Fig. 4.19), using inexpensive and off-the-shelf painting and image processing programs. Image sampling also allows architects to explore a variety of textures and finishes for a building. We can even paint the wall with images of popular soft drinks or shoes. Images and three-dimensional models with associated data provided by manufacturers are available for use/capture from the Internet. An architect can, in fact, create a convincing image of almost anything. It becomes the responsibility of the designer to create textures and images of materials that are supported by logic and are appropriate to the design concept.

FIGURE 4.19
Image sampling. These illustrations are two-dimensional images created from the same kit from parts (scans of a photograph) that were composed to create new buildings and sites without the use of three-dimensional modeling. (Courtesy of Ana Aznar and Lori Ryder.)

Serendipity

❏ The closest a designer can come to random exploration with traditional media is to doodle. Nevertheless, even doodling has a long tradition and is generally done with a purpose. The fact that a hand has to take a pencil to paper and then move the pencil for each stroke forces some degree of forethought. It is possible, of course, for an architect to lie down in the grass, look at clouds, see shapes of buildings in the sky, and then quickly sketch a variety of interpretations of what is seen (or what one thinks one sees). Building physical study models out of pliable materials (like clay) can also lead to discovery along the way during the design process. The computer, however, can be used to generate a variety of alternatives for the designer to evaluate.

Those individuals who support the development and use of artificial intelligence in computer-aided design seek to have the computer develop solutions for the architect to implement. At the other extreme, computers can be used to empower the designer. Designers, using all the knowledge and experience at their disposal, can then evaluate the many alternatives created and generated by the computer. This ultimately causes a slight shift in some of the skills needed by an architect. Analytic skills—the ability to carefully critique and evaluate alternatives—become increasingly important.

Computer images are generated by algorithms that, in general, translate the input from the creator into a graphic display. There are additional algorithms and programs that, when compiled, approximate various laws of physics (laws of reflection and refraction when dealing with light, of gravity and wind when dealing with scientific visualization), mathematics (linear perspective, vertices manipulation), etc.

Almost every computer program can provide some level of automation. Paint programs provide opportunities for color swapping, smoothing or blending, sharpening, and so on. Image-processing programs provide a myriad of filters that can be used to turn an image (or photo) into another image of a completely different style. Algorithms are being written that will even generate well-known patterns that will scale or tile to fit the appropriate space. Modeling software can be used to generate multiple perspectives with varying lighting conditions, and so on. Rapid and automatic sequencing of alternatives is possible.

There are also "nonpredictive" images that may result from preprogrammed random operations and error (human and/or mechanical). Unintended images can be the catalyst for future design development in almost any project. With the advent of word processing programs, writers no longer needed to have a clear organizational scheme prior to the start of a project. The ease with which words, sentences, paragraphs, and whole sections could be moved and rearranged allowed the organization to come later without any loss of efficiency. Authors could enter their ideas as they came, knowing that they could be moved. In this way, random thoughts that initially might not have had a place would not be lost. The creation of computer imagery and the utility of randomly generated images have also had a similar impact. The computer, with multiple originals, provides an almost infinite array of possible alternatives (limited only by time and digital storage capabilities). Furthermore, architecture can now be created accidentally, rather than necessarily originating with intent. Meaningful intent may be discovered during a spontaneous or automated process if the designer is capable of evaluating that which appears on screen.

Animations are created with the process of *tweening*—filling in the intermediate frames between selected key frames. If one object is transformed into another during tweening, the process is more widely known as *morphing*. Made popular in the movie *Terminator 2* and a Michael Jackson music video, morphing is now an accepted digital special effect. Architects can look at two alternatives and automatically generate in-between states for evaluation. Initially, only the number of intermediate steps is asked of the designer. Evaluation, however, is completely in the hands of the architect!

Virtually everyone is familiar with the phrase *twiddling with the dial*. It commonly means to play with, or turn lightly, the dial of a radio or television (before digital tuning became commonplace) to see what is on. This concept can easily be transferred to a three-dimensional computer model. Without any automated random generating program, the designer is responsible for the random manipulation of a model. Vertices may be pushed or pulled, planes warped, and objects collaged, in a "negligent" or random manner. The process is completely reversible (as long as the designer saves intermediate models or the software has sufficient undo capabilities), and again, the evaluation of the results is left to the architect. The newly created models may not result in a radically new design. However, the generated alternatives may stimulate the designer to think of a new (and better) alternative solution. Alternatively, the play with the model may confirm to the architect that the current solution is the proper one to pursue. The entire process may take only minutes, yet create a large number of possibilities. The cost is low, the potential reward high. New processes and the new premium placed on analytic skills may begin to redefine the idea of creativity.

Conclusion

❏ The possible uses of digital media for architectural design have not all been discovered. Each architect is likely to find a method, or combination of methods, comfortable. Furthermore, as the capabilities of both hardware and software increase, new opportunities arise and the computing overhead required by easier-to-use interfaces is accommodated. It is clear, however, that to take advantage of these opportunities, all of the basic types of software (modeling, rendering, animation, painting, image processing, drafting, and illustration) must be available to the designer. Moving readily back and forth between applications is necessary. Almost everything discussed here is commercially available to architects now. The designer must be cautious, however. It is much too easy to create anything in a three-dimensional model or a two-dimensional collage. Issues of gravity and appropriateness of imagery should be considered. Common sense needs to be brought to the workstation by the architect.

One can read about the possibilities, but it is necessary to try to use digital media in order to make computers part of the design process. With practice comes proficiency. With comfort comes utility for design.

References

Arnheim, Rudolf. *Visual Thinking*. Berkeley, CA: University of California Press, 1974.

Arnheim, Rudolf. *The Dynamics of Architectural Form*. Berkeley, CA: University of California Press, 1977.

Goldman, Glenn. "Computer Graphics and Architectural Design." *Computer Graphics*, July, 25(3):174–177, 1991. [Additional contributors: Elizabeth Bollinger, Richard Norman, James Turner, M.S. Zdepski.]

Goldman, Glenn. "Reconstructions, Remakes and Sequels: Architecture in Motion Pictures." In *Design Computation: Collaboration, Reasoning, Pedagogy. Proceedings of the Association for Computer-Aided Design in Architecture Annual Conference*. Tucson, AZ, November 1996, pp. 11–21.

Goldman, Glenn. *Architectural Graphics: Traditional and Digital Communication*. Upper Saddle River, NJ: Prentice Hall, 1997.

Goldman, Glenn, and Hoon, Michael. "Digital Design in Architecture: First Light, Then Motion, and Now Sound." In *Re-Connecting. Proceedings of the Association for Computer-Aided Design in Architecture 14th Annual Conference*. St. Louis, MO, October 1994, pp. 27–37.

Goldman, Glenn, and Zdepski, M. Stephen. "Abstraction and Representation: Computer Graphics and Architectural Design." In *Computing in Design Education. Proceedings of the Association for Computer-Aided Design in Architecture 8th Annual Workshop*. Ann Arbor, MI, October 1988, pp. 205–215.

Goldman, Glenn, and Zdepski, M. Stephen. "The Three Dimensional Design Studio: Pre-Visualization and Dynamic Modeling." In *Debate and Dialogue, Architectural Design and Pedagogy. Proceedings of the Association of Collegiate Schools of Architecture National Conference*. Chicago, IL, March 1989, pp. 137–152.

Goldman, Glenn, and Zdepski, M. Stephen. "Twiddling, Tweaking and Tweening: Automatic Architecture." In *Architecture of* the In-Between. Proceedings of the Association of Collegiate Schools of Architecture National Conference. San Francisco, CA, March 1990, pp. 98–107.

Goldman, Glenn, and Zdepski, M. Stephen. "Image Sampling." In From Research to Practice. Proceedings of the Association for Computer-Aided Design in Architecture 10th Annual Conference. Bozeman, MT, October 1990, pp. 18–21.

McCullough, Malcolm. "Representation in the Computer Aided Design Studio." In Computing in Design Education. Proceedings of the Association for Computer-Aided Design in Architecture Annual Conference. Ann Arbor, MI, October 1988, pp. 163–174.

Mitchell, William J. "A New Agenda for Computer-Aided Architectural Design." In New Ideas and Directions for the 1990s. Proceedings of the Association for Computer-Aided Design in Architecture Annual Conference. Gainesville, FL, October 1989, pp. 27–43.

Zdepski, M. Stephen, and Goldman, Glenn. "Form, Color and Movement." In Integrating Computers into the Architectural Curriculum. Proceedings of the Association for Computer-Aided Design in Architecture 7th Annual Workshop. Raleigh, NC, October 1987, pp. 39–50.

A case study from the New York City–based firm Resolution: 4 Architecture involving design computing follows. (Project credits: Joseph Tanney and Robert Luntz, principals; Michael Andersen, project architect; Eric Fauerbach, Clay Collier, and Michael Syracuse, project team; David Freeland, case study layout.) (Visit Resolution: 4 Architecture's Web site at www.re4a.com.)

Resolution: 4 Architecture believes in architecture's ability to resonate with the human psyche, evoking and amplifying both emotional and intellectual responses. Acknowledging programmatic, economic, political, and social requirements, the firm seeks to establish a dialogue between the idealized and the pragmatic, the general and the specific. The development of this discourse through digital and drawn process allows for aesthetic

**McCann Erickson
20th Floor
Conference Center**

Representation and communication, the two central components of the science of advertising, formed the conceptual basis of the interior renovation for this worldwide advertising agency. The computer became a means for exploration of new representational possibilities between architect, client and their potential customers. Ideas communicated through the virtual realm have inspired provocative spatial investigations through the essential freedom allowed by digital media.

worms eye view

The simple existing sequence of spaces demanded a focus on each of the rooms as seperate spatial events; totemic elements rationalized by the simplicity of the strucural armature.

dining

Initial abstract wireframe studies explored the formal foundations of the project, structuring and filtering further investigations.

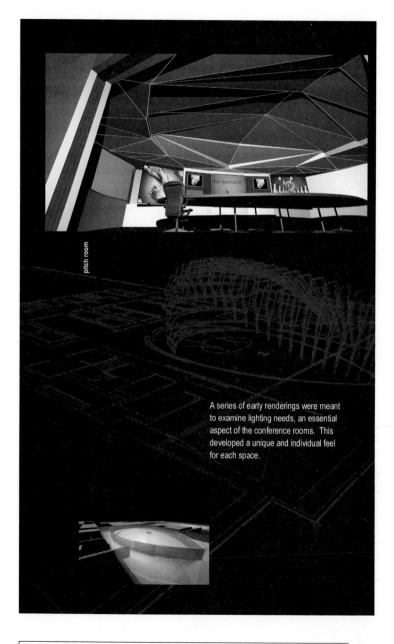

pitch room

A series of early renderings were meant to examine lighting needs, an essential aspect of the conference rooms. This developed a unique and individual feel for each space.

reception

More finished renderings became the projector for each spatial concept, facilitating an open dialogue between client and architect on programmatic intention, as well as an effective representation for construction.

animation key frames

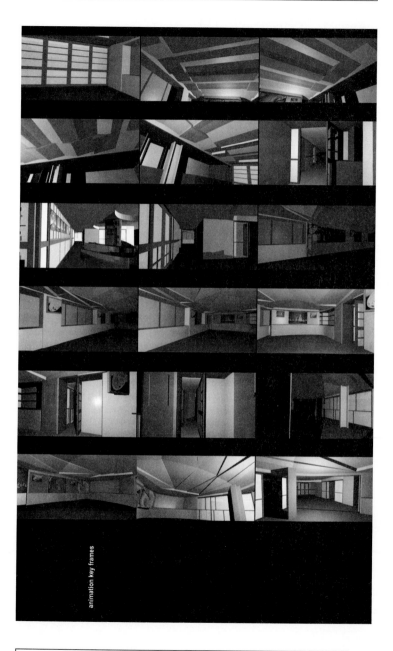

animation key frames

choices that are for the firm a rigorous reinterpretation of formal relationships. Analysis of existing context is a foundation used to formulate an intentional response that connects or disconnects the new intervention. It establishes relationships between form, use, and materials, and ultimately expresses an idea illustrative of the uniqueness of each client.

Construction Technology

"From the outset of every project, he keeps in mind the global vision and the nuts and bolts at the same time."
> —**Shunji Ishida, talking about Renzo Piano, with whom he has worked for almost 30 years**

❏ Knowledge of how buildings are assembled is obviously and critically important, but often overlooked (and therefore a potentially missed opportunity) in the most important beginning phases of the design process.

Designing in the office physically removes the architect from the action of construction. (See Supplement 4.3, which describes how one architect reconciles this issue.) Therefore, it is easy for the products of design—drawings and models—to become too much of an abstraction of reality, too much ends in themselves. This is a problem; the architectural design process is meaningless and myopic if it is not truly and completely informed by the construction process. And, as with all the other myriad influences impacting design, awareness of the building industry and its practices can support and define design excellence. Always keep in mind what that piece of cardboard or that crosshatched wall really represents, how it is going to get to the site, who is going to put it in place, and how it will be joined to the adjacent component.

Supplements 4.3 and 4.4, by Geoff Adams and John Brittingham, respectively, speak directly to the issue of the art of detailing and construction as integral to thinking about architectural design.

Thinking and Making
With Geoffrey Adams

Geoffrey Adams

SUPPLEMENT 4.3

Geoffrey C. Adams is an assistant professor of architecture at the University of New Mexico and maintains an independent practice in Albuquerque. He received a BA in studio art from the University of California at Davis in 1982 and an MArch from the University of New Mexico in 1992. After completing an internship with Antoine Predock in 1993, he has pursued design/build projects both in partnerships and independently.

❏ There exists a divide between the act of design and the craft of building in the architectural profession. Many aspects of this division are endemic to architectural practice: buildings are necessarily large, complex, and expensive endeavors requiring collaboration among disparate specialists. A seemingly natural collaboration exists between designer and maker. Yet it is precisely this divide between thinking about making and making that occupies a most treacherous terrain for the architect, for it is between the mental construct of a building (imagined, modeled, and drawn) and its physical presence that our success or failure is measured. Architecture potent in concept, rooted in place and time, measured in its economies, and fine in the service of its inhabitants relies, in the end, solely on its construction in material to bear witness to these attributes. The material envelope explicitly describes a spatial volume, modifies conditions of light and atmosphere, and creates a boundary condition in which the dialogue between the site and the situated resides. The thoughtful construction of this interface provides the physical means by which the designer controls these relationships and may elucidate the conceptual. The way in which materials are chosen and interwoven marks the precise location of the architectural act. The fidelity with which this traverse is navigated is an essential link in the continuum between an idea and its realization as a physical presence.

In this brief essay I propose to investigate the nexus between designing and building by discussing an ongoing project of mine, the construction of two studios (Fig. 4.20). Specifically, I'm interested in ways of thinking about making that come out of

FIGURE 4.20
Work in progress: backyard studios under construction. (© Geoffrey Adams.)

making. This is necessarily an incremental process that revolves around the physical presence of the work. It is an opportunity that I afford myself as a designer. By limiting scale and expense, one can expand time and allow for inefficiencies that would otherwise be intolerable. This project serves as a lens to focus previous efforts and project discoveries about thinking and building into future work.

This work evolves from concerns that have preoccupied my thinking regarding architecture for some time: (1) a deep-seated affinity for the elegance of economy, the judicious construction of a few carefully chosen common industrially produced materials; (2) a desire to find order and rhythm in the module of these materials, to take what the materials have to offer as an ordering device; and (3) a means to make the method of construction explicit, to expose to the eye the beauty of how the thing is made. In concert with these concerns is a group of no less important practical issues—that the project be built by a single person with idiosyncratic construction skills (i.e., myself) and that the project adhere to a somewhat austere budget ($10,000 for materials).

The North Valley of Albuquerque, New Mexico, is a landscape that can be read as a series of cultural overlays made possible by the life-giving waters of the Rio Grande. Located in a rural 1950s subdivision with access to a gravity-fed agricultural irrigation system, a verdant oasis of exotic flora is maintained. The tenuous nature of this landscape, now engulfed by a sprawling, thirsty western city, is manifest in the two-studio project. Built on piers, which allow flood irrigation waters to flow freely beneath, these lightweight bolt-together structures are designed to be disassembled and transported, itinerant as the landscape they inhabit. The buildings are made of four materials: (1) cast-in-place concrete for pier construction; (2) wood for framing, sheathing, and millwork; (3) galvanized steel for sheathing and break metal; and (4) glass for fenestration. With the exception of the concrete, the materials are imported from some distance, and while their industrial production and relative lightness makes building with them economically feasible, they also reveal the structures as exotic inhabitants. Like the flora, they are transported from another place and rely on human intervention for their existence in this locale.

Emulating the rhythm of the trees lining the irrigation ditch, five redwood frames deployed on four-foot centers set the structural module. This affords a number of efficiencies: (1) the number of primary supports allows the building load to be comfortably supported by small bell-shaped piers (16 inches in diameter at the base), facilitating excavation with manual posthole diggers; (2) the running of sinusoidal steel sheathing horizontally and perpendicular to the redwood columns creates structural rigidity (in the long dimension) and serves as a cross-frame that allows a thin plywood skin (½ inch) to be through-bolted, sandwiching a layer of rigid insulation (the resultant stress skin structure is very strong in relation to its weight); (3) the module provides for the logical exposure of the redwood structure to the interior, each module being filled with a single piece of sheet material allowing a simple edge detail of a J-metal strip to finish all vertical intersections; and (4) the resultant wall system protects the vulnerable wood elements from the harsh assault of the New Mexico climate, allowing the steel siding to act as an exterior bark protecting the fragile interior heartwood (Fig. 4.21).

Terminating the wall system is a corner detail that evolved from several efforts. Typical metal building corner details

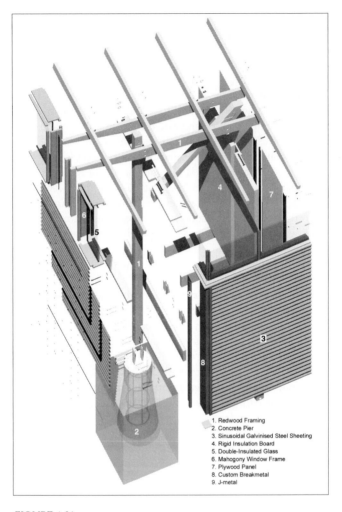

1. Redwood Framing
2. Concrete Pier
3. Sinusoidal Galvinised Steel Sheeting
4. Rigid Insulation Board
5. Double-Insulated Glass
6. Mahogany Window Frame
7. Plywood Panel
8. Custom Breakmetal
9. J-metal

FIGURE 4.21
Exploded axonometric showing composite construction of studios. (© Geoffrey Adams.)

involve a rather large (6-inch) corner closure screwed to the outside of the metal sheathing. While serviceable, this detail has a visual heaviness that runs contrary to the inherent lightness of the steel siding. Inspired by Mies van der Rohe and Glenn Murcutt, I looked for a way to turn the corner simply with visual balance. My first efforts, while visually derivative of my models, were unsatisfying. It was a difficult corner to construct, as it was built out of too many pieces and relied on hidden means of questionable effectiveness to ensure weathertightness. The experience of building exponentially improved the ensuing efforts, leveraging design investigations and critical revisions based on the salient issues of making rather than mimicry. The solution devised is a composite built-up corner consisting of two Js and an L of light-gauge steel break metal. It is weathertight, is inexpensive to manufacture, serves as a framing member, and facilitates installation of the metal sheathing (Fig. 4.22).

Another example of an iterative hands-on approach to designing and making involves the connection between the window frame and the structural post. The desire to expose this meeting to both the interior and the exterior led to a single spacer board bridging the 1-inch gap formed by the roof structure. This solution had a couple of inherent flaws: (1) the tight tolerances required to build and fit the elements together and (2) infiltration—even when well fitted, the shrinking and swelling of the wood due to changes in moisture and temperature opened cracks. Only after building the connection and observing the performance was I able to develop a suitable solution. A simple rabbit let in on either side of the spacer board allows for the insertion of a closed-cell backer rod that has enough elasticity to close whatever change may take place in the gap. This detail also reduces the tolerances for fitting, giving the work a reasonable margin of error. Further, the detail is explicitly exposed to view. One can see not only how the building is constructed but also how when materials meet they must be given a way to expand and contract (Fig. 4.23).

Tracking the exact path of my thinking in developing even a single detail in these buildings is impossible and in the end would become a more or less boring disclosure of my limitations as a

FIGURE 4.22
Detail of corner construction. (© Geoffrey Adams.)

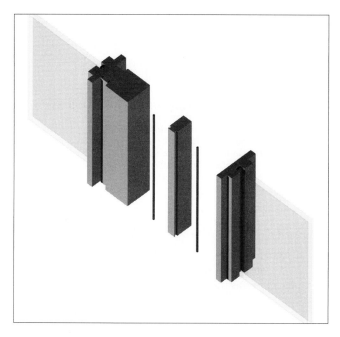

FIGURE 4.23
Detail of column and window connection. (© Geoffrey Adams.)

designer and builder. By presenting specific intentions and observations of this work, I attempt to cast some light on my experience of the relationship between design and making. The development of the intricate interdependencies that make up a building blossoms with the opportunity to test design ideas directly. Immediate redesign is possible—in fact, unavoidable. Hammers, saws, and drills coexist with pencil, paper, and computer and begin to blur the distinction between designing and building. That this approach runs against the grain of commercial architectural practice does not of necessity devalue it. While finding space for thoughtful experimentation in architecture may be difficult, I have found the rewards indispensable and critical to the practice of both thinking and making.

Tectonics: Art/Techne
With John Brittingham

John Brittingham

John C. Brittingham, associate professor of architecture at Montana State University, received a Bachelor of Arts in art history from Bowdoin College, and a Master of Architecture from Harvard University. He has worked with Peter Eisenman, Machado-Silvetti, and Antoine Predock. John is a practicing architect. Prior to teaching in Montana, he taught at the University of New Mexico and the University of Texas at Austin. John's current writing and design research are concerned with relationships of architecture and landscape.

SUPPLEMENT 4.4

"God is in the details."

—Mies van der Rohe

❏ The term *tectonic* is Greek in origin and is derived from the word *tekton*, meaning carpenter or builder. The Greek verb *tikto* (to produce) means the simultaneous existence of both art and craft. Further references are found in Greek, where *tikto* alludes to the art of construction. *Merriam-Webster's Collegiate Dictionary* defines tectonics as something pertaining to building or construction. Further, the dictionary notes that tectonics is the art of constructing with utility as well as taste. The word *tekton* eventually leads to the concept of the master builder or *architectus* in the Renaissance, as described by Vitruvius and Alberti, and systematically continues to appear throughout the Beaux Arts tradition and the Arts and Crafts movement under varying guises. In the 1800s, notions of the tectonic were refined, and the term now refers to a complete system binding all the parts of a building into a single whole.

Techne is the Greek word for art or skill. It has been defined by Martin Heidegger as something that is "poetic and revealing," and further suggests that the act of revealing "makes something palpable according to knowledge of something that has precedent, something that is 'the same' as the thing to be made." Hence, the term *tectonic* comes to mean the poetics of the craft of construction, or art/techne (art making art), and appears as far back as 2500 years ago with a clear marriage of aesthetics and technology.

The unusual common ground in this lengthy history begins to suggest that the role of the detail might be reconsidered as a generator that has been traditionally ascribed to plans. Elusive in the traditional sense, the architectural detail might be thought of instead as pragmatically solving a construction problem of joinery, but more importantly it might be considered as a microrendering of the idea behind the architecture.

Details can be much more than subordinate elements that merely resolve a problem. They can in fact be regarded as the most distilled element of meaning in architecture. Detail should be treated as a kind of tectonic condensation embodying the whole in the part where the whole is greater than the sum of its parts. When thought of in this way, detail begins to operate simultaneously in interlocking dialectical realms: the theoretical and the empirical, the conceptual and the pragmatic, the artistic and the technolog-

FIGURE 4.24
The story begins with the precise positioning of a ranch sign relative to the threshold of a cattle guard and the distant horizon. (a) The sign is placed such that when one crosses the threshold of entry to the ranch, the subtracted pattern from the steel plate aligns with the horizon. The decision to use a subtractive process in the rendering of the steel plate as well as the letters in the concrete wall was dictated by the erosive quality of the landscape.

FIGURE 4.24 (Continued)
(b) Just as the distant caprock appears to balance precariously on the ground underneath it, the 1000-pound steel plate reacts sympathetically with the concrete wall that supports it, with a continuous weld plate serving as the connection. (Courtesy of John C. Brittingham, Architect.)

ical. In sum, the conceptual identification of detail is with the making of the joint between things and the recognition that details themselves can impose order on the whole through their own order. A good analogy is that details can be seen as words composing a sentence. As the selection of words and styles gives character to a sentence, the selection of details and their manifestation gives character to the architecture of buildings. From this standpoint, architecture becomes the art of the appropriate selection of details in the telling of the story behind an idea.

Architecture is always faced with the challenge of developing a whole out of innumerable details—of various functions and forms, materials and joints—for the points where surfaces intersect and different materials meet. These formal details determine the sensitive transitions within larger proportions of the building. The details establish the formal rhythm, the building's finely fractionated scale. Details express what the basic idea of the design requires at the relevant point in the object: belonging or separation, tension or lightness, friction, solidity, fragility. Details, when they are successful, are not mere decoration. They do not distract or entertain, as nothing can be added or taken away. Each and every component is essential to the final outcome, as they all lead to an understanding of the whole of which they are an inherent part.

In accepting the notion of detail as a microrendering of the idea behind architecture, it is useful to restate that architecture is an art as well as a profession. Appropriate and sensitive detailing are the most important vehicles for avoiding failure in both dimensions of the architectural profession—the ethical and the aesthetic. This is because of the understanding generated by the detail as joint. Architecture is an art because its charge in practice is not only to provide shelter but also to put together spaces and materials in a meaningful and sensitive manner. This happens at the intersection of both formal and actual joints. The joint becomes the site, or opportunity, for the fertile detail and is the place where both the construction and the meaning of architecture take place.

Not only can a building's conception determine its form, but also notions of construction and detail can directly inform the conception. Conception and construction can conspire together to give rise to form. If one looks at architecture and tectonics in this way, what surfaces is investigations into the qualities latent in the architectural artifact—of materials and their assembly, of site and program. Meaning and value become vested in the artifact—the building, the detail.

By acknowledging that the nature of things is best described as a series of relationships developed through interconnectedness, one verifies that the part should be related to the whole. Detailing should always be regarded as an asset or opportunity instead of a liability. If we as architects take the time to explore the site of tectonics in the making of architecture, and it becomes integral to the design process instead of being regarded as a necessary afterthought, we will by default empower ourselves with the ability to distinguish ourselves simultaneously as artists and problem solvers. The art of detailing is really the joining of materials, elements, components, and building parts in a functional, appropriate, and aesthetic manner. Hence, the understanding and execution of details should constitute one of the fundamental processes by which architectural practice and theories evolve.

FIGURE 4.25

This project, being constructed in the summer of 2000, is titled "The Gathering House." The site in Throckmorton County, Texas, is situated in an area rich in game habitat and highly productive ranching country. This building's hybrid concept is derived from two types typical of the area: the cookshack and the hunting blind. The tectonic expressions of these two types are radically different: one is a load-bearing limestone construction, while the other is typically an elevated, porous wood construction with exposed connections. A detailing dialogue between elements in compression and those in shear, or tension, informs the project. (Courtesy of John C. Brittingham, Architect.)

FIGURE 4.25 (Continued)

In conclusion, it is interesting to note that the original root of the word *art* is the Indo-European word for *joint,* and as Louis Kahn so poetically stated in *Light is the Theme* (Kimbell Art Foundation, 1994), "The joint is the beginning of ornament and that must be distinguished from decoration, which is simply applied. Ornament is the adoration of the joint."

Endnotes

Alter, Kevin, et al. *Construction Intention Detail.* Zurich: Artemis, 1994.

Frampton, Kenneth. "Rappel a l'Ordre: The Case for the Tectonic." In Nesbitt, Kate (ed.), *Theorizing a New Agenda for Architecture.* New York: Princeton Architectural Press, 1996.

Frampton, Kenneth, and Cava, John. *Studies in Tectonic Culture.* Cambridge, MA: MIT Press, 1995.

Frascari, Marco. "The Tell-the-Tale Detail." In Nesbitt, Kate (ed.), *Theorizing a New Agenda for Architecture.* New York: Princeton Architectural Press, 1996.

Gregotti, Vittorio. "The Exercise of Detailing." In Nesbitt, Kate (ed.), *Theorizing a New Agenda for Architecture.* New York: Princeton Architectural Press, 1996.

Hartoonian, Gevork. *Ontology of Construction.* Cambridge, UK: Cambridge University Press, 1994.

Norberg-Schulz, Christian. "Heidegger's Thinking on Architecture." *Perspecta: The Yale Architectural Journal* 20, 1983.

Zumthor, Peter. "A Way of Looking at Things." *Architecture and Urbanism*, Special Edition, February 1998.

Working with Constructors
With Raymond Worley

❏ Construction technology and detailing, to some extent (depending on the exigencies of a specific project), is a subspecialty within the field of architecture. Atlanta-based architect George Heery, FAIA, offers a different perspective and states: "The construction technology frontier—where practical, cost-effective construction methodologies are to be found—lies with specialty subcontractors and building product manufacturers, not with the architect, engineer, or even general contractor." It is the role of the architect to know where and how to get appropriate information and how to apply that information to the circumstance, communicate it, and finally, coordinate it with other construction trades. (See Supplement 4.5.)

Robert Singleton, a builder in central Florida, believes that architects must somehow acquire field experience; a thorough appreciation of construction techniques, which of course have regional variations, is essential to the success of a project. Singleton says, "An architect has to be flexible. Take full advantage of a well-seasoned constructor's knowledge and insight! Listening to and respecting their special point of view is another means to understand construction and hence move toward excellence in design."

Nagle, Hartray & Associates, Ltd. in Chicago maintain that the best decorative and cost-effective details are derived from construction technology. Of course, there are other stances, for example the use of ornamental details to convey or recall a particular image that may mask actual construction details.

Raymond Worley

Raymond A. Worley is executive vice president of Morse Diesel International. Morse Diesel, founded in 1936, ranks among the largest U.S. construction firms. Worley, a 40-year industry veteran, oversaw construction of Chicago's Sears Tower, one of the world's tallest buildings.

SUPPLEMENT 4.5

Building a Foundation of Teamwork

❏ Every building project has three common elements: goals, time, and money. Meeting the owner's programmatic objectives within the established schedule and budget requires an understanding of the construction process as well as teamwork between the architect and the constructor. (Because so many terms describe contractual arrangements with the builder—*general contractor, construction manager,* and so on—we have elected to use the word *constructor* throughout this discussion.)

A successful project depends on the efficient utilization of materials, methods, and manpower to transform design into reality. The more thought the architect gives to this process, the more smoothly it will run.

In designing a project, the architect should examine the most challenging aspects first, allowing time for solving problems, ordering special materials, and assembling equipment and personnel. Consider how structural elements will meet. Two walls join—how? The flooring joists come together—where? The reality of construction will inevitably affect the aesthetics of design; plan accordingly.

Cost factors, too, have an impact on the realization of design. Achieving design intent within budget constraints takes pragmatic creativity. Currently, the catchphrase in cost management is *value engineering*—which is not synonymous with cutting corners. Rather, it means determining what systems and materials will prove most cost-effective over the life, and for the purpose, of the project. For example, a bargain-priced HVAC system may need frequent, costly repairs, while a more expensive alternative may pay for itself in fuel efficiency. Spectacular illumination may play a critical role in establishing a building's identity, but expensive lighting fixtures in stairwells and machine rooms only burn money that could be used to better effect in public areas.

The project construction team can offer valuable assistance in identifying opportunities for value engineering and other cost savings. Because constructors have daily, hands-on experience with purchasing, they know the latest materials and prices. Constructors can also help hold down the bottom line through scheduling techniques. A large part of any project budget lies in personnel requirements. By developing strategies to use time and personnel efficiently, the constructor can achieve significant savings.

Clearly, to make the most of these opportunities, the architect should involve the constructor early in the project. Teamwork is critical. All too often, the relationship between architect and constructor takes an adversarial tone. Yet the two are mutually dependent: the builder on the designer for concept, and the designer on the builder for execution. To work effectively together, both must recognize that expertise is found throughout the construction field, from heavy hitters in the architectural arena to heavy-equipment operators on the job site.

Only by working in concert can the team achieve the highest benefit for the project and the client. Only with teamwork can the architect and constructor manage the project's schedule and budget to reach the owner's goals.

Materials

❏ Selection and application of materials should be considered an important part of the design process. (See Supplements 4.6 and 4.7.) Certainly there are inherent color and textural qualities across a range of finishes and materials that would enrich work regardless of budget. Consider a materials palette in relation to typology (research what is typically used and why) and

Sketches

locality (use of readily available, indigenous materials can be economical and tie the building to its site, and local climatic factors may play a major role in material selection to enhance weathering properties and energy conservation). The design concept itself has a bearing on materials. Much innovation is possible in specification and use; for example, take a precast concrete T and turn it sideways to form a sculptural parking screen or a bench.

Note also that materials include interior finishes. To reiterate an idea from Chapter 3, indoor-outdoor transitions can be controlled—blurred or contrasted—by extending or changing materials from inside to outside. It is self-evident that more durable and easy-to-maintain materials should be chosen for areas of frequent use (i.e., circulation paths). Also, areas can be zoned by using similar finishes. Other selection criteria range from the obvious to the subtle and should include acoustical characteristics. Interior finishes can end up inflating construction budgets perhaps more than any other single factor, so be judicious in the use of extravagant and expensive materials!

The Nature of Materials
With Terry Patterson

Terry Patterson

Terry L. Patterson, AIA, professor of architecture at the University of Oklahoma, is an expert on the use of materials in architecture. Refer to his relevant and important book, Construction Materials for Architects and Designers *(Prentice Hall, 1990), in which reasoning and conclusions regarding the nature of wood, masonry, steel, and concrete are explored in detail. Patterson is also the author of* Frank Lloyd Wright and the Meaning of Materials *(Van Nostrand Reinhold, 1994).*

❑ Building materials have properties that manifest themselves visually. Consequently, they project a discrete image that may be compatible or incompatible with other visual goals of architectural design. Building character derived from functional demands, geometrical relationships, site characteristics, environmental concerns, artistic concepts, or other influences will be

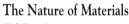

embellished or diluted by the separate message from the building's materials. For example, if general harmony is promoted, the materials may reflect discord. If chaos is desired, the materials may embody order. If clarity and sureness of purpose are intended, the materials might declare uncertainty and ambivalence. Understanding the relationship between material properties and their visual impact lets the designer manipulate their contribution to the architectural goals with certainty. Regardless of one's theoretical persuasion, control of all visual aspects is imperative for a predictable cause-effect relationship in the design.

To maintain control of material expression, one must understand a material's spirit. Only then may building form and detailing purposefully express or violate the nature of the materials. Sensitivity to materials in the broadest sense does not require designing within their nature. This is only one philosophical attitude, which, like any stylistic approach to design, does not have inherent correctness or incorrectness but only cyclical popularity. It is haphazard and accidental relationships between material expression and the larger aesthetic order that demonstrate insensitivity to materials and, consequently, a loss of control over part of the design.

Material nature is defined by four categories of properties: form, strength, durability, and workability. A material's form is linear, planar, or blocklike. Its section is simple or complex. Form is precise or imprecise. Architecture that expresses the essence of material form will express these characteristics in its structure, connections, surfaces, and edges. Expressing strength involves a demonstration of the stress-resisting ability (tension, compression, or bending) most representative of each material's limitations or potential. Consequently, a building's sedate or heroic expressions of strength can match or oppose the natural tendency of its materials to be structurally sedate or heroic. The expression of a material's durability requires its weathering ability to be clearly challenged or accommodated. Expressing the protective systems for the less durable materials is a positive demonstration of low durability. Workability, being the ease of reshaping a material, tends to oppose the expression of a material's basic form. When the expressions of properties are in conflict (which they are in several circumstances), another level of judgment is required of the designer. The appropriate degree of balance between the expressions of opposing properties must be determined and justified given the material context.

Frank Lloyd Wright is known for his sensitivity to building materials, through both his claims and his architecture. For the most part, his use of materials verifies a respect for their basic forms, strength potentials, and even durability limitations—his leaky roofs notwithstanding. His rejection of workability as a property suitable for expression in both words and practice was an attitude compatible with his focus on basic material form.

His brick, stone, and concrete block, for example, tended to express the blockiness of masonry in massing and detail. Brick thickness and rectangularity are often emphasized (Robie House pilasters, Morris Gift Shop detailing). Stone's compact shape and roughness is typically featured by projected units (Fallingwater, Jacobs II House). Concrete block's mass and rectangularity are often demonstrated in stepped forms and projecting units (Ennis and other block houses). His masonry typically demonstrates its affinity for compression in deep arches (Dana House, Heurtley House), in extensive direct compressive contact with the earth (Fallingwater, Taliesin North), in the stability of massing (Jacobs II House, Winslow House), and in its setting on lintels (or apparent lintels) at openings instead of setting on "air" (Robie House, Martin House).

Laying brick on a broad stone base and capping it with thick overhanging stone copings (Robie House, Martin House) framed the units in a protective sandwich. Philosophically at least, the walls are therefore safe from the deleterious effects of moisture from above and below. Thus a limitation of masonry durability (the vulnerability of the joints) is visually expressed regardless of the actual inspiration for the detailing. As is typical for all of Wright's materials, the basic forms of his masonry are not extensively worked (reshaped), which goes mostly unnoticed until an obtuse-angled corner causes the right-angled brick to yield up a texture of partially lapped units (Hanna House). His occasional violations of material compatibilities remind us that Wright was always sympathetic to the visual needs of the circumstances even if they forced a material to do something that it did not want to do. Hidden steel, for example, sometimes helps his masonry and wood achieve remarkable spans that they could never attempt on their own.

Whether or not a designer believes that building materials are central to design, he or she must control their visual impact so as to avoid compromising other visual goals. This requires consideration of the materials' expressive ramifications in all phases of design from schematics through detailing.

Using Common Materials in Uncommon Ways
With Christopher Jofeh

SUPPLEMENT 4.7

Christopher Jofeh

Chris Jofeh, a civil and structural engineer, is director of Ove Arup & Partners' Cardiff Bay Office. Prior to joining the Cardiff Bay branch in 1991, he served as structural principal in Los Angeles for three years. Chris is the author of Structural Use of Glass in Buildings *(Institution of Structural Engineers, 1999). He leads multidisciplinary design teams and has been responsible for the engineering design for a wide range of projects including the Arup Office Building, Cardiff Bay; the Millennium Dome, London (as planning supervisor); and the Terminal Building, Stansted Airport, London.*

Introduction

❑ For many of us, progress means using new materials for old tasks. Ashby (1997) describes the evolution of the design of an everyday object—the body of a domestic vacuum cleaner. At the beginning of the twentieth century its primary materials were wood, canvas, leather, and rubber. By midcentury it was mostly mild steel, and by the end of the century it was made primarily of molded polymers. Ships have progressed from timber to iron to steel to plastic. Airplanes have followed a similar pattern.

In contrast, the theme of this brief essay is that progress can equally be demonstrated in those projects in which old materials are used in new, uncommon ways. Particular technical solutions exist in a broader context. We become familiar with ways of using materials and take them for granted without questioning their validity when circumstances have changed. Sometimes the circumstances allow or encourage a fresh look that leads to a different kind of progress.

The examples that follow deal mostly with some recent building structures in which, by thinking afresh about material properties, by being able to analyze beyond the conventional, by employing intuition and curiosity, and sometimes by taking advantage of improvements in the manufacturing techniques of the materials themselves, creative designers have used common materials in uncommon ways. In doing so they have enriched the built environment.

Ceramics

❑ Ceramic structures have been around for thousands of years: the pyramids in Egypt, the Great Wall of China, and the Parthenon in Athens are all ceramic structures. These are all objects that weigh hundreds, thousands, or even millions of tons and don't move an inch.

Weighing at the most a few tens of kilograms, vitreous ceramics are in everyday use in huge quantities in plates, cups, tiles, and bricks.

Fifty years ago, no one would have predicted that ceramics would be used in place of metals in many demanding applications. Modern developments in high-performance engineering ceramics have led to the use of ceramics in cutting tools, artificial joints (to replace worn-out human ones), engines, turbines, and body armor.

Brick and Stone

Opera House, Glyndebourne, U.K. This new opera house is, for architectural and acoustic reasons, massively constructed in load-bearing masonry. The design of the external wall began to develop as a series of flat arches spanning onto brick piers, and it soon became clear that it would be very difficult to introduce movement joints, as is common in modern brickwork. To avoid the joints, engineer Ove Arup & Partners and architects Michael and Patty Hopkins decided to return to the old tradition of lime-putty mortar. This took the team out of the realm of modern codes or even conventional good practice. After much testing, analysis and historic comparison, engineering judgment allowed the omission of the joints in the brickwork. The structure was built and has performed well.

Inland Revenue Building, Nottingham, U.K. This building was designed by the same team that created Glyndebourne's opera house. Instead of walls, at Nottingham, the vertical structure is load-bearing brick piers that support folded plate floors. Expansion was not a concern, but strength and robustness during the handling of the piers (which were prefabricated off site) was an issue, so a more conventional mortar was more appropriate.

New Parliamentary Building, London. Also designed by Arup and Hopkins, this building uses load-bearing piers (and folded plate concrete floors), but this time the piers are sandstone, with a few in granite. The early test programs left considerable doubt in the designers' minds about the properties of the stone but did establish the relationship between cube strength and design strength. They were also of benefit in identifying the failure mode of the stone and the possible consequences of irregularities in the form of the blocks.

Load testing of full-scale prototypes was not feasible, so the engineers had to proceed on the basis of their limited data. Confidence in their analysis and belief in the precision with which the blocks were cut and assembled were sufficient to permit the engineers to design a building with a different structural system from traditional stone buildings, and with higher working stresses.

Glass

Parc de La Villette, Paris. The Serres at Parc de La Villette (architect: RFR; engineer: RFR and Ove Arup & Partners) owe much to the late engineer Peter Rice of Ove Arup & Partners. They are a series of glass-clad enclosures, supported by a structure of remarkable clarity.

From his study of the brittle nature of glass, Rice decided that it was crucial that the design of a structure using glass should not impose forces or movements on the glass that could not be predicted. In the jargon beloved of structural engineers, the structure should be fully determinate.

This led to an extraordinary structure beautifully described by Rice and Dutton (1995), in which each pane of glass is suspended by a pair of bolted connections from the pane above, with the uppermost pane suspended from the steelwork by a single central bolt.

Much of the façade architecture and engineering of the years that followed was characterized by designs that sought to emulate what Rice's team had achieved. All this came about because an engineer thought about a traditional material in a new way.

The Millennium Dome, London. The British scientist A.A. Griffith is responsible for our basic understanding of how cracks propagate, and this is described in many materials and fracture mechanics textbooks. In a pioneering series of experiments, Griffith showed that thin glass fibers, if produced in a way that discouraged the initiation of even the smallest (subvisible) cracks, had tensile strengths of around 750,000 psi (5,100 N/mm^2). By comparison, the steels generally used in the beams and columns of modern buildings have tensile strengths of about one-tenth of that figure.

The Millennium Dome (architect: Richard Rogers Partnership; engineer: Buro Happold) is the latest and biggest structure to use glass fibers in its construction. Its skin is a fabric of woven glass fibers coated in Teflon.

A material traditionally used for windows and drinking vessels has been used for the last 25 years as a high-performance architectural fabric.

Sight Screen Spanning 15 Meters, London. In the design of a law office in London, it was decided to incorporate a sight screen within the atrium in order to provide greater privacy for clients on opposite sides of the glass-walled atrium. The architects wanted a 15-meter-long, slender, ribbonlike screen, which they expected would need to be suspended by cables from high-level beams.

By using the materials selection techniques described by Ashby, I deduced that the structural material most suitable to span this width unaided was glass. A simple ceramic frit or a translucent interlayer would provide enough diffusion to ensure privacy.

Slate

The Wales Millennium Centre, Cardiff. The Wales Millennium Centre (see Fig. 4.26) is a major new multifunctional arts project under construction (2000–2002) in the capital city of Wales. At its heart is an 1800-seat lyric theatre, designed to provide a wonderful acoustic environment for both opera and for musicals that use amplified sound. Percy Thomas Partnership is the architect, and Ove Arup & Partners are the engineers.

The 20-meter (76 feet)-tall main elevations of the building are clad in stone, but it is not stone cladding in the traditional or even the modern sense. The chosen material is slate from quarries in North Wales. The slate used is not thin roofing slate but large blocks, generated as a by-product of the manufacture of roofing slates.

Figure 4.27 shows a mock-up of how the walls will look. Much careful design development has led to a simple design in which the slate blocks, embedded in a soft mortar, provide the outer skin of a cavity wall. A variety of different structural solutions enable the slate walls to span up to 16 meters (52 feet). The outcome will be a powerful romantic appearance for a building that strongly expresses its Welsh identity.

Steel

Millennium Footbridge, London. On May 9, 2000, Her Majesty the Queen inaugurated London's first new crossing of the River Thames in over 100 years. The Millennium Footbridge (see Fig.

FIGURE 4.26
Wales Millennium Centre, Cardiff, Wales. Interior rendering (a) shows the main concourse with shops, bars, and cafes supporting small-scale performances and exhibitions. (Courtesy of Percy Thomas Partnership, architect.)

FIGURE 4.27
Wales Millennium Centre. Mock-up of wall of slate blocks embedded in a soft mortar. (Courtesy of Percy Thomas Partnership, architect.)

4.28) spans between St. Paul's Cathedral on one side and the new Tate Modern art gallery on the other. In 1750 London had only one bridge. It now has 28.

The design of the Millennium Footbridge is the product of a remarkable collaboration between architect Foster and Partners, sculptor Sir Anthony Caro, and engineer Ove Arup & Partners, and is described by Norman Foster as "a blade of light."

Its principal structural material is steel, a material that has been used in bridges for many years. What is different about this bridge is the extraordinary flatness of its suspension cables. This has been made possible by a creative design team playing to its strengths, the use of very-high-strength steel cables, and three-dimensional nonlinear structural analytical techniques that provided the certainty to allow the design to be pared to the minimum.

FIGURE 4.28
Millennium Footbridge, London. (Courtesy of Ove Arup & Partners, Engineers.)

Conclusion

❏ For more examples of innovative uses of common materials, see Dunster (1996). Do not underestimate the role of intuition. Sometimes the new use of a traditional material can be achieved by the designers simply thinking their way through the problems. At other times physical testing and the power of modern structural engineering analytical software are required to provide the confidence to build.

A novel design requires an approach that is based on a clear understanding of the problem itself rather than the rules embodied in codes of practice. It also requires the engineer to face the possibility of going down a blind alley. This holds true whether the materials are new or traditional.

References and Further Reading

Ashby, Michael F. *Materials Selection in Mechanical Design.* Oxford, UK: Butterworth-Heinemann, 1997.

Dunster, David (ed.). *Arups on Engineering*. London: Ernst & Sohn, 1996.

Jofeh, Christopher G.H. (consultant). *Structural Use of Glass in Buildings*. London: Institution of Structural Engineers, December 1999.

Rice, Peter, and Dutton, Hugh. *Structural Glass*, 2d ed. London: Spon, 1995.

Color
With Deborah Sussman

❏ Ricardo Legorreta describes his fascinating approach to using color in the design process: "I do not say I will make a wall and paint it red. I say I will make something red and it may be a wall."

The wonderful world of color and texture is at the architect's disposal, another potentially powerful (and relatively inexpensive) factor to plug into the design equation, once again in support of project goals. Sometimes (but not always) there is more to life than gray and white! This can be tied in with a materials selection; certainly the two should not be considered independently. Alas, as with aesthetic criteria, there are no rules for developing a successful color scheme. And try not to consider it only as decoration or something to apply after the design is developed. Color, like any other element, should be part of an integrated and multidisciplinary approach to the design process.

Legorreta reinforces the point by suggesting that color is not simply an adjunct to form making. Rather, "it is a fundamental element." He continues, in an interview in *Architectural Record* (May 2000), by stating that color dramatizes form, turns walls into paintings, and stirs emotions. He gathers elements from the building site—rocks, soil, even vegetation—to evoke a feeling in color specific to the location.

Deborah Sussman has commented on collaborating with architects: "The architect may want to separate one form from another or to have the envelope read differently from the structure." The sources of her color schemes, as in one of her projects described in *Architecture* (January 1992), are quite compelling. Chicago Place on North Michigan Avenue, for example, was based on the "cultural heritage of Chicago," including a "color palette from the works of Louis Sullivan." (Sussman elaborates on her work in Supplement 4.8.)

Deborah Sussman

Noted graphic designer and color consultant Deborah Sussman, of Sussman/Prejza & Company, Inc., Los Angeles, writes this essay on the use of color in architecture. The firm's work has been published extensively, including a profile in Graphis *(September/October 1992).*

❏ Color in the built environment plays a powerful—if often unrecognized—role. Color is always there, even when it seems to be absent. Color can evoke memory; it can be a metaphor; it is able to arouse the emotions, stimulating pleasure, comfort, curiosity, confusion, and even anger.

Color is a companion to structure, and it is always affected by and in turn affecting light. It can express the dynamics of a building's structure. It can also perform a provocative and challenging role when interacting with structure, massing, and volume. There can be irony in the use of color in architecture. In practical terms, color often plays a role by identifying architectural components as well as by helping users find their way around. Manipulation of color in the practical manner can be studied and learned.

However, the experience of color (reactions to and selection of it) is very personal. Almost everyone seems to dislike certain colors and love others—unanimity is out of the question.

As Josef Albers taught, color is relative: relative to what is around it, how big it is, how much of it is used (a question of scale), what material it is put on. Also, one's memory of color while moving through an environment affects one's perception of color. In other words, time plays as much of a role as space, light, volume, quantity, and all the other factors that influence perception of color.

To be able to manipulate color as fully as possible, feel free and adventurous when experimenting. Applied colors are infi-

SUPPLEMENT 4.8

nite in number, whereas colors of natural building materials—stone, metal, wood, brick, and so on—are limited. The juxtaposition of both manufactured and available colors can yield the joy of discovery forever. It is interesting to consider the use of color throughout history and observe how radically it can differ in different hands at various times, and how valid such radically different approaches can be. Consider the "absence" of color in the work of Mies van der Rohe and in the International Style he pioneered, versus the personal, cultural, and emotive colored statements of the Mexicans Barragan and Legorreta. In each case, color is part of what the architecture is about. In simplified terms, Mies is about clarity of structure and abstract universal form. Color is a by-product of structure and is handled similarly anywhere in the world. By contrast, the Mexican architects use color to speak about their particular culture and their personal statements as architects and as artists. In each of these cases, the palette is fairly consistent over time.

In working with many architects for several decades, I have dealt with an interesting and provocative range of attitudes. Some deal with color largely as an adjunct to structure, avoiding any references to history, building type, or story. Others embrace the emotive, graphic, or evocative qualities of color. Many look to cultures where color plays a major role in the urban fabric. Color can be so integral to a city that its very name is inseparable from its origin, as in *siena*.

Finally, what matters when working with color is conviction, the knowledge that one has engaged with it as fully as possible, that one has emerged from the creative struggle with a feeling of rightness. Then one's choices have the power to move others.

Building Systems Integration

❑ The creation of architecture is a multidisciplinary endeavor and a collaborative effort on anything but a tiny scale. The ancient "master builder" definition of the architect no longer applies, due to the complexities of design and construction and to constantly evolving new technologies. Obviously, this is not to suggest that it's okay to be poorly versed in the more technical aspects of design and building. Quite the contrary: we must be able to conceptualize, fully appreciate, and effectively communicate and coordinate with structural, mechanical, electrical, and geotechnical engineers; lighting, acoustical, curtain wall, security, food service, graphics, and cost consultants; landscape architects, interior designers, constructors, material manufacturers; and other specialists, depending on the project. Like the good family physician, you need to know when to ask for specialized consultation.

The analogy of architect as captain of the design team is a good one; he or she must possess a balanced view and have a broad knowledge base in order to derive the most from consultants, make informed decisions about building systems that strengthen design concepts, and lay the foundation for continuing, lifelong learning. Whatever design philosophy is invoked, collaboration, coordination, and understanding of engineering aspects of architecture are required by the architect.

Architect Yann Weymouth summarizes eloquently: "Any architect is trying to make a beautiful building, a wonderful place. To do that you need technology—you need to understand the materials, the structure, the air conditioning, the solar load, the seismic problems. You can't have design without the engineering. It's a whole thing." Indeed, as Mike Crosbie says, "everything an architect does is design."

The following topics include a series of supplements (see Supplements 4.9–4.11) conceived as miniconsultations that may offer a new perspective on some of the engineering disciplines and how they affect schematic design.

The Technical Integration Game
With Carl Bovill

❑ The importance of thinking about integrating (or deintegrating) building systems very early in the design process is underscored in Supplement 4.9 by Carl Bovill, who has written a unique and valuable studio reference, *Architectural Design:*

Integration of Structural and Environmental Systems (Van Nostrand Reinhold, 1991).

SUPPLEMENT 4.9

Carl Bovill

Carl Bovill is an associate professor of architecture at the University of Maryland at College Park. He has taught at California State University in San Luis Obispo and at the University of Tennessee in Knoxville. He has received from the AIA both an Education Honors Award for technical systems integration in design instruction and the AIA School Medal for excellence in the study of architecture. Recent publications include Fractal Geometry in Architecture and Design *(Birkhäuser, 1996).*

❏ It is while the building is first forming out of the architectural program that there is the greatest opportunity to integrate the structural and environmental control systems into the architectural design. These systems need to be considered at the same rough sketch abstracted level as the architectural design. Detail is inappropriate at this stage. At the concept formation level, the design process should be primarily concerned with the qualitative evaluation of the interacting wholeness of the design. Therefore, the technical sizing information used should be just quantitative enough so that the qualitative features of technical system integration in architectural concept formation can be explored.

Technical system knowledge can be used as a constraint aid to architectural concept formation but cannot replace the creative leap at the core of the architectural design process. Once the creative leap has occurred, however, it is essential that the designer have a method of easily simulating technical constraints so they can be included in design.

The integration of the many components that are required to design a constructible building is a complex problem that has no direct algorithmic solution. The problem is beyond logic. A tool that can take the designer beyond logic is play. Technical integration can be conceived as a cooperative game played between the technical systems, interlinked with a cooperative game played between the designer's logical and intuitive minds (Minai, 1989). It is the combination of rule systems explored with logic and chance provided by the intuitive leaps of a well-

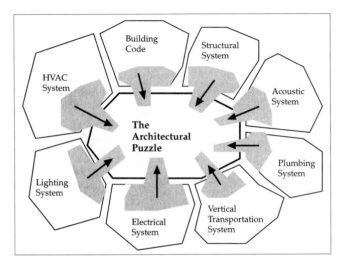

FIGURE 4.29
The architectural puzzle. (Courtesy of Carl Bovill.)

prepared mind that is responsible for creation of harmonious form. (See Fig. 4.29.)

Two Sides of Existence

❏ The world of phenomena presents itself in two forms (Rucker, 1987). One aspect is digital, like the number of trees in a row, the number of pebbles I am holding in my hand, or the amount of money I should be paid to do a certain job. The other aspect is continuous, like the area of the lawn in front of a house, or the volume of water in a glass, or how happy I am with the way my life is going. Our minds have the structure to deal with this situation. The mind has a digital, logical side and a continuous, intuitive side. The digital, logical side has become very powerful in recent history. The scientific method has allowed the digital, logical side of the brain to achieve important tasks on demand. It is the continuous, intuitive side of the mind, always monitoring the continuity of life, from which new creative ideas come, however. We need both sides of the mind to function.

Cooperative Games

❏ In *The Laws of the Game*, Eigen and Winkler (1981) explore the ways in which the combination of game rules and the element of chance create form. The authors introduce the reader to games and play in the following manner:

> *Chance and rules are the elements that underlie games and play. Play began among the elementary particles, atoms, and molecules, and now our brain cells carry it on. Human beings did not invent play, but it is play and only play that makes man complete.*
>
> *All our capabilities arise from play. First there is the play of limbs and muscles. The aimless grasping and kicking of an infant develops into carefully coordinated movements. Then there is the play of our senses. Playful curiosity sends us in search of profound knowledge. From play with colors, shapes, and sounds emerge immortal works of art. The first expressions of love take the form of play: The secret exchange of glances, dancing, the interplay of thoughts and emotions, the yielding of partners to each other. In Sanskrit, the union of lovers is called* kridaratnam, *the jewel of games.*

Games do not have to be a competition, with one player trying to beat another. In cooperative games, the players coordinate strategies to achieve some larger goal. An example of a cooperative game is warming up for a volleyball game with a group of players in a circle. The object is to keep the ball in the air. All the players win as long as the ball stays in the air. All the players lose if the ball falls to the ground.

Playing the Technical Integration Game

❏ Technical integration is a cooperative game played on two levels. The architectural, building code, structural, HVAC, lighting, acoustic, vertical transportation, plumbing, and electrical systems are playing together to create a harmonious composition. Overlaid on top of this game, the designer's digital, logical mind is playing a cooperative game with his or her continuous, intuitive mind.

The rules of the game are the architectural program, the site constraints, and the technical system sizing and composition constraints. The chance element comes from the continuous, intuitive side of the designer's brain. Where constraints conflict, intuition often leaps in to reconfigure the situation. These creative leaps are unpredictable in timing and in where they lead. Creative leaps do not come out of nowhere. They emerge from a well-prepared mind.

The game structure outlined in the following text is an attempt to coordinate the logical rule structure of technical system constraints with the chance event of the creative leap from a prepared intuition.

- Begin the game with the architectural concept and the organization of spaces to meet that concept. Developing the basic concept of the architecture is a game in itself that must be played before but also during the technical integration game.

- Over the concept layout of spaces, sketch a solution to each of the technical systems. Keep the drawings small enough to be drawn quickly and changed easily but large enough to present the needed information. Annotate the drawings to store information. Do not worry about conflict between systems on this first pass.

- After all the technical systems have been initially laid out, identify and expose the conflict points between systems. Creative inspiration lives on conflict. Learn to follow intuition as well as logic.

- Do not be afraid of intuitive leaps that restructure things. Chance is as important as rules in the creation of form.

- The technical system integration should aid the design concept of the building. The following visual design scales (Dondis, 1973) can help produce ideas of organization contrasts: balance–instability; symmetry–asymmetry; regularity–irregularity; unity–fragmentation; economy–intricacy; understatement–exaggeration; predictability–spontaneity; activeness–stasis; subtlety–boldness; neutrality–accent; transparency–opacity; consistency–variation; accuracy–

distortion; flatness–depth; singularity–juxtaposition; sequentiality–randomness; sharpness–diffusion; repetition–episodicity.

- The heart of a cooperative game is the development of coordinated strategies between the players. Develop strategies of relative importance. In a cooperative game, any player or group of players might become dominant.
- Play the game. Do not settle on the first solution or force system interactions that do not feel right. An old piece of design advice applies here. When the design concept is right, the pieces start falling easily into place.
- Remember that this is a multiplayer game. The designer cannot ignore any of the players. He or she can let some dominate others but cannot ignore some. All the players have to play to reach a solution.
- Remember that play is fun.

References

Dondis, Donis. *A Primer of Visual Literacy*. Cambridge, MA: MIT Press, 1973.

Eigen, Manfred, and Winkler, Ruthild. *Laws of the Game: How the Principles of Nature Govern Chance*. New York: Knopf, 1981.

Minai, Asghar. *Design as Aesthetic Communication: Structuring Random Order: Deconstruction of Formal Rationality*. New York: Peter Lang, 1989.

Rucker, Rudy. *Mind Tools: The Five Levels of Mathematical Reality*. Boston: Houghton Mifflin, 1987.

Structures
With Denis McMullan and Mete Turan

❏ Herman Spiegel, structural engineer and former dean of the Yale School of Architecture, explicitly defines why there is a need to be fluent in at least the qualitative aspects of structural design. "If the structural engineering accounts for 20 to 30 percent of a building, it will have profound influences on the design, the aesthetics, the manipulation of all the resources to make the most beautiful project."

Obviously, the use of structure is a key factor in the successful completion of projects. The following two very different supplements on structural engineering suggest that there is a genuine art in its integration with the overall architectural intent and project development—first, from a noteworthy and active engineering firm (Supplement 4.10) and second, from a noteworthy and active expert in the academy (Supplement 4.11).

Denis McMullan

SUPPLEMENT 4.10

McMullan & Associates, Inc. is a leading consulting structural engineering firm in the Washington, DC, area. President Denis J. McMullan, PE, assisted by colleague David Linton, PE, provides some inspirational words to help young architects see what it may be like to develop future relationships with structural engineers.

❏ Skill and art in structural engineering stems from the conceptual design, which complements the architecture and brings it to completeness. In working with structural engineers, be positive, think creatively, and listen carefully. There is nothing more discouraging to an engineer than to work with an architect who either has adopted a very conservative structural approach requiring the engineer to do nothing more than size the beams and columns, or has no idea how to make the structural system work and hopes that the engineer will magically solve the problem. Better to have early miniworkshops with the engineer. This usually takes very little time and can provide valuable insight and a guide to how the architect can proceed without falling into any of the traps just noted.

The most useful topics that should be discussed early in the design fall into two categories—lateral stiffening elements and gravity load systems. At the initial meeting, the structural engineer will be looking for ways to incorporate lateral bracing such as plywood shear walls, masonry walls, steel cross-bracing or rigid structural steel, or reinforced concrete beam and column connections. An architectural layout that can naturally accommodate such items, especially the more efficient structural walls, will provide a cost-effective and efficient structural system. The more symmetrical the arrangement of these elements, the better. If the architect has plans for extensive door openings, large floor openings, two-story spaces, or extraordinarily large open rooms, this is the time to share these ideas with the structural engineer, even though they may not be reflected on the current concept plans. Glass walls will require a more rigid lateral bracing system since they are more sensitive to displacement. Large floor openings cause problems in transferring lateral loads to the resisting elements.

Gravity load systems are easier for most architects and engineers to visualize. To avoid expensive and perhaps unacceptably heavy structural solutions later in the design process, the design team should be trying to line up load-bearing elements from one floor to the next. Using vertical supporting members such as columns and walls is generally less expensive than trying to span floor systems for excessive distances. Although contractors naturally build from the ground up, engineers design from the roof down. It is a very useful exercise to have the structural engineer explain the load path from snow on the roof down through rafters, beams, columns, and walls, and eventually, to the foundations. This will give the architect a feel for the structural design and will guide the decision-making process as the design unfolds.

Meaningful challenges need to be presented to achieve the best team performance. Mundane solutions should be rejected in favor of innovative thinking. Lean on the engineer for original solutions; even the most stubbornly conservative engineer can be persuaded to meet one more challenge.

Be aware when the design changes from concepts and schematics to real working drawings that cannot be changed easily without extra effort and additional expense. Remember—everyone wants to benefit financially from the project!

Throughout my career, I have encountered many different types of architects. There is the architect who believes that if he or she just had my computer, he or she would not have need of my services! There is also the architect who really wishes that skyhooks existed so that he or she would not have to compromise his or her dream in order to make it stand up. Meetings with a structural engineer should not be like going to the dentist. My favorite type of architect can share in the challenge of excellence in engineering blended with wonderful architectural design.

It is invigorating to work with an architect who challenges my skill in engineering and diplomacy. This architect may design pyramid roof structures that have no bottom chord tie and that may need to be supported on hip rafters that come down over little more than very large glass windows or glass doors at the corner. A structural engineer's basic instincts scream for a post at this corner, but if a post would compromise the design, another solution must be found.

Usually, in this instance, I end up cantilevering a beam over glass doors or windows to pick up the gravity load supported on very small columns. A tension ring is used to resist the outward thrust of the hip rafters. An architect once asked me if I could keep the columns to less than 2 inches in size! I think he was joking. For the most part, nothing is impossible. The solutions just become prohibitively expensive. In some cases, the addition of a column could save thousands of dollars in engineering costs and materials. It is the architect's and engineer's responsibility to balance the client's budget with the aesthetics of design.

The challenge before any architect in this relationship with his or her structural engineering consultant is to achieve the design solution within the bounds of physical possibilities, yet stretch those boundaries when necessary.

Mete Turan

SUPPLEMENT 4.11

Design professionals often experience a disjunction between their visual sense—what they like to look at—and their rational sense—what they know is good or appropriate design. Mete Turan, PhD, is one of those whose seeing and thinking are based on the same principles; even more rarely, he is devoted to teaching those principles, which are outlined in this essay (© Mete Turan). He holds a PhD from Columbia University, and is a professor at the School of Architecture, Art and Historic Preservation at Roger Williams University.

Poetics of Structures: Force Follows Form

"Now, since architecture is an art (techne) *and essentially a reasoned state of capacity to make* (poietike), *and there is neither any art that is not such a state nor any state that is not art, art is identical with a state of capacity to make, involving a true course of reasoning. All art is concerned with coming into being, i.e., with contriving and considering how something may come into being which is capable of either being or not being, and whose origin is in the maker and not in the thing made. . . . Art, then, . . . is a state concerned with making, involving a true course of reasoning."*
—**Aristotle (384–322 BCE),** ***Nicomachean Ethics***
[1140a:7–20]

❏ Structural design is composed of two distinct but related procedures: configuration and computation. One is intuitive, subjective, and synthetic; the other is rational, objective, and analytical. A union of the two is essential to minimize the disadvantages of each and to avoid reducing structural design to either mere aesthetics or mere technique. The goal of this essay is to illuminate this relationship by discussing the nature of design and structure in general, and individual structural typologies in specific.

The Nature of Design and Structure

❏ The Greek verb *poiein*, the root of our word *poetry*, has a range of meanings, including ideas of production, doing, making, bringing forth; it implies an action that has some end (e.g., a building). In its original classical usage, *poietike*, poetics, had more to do with the arrangement of materials and structure than does its present use, which refers to discourse about the essence of beauty and rhapsodic expression. The root of our word *technology* is the Greek noun *techne*, meaning art, craft, knowledge of making; it refers to instrumentality and a rational discipline that aims at production. Unlike the modern opposition often drawn between technology and art, there is a very close affinity in classical Greek thought between *poietike* and *techne*. This essay is about the giving of form to materials in the field of structures, hence the term *poetics of structures*.

Art, as used here, is not the self-important form that has increasingly disassociated itself from knowledge and cultural reality, nor is it a matter of private taste; but it is the making of things that belong together. Different components and characteristics are configured and assembled with economy of design so that the resulting form has a dynamic union in which components are related to each other meaningfully, and so that the final product is a rational whole.

Understanding structures as the products of art rather than mathematical computation can alleviate misconceptions caused by the bifurcation of the one building art into the professions of architecture and engineering. As architecture developed as a profession, it began to regard the practicalities of building, of structural design and construction, as less significant, and reduced itself to creating appearances. These practicalities were devolved, not surprisingly, upon a newly emerging engineering discipline, which concerned itself with rationality in the art of construction. This transfer of professional responsibility and authority generated new understandings and two significant misunderstandings. The first misinterprets the essence of structural design; the second results from the seductive power of computation, similar to the enticement that the rendered drawings arouse in architectural representation.

The first misconception is a tendency to view structural design as an abstract mathematical procedure. However, structural design, as Harris (1961) points out, has more to do with knowledge of materials than with knowledge of mathematics. From the composition and properties of materials to their structural behavior, from the proportioning of individual members to the overall performance of the structure, material plays a decisive role in the design process. In this process, mathematics is a powerful decision-making tool. It shortens the trial-and-error process inherent in the building craft tradition by a remarkable margin, and also empowers the designer with more choices and means of economy. However, mathematical analysis can only be performed upon a preexisting form; therefore form is at the basis of all operations and constitutes the essence of structural design. Configuring or shaping the material is the critical step in design, both temporally and logically prior to computation. However, the results of computation are crucial in affirming, reconsidering, and/or redirecting the earlier decisions.

This leads to the second misconception, which views computational results as inherently scientific. Confidence in scientific methods or the reliability of mathematical techniques is not being questioned here. However, the input for the computations—subjective design decisions and equivocal assumptions about materials and loads—is often less than scientific, and raises doubt about the results of the process. Regardless of the strict mathematical reliability of computations, the result of a process admitting so many imprecise variables cannot be represented as the output of a scientific or mathematical approach.

When the formal characteristics of structure are emphasized, the dominance of computation dissolves, giving equal opportunity to architectonics to shape the structure. The entire quality of design depends as much on visual attributes as it does on the rationality of analytical tools. A conception of structures that transcends computation elevates architectonics in the design process and subsequently the overall quality of design.

Design

❏ Aesthetics is not the prerogative of any one profession but the responsibility of everyone concerned with design. Every artifact is a product of design, which is not specific to selected objects. Objects may be distinguished by the quality of their design, not whether one has been designed and the other has not been designed. Design of all kinds is carried out to fulfill or improve fulfillment of a function, to solve a problem and reach a practical result. The other side of the design coin is solving the problem artfully, so that the end product is handsome, elegant, visually pleasing. Design is not distinct from art; hence it is both a problem-solving activity and an art.

A broader definition of art in the classical sense is an activity where a balance between form and technical rationality is exercised by "a reasoned state of capacity to make." Design is neither a problem-solving activity alone, nor is it entirely art by itself. Making is a purposeful activity with an intended result, an iterative process of selecting between different options for configuration and connection. In shaping the artifact the designer can choose freely among possibilities at every step of the design. Regardless of the number and degree of the constraints, the freedom of choice about what the designed object will look like is something that the designer must confront throughout the process.

The modern polemic has drawn a dichotomous relationship between aesthetics and utility. In spite of this nominal divide, imagination and reason, aesthetics and rational design, are correlatable. The point at which elegance ceases to be utilitarian and the point at which form is divorced from material and structure are issues whose articulation will delineate the difference between the object whose sole end is the mere expression of aesthetic ideas and the object with a purpose, as in architecture and structure, whose suitability for a certain function is the essential thing. The product of an arbitrary will with an aesthetic purpose alone, or an aesthetic end without serious concern for practical use, cannot apply to architectural or structural design. Design must explore the relationship between aesthetic intentions and utility, materials and technological requirements.

Architectonics

❏ To emphasize the relationship between architecture and engineering in general, and architecture and structure in particular, Collins (1960) proposed, four decades ago, the use of tectonics. He optimistically considered the new relationship between architecture and structure a "new science" that needed an "identity." He praised the works of engineers Eugène Freyssinet, Robert Maillart, Pier Luigi Nervi, and Felix Candela for their beauty, which "depends as much on intuitive imaginative genius as that of any temple or palace," but "beauty of a different order, deriving its emotive power from a precision of calculation and an audacity of execution."

The term *architectonics* is used here with the same spirit. Architectonics is the art of reason specific to how material is arranged and how building systems and components are assembled. This art of building systems itself is a construct, an aesthetic form that is the product of a series of design decisions and judgments. It is the necessary design intermediary between the laws of nature and the art of construction. Writing in the late eighteenth century, the poet and philosopher Friedrich Schiller (1902) defined "architectonic beauty" as "the visible expression of a rational conception." A structure's material, form, and production constitute the basis for this rational conception.

Structure

❏ Structure—from the Latin *struere*, "to put together, to assemble, to build"—takes its value, function, and meaning from the relationship between whole and parts within the system. The corollary to this principle of interdependence is that a structural component's significance comes only from the connections between it and other components. A hierarchy of interdependence, established between and within the parts by arranging and configuring the structural components, determines how the force is transferred throughout the form in whole or part; hence *force follows form*. The structural component as a unit of meaning, and its behavior, cannot be understood in its entity as a unit but in its relationship to the architectonic whole, which is in turn an interplay of formal interdependence between the components.

Form, as an idea or concept, precedes structure, and then matter is employed to manifest the form. There can be no structural form divorced from the material of which it is made. The essential nature of structure can only be apprehended after this union of form and structure. Structural art is the making of order with the given constraints; it is the effective synthesis of materials and form, arrived at as a result of the iterative process of configuration and computation. Without structure, architecture is fantasy at best.

Structural Design

❏ Structural design starts with a conception of form that is both intuitive and logical—the result of past experiences, knowledge, observation, imagination, and symbolism. Only at this investigative stage of design, the form, in part, is disjoined from matter, and is a product of subjective judgments, usually generated by a method of elimination rather than any objective method. The rational justification of structural design emerges later in the design process when the form's structural behavior is tested and the form is revised accordingly. Analysis informs this judgmental process to refine the form, to discard the capricious, the irrelevant and the irrational, providing quantifiable understanding of the form. Everything from geometrical configuration to material selection to refinements in cross sections and connections may be adjusted, and this iterative process continues until a satisfac-

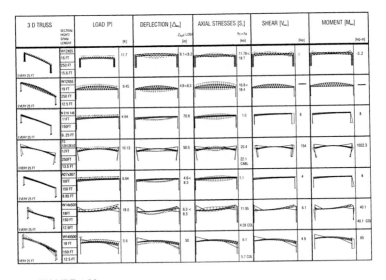

FIGURE 4.30

Comparative results of different configurations for a large span truss. (Courtesy of Lilianna Wawrzyniak and Maria Kalea.)

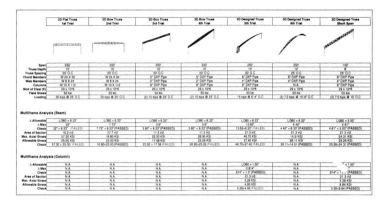

	2D Flat Truss 1st Trial	2D Bow Truss 2nd Trial	3D Box Truss 3rd Trial	3D Bow Truss 4th Trial	3D Designed Truss 5th Trial	3D Designed Truss 6th Trial	3D Designed Truss Short Span
Span	250'	250'	250'	250'	250'	250'	150'
Truss Depth	10'	15'	10'	15'	10'	12'	8'
Truss Spacing	20' O.C	20' O.C	20' O.C	20' O.C	20' O.C	25' O.C	25' O.C
Chord Members	W 24 X 55	W 24 X 94	5" DXP Pipe	5" DXP Pipe	8" DXP Pipe	8" DXP Pipe	8" DXP Pipe
Web Members	W 8 X 24	W 8 X 24	2" DXP Pipe	2" DXP Pipe	4" DXP Pipe	4" DXP Pipe	4" DXP Pipe
Columns	W 10 X 112	W 10 X 112	8" DXP Pipe	8" DXP Pipe	8" DXP Pipe	N.A.	8" DXP Pipe
Mod of Elast (E)	29×10^6	29×10^6	29×10^6	29×10^6	29×10^6	29×10^6	29×10^6
Yield Stress	50 ksi	50 ksi	50 ksi	50 ksi	50 ksi	50 ksi	50 ksi
Loading	30 kps @ 25' O.C	30 kps @ 25' O.C	(2) 15 kps @ 25' O.C	(2) 15 kps @ 25' O.C	15 kps @ 6'-4" O.C	(2) 7.2 kps @ 10'-6" O.C	(2) 7.5 kps @ 10' O.C

Multiframe Analysis (Beam)

Δ Allowable	L/360 = 8.33'	L/360 = 8.33'	L/360 = 8.33'	L/360 = 8.33'	L/360 = 8.33'	L/360 = 8.33'	L/360 = 5.00"
Δ Max	32"	7.73'	3.6'	3.6'	13.63'	4.42"	4.61"
Check	32" > 8.33' (FAILED)	7.73' < 8.33' (PASSED)	3.60' < 8.33' (PASSED)	3.60' < 8.33' (PASSED)	13.63>8.33' (FAILED)	4.42" < 8.33' (PASSED)	4.61" < 5.00' (PASSED)
Area of Section	16.2 in2	27.7 in2	11.3 in2	11.3 in2	21.3 in2	21.3 in2	21.3 in2
Max. Axial Stress	57.30 KSI	16.80 KSI	22.00 KSI	26.95 KSI	46.70 KSI	14.51 KSI	24.31 KSI
Allowable Stress	25.00 KSI	25.00 KSI	17.58 KSI	25.25 KSI	27.40 KSI	26.11 KSI	25.26 KSI
Check	57.30 > 25.00 (FAILED)	16.80<25.00 (PASSED)	22.00 > 17.58 (FAILED)	26.95>25.26 (FAILED)	46.70>27.40 (FAILED)	26.11>14.51 (PASSED)	25.26>24.31 (PASSED)

Multiframe Analysis (Column)

Δ Allowable	N.A.	N.A.	N.A.	N.A.	L/360 = 1.30"	N.A.	" = 1.00"
Δ Max	N.A.	N.A.	N.A.	N.A.	0.814"	N.A.	"
Check	N.A.	N.A.	N.A.	N.A.	.814" < 1.3" (PASSED)	N.A.	.814" < 1.0" (PASSED)
Area of Section	N.A.	N.A.	N.A.	N.A.	21.3 in2	N.A.	21.3 in2
Max. Axial Stress	N.A.	N.A.	N.A.	N.A.	5.28 KSI	N.A.	5.28 KSI
Allowable Stress	N.A.	N.A.	N.A.	N.A.	4.93 KSI	N.A.	8.84 KSI
Check	N.A.	N.A.	N.A.	N.A.	5.28>4.93 (FAILED)	N.A.	5.26<8.84 (PASSED)

FIGURE 4.31
Comparative results of different configurations for a large span truss. (Courtesy of Jason B. Wise and J. Carter Bean.)

tory solution is reached. Figures 4.30 to 4.35 display the different phases of this iterative design process.

Structural design melds the results of these iterative cycles of configuration and computation, also joining these two distinct but closely related processes. Computation, or analysis, is necessarily complemented by configuration, the formal concept, and its incorporation in matter. Multiple iterations reconcile the disjunction between form and matter, transforming the freest, most subjective and synthetic activity in the direction of necessity, objectivity, and analysis. Without configuration, computation would be an abstract and an empty system. Without computation, configuration would be isolated and meaningless architectonic expression.

Since architecture and structural engineering drifted apart, conventional structural design has been primarily concerned with the behavior and analysis of given structures, giving rise to an apparent difference between the engineer's aesthetics and the architect's aesthetics. This is not, however, as the architect Le Corbusier contended in his early writings, to be understood simply as a difference in the degree of artistic competence, whereby the engineer's forms are purely rational and the architect's are

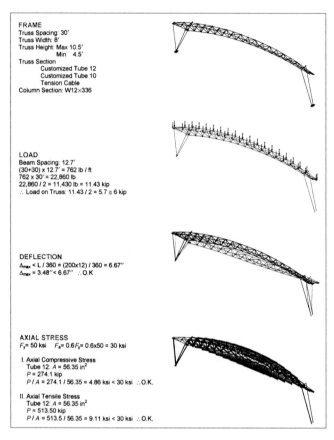

FRAME
Truss Spacing: 30′
Truss Width: 8′
Truss Height: Max 10.5′
              Min   4.5′
Truss Section
        Customized Tube 12
        Customized Tube 10
        Tension Cable
Column Section: W12×336

LOAD
Beam Spacing: 12.7′
(30+30) x 12.7′ = 762 lb / ft
762 x 30′ = 22,860 lb
22,860 / 2 = 11,430 lb = 11.43 kip
∴ Load on Truss: 11.43 / 2 = 5.7 ≅ 6 kip

DEFLECTION
Δ_{max} < L / 360 = (200x12) / 360 = 6.67″
Δ_{max} = 3.48″ < 6.67″ ∴ O.K

AXIAL STRESS
F_y= 50 ksi F_a= 0.6F_y= 0.6x50 = 30 ksi

I. Axial Compressive Stress
   Tube 12: A = 56.35 in^2
   P = 274.1 kip
   P / A = 274.1 / 56.35 = 4.86 ksi < 30 ksi ∴O.K.

II. Axial Tensile Stress
    Tube 12: A = 56.35 in^2
    P = 513.50 kip
    P / A = 513.5 / 56.35 = 9.11 ksi < 30 ksi ∴O.K.

FIGURE 4.32
A typical analysis for each configuration of a truss. (Courtesy of So Young Sun and Seon Woo Kang.)

packed with emotional power. Although the expression *engineer's aesthetics* conjures up an image of hopelessly inept design entirely without artistic quality, art manifests itself in any action of making. Structural design, the engineer's art, reveals its essence through the relation of load and support, the conflict between gravity and resistance, the liaison between material and form, the reciprocity of lightness and span.

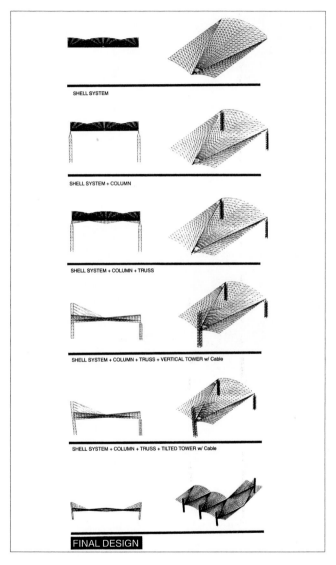

FIGURE 4.33
An iterative process towards a final design. (Courtesy of Chun-Ling Daphne Lin and Kuo-Chin Weng.)

FIGURE 4.34
Three-dimensional modeling of the final design in its context. (Courtesy of So Young Sun and Seon Woo Kang.)

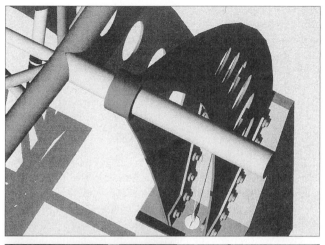

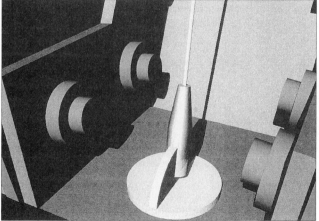

FIGURE 4.35
Details from a final design. (Courtesy of So Young Sun and Seon Woo Kang.)

This art is not well served either by the way structural design is taught to design and building professionals or by the way it is often practiced. Teaching of structural design in both architecture and engineering schools typically involves a given structure, with predetermined global geometry and end conditions, which allows, at best, informed guessing at local geometry or member size. This procedure rarely involves a comprehensive global geometrical configuration or exploration of structure and form.

At the other end of the structural design spectrum is the optimum structural design, which does not begin with predetermined dimensions but searches for them as variables under minimum weight or cost requirements while satisfying equilibrium conditions and functional objectives. In the mid-nineteenth century, physicist James Clerk Maxwell's minimum-weight strength design laid the foundation for a general theory of optimization in structural design. Since then, other behavioral criteria—stability and stiffness—have been used to further develop the theory. The complex problem of simultaneous satisfaction of all three criteria—minimum weight, stability, and stiffness—under multiple loading conditions was not possible until the advent of computers. However, even the computerized synthesis capability does not provide a true optimum solution because of its inability to demonstrate the convergence to an absolute minimum. One other problematic area lies with the practical application of the rather unconventional forms derived as optimal shapes, since design conventions are not designated as mathematical parameters. These new shapes can lead to new design forms; however, the optimal shapes often do not lend themselves to widespread applications because of economic, technological, and functional limitations.

In spite of these shortcomings, the results of such procedures improve structural design in ways that would not otherwise be possible. Yet there are other shortcomings in both of the approaches just discussed, and neither can be truly called scientific. There are too many uncertainties about assumptions used to simulate real-life conditions; limitations of the analysis; compatibility constraints; architectural requirements; and construction materials, methods, and capabilities. While a unique scientific solution is conceivable under strictly controlled conditions and well-defined constraints, there can be no such solution in actual structural design. At best, these methods provide a rational, informed procedure resulting in a number of design solutions, each one an approximation. As Harris (1961) declares unequivocally, "Engineering is clearly an art and not a science."

Here, art is used "to be any direction of the practical intellect to the making of things, imposing an idea or a form upon material, upon matter." Mathematical analysis should be used only to judge the empirical use of understanding; therefore its use is distorted and misleading when substituted for design, which is an art of both the quantifiable and the nonquantifiable. "Imposing an idea or form upon material" can best be achieved with a comprehensive approach in which the analysis informs and enriches the synthesis.

Forces and Basic Structural Actions

❏ A force is a push or a pull; it is a mechanical action exerted by one physical body on another. Force has a magnitude and a direction, which make it a mathematical entity called a *vector*. The function of a structure is to resist external forces without undesirable deformations and displacements occurring in the individual members or the whole of the structure. A force developed by the structure, one equal in magnitude and opposite in direction, resists each external force exerted on a structure. An example is the force acting vertically downward and caused by gravity. This includes the structure's own weight as well as the loads it supports, which are also subject to gravity and are transferred to the structure. The structure must resist this downward force with an equal upward force. Examples of lateral forces, perpendicular to those caused by gravity, may be the forces created by wind pressure on the surface of a tall structure, or the forces generated by an earthquake on the foundations of a structure. All of these forces must be resisted by equal and opposite support reactions within the structure.

There are four basic structural actions: compression, the act of pressing or squeezing together; tension, the act of stretching or straining; bending, the act of flexing or deforming along a plane mainly perpendicular to the direction of the force; and shearing, the act of deforming or rupturing along a plane parallel to the direction of the force. Structural behavior is due either to one of these actions (e.g., an individual member in a truss subject to compression) or a combination of these actions (e.g., a column subject to bending and compression at the same time).

Stability, Strength, and Stiffness

❏ To maintain the shape and the position of the structure, the structure must be in equilibrium with the external forces acting upon it. This condition of stability, known as *translational equilibrium*, requires the summation of all forces acting upon the whole or any part of the structure to be zero. There is also a *rotational equilibrium* in response to the moments developing at any part of the structure, which requires that the summation of all moments effective at any part or whole of the structure must be zero.

The structure achieves stability through a combination of material and geometry. The structural property of the material provides the strength, and the material and the geometrical composition of the structure provide the stiffness. Together, strength and stiffness generate internal forces to resist external forces and achieve stability.

Force Follows Form

❏ One of the functions of a structure is to direct the forces that are applied to it safely to earth. A structure resists its own weight and other forces applied to it by generating internal forces, whose nature is a function of the form and geometry of the structure. Hence force follows form in one way or the other. Some forms allow more efficient force transfer than others; some are not suited for every function. Regardless of the structure's size or span, the relationship between geometry, material, and loading determines an appropriate structure-form combination.

A structure or structural component transfers force in four primary modes: axially along the length of a straight structural member; axially along the length of a curved structural member, generating thrust at the end of the member; in flexure, where forces perpendicular to the longer axis of the member generate bending and shear stresses that vary over the length of the member; and through membrane action, in which the internal forces are distributed across the surface of the structure. Some structures combine more than one type of force and thus have a composite behavior; however, the behavior of most individual components falls within one of these four categories.

This classification of load transference and internal forces generated to respond to external forces allows us to classify structure systems in four categories, related to the four internal modes just listed: lineated, arcuated, trabeated, and reticulated.

Lineated Structure Systems

❏ Lineated structure systems are those in which forces transfer along the length of structural members, generating stresses perpendicular to the cross-sectional area of the member. These axial forces that develop as the members redirect the external forces are either compressive or tensile. Typically, members in lineated structure systems are short, solid, and straight-line elements, which respond to the transferred axial force with their cross-sectional area. Hence, material strength is a prime design criterion.

The member's length is not at issue if the force acting on it is a tensile force; however, if it is a compressive force, then behavior other than the axial stresses developing may be critical, possibly resulting in buckling.

Lineated structural systems typically include compression components such as columns, struts, buttresses, walls, or tension components such as stayed cables, ties, or hangers. Two- or three-dimensional trusses are the most common structures in this category, which also includes geodesic domes and curved space frames.

Arcuated Structure Systems

❏ Arcuated systems include curved rigid forms such as arches or vaults, characterized by compressive stresses that develop to redirect external forces; and curved flexible structures that take exactly the shape of the pressure line of the external loading and generate tension forces in response to external forces. Arcuated structure systems are those in which forces transfer along the curvature of the structural component, generating stresses perpendicular to the component's cross section, analogous to the stress distribution in a lineated system. In addition to the stresses developed by the axial force along the component's curvature, arcuated structure systems also generate a horizontal thrust at the member's ends, which must be transferred to the support. This horizontal thrust is an outward force in arches and vaults, and an inward force in cables, and its magnitude is proportional to the span length, the rise in arches, and the sag in cables.

As long as the natural path of the forces remains within the depth of the member, no stresses other than the normal stresses will develop in the cross section. If the pressure line of the external forces has a trajectory outside the form of the structure—for example, in the case of a large point load applied to an arch—then the structural action will include bending in addition to the other stresses. Arches and barrel vaults are the most common compressive arcuated structures, and catenary and suspension structures are the most common tensile versions. The geometry of the arch, or the sag of the cable, are significant design criteria.

Trabeated Structure Systems

❏ Trabeated structure systems are those in which the external forces are redirected by bending and shearing actions. The members of trabeated structure systems are generally subject to external forces that are perpendicular to the longer axis of the member. Hence the member, while transferring the forces, develops a pair of tensile and compressive stresses simultaneously in order to react to the moment or rotation that develops as result of the external forces. As bending takes place in the member due to the moment created by the external forces, shear stresses are also generated simultaneously to establish equilibrium in rotation as the member develops resistance by its material strength. The shear stresses, both in vertical and horizontal directions, cause a square element of a member to be deformed into a rhombic shape, i.e., as the square on one diagonal is put in tension (elongated), on the other it is put in compression (shortened). The geometrical properties of the member's cross section determine its stiffness and therefore its ability to withstand all of these forces. The most common structures or structural components in this category are beams, frames (e.g., portal or Vierendeel), one- and two-way slabs, grillages, and coffered and ribbed slabs.

Reticulated Structure Systems

❏ Reticulated structure systems are those in which forces are dispersed along the membrane, or the surface, primarily in two directions, as opposed to the unidirectional transfer that takes place along the length of the member in the other systems. A characteristically small dimension in one direction distinguishes reticulated structures. The three main categories in this type—namely plates, shells, and tensile structures—are also known as *surface structures*.

Compressive, tensile, and shear stresses are resisted within the thickness of the membrane; hence a structural continuity in two axes is a prerequisite. Because of the very small thickness-to-span ratio of this structural type, the form of the membrane is critical, since it determines the bearing mechanism. The main resisting mechanism relies on thrust developed in both directions along the surface, although shear, moment, and torsion are still present. Structure-form relationship is very critical since the economy of the structure depends very much on the correct form. Most three-dimensional structures can be cited in this category: space and lattice trusses, ribbed and fan vaults, domes, thin and grid shells, plates, tensile structures, fabric membranes, and cable nets.

"To build means to make use of solid materials in such a way as to create a space suited to particular functions and to protect it from the external elements. The structure, be it large or small, must be stable and lasting, must satisfy the needs for which it was built, and must achieve the maximum result with the minimum means.

"These conditions: Stability, durability, function, and maximum results with minimum means—or in current terms, economic efficiency—can be found to an extent in all construction from the mud hut to the most magnificent building. They can be

summed up in the phrase 'building correctly,' which seems to me more suitable than the more specific 'good technical construction.' It is easy to see that each of these characteristics, which at first seem only technical and objective, has a subjective—and I would add psychological—component which relates it to the aesthetic and expressive appearance of the completed work."

—**Pier Luigi Nervi, *Aesthetics and Technology in Building: The Charles Eliot Norton Lectures, 1961–1962* (Harvard University Press, 1965)**

Conclusion

❏ A structure's legibility depends on effectiveness of communication, the interplay of size, form, mass, scale, texture, color, proportion, simplicity, delicacy, elegance—in short, its visual authority, a function of the designer's understanding. Generation of structural form begins with knowledge of the basic structural systems and their components, materials and their inherent properties, and the forces to which a structure must respond. These are the beginnings of a vocabulary that becomes richer and more complex as the designer learns to understand both sides of the dialogue between form and mathematics, between configuration and computation. Only by the union of these two tools can the designer transcend both empty form making and rote calculation and create a structure that is both rational and expressive.

Notes/References

Collins, P. "Tectonics." *Journal of Architectural Education*, Spring, 15(1):31–33, 1960.

Harris, A.J. "Architectural Misconceptions of Engineering." *RIBA Journal*, 3rd Series, 68(4):130–136, 1961.

Schiller, F. *Aesthetical and Philosophical Essays* (2 vols.), Dole, N.H. (ed.) Boston, MA: Niccolls, 1902.

Mechanical Systems
With Norbert Lechner

❏ Environmental controls, including heating, ventilating, and air conditioning (HVAC), should be thought of as integral to the early stages of design. Donald Watson, FAIA, has pointed out that buildings consume about 40 percent of the national energy budget for heating, cooling, and illumination. In view of this fact, Watson observes how surprising and disturbing it is that many buildings are not maximizing energy efficiency and environment-conserving potentials. One broad explanation for this may lie in our failure to sufficiently stress early integration of environmental systems with design concepts.

The HVAC system is composed of many elements, some requiring many square feet of floor space. Carl Bovill says, "For the creative manipulation of the HVAC implications in architectural design the architect needs to consider the relationship between spatial organization, structural requirements, and the HVAC needs in an overall way. In order for this to happen at the highest levels of design intent, detail must be suppressed and strategic concept emphasized."

One way to emphasize this strategic concept development is to incorporate the efforts of the entire project team—including many of the key engineering consultants—into the early phases of the design process. This will greatly enhance systems integration in support of the broad design concepts, and likely promote the highest-quality effort and investment from consultants to reach project goals.

In Supplement 4.12, Norbert Lechner demonstrates why he is a champion in helping architects to design more energy-efficient buildings.

SUPPLEMENT 4.12

Norbert Lechner

Professor Norbert M. Lechner, of the Building Science Department at Auburn University, contributes this lucid three-tier approach to designing mechanical systems in buildings. Professor Lechner believes that such a method is being used implicitly on most good buildings and suggests that it be used explicitly. (Refer to his excellent book, Heating, Cooling, Lighting:

Design Methods for Architects, recently published in a second edition by Wiley, for more information.) Lechner's material is especially salient for the schematic design phase, which is most appropriate for the theme of this book.

Mechanical Systems/Equipment

❏ Is the architect or the engineer the primary designer of the heating, cooling, and lighting systems? The surprising answer is the architect, and for two different reasons. First, the size of the heating, cooling, and lighting systems is determined almost completely by the architect's design of the building. A well-designed building will have less than half the heating, cooling, and lighting loads of a conventional building. Energy-efficient buildings using only 10 percent as much energy as a conventional building are technically and economically feasible—they have been built.

Second, the architect is the primary designer of the type and layout of the mechanical systems. The building design determines the number of zones as well as the location of mechanical equipment rooms, duct runs, cooling towers, and so on. Although the engineer makes the actual specifications, his or her options are greatly limited by the architect's design. The best approach is for the engineer to have input at the early stage when the architect is making all the important decisions that impact the design of the mechanical equipment.

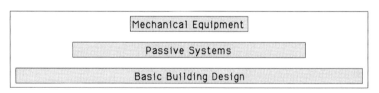

FIGURE 4.36
The three-tier approach to designing the heating, cooling, and lighting systems of a building. (Courtesy of Norbert Lechner.)

The Three-Tier Approach

❏ It is useful to see the design of the heating, cooling, and lighting systems as a three-tier approach (Fig. 4.36). Tier 1, *basic design*, includes such considerations as building form (degree of compactness), orientation, interior and exterior colors, size and location of glazing areas, window shading systems, envelope construction (thermal resistance), massiveness of construction (thermal mass), and so on. These are all major factors in sizing and selecting mechanical systems, and they are all the primary responsibility of the architect. The proper design of the tier 1 considerations will greatly reduce but not eliminate the size of the mechanical equipment. Thus the strategies of tier 2, *passive systems*, are used to further reduce the size of the mechanical systems.

In tier 2, natural energy sources are used for passive heating, passive cooling, and daylighting. Passive heating strategies use south-facing windows and clerestories along with thermal mass to collect and store up excess solar heat collected during the winter day for nighttime use. Passive cooling strategies include the use of wind for comfort ventilation or convective cooling, the use of water for evaporative cooling, and the use of radiators for nighttime radiant cooling. Daylighting strategies bring good-quality daylight into the building to make it possible to turn off the electric lights during most of the daytime hours. The energy-saving potential is tremendous when you consider that there are about 4400 hours of daylight per year, and that most working hours—about 2000 of them—are daylight hours.

Even well-designed buildings fully utilizing the strategies of tiers 1 and 2 will in most cases still require some mechanical equipment, but the size, cost, and energy demands of this equipment will then be quite small. Thus, tier 3, *mechanical equipment*, consists of designing the small amount of equipment still required. Although this tier is mainly the responsibility of the engineer, the architect must still be involved in many important considerations:

- Sizing and locating mechanical equipment rooms
- Exposing or hiding the ductwork

- Establishing floor-to-floor heights and clearances with the structure for the ductwork
- Locating intake and exhaust louvers on exterior walls
- Locating the condenser unit (cooling tower) on the roof or on grade next to the building
- Deciding whether to use active solarpower, photovoltaic cells, wind power, and so on
- Selecting the type of ceiling diffuser, with its strong aesthetic implications indoors

Because the heating, cooling, and lighting of buildings is largely determined by the architect, it is very important that he or she understand the basic concepts involved. For example, cooling is the pumping of heat from a building into a natural heat sink (Fig. 4.37). In large buildings this is accomplished with cooling towers (Fig. 4.38), and in small buildings with just a condenser unit (Fig. 4.39).

The plumbing and electrical systems are not discussed here because they have little impact on the schematic or conceptual design stages. These systems have minimal space needs and are quite flexible in layout. Consequently, there is usually little problem in designing them at the working drawing stage. The main

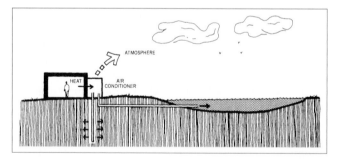

FIGURE 4.37
Air, water, or the ground can act as the heat sink for a building's cooling system. (From Heating, Cooling, Lighting: Design Methods for Architects, *by Norbert Lechner, © 1991 John Wiley & Sons, Inc. Reprinted by permission of John Wiley & Sons, Inc.)*

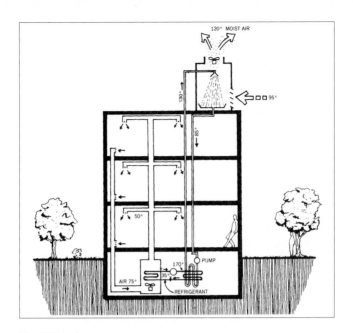

FIGURE 4.38

A cooling tower cools water by evaporation. This cooling water is then used to cool the condenser coil, located elsewhere. (From Heating, Cooling, Lighting: Design Methods for Architects, *by Norbert Lechner, © 1991 John Wiley & Sons, Inc. Reprinted by permission of John Wiley & Sons, Inc.)*

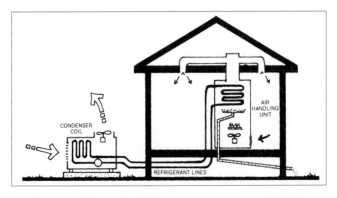

FIGURE 4.39

A schematic diagram of a split system. (From Heating, Cooling, Lighting: Design Methods for Architects, *by Norbert Lechner, © 1991 John Wiley & Sons, Inc. Reprinted by permission of John Wiley & Sons, Inc.)*

exception is the need for some small electrical and telephone closets in larger buildings.

Lighting

"There is no end to the possibilities of light—for it is the source of magic in architecture. I believe that light is the ultimate determinant of design. I am convinced that how we see things as a consequence of light is fundamental to the formation of human perception and imagination."

—Arthur Erickson

❏ In addition to Erickson's words, which capture some of the more intangible and even biological correlates of lighting, there are a host of technical and economic aspects addressed in the following material. Lighting is truly a multidimensional field that legitimately contains as much metaphysics as it does physics. (See Supplement 4.13.)

It has always struck me that William Lam's work represents architectural wisdom in general as much as it does fine lighting design in particular. The interview that follows can be described in much the same fashion. Lam was one of the pioneers in the relatively new specialty of architectural lighting. His classic books, *Perception and Lighting as Formgivers for Architecture* (McGraw-Hill, 1977) and *Sunlighting as Formgiver for Architecture* (Van Nastrand Reinhold, 1986), emphasize the importance of the design process, elaborate on theoretical concepts, and illustrate practical design methods and their application to projects.

I asked Lam what he finds most frustrating about the way projects are developed in terms of lighting. He spoke of a natural but dangerous sort of nearsightedness from which many practitioners seem to suffer. Lam observed, "Designers often start by focusing only upon some parts of the problem." While he admitted that a certain amount of this compartmentalizing is necessary, the point to be constantly aware of is "translating the overall objectives into a building—an integrated form." The problem, Lam believes, is compounded by the order in which lighting is considered. He says: "There is the tendency to design the structure in relation to the plan, and then the mechanical systems, *and then* lighting—in that sequence. They're add-ons rather than part of the first concept." Lam urges that architects try to conceive of all the issues from the first efforts to develop a design solution. Imagination then is not limited and the process becomes an "integrative" one rather than one of "erosion."

Lam was quick to point out that a multidisciplinary team is less likely to get stuck in one approach or preconception: "Even when there are structural and plan concepts before a team is brought aboard, there is something to react to—other people are in the position to remind the architect that if you do X, it has certain implications for daylight or mechanical systems, for example, that he or she may not have considered."

Most preferable, however, even in a team effort, is the condition in which there are no preconceptions. Lam described the ideal stage in which "Nobody has anything except a bubble diagram of where things want to be—you have the site, and if everyone's open to ideas—you get a kind of synergism. You don't know who the ideas came from; it's a little bit of everybody. You do need to be thinking of the whole problem, and try to be at least conceptually aware of all the issues simultaneously."

I asked Lam to comment on the value of building rough chipboard study models. He responded emphatically: "Rough models are extraordinarily valuable for practicing architects. To me, a good model is one that's done crudely enough that it's a tool for study rather than a tool for documentation. In this way, you don't mind knocking it apart and what you can't avoid is learning something from it—you build a model, you see what's wrong with it, and try to fix it. But if you build it too carefully, you've got this beautiful thing, and of course you don't want to destroy it. Eventually, you get to a more finished model, but the first model should be very conceptual. If you're afraid to destroy the model, cut a hole in it, move something, then why build it? If you want to explore or test something, and you find it's perfect to start with, then fine. I find that many times building models is a marvelous way to get around misconceptions."

"I suggest that the best thing is build a model, put some scale furniture or people in it, and photograph it as realistically as you can. If you have the actual model and come to present it, you may not have the time or the desired lighting conditions—for example, it might be at night and you may be trying to demonstrate a sunny condition. So you better have photographed the model with the sun; actually take it outside, see it, and take the photographs. It's not a representation or simulation of environmental conditions. It *is* the environmental conditions!"

Finally, I asked Lam to be a bit more specific about lighting, to go back even before one thinks about making a model. He replied by saying that we first should recall the potential impact of good lighting, "to facilitate orientation, to provide focus, sparkle, even essential character of a space, and to satisfy fundamental biological needs for view and for sun as well as for the activity needs." Keeping all this in mind, Lam implores that we "ask the right questions about the spaces to be designed—just what are the qualities you want?" Lam mandates that we think about lighting early and start with diagramming early. He explained: "Freehand schematic diagrams and diagrammatic sections especially can be readily used to explore design concepts and develop designs in advance of model building. Sketch lines of illumination and probable reflection and glare. Evaluate possible lighting designs according to advantages and problems of each solution. It's amazing how well the diagrams can help catalog real conditions and in turn lead one to good *concepts* for lighting, which can then be tested in the model."

"Most important is to recognize that lighting design is not a technical engineering–based discipline; it is applied perception psychology. A designer needs to know why things are perceived the way they are. If you know what a good environment is, you can design one. Think concept first, hardware last. Think about what wants to be lit, why, and how it should appear. Think and diagram in three dimensions. Diagram light in relation to architectural features, to artwork, to the furnishings and the projected activities in the space, and then where the light may come from. The reflected ceiling plan comes last. I am amazed how many architects, engineers, and, not surprisingly, their students start and end their lighting design with a reflected ceiling plan."

Our time was up, and I invited Lam to add anything else he believed appropriate. With characteristic wisdom—and, I'm certain, a wry smile—he said, "I would always emphasize the application of common sense—an underrated commodity."

Lighting Design
With Charles Linn

Charles Linn

Charles D. Linn, AIA, is a Senior Editor for Architectural Record *and is the editor of "Record Lighting," the* Record's *quarterly special section on lighting. In addition to writing design features and essays, he occasionally takes photographs for the magazine.*

SUPPLEMENT 4.13

❑ Lighting designers are people who are usually not architects but independent designers who have been hired just to design the lighting for architects' buildings. This is a curious practice—one might even say a disturbing one. Light is the most important stimulant to the human's sensory receptors—more information is conveyed by the lighting that reflects off surfaces into our eyes than by the stimuli to any of the other senses.

Yet architects usually leave the important activity of designing lighting to somebody else, neglecting it until after their buildings have been more or less completely designed. Often ellipses or vague grid markings are added to the ceilings of interior perspectives at the eleventh hour to give them a more realistic appearance, but seldom is much thought given to what the light in the room will really be like if downlights or troffers are actually installed there. These renderings make no attempt to show this.

So, the ways in which the lighting will affect the mood and feel of interior spaces is something that architects must learn to be aware of as they design, just as they become aware of building materials, texture, color, and other design elements. Façade lighting also offers many options for distinguishing the appearance of a building. But whether the lighting is interior or exterior, designers should begin by understanding what light fixtures are capable of doing, so that their renderings do not illustrate the improbable or unfeasible!

For example, nighttime renderings of a high-rise office building show 60 stories evenly illuminated from top to bottom. Where would the spotlights be located? Evenly spaced up a 60-story light tower across the street? Improbable. Renderings of interiors are often illustrated using inappropriate light fixtures—or worse, none at all. For example, row upon row of track lighting is shown in a retail shop design, with no fluorescent troffers or downlights for general illumination. Although track lights are good for accenting merchandise, they are inefficient for general space illumination, and, if incandescent, not energy efficient. Yet the renderer will show the room bathed in an even pool of light. That is visually dishonest.

I suggest two ways that designers can become more aware of light in buildings. The first is the easiest: make a point to look at lighting. Go into stores, churches, office buildings, museums, or out on the street and observe the lighting. Look at what fixtures are like and what they do. What color is the light? What are the shadow patterns like? Does the light make harsh shadows, or is it diffuse? What is the light source? What is the color rendering of the light? Does it make the skin look rosy or pale or green?

It really isn't difficult to distinguish pleasant lighting from unpleasant. All that remains is understanding the lighting systems that create each kind. For this, advanced study of lighting systems is required.

The emergence of more complex energy efficiency codes and regulations, coupled with an ever more bewildering array of lighting equipment choices, makes it critical that architects make an effort to learn to design lighting systems to accompany their design projects. Some say that "How will I light it?" should be asked even before "How will I keep it from falling down?" With at least 20 different types of light sources commonly available today, informed architects can illuminate beautifully, while inexperienced ones may create caverns of misery for their clients.

Acoustics

With Gary Siebein

"By intention or default, designers engender their buildings with acoustical environments. When the acoustic characteristics are appropriate for a given interior, they tend to go unnoticed. When room acoustics are unsatisfactory, however, owners and users suffer, and the architect is held responsible."

—Darl Rastorfer

❏ Sound represents an early design opportunity that should be consciously exploited. To achieve this goal, architects must learn about applying some essential principles, as deftly outlined by Gary Siebein in Supplement 4.14.

Gary Siebein

Gary W. Siebein is a registered architect, and is principal consultant with Siebein Associates, Consultants in Architectural Acoustics. He is also professor and director of the Architecture Technology Research Center at the University of Florida, which specializes in architectural acoustics. (© Gary W. Siebein, 2000.)

SUPPLEMENT 4.14

Ten Things Every Architect Should Know About Acoustics That Your Teachers Never Told You

❏ Architectural acoustics is considered by many people to lie somewhere between an art and a science. On the one hand it is viewed as a mysterious art whose secrets have been handed down from master to apprentice through the years. Many architectural firms have their own experience of the vagaries of the black art of acoustics, where one project was executed successfully and a subsequent one did not meet expectations even though the situations appeared to all involved to be similar. On the other hand, acoustics is considered a complex science whose basic laws are difficult to interpret.

The history of architectural acoustics as a deliberate design discipline, where results determined in the programming phase of a project can be achieved in completed buildings, is only 100 years old. The pioneering work of Wallace Clements Sabine at Harvard University at the beginning of the twentieth century was the first serious inquiry in the specific architectural applications of acoustics. There has been a significant multifaceted research effort that has occurred from 1960 until 2000 that has expanded the knowledge base in "the science of sound as it is applied to buildings" (Sabine, 1922; Siebein and Kinzey, 1999).

There are many excellent textbooks that cover basic principles of acoustics that architects should be familiar with. However, there is also a substantial body of practical knowledge that people must learn on a job-by-job basis that affects the acoustic environment of buildings in ways that are not discussed in the architectural literature due to the overwhelming focus in architectural education and practice on visual and spatial phenomena (Siebein, 1994). Ten of these issues that were learned by the author through research and consulting projects (in the school of hard knocks) are discussed in this essay. Hopefully, the discussion will expand the theoretical basis for the architectural applications of acoustics.

1. Floor-to-Floor Height Is an Acoustical Decision. As the height of the structure above a suspended ceiling is decreased, there is less room for heating, ventilating, and air conditioning (HVAC) ducts and other building services. This often causes the air ducts to be reduced in size. As the ducts are reduced in size (for a given air flow), the velocity of air in the duct is increased. This increase in air velocity causes noise from turbulent air flow to increase within the ducts. This is especially true in confined spaces where there are many duct elbows and transitions that have not been designed to meet American Society of Heating, Refrigerating and Air-conditioning Engineers (ASHRAE) and Sheet Metal and Air-Conditioning Contractors National Association (SMACNA) guidelines for smooth air flow.

Furthermore, as the ceiling height is reduced, there is less room available to accommodate silencers and other noise control devices due to the rising velocities and excess pressures that result. For example, wide-radius elbows coming off an air han-

FIGURE 4.40
Exterior view of a high school. The exterior view of the building presents the image of satisfactory architectural design. The ceiling height was reduced by over 12 inches during value engineering to reduce costs. The acoustical consultant was never notified of the consideration of this decision until it was irrevocable. The air ducts were reduced in size to fit within the suspended ceiling height. Air velocities are such that noise levels in the first two classrooms in each wing near the mechanical rooms are at noise criterion (NC) 40 and above.

dling unit cannot be accommodated to help smooth air flow and reduce noise. (See Fig. 4.40.)

2. The Location, Size, and Arrangement of Mechanical Rooms Are Aesthetic Decisions, Not Functional Ones (Relative to Sound). The aesthetics of sound, and especially control of sound from air conditioning systems, is inherently tied to the distance the units are located from critical spaces. Sufficient duct length is required between air handling units and rooms that must be kept relatively quiet. As rooms must be kept quieter, the distance of duct required to achieve the background noise level in a room increases.

Background noise levels in rooms are usually classified by noise criterion (NC) or room criterion (RC) curves. Noise criteria and room criteria are a family of curves that describe design background noise levels in 5-dB increments (NC 20, NC 25, NC 30, NC 35, etc.). The NC curves allow greater amounts of low-frequency sound in a room than middle- and higher-frequency sounds, because the human ear hears high-frequency tones as louder than low-frequency tones. (See Fig. 4.41.)

For example, one can read the planning data for the following two case studies from Table 4.1. A television or radio recording studio might be designed to have background noise levels of NC 15 to NC 20. This would require approximately 120 feet of duct between a typical air handling unit and the first inlet or outlet in the system, a 10-foot-long duct silencer, and 8 to 10 feet of acoustical flex duct at the inlet or outlet to reach this level. A school auditorium might be designed to reach levels of NC 25 to

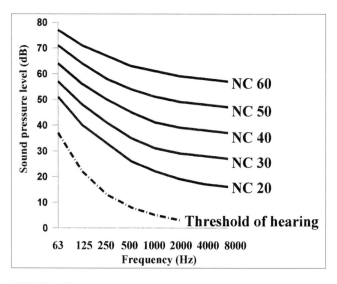

FIGURE 4.41

A family of NC curves plotted as sound level (in dB vs. frequency [in Hertz]).
For a room to be classified as NC 35, for example, the background noise level in
the room must be less than or equal to the NC 30 curve. Usually a tangency
method is used to determine the NC level of a room: a tangent line drawn to the
background noise curve at its highest point defines the NC of the room.

Table 4.1
SUMMARY OF DUCT LENGTH, SILENCER SIZE, AND FLEXIBLE
DUCT REQUIRED TO ACHIEVE VARIOUS NC LEVELS

Design NC Level for Room	Velocity in Duct Near Terminal Supply/Return	Silencer Length	Duct Length to First Inlet	Acoustic Lined Flex Duct Required
NC 20	300/360 fpm	10 ft	90–120 ft	8 ft
NC 30	400/500 fpm	3–7 ft	50–70 ft	6–8 ft
NC 40	600/650 fpm	3 ft	30–50 ft	6–8 ft

NC 30. This would require 90 feet of duct between the first inlet or outlet and the air conditioning unit, a 7- to 10-foot-long silencer, and 6 to 8 feet of acoustical flex duct at each inlet or outlet to reach these levels. One could read similar data for an office with a design background noise level of NC 35 or an open-plan office with a design background noise level of NC 40. Please refer to ASHRAE (1999), Egan (1989), or Cavanaugh and Wilkes (1999) for design NC or RC values for other occupancies.

The size of the mechanical rooms must not only account for the size of the unit and distances required for servicing it, but must also allow for smooth duct transitions particularly on the outlets, lengths of straight duct to smooth air flow before silencers, silencers located before entering critical spaces, and adequate vibration isolation of units. (See Fig. 4.42.)

Both the distance that mechanical rooms are located from acoustically sensitive spaces and the size and planning of the mechanical rooms themselves affect the sonic aesthetics of buildings. If these planning guidelines are adhered to, buildings will be appropriately quiet for their intended uses. If these guidelines are not adhered to, the building will be uncomfortably loud or expensive to keep quiet.

3. You Cannot Understand What the Priest Says in a Cathedral. Cathedrals were designed around the acoustics of the liturgy and theology of the medieval Catholic Church. There was an interest in creating an ambience of otherworldliness, or the ethereal aura of a Supreme Being manifest in light, space, and sound. Choirs sang

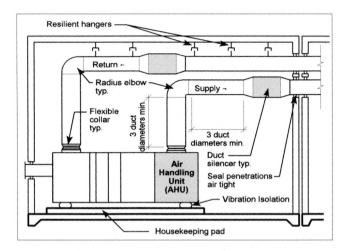

FIGURE 4.42
Schematic section of a typical mechanical room on grade showing a packaged air handling unit mounted on spring isolators on a housekeeping pad. There is adequate ceiling height for 2 to 3 diameters of straight duct to be installed before the duct makes the first 90 degree turn. Silencers are installed another 2 to 3 diameters of straight duct after the elbow before the ducts leave the mechanical room. There is a flexible collar installed between the air handling unit and the ductwork to reduce transmitted vibration. Electrical conduits and piping are also connected to the unit with flexible connections. Space must be provided in mechanical rooms to accommodate not only the footprint of the air handling unit, but also the associated ductwork to achieve quiet operation. Masonry walls or gypsum board and metal stud walls with adequate transmission loss are installed between the mechanical room and adjoining occupied spaces. An expansion joint is provided in the floor slab around the room when it is located on grade.

Gregorian chant. The Mass was celebrated in Latin with the priest facing away from the congregation. There was little need for people to hear clear, intelligible sermons. The large room volume, the acoustically coupled transepts and naves, the great ceiling heights, and the lack of acoustical shaping all contribute to the wonderful acoustics of cathedrals.

However, in the late twentieth century, churches have a different program. Articulate communication between the celebrant and congregation is essential in many religions. The congregation often joins in singing hymns whose words are intended to be understood. There is a need for a new conception of architectural and acoustic space in the church of the twenty-first century that recognizes the roots of the religions they serve. This requirement should transform the architectural form of the church into one that serves its modern needs. The form of the church of the twenty-first century should be changed from its earlier vocabulary into one that has a shape and volume to project sound to the congregation. There are surfaces to reflect sounds from the pulpit, podium, and choir to the congregation, and there are strategically placed sound-absorbing materials to absorb potential echoes and other acoustical defects and limit reverberation times to appropriate values. (See Fig. 4.43.)

4. Concert Time Is Measured in Milliseconds (Not ¼)! Sound travels only 1128 feet per second in air. This is extremely slow when compared to light, which travels at 186,000 miles per second. When one turns on the light switch at the wall, the lamp is illu-

FIGURE 4.43
Photograph of a cathedral, illustrating the large room volume and hard surfaces that contribute to the long reverberation time in the room.

minated instantly. When one speaks or plays an instrument in a large room, the sounds take a relatively long amount of time to move through the space. One millisecond is $\frac{1}{1000}$ (0.001) of a second. This is approximately the amount of time it takes for sound to travel 1 foot.

A sound reflection from a ceiling that arrives at a listener's location shortly after the direct sound (within approximately 50 milliseconds) will be heard as increasing the apparent loudness of the direct sound. This was discovered by Haas (1972). This principle explains why the loudness in an acoustically designed theater may be almost the same from the front of the room to the rear. An angled ceiling can be designed to reflect multiple sounds to seats at the back of the room to add to the perceived loudness there. Sounds are usually heard as less loud as one moves farther from someone who is speaking, due to the increased distance between the speaker and the listener. These important sound reflections are called *early reflections* by acoustical consultants.

Sound reflections that arrive at listeners' ears from the sides within 80 ms of the direct sound have been found to increase the apparent width of the source and to increase the sensation of listening in a three-dimensional acoustic space. This phenomenon is often described as creating a sense of acoustic spaciousness or envelopment (Barron, 1993). These reflections are called *early lateral reflections* by acoustic consultants.

The prolonging of reverberant sound in a room is often used to deliberately enhance the fullness or liveness of musical sounds. Concert halls may have reverberation times of 2 seconds or longer to create the rich, full sounds musicians prefer. This reverberant sound is combined with a strong direct sound, early reflections from the ceiling for loudness, and early reflections from the side walls for spaciousness and source width, to create the beautiful natural sound of a concert hall. (See Figs. 4.44, 4.45, and 4.46.)

5. The Selection and Design of HVAC Systems Is an Acoustical Decision.
In research conducted by the Classroom Acoustics Group at the University of Florida, it was found that the initial selection of the HVAC system for classrooms was directly linked to noise levels inside the room. Self-contained, packaged air conditioning units

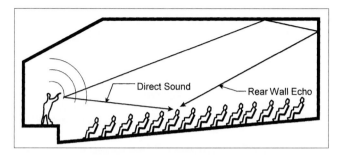

FIGURE 4.44
An echo is a sound that is reflected from a room surface such as a high ceiling or the rear wall that reaches a person listening in the room long enough after the direct sound from the person speaking that it is heard as a separate sound. In the discussion of time, an echo is usually heard when the reflected sound arrives 70 milliseconds or more after the direct sound.

mounted on the walls or roofs of classrooms produced very high noise levels (NC 45 and higher) because of the short distance between the units and the rooms, the high air velocities at the air inlets and outlets, and the typical omission of noise control devices such as silencers in the duct path. Many of these units

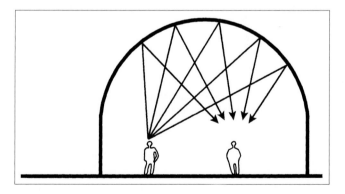

FIGURE 4.45
A large dome focuses sound at its geometric center, creating an acoustic hot spot where it is very loud with acoustic dead spots at other locations where it is difficult to hear.

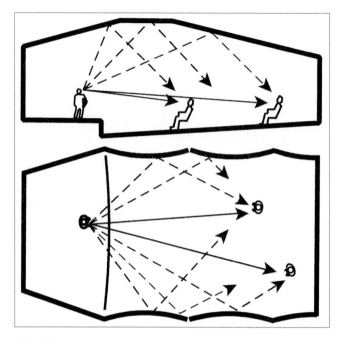

FIGURE 4.46
Reverberation is the prolonging of sound in a room after the source has stopped due to repeated reflections from the room surfaces. Reverberation is related to the volume of a room (in cubic feet or cubic meters). The larger the room volume, the longer the reverberation. As the reverberation time (RT) in a room increases, it becomes increasingly difficult to understand speech because the reverberation from the first word "masks" or covers up the next words. RT is also related to the amount of absorbing material in a room. A room with sound-reflective surfaces will have a longer RT than a room with sound-absorbing surfaces.

have no ductwork associated with them. The air inlets and outlets for the units are directly connected to the room.

Fan coil units, unit ventilators, and rooftop units located within the classrooms or in a mezzanine or closet directly adjacent to the room often produced noise levels of NC 40 to NC 50 in the classrooms. There is often more ductwork and therefore distance between these units and the classrooms. The units are often enclosed in a closet or attic space to reduce noise transmitted from the unit casing. There is often vibration isolation provided for these units as well.

Central air conditioning systems designed with short duct runs with classrooms clustered around them had noise levels of NC 40 and above due to the short duct runs between the units and the inlets and outlets. Central air conditioning systems designed in accordance with items 1 and 2 in this essay had noise levels of NC 35 and less.

Audiologists have presented data showing that young children need classrooms with low background noise levels (NC 25 to NC 35) in order to hear and understand what teachers are saying. (See Fig. 4.47.)

6. The Design of Cafeterias, Classrooms, Music Rooms, Restaurants, and Lobbies Is a Room Acoustics Design Problem. In a cafeteria there is generally not enough wall area on which to locate sound-absorbent material to reduce all the noise that large numbers of children will make when they use the room for lunch. The same

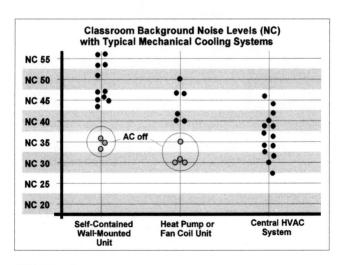

FIGURE 4.47
Graph of background noise level plotted vs. type of air conditioning system measured in a school. (Siebein, Gold, Ermann, and Walker, 1999.)

is often true of lobbies, classrooms, restaurants, and other building types where occupants may create large amounts of noise. It becomes necessary to use room acoustic design principles borrowed from concert hall acoustics to combine the controlled use of acoustical materials with strategies such as limiting the room volume; canting, splaying, or otherwise shaping walls to redistribute sound in the room; and breaking up sound with diffusing panels. (See Fig. 4.48.)

7. The Acoustics of the New Urbanism Is a Potential Nightmare. As urban areas are revitalized with new commercial activities, there are a number of serious acoustical concerns that become evident as this process begins. Often the first businesses to move into a revitalizing downtown area are nightclubs and other entertain-

FIGURE 4.48
This music practice room incorporates several important acoustical design features. Absorbent materials are located on both the walls and the ceiling to reduce the overall loudness of reverberant sound when the entire band of 70 to 100 students plays. The angled wall panels are designed to diffuse or break up standing waves and prevent the boomy reflections that can occur in rectangular rooms. The angled ceiling and wall panels also diffuse or scatter reflected sounds so the teacher can hear each student playing. These room acoustic principles help to achieve satisfactory sound quality.

ment venues. Deep bass thumping sounds propagating from the nightclubs into nearby residential units is a particular problem that must be addressed at the planning stages of a rejuvenating downtown. Once a nightclub or outdoor patio is designed, the owner can buy enough amplifiers and loudspeakers to produce high-quality sounds for his or her customers at very economical costs. The acoustic power of the amplifiers and loudspeakers, especially the subwoofers that are used to amplify the bass or low-frequency sounds, is great enough to disturb people for over half a mile from the nightclub, especially if there is an open area of water between the club and residences or if there are other buildings that can reflect sounds to residences. There are five strategies that can be implemented to reduce the noise impact from nightclubs and other activities that use amplified sound as part of their operations.

■ Communities must have effective noise ordinances to control the potential noise impact from entertainment venues on residences as the first line of defense.

■ Zoning ordinances or land management ordinances might require minimum distance separations between entertainment venues, particularly those with outdoor entertainment and residences.

■ The transmission loss or sound transmission class (STC) rating of the source property should be designed to effectively reduce sounds produced within the facility.

■ The STC ratings of nearby residences should be upgraded from traditional construction assemblies to effectively reduce sounds within, especially in bedrooms and sleeping areas.

■ The plan approval and building permit processes should be tied into the noise ordinance. Activities that might have a potential noise impact on neighbors should be identified early in the design process, and appropriate mitigation measures should be designed in. Verification of performance should be required as a part of the certificate of occupancy process.

When homes and businesses are located very close to each other, the placement of central air conditioning plants becomes a critical problem. This is especially true in areas such as the southeastern United States, where the hot, humid climate requires extensive air conditioning systems for much of the year. Air-cooled condensing units of the sizes required by schools, civic buildings (such as courthouses, post offices, municipal auditoriums, libraries, etc.), office buildings, multistory condominiums, and other larger buildings create enough noise to disturb residences located nearby. The low-frequency sounds are particularly annoying to residents at night, when commercial properties may run their air conditioning plants to take advantage of off-peak electric rates. Commonsense site planning for the utilities is the most effective acoustic control that can be implemented. Noise control devices such as carefully designed barrier walls, sound-absorbing equipment enclosures, and specially designed noise abatement enclosures are often required to provide a suitable sonic environment for neighbors. The noise control elements become very expensive to implement and are at the state of the art of the industry to provide suitable noise reduction.

8. Beware of STC Ratings for Selection of Partitions. The sound transmission class or STC rating is a single-number weighted average of the sound transmission loss measured in frequencies from 125 to 4000 Hz. The higher the STC rating, the more the sound is reduced as it travels through the wall. This presents a simple method to rate or rank the relative reduction of average sounds (usually speech sounds) as they pass through a wall or ceiling. In simple terms, the STC rating represents the amount of middle-frequency sound that is "lost" or reduced as it travels through a partition. Low-frequency sounds associated with amplified music or HVAC equipment are outside the frequency range that is considered by the STC rating. Therefore it is possible to select a wall assembly with a high STC rating and still have disturbing sounds be heard on the other side of it.

It is also possible to have two walls that have the same STC rating but behave differently for specific sounds due to the way in which the STC data is weighted to form the average. For example, a wall with an STC rating of 55 might be used between a mechanical equipment room and an adjoining conference room.

If the equipment in the room is a large air handling unit with an air compressor, such as might be found in a hospital, an STC 55 wall consisting of 2 layers of ½-inch gypsum board on each side of metal framing with glass fiber batts in the cavity will likely not have adequate transmission loss in the lower frequencies to reduce the noise to acceptable levels. For instance, in the 63-Hz octave band, the gypsum board wall just described has a transmission loss of approximately 10 to 20 dB. A masonry wall consisting of 8-inch lightweight concrete masonry unit with gypsum board on one side and a plaster coating on the other side would have the same STC rating as the gypsum board wall. However, the transmission loss in the low frequencies (63-Hz octave band) is 35 dB. This is almost 20 dB greater than the gypsum board wall with the same STC rating. This would result in low-frequency sounds being one-fourth as loud on the other side of the wall. (See Fig. 4.49.)

Contractors often request that acoustical consultants provide STC ratings so they can value engineer partition selections by selecting less costly, less massive partitions with equivalent STC ratings. It is essential to realize that many partitions are selected

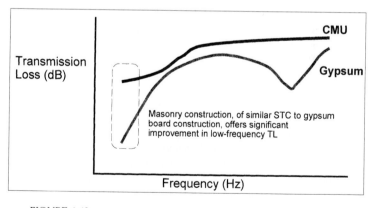

FIGURE 4.49
Graph of sound transmission loss in dB vs. frequency for a concrete masonry wall and a gypsum board wall. Notice the increased transmission loss in the lower frequencies for the masonry wall.

on the basis of the actual sound transmission loss in each frequency band and not on the basis of the STC rating.

9. One Person's Music Is Another Person's Noise; or Is It? There is a substantial body of literature describing the subject of noise-induced annoyance and acoustical preferences for music. The general consensus of this work is that neither annoyance nor acoustical tastes are as idiosyncratic as many people believe. In other words, there are significant areas of agreement among people as to what sounds they find annoying. There is also a substantial agreement as to what many people define as good acoustics.

Noise-induced annoyance has been identified by Fidell and Green (1991) as an adverse mental attitude toward noise. There are several acoustic and nonacoustic factors that contribute to annoyance. As the loudness of a disturbing sound is increased, most people will find it more annoying. However, just the presence of a disturbing sound, such as a dripping faucet or low-level bass thumps from amplified music, even though heard at low levels, will be severely annoying to many people. Intermittent sounds, especially those like the dripping faucet or the bass beats from amplified music, are usually more annoying to people than continuous sounds such as noise from an air conditioning unit or cars on a distant highway—even if the air conditioning unit is heard at a louder level than the drip. This is especially true when the annoying sound is different in pitch, loudness, or duration than the background or ambient sounds.

Annoyance is generally proportional to the time people are exposed to the noise. The longer one is exposed to noise, the greater the annoyance. Changes in the sound level over time or changes in the pitch of sounds over time are also annoying because these sounds stand out as distinct events in the sonic environment. This is why changing sounds are used for emergency warnings. The spectral content or pitch of sounds contributes to the potential for annoyance.

People will gradually become used to some sounds. When people are involved in the making of noise, they will usually not be annoyed by it. For instance, those listening to amplified music in a teenager's bedroom will find the music enjoyable, while parents trying to read or sleep or talk in a room down the hall may be disturbed even though they are hearing the sounds at lower levels than the teens. When the noise is perceived as necessary, people will often not register annoyance with the sound, even though it is loud or otherwise might be disturbing. For example, a neighbor using lawn equipment such as power mowers, leaf blowers etc., may disturb the university professor trying to read Plato on his patio next door, while the neighbor on the other side, who might be hammering nails or sawing wood or have just completed mowing his grass, might not register annoyance even though the sound level at the two homes is identical. The subtleties of noise-induced annoyance are a match for the subtleties of concert hall music quality.

In concert halls, four primary qualities have been identified as contributing to most people's notion of what good acoustics are. Loudness is essential in order for people to hear well. Fairly small ranges of preferred loudness levels have been found that vary slightly with the type of music (for natural or unamplified music). Fullness or liveness, measured by the presence of reverberation, is a second major contributing factor to good acoustics. Acoustic intimacy, identified by how soon after the direct sound reflections from the walls and ceiling arrive, is the third factor. The fourth primary factor is the relative difference in the reflection pattern of sounds that arrive at the left and right ears of listeners. This difference in the detailed configuration of sounds at the two ears, called *binaural dissimilarity* by acoustical consultants, contributes to the acoustical qualities of source width, envelopment, and spaciousness just described. Secondary factors include clarity, providing suitable levels of quiet in the room so performers can be heard, the ability to locate the sound source in the three-dimensional space of a room, the ability of performers to hear each other to play in ensemble, maintaining proper timbre or frequency balance among performers, maintaining a balance in loudness between soloists and the ensemble, avoiding the acoustical defects just described, providing adequate support for bass sounds, and providing adequate support for treble sounds, among others (Siebein and Kinzey, 1999).

10. Concert Halls Today Are Designed by Impulse (Response). Recent research has defined the notion of an impulse response that represents the pulsing of a room caused by a single, loud sound. The impulse response provides a convenient way to describe and measure acoustical situations in rooms. The impulse response obtained in a room describes sound propagation and reflections within that room that arrive at a specific listener's location. It is hypothesized that each note of a piece of music or each syllable of spoken words excites the room in a similar way (Cremer and Muller, 1982). The impulse response will vary at each seat in a room because it represents the unique signature of sound that arrives from a given source to a specific listener. The contribution of the direct sound and reflections from each of the walls, the ceiling, and other architectural elements is depicted in the impulse response as shown in Fig. 4.50.

Figure 4.50 is organized into two columns. The column on the left shows the path of sound travel between the source and the receiver in a small room. The column on the right shows the impulse response as a graph of sound amplitude or loudness (in decibels) on the vertical axis plotted versus time (in milliseconds) on the horizontal axis. The figure starts at the top with no communication between the people. Only the background or ambient noise exists in the room. In the second sketch, the person on the left speaks. The direct sound travels from the person speaking through the air to the listener. It does not strike any of the room surfaces.

In the third sketch, the reflected sound path from the ceiling is shown as it arrives shortly after the direct sound in time at a reduced amplitude. Both the decrease in loudness and the increase in arrival time are due to the longer path length this sound travels compared to the direct sound. The sound reflections from the ceiling increase the apparent loudness of sounds when the delay time between the reflections and the direct sound is less than 550 ms for speech and 80 ms for music. If the delay time is greater than 70 ms, the sound will be heard as an echo.

The fourth sketch shows sounds reflecting from the walls of the room. These reflections arrive after the ceiling reflection and at a lower amplitude due to the increase in path length. If these

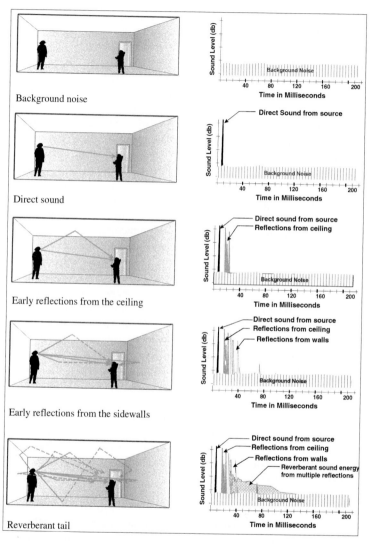

FIGURE 4.50

Concept diagram of how the impulse response of a room is constructed of the background noise, direct sound, early reflections from the ceiling and side walls, and reverberant sound.

reflections arrive within 80 ms after the direct sound, they will increase the perceived width of the sound source and create a sensation of acoustic spaciousness or envelopment.

The fifth (bottom) sketch shows sounds that strike multiple surfaces in the room. This is the reverberant energy that persists for some extended period of time (the reverberation time [RT]) after the direct sound. Two seconds of reverberation is desired to enhance the natural sounds of an orchestra in a concert hall. One second of reverberation is desired for increasing the loudness of speech in a theater, yet still providing sufficient clarity or intelligibility.

As the architectural characteristics of a room are altered, the impulse response and the qualities of what people hear and how well they hear are also changed. The impulse response can be used as a basis for suggesting possible architectural approaches to the design of a room or can help determine which modifications can be made to an existing room (Cremer and Muller, 1982; Siebein and Kinzey, 1999).

The use of the impulse response as an acoustical diagnostic tool is analogous to an electrocardiogram of a heartbeat that a physician might use to evaluate the health of a patient. By looking at the relative amplitude and timing of a sequence of pulses (like the series of peaks and valleys one observes on an electrocardiogram), the acoustical consultant can diagnose the acoustical conditions in a room. He or she can then recommend design changes to improve communication in the room (Siebein and Kinzey, 1999).

The impulse response can help to provide a conceptual understanding of the links between perceived acoustical qualities and the architectural features of rooms. Additionally, it is used extensively to characterize sound fields in computer models, scale models, and full-size rooms. Once the impulse response has been obtained, the information can then be translated into a virtual sound field. This makes it possible to actually hear how architectural changes to a computer model or scale model of a room that are indicated in the impulse response might be perceived by listeners in the room (Siebein and Kinzey, 1999).

References

Barron, M. *Auditorium Acoustics and Architectural Design*. London: Spon, 1993.

Cavanaugh, William J., and Wilkes, Joseph A. (eds.). *Architectural Acoustics: Principles and Practice*. New York: Wiley, 1999.

Cremer, L., and Muller, H.A. *Principles and Applications of Room Acoustics*, vol. 1. London: Applied Science, 1982. Translator: Theodore J. Schultz.

Egan, M.D. *Architectural Acoustics*. New York: McGraw-Hill, 1989.

Fidell, Sanford, and Green, David M. "Noise-Induced Annoyance of Individuals and Communities." In Harris, Cyril M. (ed.), *Handbook of Acoustical Measurements and Noise Control*. New York: McGraw-Hill, 1991.

Haas, H. "The Influence of a Single Echo on the Audibility of Speech." *Journal of the Audio Engineering Society*, 20(2):146–159, 1972.

Sabine, Wallace Clement. *Collected Papers on Acoustics*. Los Altos, CA: Peninsula, 1922.

Siebein, Gary W. *Acoustics in Buildings: A Tutorial on Architectural Acoustics*. Unpublished manuscript, 1994.

Siebein, G.W., Gold, M.A., Ermann, M.G., and Walker, J. "Background Noise Levels in Classrooms." In *Proceedings of the 137th Meeting of the Acoustical Society of America and the 2nd Annual Convention of the European Acoustics Association: Forum Acusticum*. [machine-readable data file]. Sigrid Bärndal, assisted by Ulrich Redlich and Julia Harman (producers).

Siebein, G.W., and Kinzey, B.Y. "Recent Innovations in Acoustical Design and Research." In Cavanaugh, W.J., and Wilkes, J.A. (eds.), *Architectural Acoustics: Principles and Practice*. New York: Wiley, 1999.

Orchestrating Design

❏ One aim of this chapter is to elaborate on the multidisciplinary nature of designing buildings, especially large buildings. While expertise from other disciplines is required on all projects, executing smaller-scale work is likely to be well within the province of most architects.

Designing buildings involves consideration of a potentially enormous number of factors, each weighted differently, and of course artfully integrated, according to the project. Those factors deemed relevant (and described throughout the book) must be explicitly determined and addressed from project inception.

While teamwork and collaborative effort have been stressed, the architect is still the leader. The architect's conceptions must remain true, without undue compromising. It is in the development of those conceptions where input from and management of consultants reinforces, informs, or in some cases establishes the means for implementation. That is why it is so important for architects to have a broad knowledge base. The architect is the direct liaison to the client; in most situations, he or she alone has the opportunity and privilege of learning about the client's issues—often in a personal manner—and has the ultimate responsibility for translating these issues to an architectural solution.

All architects view collaboration as an essential part of the design process; some regard concept development as collaborative, while others see collective effort as diluting the strength of a solution in some instances. The way in which consultants (and colleagues, for that matter) are worked into the design process is part of the architect's personal philosophy. Just as there is no single right way to create a concept, it must be clearly and absolutely stated that there is no disputing the value and importance of consultants' participation during the design process.

The Symphony

❏ In terms of the five senses, nothing compares to the feeling of standing in the center of a building in progress, particularly if you've had anything to do with creating the project. For some, even the triumph of the completed work stands as a lesser thrill. Perhaps the open framing, the columns and beams, the pipes and wiring, the shapes, textures, voids, and smells work together and suggest motion and even life. To have a hand in orchestrating all these components is a truly remarkable privilege.

My first experience as a sole proprietor, nearly 20 years ago, involved the expansion and renovation of a corporate travel consulting office located in a windowless space in a mall. The sequence of drawings and photographs that follow is my attempt to communicate that feeling of creating, nurturing, and witnessing various phases of a small-scale yet special "everyday" project.

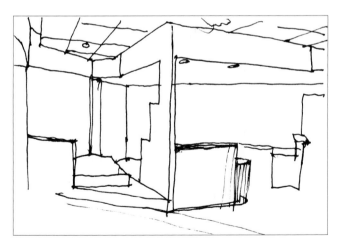

FIGURE 4.51
Early perspective sketches of the angled reception desk and ceiling configuration.

FIGURE 4.51 (Continued)
(Courtesy of Andy Pressman.)

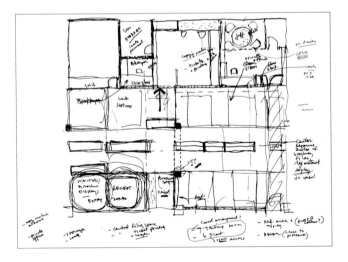

FIGURE 4.52
(a) Sketch illustrating the transition between a bubble diagram and a more resolved plan.

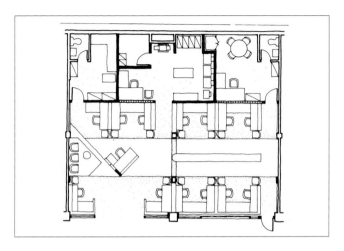

FIGURE 4.52 (Continued)
(b) Floor plan presented to the client as the final layout. (Courtesy of Andy Pressman.)

FIGURE 4.53
(a) A view of the existing condition and the wall that will be demolished to expand the space.

FIGURE 4.53 (Continued)
(b) Study model of chipboard and corrugated cardboard. Note container of glue in the background for scale. I'm certain this was the model that sold the client on the design in this case.

FIGURE 4.53 (Continued)
(c) Construction progress photo; note that the view is similar to that of the study model. At this stage, I virtually felt the bold lines of the drawings coming to life. (Courtesy of Andy Pressman.)

FIGURE 4.54
(a) Reception desk and waiting area; view upon entering the office.
(b) Diagonal orientation of reception desk directs clients toward workstations or waiting platform. (Photos © Norman McGrath.)

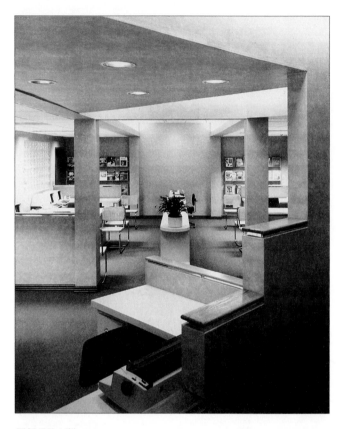

FIGURE 4.55
View from waiting platform. The reception area is the focus for the design.
(Photo © Norman McGrath.)

FIGURE 4.56
An image of the general contractor for the project as I first experienced him. Later, our adversarial relationship gave way to one of mutual respect. (Photo: Andy Pressman, during an early construction observation meeting.)

Community Design
With Richard Nordhaus

❏ Concluding the chapter on architectural design, Richard Nordhaus provides a primer and rationale for the reenergized discipline of community design. In Supplement 4.15, he examines the role of community design as a catalyst for an expanded, more inclusive vision for the profession. The directives for enhancement of both environmental and practice quality are as much timely social and political statements as they are substantive design conceptions.

Richard Nordhaus

Richard S. Nordhaus is a regents' professor at the School of Architecture and Planning at the University of New Mexico, where he teaches design and directs the school's Design and Planning Assistance Center. He holds a Master of Architecture from the University of Pennsylvania.

SUPPLEMENT 4.15

Why Community Design?

❏ There is little doubt that our cities, suburbs, and rural communities are in trouble, confronted by disinvestment, crime, poverty, racism, gridlock, environmental degradation, and hopelessness. The problem is most severe for low-income people who have no choice and little voice in decisions that impact their communities. In a democracy, community development can only take place when local residents are committed to investing themselves and their resources in the effort. But the communities with the greatest need are often excluded from the planning and design process, lacking access to professional collaborators who support a bottom-up, inside-out process. Community design has evolved as an alternative mode of architectural and planning practice that aspires to fill the gap.

Community design is a philosophy and a methodology of planning and design practice that endeavors to focus professional knowledge and skills on social issues. While rooted in the professional traditions of architecture, landscape architecture, and plan-

FIGURE 4.57
Courtesy of the Design and Planning Assistance Center, School of Architecture and Planning, University of New Mexico.

ning, it proposes alternative modes of practice that address issues of social and environmental equity, engaging in projects that are community based, empowering, participatory, and sustainable.

Social equity is the core value of community design, recognizing that improvement of the physical environment is essential for community development and social change. Dialogue through user participation is the core methodology, enhancing both process and products through collaboration. When partnerships are established between residents, professionals, and institutions, and when residents are effectively engaged in the whole design and development process, the outcomes are more likely to fulfill the aspirations of the residents, build community capacity and confidence, develop project support, and improve occupant satisfaction.

The planning and design professions have a professional and ethical responsibility to promote healthy communities, but they can only exercise that responsibility effectively in collaboration with other stakeholders. The potential benefits to professionals are substantial: professionals gain otherwise inaccessible insights, information, and values; access to new markets and professional opportunities; and the personal satisfaction that their work can make a difference.

A Brief History of Community Design

❏ The community design movement emerged during the late 1960s and early 1970s in reaction to a variety of social, political, philosophical, and professional pressures—the abuse of urban renewal, the decay of the inner cities, the civil rights movement, and disillusionment with the top-down, modernist approach of the planning and design professions. Whitney Young's famous speech to the 1968 National AIA convention provided the impetus for action by the architectural profession. As president of the Urban Coalition, Young told the convention:

"You are not a profession that has distinguished itself by your social and civic contributions to the cause of civil rights, and I am sure

FIGURE 4.58
Courtesy of the Design and Planning Assistance Center, School of Architecture and Planning, University of New Mexico.

this does not come to you as any shock. . . . You are most distinguished by your thunderous silence and your complete irrelevance. . . . You are employers, you are key people in the planning of cities today. You share the responsibility for the mess we are in—in terms of the white noose around the central city. We didn't just suddenly get this situation. It was carefully planned."

Community design centers were established by activist professionals and academicians as a vehicle for community design. While a few centers were operating at the time of Young's speech, most were established in the years immediately following. By 1971, between 60 and 70 centers had started up, rising to over 80 by 1978. An association of community design center directors was established in 1978 and later became the Association for Community Design (ACD). During the 1980s, the numbers fell radically. By 1987, the ACD could identify only 16 active centers (Cary, 2000).

The early centers were predominantly ideological and adversarial in nature. They were established to provide professional technical assistance to disenfranchised communities and groups battling to save their communities from imposed urban renewal, highway construction, inhumane housing conditions, and a host of other threats. Client communities lacked the technical resources needed to argue their case effectively and professional activists believed technical assistance would level the playing field. During the process, neighborhood leaders would become effective advocates for the neighborhood's agenda, eliminating the need for outside professionals. Much of the work addressed broad planning and social policy issues. Architectural work was usually limited to programming and preliminary design proposals intended to articulate needs and raise funds.

During the 1980s, the focus and structure of community design and community design centers shifted to a more pragmatic and entrepreneurial stance. The dismantling of the Great Society dried up critical sources of support for community-based initiatives. Many surviving design centers shifted their focus to work on housing and local projects with neighborhood community development corporations. The philosophy shifted from political empowerment to economic empowerment (Comerio,

1990). This phase recognized the importance of concrete, visible success—no matter how small—to build the capacity of grass-roots organizations and community development corporations.

Community design practice has experienced a resurgence in the 1990s. A recent survey by the Association of Collegiate Schools of Architecture (Cary, 2000) has identified more than 70 community design organizations including professional schools, nonprofit, and for-profit organizations. This figure does not include the many professionals who commit their time and skills to pro bono work.

While the philosophy and methodology of community design continues to evolve, the tenets of social equity and user participation persist. The poverty focus of the 1970s has broadened to incorporate issues of environmental justice, multiculturalism, and gender. Many community designer organizations search for a balance between the ideology of the 1970s and the pragmatism of the 1980s, recognizing that neither approach is sufficient to improve the conditions of distressed communities and effect social change. Collaboration between neighborhood and project residents, local institutions, and professionals is essential to build communities and effect beneficial change.

Types of Community Design Centers

❏ Community design is practiced in a variety of formats and settings. Centers may be institutional or private, may be for profit or nonprofit, may operate locally or regionally, may provide front-end design or full architectural services, and may work on broad planning and social advocacy issues or specific building projects. While centers vary in structure and services, most follow a few organizational models.

■ *University-sponsored community design studios* are staffed by faculty and students who generally work on specific projects with community or neighborhood groups. Projects may be initiated by the community or by the studio, and usually last for one semester. Typically, the scope of service is limited to planning and front-end programming and design,

FIGURE 4.59
Courtesy of the Design and Planning Assistance Center, School of Architecture and Planning, University of New Mexico.

although some schools conduct design-build studios where students carry projects through to construction.

■ *University-based research and service institutes* are usually operated by faculty and staff who are engaged in community-based contract work. These organizations may be supported by the university, public agencies, foundations, and/or contracts. University institutes are not limited to the constraints of the academic calendar and can undertake long-term projects. Most do not provide full architectural services.

■ *Nonprofit community design centers* are professionally staffed organizations that provide a variety of planning and architectural services to low-income communities and nonprofit development corporations. Centers are funded by a variety of sources—foundation grants, public monies, agency contracts, client reimbursement, and fees. Projects include the full range of services, from planning and programming through full architectural services.

■ *Nonprofit multiservice design centers* offer a variety of services in addition to planning and design, which may include development services, employment training, youth programs, and housing counseling. Multiservice centers often start with planning and design, expanding their capacity to fill urgent community needs. Funding sources are as varied as the services provided.

■ *Professional volunteer clearinghouses* are normally sponsored by local professional chapters. A small staff acts as broker for community groups and low-income individuals who seek professional assistance for qualifying projects, often providing training and guidance to volunteer practitioners.

■ *For-profit community design firms* provide full architectural services to community groups and nonprofit community development corporations, charging professional fees. Successful firms address the needs of their community clients by developing the knowledge and techniques required to work collaboratively throughout the design and development process, usually providing assistance beyond normal professional services.

Community Design Process

❏ Four fundamental roles—sponsor, user, designer, and builder—structure the community design process. How these roles are defined and played out strongly influences the design outcomes. The distinction between sponsor and user is particularly important

FIGURE 4.60
Courtesy of the Design and Planning Assistance Center, School of Architecture and Planning, University of New Mexico.

for community design projects where the sponsor exercises substantial control while the user has neither voice nor influence in the process. Effective community design process requires that project residents have a clear voice and substantial role at all stages.

In conventional practice, the design professional must serve the interests of the sponsor, who signs the contract and pays the bills. In situations where the interests of the sponsor and the user conflict, the interests of the sponsor will prevail. While many practitioners recognize the predicament, they are often powerless to change it. Participatory methods are sometimes employed in conventional practice, but their application tends to be limited to the programming and schematic design stages. Users seldom have a voice at the initial problem identification stage, when project direction is set, or at the later development and construction stages, when final decisions are made. Even when users are consulted, institutional barriers that limit direct dialogue between designer and users often filter input.

Community designers identify users as their primary clients, seeking alternative forms of practice that support effective engagement of users throughout the process. Many community design problems are ill defined and value based, encompassing multiple, often conflicting interests. Diverse participants contribute their own distinct skills and knowledge to the process, which is best conceived as a mutual learning process, a dialogue that allows solutions to emerge from the give-and-take between all of the actors.

When design is conducted as a sustained dialogue, the designer and the user play essential roles and neither can displace the expertise of the other. The designer can conceptualize and delineate many possibilities. But the professional does not know and can never fully understand the user's stories, dreams, and beliefs. The user best knows the realities of the situation and can choose preferable solutions, but does not have the skill and experience to pose a broad range of alternative solutions or the technical competence required for implementation.

Figure 4.61 illustrates the conceptual difference between conventional design and community design. The roles and influence of the actors in the process (designer, sponsor, user, and builder) are presented for the six stages of conventional and community design (problem identification, problem definition, schematic design, design development, construction, and occupancy). The shades indicate the hierarchy of control in a conventional design process. The numbered circles show the reallocation of influence required for an effective user voice in the design dialogue.

Problem identification establishes the scope and focus of the project, determining which issues will be included and which will be excluded. Framing problems to include the concerns of disadvantaged communities requires their active participation in the problem-setting phase. The relevance of community concerns cannot be determined from the outside in or from the top down.

Active participation during the programming/problem definition phase requires user involvement that extends beyond normal programming research. The user, sponsor, and designer need to collaborate on the full range of programmatic decisions. The residents are the experts about their needs and their community. They know what is important, what is realistic, and what will work. On the other hand, they do not have the technical knowledge or the experience necessary to ensure a productive process.

Collaboration between sponsor, user, and designer is essential during the schematic design phase. The translation of program-

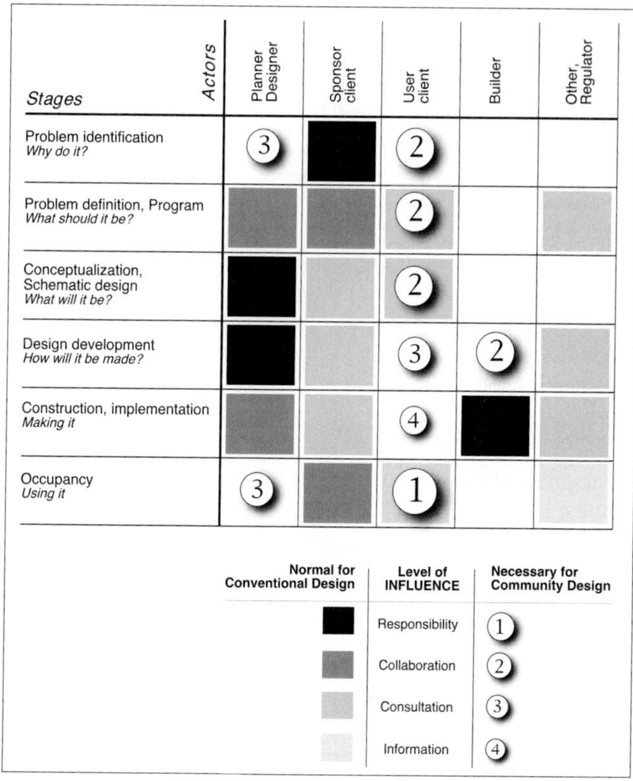

Stages \ Actors	Planner Designer	Sponsor client	User client	Builder	Other, Regulator
Problem identification *Why do it?*	③	■	②		
Problem definition, Program *What should it be?*			②		
Conceptualization, Schematic design *What will it be?*	■		②		
Design development *How will it be made?*	■		③	②	
Construction, implementation *Making it*			④	■	
Occupancy *Using it*	③		①		

Normal for Conventional Design	Level of INFLUENCE	Necessary for Community Design
■ (black)	Responsibility	①
■ (dark gray)	Collaboration	②
■ (light gray)	Consultation	③
■ (lightest)	Information	④

FIGURE 4.61

Role influence in conventional and community design processes. The background shading and numbered circles indicate the level of influence of the actors at each stage of the design process. The background shades indicate normal influence in the conventional design. The numbered circles indicate the restructured influence necessary for community design. (Courtesy of Richard Nordhaus.)

matic decisions to design concepts is subjective and tenuous. Good, acceptable planning and design solutions are seldom achieved without considerable debate. Negotiation and dialogue between designer, user, and sponsor is needed to respond to the spoken and unspoken requirements of all the participants and to discover solutions that are mutually beneficial.

Typically, user involvement during the later stages of the process—design development and construction—is very limited. While the issues are often technical, users need to be informed and consulted. Decisions made during design development and construction can have a significant detrimental effect on users if they are not consulted. The dialogue established during the earlier phases needs to be maintained to sustain user trust and confidence in the process.

A continuing role in the management of the built environment through personalization of space, participation in management, ownership, and other activities has meaning and value to residents, increases occupant satisfaction, and often develops residents' skills and capacity.

Principles of Community Design

❏ Community designers and community design organizations generally share values and beliefs about the societal role of the environmental design professions. While community design organizations vary widely in structure, philosophy, and services, there is a substantial and growing body of work that is committed to recognized principles of community design.

■ *Social and environmental equity.* The political dimension of planning and design, and the resulting allocation of space, resources, and services, is a central concern of community design. Community design focuses on planning and design projects that contribute to social and environmental equity.

■ *Empowering and enabling projects.* Community designers engage projects with the potential to empower residents to control their own environments and enable them to participate fully in their communities.

■ *User participation.* The community design process supports active user participation in partnership with professionals and institutions throughout the process of planning, designing, and developing local facilities and neighborhoods.

■ *Bottom-up, inside-out process.* Projects are internally focused on the needs and priorities of client communities. The

FIGURE 4.62
Courtesy of the Design and Planning Assistance Center, School of Architecture and Planning, University of New Mexico.

application of community knowledge and skill is essential to community design. Community design seeks to provide meaningful choices for those who have the fewest options.

■ *Design is a process of mutual learning.* Residents, professionals, and institutions have different knowledge, skills, and values. Community design requires mutual learning through an open, active dialogue.

■ *Sustainability and long-term benefit.* Planning and design investment in distressed communities must have long-term environmental, economic, and social benefit to the residents.

■ *Built projects help build communities.* The visible success of built projects can be a vehicle for community development and social change when broader social advocacy strategies are integrated in the process. Tangible physical improvements build pride and stimulate revitalization.

■ *Design matters*. Good design provides a message of hope and pride to distressed communities. Good design can provide a catalyst for creating a sense of place and identity that is an important component of social communities.

Bibliography

Comerio, Mary C. "Community Design: Idealism and Entrepreneurship." In Sanoff, Henry (ed.), *Participatory Design: Theory & Practice*. Raleigh, NC: Sanoff, 1990.

Cary, John M. Jr. (ed.). *The ACSA Sourcebook of Community Design Programs*. Washington, DC: ACSA Press, 2000.

Kretzmann, John P., and McKnight, John L. *Building Communities from the Inside Out*. Chicago: ACTA, 1993.

Lawson, Bryon. *How Designers Think: The Design Process Demystified*. London: Butterworth Architecture, 1990.

Mehrhoff, W. Arthur. *Community Design*. Chicago: Sage, 1999.

Sanoff, Henry. *Community Participation Methods in Planning and Design*. New York: Wiley, 2000.

Sanoff, Henry. *Participatory Design: Theory & Practice*. Raleigh, NC: Sanoff, 1990.

Schon, Donald A. *The Reflective Practitioner: How Professionals Think in Action*. New York: Basic Books, 1982.

chapter 5

Presentations

*"I really didn't
say everything I said."*
"90% of the game is half mental."
—Yogi Berra

Sketches

❏ "I'm going to *die* if I don't get this job!" Antoine Predock exclaimed, then continued, with a big smile, "If there's something wrong, I'll fix it—just tell me!" This was how he began his required one-minute concluding remarks for the presentation of a new School of Architecture and Planning building at the University of New Mexico in April 2000.

Predock developed great rapport with the audience. It was as if he was connecting personally to each individual in the group. Straight talk about the substance of the design (without notes), and humor, of course, were woven throughout. He won the crowd (and eventually the invited competition) with his casual and nonthreatening style, without pandering. And a tough crowd it was: other architects, architecture faculty, and students. Predock was self-assured, confident without being arrogant, and informal, yet he addressed the necessary issues. His sincerity was absolutely convincing. He brought along an army of about a half-dozen interns and associates from his office who had worked on the scheme, and who also participated in the question-and-answer period. Great tactic, great drama. The enthusiasm, excitement, and investment in the project were quite clear, and had a very positive impact.

This chapter dissects the art of persuasion necessary for effective presentations. Karen Greenstreet and Bob Greenstreet provide the definitive supplement on presenting for pros. Kathryn Anthony, author of the critically acclaimed *Design Juries on Trial* (Van Nostrand Reinhold, 1991), elaborates on best communication methods with clients, and what to do before, during, and after the presentation. Information on trends in reprographics, printing, and imaging follows in an interview I conducted with Jim Maitland, a leader in the field from the Charrette Corporation. The importance of architectural photography as perhaps the final step in the whole design process is discussed by Steve Rosenthal, one of the top photographers in the world. And James P. Cramer, former executive vice president/CEO of the American Institute of Architects (AIA), summarizes the chapter with a brief commentary on the importance of acquiring the ability to negotiate (i.e., communicate, present) for good design. This is crucial because otherwise the opportunity to raise the bar is missed, even if the quality is there.

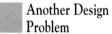 **Another Design Problem**

"Rather than imagining the audience or the client in underwear (which never works—never demean your audience), imagine them cheering you and bubbling with approval."
—**John S. Lyons, PhD**

"The process is communication. The objective is to project a fresh idea and have it acted upon. The name of the game is salesmanship. The techniques used will vary considerably according to the nature of the idea and the audience to be reached."
—**Weld Coxe, Hon. AIA**

"Communication among three categories of participants is needed to see a design project through to completion. (1) The architect or designer, with colleagues, staff, and consultants. (2) Builders, manufacturers, fabricators, and tradespeople. (3) Clients, financiers, competition jurors, enforcement officials, users, and the public."
—**Paul Stevenson Oles, AIA**

I always like to view the presentation of a project as another design problem. But then, I view almost every challenge in life as a design problem—that's one of the good and powerful side effects of being an architect! You should be able to communicate your project visually and verbally in a manner that is consistent with the character of the design. This requires planning and time management (see Chapter 1). My guideline is to seek ways in which design time can be maximized without sacrificing the time and effort needed to produce the most compelling presentation possible.

One way to accomplish this goal is to make design tools and presentation tools or media the same. In fact, there is a personal and alluring quality to original drawings that can rarely be duplicated in a set of presentation drawings (see Figs. 5.1 and 5.2). In many instances, it doesn't seem logical to redraw painstakingly—the results are sometimes sterile in feeling and, of course, take up precious time. With careful planning at the outset of projects, it

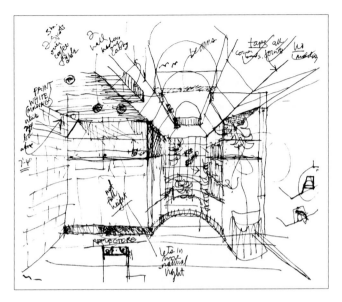

FIGURE 5.1

An early design sketch of a new family room that was eventually shown to the client as part of a preliminary design presentation. The basic elements of the design—barrel-vaulted skylight, splayed ceiling forms, and rounded glass block terminus—are all very loose, but convey the overall intent. (Courtesy of Andy Pressman.)

may be desirable to make use of process drawings as a major presentation element. Explore the various printing and imaging options available—for example, a print of a design sketch can be experimented with and rendered (using color pencils or markers) to read as a seductive presentation graphic. Similarly, xerography can offer more possibilities for translating the range of design sketches, from analysis diagrams to more elaborate perspective drawings to an impressive and coherent presentation. Play with cheap copying machines and scanners! Reduce, enlarge, try different papers, and then experiment with rendering the copies. There is also an inherent beauty in pencil or pen on yellow trace—witness the many original design drawings being sold at galleries for enormous sums of money.

FIGURE 5.2
Another quick and conceptual drawing. A newly exposed hip roof is revealed for a residential renovation, with a lounge in foreground and a home office beyond. This, too (in an enlarged form), was a helpful adjunct for the client presentation. (Courtesy of Andy Pressman.)

Returning to designing the presentation, a helpful tip is to block out all the drawings at small scale. A set of miniature presentation drawings will help to arrange (and size) individual sketches in the most effective sequence and produce dynamic layouts with focus and unity. Mock-ups like this have been a common office practice regarding working drawings, and the technique has great applicability for presentations as well.

The Show

❏ If you know what you're talking about, and can say it directly to your audience (i.e., with as much eye contact as possible), you will radiate confidence. Try not to patronize people by an exaggerated or simplified lecture; encourage any questions and respond with a level of detail consistent with the inquiry. John Lyons, PhD, states, "The key to a presentation, whether it's before a small-town client or the Congress of the United States, is to define what you want to say. One or two points should be identified, and those are the ones you amplify. More than this and most people tend to become ineffective and lose their audience. Present with confidence. Self-confidence is a most important metric of the effective presentation. The worst thing presenters do is to become their own audience, to get idiosyncratic. Stay basic, stay confident, and keep it brief. There will always be time to elaborate if that is called for." The overarching message is to project confidence if not charisma, express enthusiasm, "grab" the audience, and try to enjoy the experience! View and convert any initial nervousness into excitement and enthusiasm for your work. Residual anxiety that can't be transduced or concealed will usually vanish as you become caught up in the momentum of the presentation and the response of the audience.

The conventional wisdom has always held that if you make a mistake, don't apologize, and at the same time don't be defensive. Move on. Maintain a sense of humor. A few years ago, I designed a high-end kitchen for a celebrity client who was always adding last-minute changes. When construction was 90 percent complete, she informed me that her oversized computer keyboard didn't fit in the custom home-office casework I

FIGURE 5.3
© *The New Yorker Collection 1991, John O'Brien from cartoonbank.com. All Rights Reserved.*

designed. I never knew anything about such an oversized component—so, paraphrasing Frank Lloyd Wright, I advised her to get a smaller keyboard! We all had a good laugh (and I called my lawyer).

Try not to present at 5:00 P.M. Unfortunately, scheduling presentations is such that you may end up doing it at the end of the day—when the attention spans of a selection committee are at a minimum and hunger is at a maximum. Be especially attuned to the audience's condition at this time and take action to prevent disinterest and discomfort resulting from sitting through a marathon session. Dorothy A. Lynn, a communications specialist, recommends speaking with varied cadence and volume, and maintaining high energy (don't slouch). Don't fidget, and maximally engage the group. Move as close as possible to your audience (don't be shy about striding away from a desk or lectern and turning to face the group), and, most important, maintain good eye contact.

Responding to Criticism

❏ The title of this section may be somewhat misleading; it presupposes that the reader understands that life in architecture and in design presentations is not singularly driven by critical unpleasantness. Criticism is very much a part of the process (see Chapter 1), but it should be pointed out very clearly that reviews and juries are by no means always tough, pressured events. A good portion of the time, the tone is relaxed, collegial, and often absorbing.

Learning how to respond to the tough aspects of criticism is central to the ease with which one returns to the critical forum. There are several truisms in this regard. The one most often repeated has to do with avoiding your natural propensity for defending yourself: in a phrase, don't do it very often. If you find yourself backed up against the ropes, there is probably a good reason for that position; try to understand just what that reason is, and carefully attend to every word the critic utters. If there is any ambiguity in what you are hearing, form a hypothesis about what is being said and try to restate the critic's comments. In this way, clarification is more likely (the critic may soften and elaborate in valuable fashion), and you demonstrate your efforts at understanding and correction.

All this is not to say that you should always be unconditionally deferential and subservient to criticism. Part of the value of presenting work to critics is in preserving your individuality while being responsive to the judgments and suggestions of others.

If you feel a particular aspect of your project is exceptional, focus on it, and be sure to justify and support it clearly, from as many angles as possible. Be ready to take the offensive, but in a selective, measured, and graceful manner. It is self-evident that it is not adequate to emphatically state that you just "like" something. Clients both need and deserve to know substantively why you have made each and every decision and why you have ruled out alternative schemes. This is not to suggest that every detail of a project should be identified and justified; it does mean that you must be prepared to field questions about any detail in order to show why it does not represent arbitrary thinking.

Presenting for Pros
With Karen Greenstreet and Bob Greenstreet

❏ Set forth in Supplement 5.1 is the definitive checklist for planning, conducting, and following up for all types of important presentations. It is a comprehensive and qualitative guide written by people who present so well themselves that they could have careers performing in Hollywood.

SUPPLEMENT 5.1

Karen Greenstreet and Robert Greenstreet

Karen Greenstreet, PhD, is president of Greenstreet Consulting and specializes in executive coaching for professionals. Bob Greenstreet, RIBA, PhD, is dean of the School of Architecture and Urban Planning at the University of Wisconsin-Milwaukee. Each has written numerous publications, including The Architect's Guide to Law and Practice *(Van Nostrand Reinhold, 1984), which they authored together. (© Karen Greenstreet and Bob Greenstreet 1999.)*

Why?

❏ Experienced architects know that quality designs do not sell themselves. They have to be presented in visual and verbal formats that persuade clients of their excellence. In today's highly competitive marketplace we have two choices: present the scheme with energy, clarity, and creativity, or increase the risk of compromising the design and/or losing the job. If you want to protect the quality of your work and the economic health of your practice, become a superb presenter.

When?

❏ Thoughts about how to present the scheme should begin as early as possible in the design process. Thinking about presentation at this stage saves time and focuses you on communicating your ideas to the client. After all, if your client doesn't get it, it is unlikely that your client is going to buy it.

Choices you make at the outset of a project should be guided by these three principles:

■ The client probably does not have your visual skills and cannot "read" drawings fluently.
■ From this it follows that, to understand the scheme, the client needs words as well as pictures.
■ The less the client understands from your presentation, the harder the questions you will have to answer.

So, whenever possible, plan to talk through the scheme using the drawings and models as props. If a verbal presentation is impossible—because, for example, competition rules forbid it—include clear, brief but interesting explanations on or with the drawings outlining the process that informed the design. Useful information includes:

■ Your understanding of the client's needs
■ Restraints and conditions imposed by site, budget, program, etc.
■ Alternative designs that were explored, showing the evolution of the final scheme
■ Simple illustrations diagramming the high points of the final scheme: circulation, climate control, structure, etc.

What?

❏ When it comes to client presentations, one size does not fit all. Obviously, clients range from small businesses to major corporations or governmental departments, from individuals with no prior exposure to the building process to large groups who have worked with dozens of architects in the past. Use this checklist to help tailor your presentations to individual client experience, style, and expectations:

■ *How many people will be at the presentation?* The answer will affect whether you present with drawings alone or use projection or video techniques. If you are presenting to more than two people at the same time, larger visual images that you can manipulate through a computer or with slides or video can be effective. Remember, though, that these devices often require that the lights be turned down, and low light can result in a loss of concentration. If you hear a gentle snoring, you will know you have lost your audience. On the other hand, if you have a tense, nervous, or potentially hostile audience, a brief video or slide show can help them to relax for your lights-up presentation.

■ *Who will be at the presentation (what roles do they play, who makes decisions, who influences decisions)?* There is little point in aiming your presentation at non-decision makers. On the other hand, some individuals are highly influential even though they have no direct decision-making power themselves. Find out who plays what role and emphasize the benefits of the scheme to them. Some selective questioning during early discussions may help to identify the key players.

■ *What professional language does the client use?* Instead of using design jargon, discover words and phrases that resonate for the individual client or client organization and mirror these in your presentations. Using the client's language is the key to rapid communication and understanding. Again, listening carefully to clients during the early meetings should give you a good idea of the language clients prefer.

■ *What is the client's thinking style?* Broadly, clients may think best through words, images, or a hands-on approach (such as handling models and testing mock-ups). The client's thinking style, not yours, should determine what kinds of props you use and how much you talk.

■ *What mix of drawings should you present?* Client thinking style and client experience govern the answer to this question. Find out how much the client knows about design, working with architects, and the construction process to ensure the right amount and mix of drawings. If in doubt, err on the side of more rather than fewer and use drawings or models that the client can understand. An exploded axonometric may be the best way to demonstrate spatial relationships to other architects, but may confuse someone not familiar with the drawing type.

Sketches

One last point on what to present: no matter what props you choose to make your presentation, they should be of the highest quality available within the financial constraints of the job and should be planned as early in the process as possible. Even experienced architects have fallen into the trap of relying on the immediate availability of materials and outside technical assistance only to find that a lack of supplies or a long wait for copies wreaks havoc with their tight timetables.

How?

❏ Once you have selected your presentation approach through careful consideration of the client's style, experience, and needs, *write down an explanation of the project* in the fewest words you can find. Think of this as writing a legal brief that explains your case in the most persuasive way possible. This will center your efforts and keep you from straying too far from the focal point of the presentation.

Next, *develop a powerful hook* that will capture your client's attention in the first few seconds of the presentation. In designing the hook, consider audience style and needs, the design solution, and the overall presentation approach. This hook can function as a touchstone device that you repeat from time to time throughout the presentation, such as "On point, on time, and on budget." When choosing a hook, think about key phrases the client has used either in discussion or in organizational brochures and mission statements. Hearing their own words in the context of the presentation will convince clients that your design is most attuned to their needs.

During the presentation, be sure to *interpret information* so that your client can readily understand. Instead of speaking just about dimensions of a space, translate that into how many people the space will accommodate for a particular function. Generally, clients are not impressed by technical language. Paint them a picture of how the scheme fits in with their personal and professional reality.

Always *prepare an outline* of your presentation with stage directions for slides or computer images. Never read a script, but do learn the key phrases and important brief statements that express your design particularly well. As you put your outline together, remember the power of three. Human brains understand information more readily when it is grouped in sequences of three. Try to arrange your material to take advantage of this simple truth. If you have five points, try to boil them down to three. If you have six images, try to pair them into three sets. Your outline should also reflect the rule of three by its structure of opening, body, and closing.

Choose your words. Clients and prospective clients watching you present are focused on their own interests. Above all, they want to know how your scheme benefits them and their organization in terms of economics, efficiency, and personal space as well as general aesthetics. To emphasize specific benefits, use *benefit vocabulary.* Here are some examples: *help; better; improve; enhance; generate; more; reduce; increase; identify; avoid; fewer; fast; rapid; validate; inform; ensure; strengthen; build; promote; clarify; add value; opportunity; empower; reward; enrich; expand; fulfill; motivate; satisfy.* Keep your own list and refer to it often. Also, be sure to use plenty of active, unpretentious verbs when explaining your design solutions: "You enter the conference area from the atrium" is preferable to "Access to the conference area is gained from the atrium."

Learn to dance, which is another way of saying you need to be ready to adapt on your feet by carefully watching your audience. What nonverbal signals are audience members sending you? Are they engrossed, keeping their eyes firmly on you and your props? Or are they showing signs of boredom or skepticism by losing eye contact or half-turning away from you? Train yourself in body language so that you can recognize what your clients are thinking and also so that you can reinforce your own verbal and visual messages with powerful nonverbal suggestions of your own (see, for example, Gerald I. Nierenberg and Henry Calero, *How to Read a Person Like a Book,* Barnes & Noble, Inc., 1994). In particular, learn to gesture appropriately and avoid a deadpan expression. Let the people in your audience see your commitment to the design if you want them to reciprocate.

Watch your pace and inflection. No client wants to be bored to tears by an architect droning on at length in a monotone. Keep the presentation moving along by varying your tone. Audiotape your presentation beforehand and listen to how well you modulate your voice and how appropriately you vary your pace. Speaking very rapidly is not the answer either, since clients are also frustrated by designers who gush so fast that they cannot catch essential points. Most importantly, though, appreciate the power of an effective pause. When you express a crucial concept or solution, pause to let that idea catch the light. Excellent presenters know how and when to pause for the greatest effect. If you can come in under budget, tell your clients and then pause to let them savor the good news.

Make eye contact with your audience. Divide the room into thirds and make eye contact with someone in each third roughly every 10 seconds. Ten seconds is actually quite a long time to maintain a gaze, so don't worry, you won't find yourself blinking around the room like a crazed pigeon. What you will do is connect with the people whose needs you are trying to meet with your scheme. This will also give you a chance to register their reactions.

See yourself through your client's eyes. That old truth, "You never get a second chance to make a first impression," still holds. By the time you make a presentation, chances are you have already met some of the people in the room. Nonetheless, be aware that we make judgments about other people during the first 30 seconds of seeing them. What does this mean in practical terms? It means taking care to make an impression that is genuinely you but that may make some outward concessions to your audience. Some clients may expect a degree of nonconformity in the dress and general appearance of architects. Each presentation requires you to make a judgment on dress that does not compromise your style, but nonetheless will make the client feel comfortable.

To get a good sense of how you come across generally in a presentation, arrange to videotape a session and spend some time watching yourself and the reactions of your audience. The very best presenters do this regularly to banish any undesirable habits (repeating phrases like "you know" too often, jangling the change in their pockets, poor posture, negative facial expressions, poor voice modulation, etc.).

Check out room and equipment. Avoid being a victim of technical or physical hitches by looking over the room where you will be presenting well ahead of time. If you are presenting at the client's place of business and the room is unfriendly for your purposes, consider requesting a different space or a rearrangement of furniture and equipment. If you will be using computer graphics, make sure that the wiring connections exist, that a screen or projectable wall is available, and that adequate blackout can be achieved. Wherever possible, use your own equipment and keep it well maintained. Take spare overhead projector bulbs and extension cords just in case. Decide whether you need amplification based on the acoustics of the space and your own voice. If a microphone is necessary, choose one that will allow you to walk around. Don't plan to pace backward and forward too much, but under no circumstances stay rooted in the spot.

Be prepared for exhibits. Check the lighting and the condition of any walls you want to use for display. Free-standing exhibits give you more flexibility and quality control as long as you have the right equipment at your disposal. Don't rely on the client to provide display units or easels—you may end up with a row of chairs to perch your drawings on. If you have to use a poor wall surface, use sturdy and attractive mounting sheets to focus attention on the drawings. Give yourself adequate time to mount the exhibit and take along all the tools and equipment you may need to do the job well, including tacks, nails, tape, Velcro, pliers, and a hammer. Don't be caught, as we were once, having to bang in nails with the heel of a shoe.

Rehearse the presentation in front of colleagues and nonarchitects wherever possible. Nonarchitects will raise issues that you may take for granted. Prepare for questions and polish the presentation by trying to think of the six most difficult and embarrassing issues a client could raise about the design. If you come up with good answers, perhaps ask the questions yourself to show you have considered every angle. If you can't answer the difficult questions, go back to the drawing board (or computer) if these issues strike you as crucial to the client's acceptance of the scheme.

Follow up after the presentation by calling the client and asking if any questions came up after you left the room. This is an effective way to clear up matters that would otherwise scuttle the project before a final decision has been made. If the client rejects the design and cannot be persuaded to continue working with you, ask for candid feedback about where you or your firm went wrong. Don't be defensive. Use the feedback to avoid similar problems in the future. If the client wants to press ahead, maintain the same quality of communication throughout the relationship. Your presentation creates expectations; be sure to meet them.

Preserve and protect the scheme. Decisions about how and where drawings and other materials are to be stored should be made early in the design process and may affect presentation choices such as size of drawings, methods of delineation, and reproduction techniques. Remember, even if you don't get the job, you want to keep the ideas for future reference. Well ahead of time, consider filing options, photographing and storing models, preserving disks, etc.

And Finally . . .

❑ *Keep a log* of presentation outlines, ideas, and feedback. The professional presenter constantly refines style by reviewing past successes and failures.

Train your colleagues and staff in both visual and verbal presentation techniques. Encourage them to read up on the subject and hold office sessions and retreats focusing on both proven and novel presentation methods.

Quality is the primary concern of the true professional. Communicating quality to the client through first-rate presentations is crucial to the reputation and economic health of your practice. Make it a priority.

Quick and Dirty Refresher Tips

❑ The following remarks may seem very obvious, but I have observed too many projects in which commonsense standards have been neglected. These quick tips are intended to promote optimal communication and understanding of your design schemes.

■ An accurate three-dimensional representation is worth a thousand two-dimensional drawings. Communication of the design scheme through a series of colorful perspective renderings, models, or animations is quite simply much easier to understand—and, for many clients, essential. Plans and sections are not easy to read—it takes considerable effort and time to coordinate and assimilate the different pieces of information. Marc Hinshaw has said, "The model is there to comfort the client so that the drawings can reach for a higher level of understanding about a project. It is like a one-two punch."

■ If you get in the habit of graphically expressing ideas for the nonarchitect (i.e., realistically, three-dimensionally), communication is invariably enhanced. Better design more than likely follows from improved dialogue between architect and client.

■ Ernest Burden, a big proponent of portraying entourage and people in a photo-realistic manner, has said that it is wise to include the context within which the building sits (see Fig. 5.4).

■ Consider developing presentation drawings as you design, and vice versa. Burden again states, "Unlike many architects, Frank Lloyd Wright considered renderings as part of the creative process." Moreover, process drawings demonstrate to the client how the project evolved and how decisions were made, which can be quite valuable in some cases.

■ Reference something the client said, squiggled on the back of a napkin, or showed as an example that appears in the design scheme. For example, point out how the client's squiggle is translated into a plan, and describe how it was influential in making a design decision. Be honest. If it represents a genuine contribution, celebrate it, and the client will be that much more invested in the project. This also demonstrates that you have listened well and responded accordingly.

FIGURE 5.4
Entourage makes this simple sketch come alive and ties it to its suburban site.
The new addition is on the right, with the new second floor on the existing house
on the left. The bird is traced, a quirky preference of the renderer. The car is
dated—it must mean that the client is a collector of vintage automobiles. Ernest
Burden has said, "Strive to create continuity and a story within the rendering
series." (Courtesy of Andy Pressman.)

■ Keep an eye on size and scale of drawings. Working smaller
  can save a lot of time. The drama of large scale can then be
  achieved by digital means.

■ This tip is almost too obvious, but surprisingly, these mistakes are made: the neighborhood, site, and floor plans
  should have the same orientation (north in the same direction), and include a north arrow. Drawings are read and
  appreciated far more easily when there is a standard orientation.

■ Lower-floor plans should be at the bottom of the sheet, with
  higher floors above, or lower floors at the left with higher
  floors to the right. Align the plans as they would appear in
  reality (i.e., a stair tower should appear in the same relative
  location on all plans, even if the shapes of the plans are all
  different).

■ Show as much of the surrounding context as possible on all
  drawings and/or model. Set the building in a place, whether

adjacent to other buildings or landscape, and include foreground and background. (This has been alluded to previously, but it is so important it is worth repeating.)

■ Include people and entourage as appropriate to the setting, season, and time—this certainly makes drawings more realistic. Tom Porter and George Dombeck caution about becoming overly stylized and standardized in "a strange drawing-board world whose bleakness is occasionally punctuated by stereotype automobiles and mass-produced trees, and peopled by odd, balloon-shaped beings." Losing contact with reality may have the consequence of misrepresenting design ideas to laypeople.

■ Provide a sense of scale in the drawings. Of course, include a graphic scale, but moreover, suggest a furnishings layout (in plan and section). This shows that you've thought about the specific functioning of the space, and it automatically gives a feeling of scale for nonarchitects.

■ In general, attempt to draw plans, elevations, and sections at the same scale. It makes comparing drawings easier. However, when time and space are very limited, or when a high level of detail is not required on a particular drawing, it may be appropriate to use a smaller scale.

■ Key in all cross sections and elevations to the presentation plans for easy reference by clients.

■ Be sure that any lettering is graphically consistent with the drawings. I've seen wonderful renderings that have obviously taken hours to construct ruined in five minutes by awful hand lettering! Hand lettering is a skill that takes time to mature. If you're not there yet, consider other options (i.e., the computer).

■ Elevation labels usually refer to the cardinal directions of the compass (i.e., the east elevation faces east). Students occasionally incorrectly label the elevation as the direction in which they are viewing it. Some clients share this perception as well.

■ Keep sheet format simple! Don't take away from your design! You may want a border (a plain freehand or hardline rule) and title block—again, simple (and small!). Include the name of the project/client, the name of the drawing (why label a perspective, *Perspective?* Everyone knows it's a perspective. Instead, indicate where the view is looking); scale (this may need to appear under separate sketches on the same drawing if there are differences in scale); north arrow; drawing number (i.e., *2 of 5*—sequence is important); and don't forget your firm name and date of the presentation. I also recommend using the same sheet size for all drawings. Again, avoid overly stylized graphic or other idiosyncratic elements here (however closely or consistently you think they follow your design themes); they draw attention away from your architectural project, which defeats the purpose of presentation graphics. You don't want a selection committee discussing some obscure element at the expense of your design.

■ Employ a hierarchy of line weights to highlight (by contrast) more important elements (i.e., walls or edges are generally thick, furnishings are thin). This can also help to give a sense of depth: for instance, closer lines and section cut lines should be heavier; objects in the background should appear lighter. If everything is equally weighted and there is no hierarchy, nothing reads prominently.

■ Use shade and shadow liberally! These qualities add depth, texture, and contrast to emphasize and animate forms, imbue two-dimensional drawings with a sense of reality, and help them to read better at a distance—where most reviewers sit. On occasion, grant yourself artistic license in developing shade and shadows to improve clarity, but be consistent within a set of drawings.

■ In floor plans, use dotted lines to indicate space above (i.e., overhangs, balconies, floors, etc.). This again helps in comparing and reading plans and sections.

■ Suggest materials. Partially render rather than draw every brick, for example. This not only saves time but can be just as effective. Concentrate the texture or value at the edges, and gradually diminish the density.

■ Generally, provide more detail in the foreground, less in the background. Overlapping objects or cutting elements (only the upper half of a person is visible behind a counter) enhances the illusion of depth.

■ If you're doing a precision hand drawing, be precise! Curves should flow into straight lines without a blotch, corners should be crisp—sloppiness can become a major issue for some clients. Usually, the degree of precision is a function of the stage of design. Very preliminary design implies an ambiguity (freehand may be comfortable), and construction details imply high resolution (hard-line may be comfortable). This is not to say that you can't have a drawing that is loose stylistically yet also precise; in fact, the combination of freehand and precision drawing is sometimes desirable for schematic design and developing details.

■ Consider cost. Paper, printing, and supplies can add up—be aware of your budget. At the same time, try not to skimp; remember, this is an investment in your practice, and materials can be recycled in portfolios for future marketing efforts.

Architectural Presentations as Graphic Art

A Conversation with Iris Slikerman

Iris Slikerman is a former promotional art director for Penguin Putnam, Inc.

Andy Pressman: *We talked about the importance of creating a focus on each presentation board; what do you do about a board that has, say, two floor plans, equally weighted? How do you give that focus and make it an interesting layout?*

Iris Slikerman: Try highlighting a certain element within each plan—for example, the circulation path. A gray tone, or perhaps some color with marker, pencil, tape, or film to show the underlying organization of the plan. It makes it easier to read—pops it out—and interesting graphically. If the project is a renovation, you could focus on the area to be renovated; render it more than areas to be left alone. Alternatively, key in to whatever it is that's particularly noteworthy in plan (since we're talking about plans) and emphasize it graphically so that it becomes the focus.

Pressman: *I've noticed a common mistake—a building design theme—for example, a stepped geometry where "stepping" appears throughout a project (in plan and section) is carried through into the presentation graphics. It appears in things like borders and tile blocks. To me, that's very annoying since it distracts from the architectural design. It's not the same thing as having a strong design concept that appears in details like the door pull.*

Slikerman: You have a good point, but what if the graphic translation is so subtle that you have pulled your viewer in just by a feeling you have evoked—consistent with your project's themes? The viewer may not even know why it's so appealing. What you're talking about is overkill—too much of a good thing—it can destroy the freshness of what you're trying to achieve. You have to be cautious in your use of design elements; I know it's cliché, but a little zip in the right place at the right time can go a long way.

Pressman: *How do you feel about the use of color in presentations?*

Slikerman: Sure, color is terrific, but only if it enhances your message. Its use shouldn't be arbitrary. You don't necessarily need to use a rainbow of colors—one or two might be most effective for any given presentation. And a *little bit* of color can have a big impact.

Pressman: *I've seen site plans where all the trees and grass are colored in a grotesque green, and brown is supposed to represent dirt. Should we consider restraint here, or is that too inhibiting?*

Slikerman: Again, it all depends on what you're trying to achieve—there needs to be a rationale behind every move. If color is an integral part of your design, the presentation demands it. If however, you're showing something more subtle, like a certain species of wood or type of stone, the beauty of it might be in its muted tones—color would be inappropriate. Take direction from the specifics of your project.

Pressman: *How would you summarize the function of graphics in presenting a design?*

Slikerman: Where selling is the name of the game, you want to distinguish your project; capture its essence and uniqueness. The package can count for a lot—at least initially.

Pressman: *So your message is to underscore the importance of graphics and presentation in selling your design.*

Slikerman: Yes, but that is not to say that slickness and sheen are sufficient, especially in the profession of architecture. You can probably make a bad design look good with super graphics, but what's the point? You won't fool anyone in the long run. You can certainly make a good design look bad by not paying enough attention to professional quality in the presentation—that's a real waste. Don't make that mistake twice! A great presentation of a great design can distinguish you from everyone else who has talent and enthusiasm.

Pressman: *In your work, how do you deal with criticism?*

Slikerman: When a project is criticized or rejected in some form, and the artist is personally satisfied with it, I always tell the artist to think of it as another completely different assignment. It just shows that there are a hundred ways to approach a problem. Sometimes—and I really hate to admit this—I'm so glad I responded to the criticism because the job usually gets better.

Pressman: *I've noticed that some architects design their own letterheads and associated graphic materials—and they're horrible! Okay, maybe not horrible, but they clearly lack a certain design sensitivity. And the architects are blind to it!*

Slikerman: It does tarnish the professional image, not to mention wasting time. Graphic design is so polished today in just about everything we see—from flyers from the local Chinese restaurant to junk mail—that anything less than high polish or quality appears glaringly bad. My advice is, quite frankly, to stick to what you do best—architecture! It's presumptuous to assume competence in another field, albeit related, without the requisite training or at least some very good experience. Subtleties are missed.

Pressman: *Any quick graphic tips?*

Slikerman: Graphic elements should be emphasized differently—that is, there has to be a "hit" or focal point, along with a gradation of values. You don't want someone's interest to be diffused.

Pressman: *Give me an example of an architectural design concept that influences or cues presentation ideas.*

Slikerman: Say that you have a tall building where the vertical lines are articulated. That may suggest a vertical orientation of drawings. Conversely, if you have a low, rambling suburban building, maybe you have a very wide format, accentuating the horizontality.

Pressman: *In terms of media, what about presenting with a computer, slides, or video instead of drawings?*

Slikerman: Depends on the situation. You certainly have more control in terms of sequence and maybe holding someone's attention by presenting one image at a time. For instance, you won't have a committee member distractedly trying to balance your precious model on his/her knee while you're pointing to one of your boards. It also depends on the size of the crowd. Computer animation is exciting. But it could turn out to be more of a gimmick, where attention is drawn to the medium and not the design. As in most design decisions, you should have a good reason for any medium you choose.

Engaging Your Client
With Kathryn Anthony

❏ Jargon-laden speech directed at the cognoscenti: this is probably something to avoid for clear communication with your client! Education about architecture goes hand in hand with the presentation of your ideas (as well as operating throughout the design process), as Kathryn Anthony so eloquently states in Supplement 5.2. Education can also be viewed as a natural extension of a professional's overall responsibility to both clients and the public.

Anthony talks about essential strategies to engage in constructive dialogue, when to be appropriately assertive for the best interests of the project and its constituents, and how to be graceful in preserving design integrity without compromising core values of client needs and preferences, among other things.

Kathryn Anthony

Kathryn Anthony, PhD, is a professor in the School of Architecture, Department of Landscape Architecture, and the Women's Studies Program at the University of Illinois at Urbana-Champaign. She is the author of the critically acclaimed book, Design Juries on Trial: The Renaissance of the Design Studio *(Van Nostrand Reinhold, 1991). She holds a PhD in Architecture from the University of California at Berkeley.*

❏ As an architect, communicating with your clients is one of your most challenging tasks. Unfortunately, with the exception of graphic communications, little is taught about oral and written communications skills in architecture school. And all too often, architects assume that they will acquire these skills through trial and error. The problem is that no matter how talented a designer you may be, too many errors will drive your firm right out of business. Conversely, success in this arena leads to satisfied clients, repeat business, and terrific references for future work. Improving your communication skills with clients is definitely a worthwhile investment.

SUPPLEMENT 5.2

It is essential that you stay in touch with your clients, as they say in Chicago, "early and often." Discuss and agree upon the scope of work, negotiate your fees, establish a starting date and a schedule, and do your best to stick to it throughout your working relationship. If your schedule changes and you are running behind, call your clients to inform them immediately. From their perspective, simply knowing you will be late is better than being left in the dark, not having heard from you at all.

Presenting design schemes to your clients is one of your most important tasks. Paul Revere Williams (1894–1980), who ran one of the most successful African American architectural practices in the U.S., earned many of his clients through his presentation techniques. Once clients were in his office, Williams asked them what kind of budget they had to spend. He would then reply that he rarely took on projects with that low a figure, but that perhaps he could offer them some suggestions "free of charge." This served as the bait that took them in. He would ask them to discuss what kind of "dream home" or building they had in mind. While he sat opposite them during their discussion, he adeptly began to sketch out their ideas—upside down. This enabled them to see their ideas immediately come to life literally from their own point of view. This unusual ability won Williams scores of clients, and he eventually became known as the "architect to the stars," designing homes for such film luminaries as Lucille Ball and Desi Arnaz, Betty Grable, Cary Grant, William Holden, and Frank Sinatra, among others. Today a myriad of computerized presentation techniques are available to help clients better visualize your designs. Use them whenever possible.

Giving clients ample opportunity to react to your designs while in progress is a key to professional success. Similarly, involving prospective building users as well as clients is even more valuable in the long run. Say your client is a large corporation, such as a health care provider. While the hospital administration may serve as your client, no doubt the perspectives of administration personnel will differ significantly from those of doctors, interns, residents, nurses, and other medical staff who use the building regularly. In addition, the experiences of patients and visitors who use the building irregularly, often as a result of life-threatening emergencies, are altogether different as well. Understanding how each type of user experiences the current medical environment as well as how each reacts to your prospective designs inevitably produces a better building. People are likely to be more satisfied with a new building or addition if they have been consulted in the design process. For a large institution, this can translate into increased productivity on the job, reduced absenteeism, less turnover, and lower costs.

How can you maximize the efficiency of your in-progress design presentations to clients and users? Here is some advice.

Before Your Presentation

- Prepare in advance. Understand your audience. Anticipate how much clients already know or do not know about your project. Select your words carefully, avoiding such architectural lingo as *fenestration* or *glazing* (choose *windows* or *glass* instead), *building envelopes*, or *building skins*.
- Find out exactly how much time your clients plan to set aside for your meeting. Be aware of any schedule constraints they may have, and plan your presentation accordingly.
- Practice your presentation with coworkers. Have them ask you questions that mimic those that your clients will ask, and be prepared with answers. Ask them for feedback on how you come across.
- Schedule a time where a coworker can videotape your presentation. Watching yourself talk about your design is an experience like no other. You are likely to be your own worst critic. Listen carefully to what you say and how you say it. Are you using filler words, like *um*, *like*, and *you know*? We all do, but rarely are we aware of them. Watch your nonverbal behavior as well. Are you fidgeting, rocking back and forth from one foot to another, or jiggling keys? All these actions distract others from what you are trying to say. Once you are aware of them, you can keep yourself from falling into the habit.

Sketches

During Your Presentation

- Make it clear that your designs are still evolving, and that you want and need feedback at this stage.
- Annotate your drawings with short pieces of text highlighting major features of your design.
- Ask for audience participation in reviewing your work. For example, offer clients and/or users different-colored dots that they can place on your drawings. Use one color to signify an aspect of the design that they like, while another to indicate a feature they dislike. Use yet another color to highlight parts of the design that they do not understand.
- After hearing the participants' comments, repeat them to make sure you understood the audience's concerns correctly. Listening carefully is half the battle.
- Note down important points that your clients make to you. From their perspective, simply seeing you write down at least some of what they have to say shows that you have paid attention, rather than dismissed them.
- If you disagree with opinions of clients and users, don't become defensive. Instead, let them finish their points. Do not interrupt. If their views have merit, say so. If they're off the wall, be diplomatic. In any case, discuss their remarks along with your own viewpoint and the rationale behind it, and say that you will take their comments into consideration.
- Be sure to offer plenty of opportunity to ask questions: "Is there anything more you'd like to ask?" "What else would you like to know about what I have in mind?"
- Maintain eye contact. Make sure your body language indicates that you are interested in what clients are saying.
- In addition to your drawings and models, offer clients a portable version of your design that they can take home and study on their own. If possible, produce a Web site that they can access on their computers. Ask for their comments by a particular date and time.

After Your Presentation

- Delegate someone in your office to be in charge of monitoring and summarizing the feedback you receive. If you do not hear from clients, call and follow up to ensure that you receive their reactions.
- Be available to answer questions about your proposed design. Often clients will have more questions after they meet you, once they have a chance to digest your ideas.

Once your design is completed and the project is built, it is important that you continue to maintain contact with your clients. Don't just design and run. Make it clear to them that you are genuinely interested in learning about how their building is working. An excellent way to do this is by conducting a postoccupancy evaluation (POE). POEs can be done in a myriad of ways. In an academic setting, POEs may involve a series of studies spanning several months or even years. In fact, scores of publications have been written about how to conduct POEs, and many involve questionnaires and complex forms of data analysis. In a professional setting, however, rarely do you have the luxury of spending several months to conduct a POE, nor do you have the expertise. So, what to do? You can either hire someone to do the POE for you, or conduct an abbreviated version yourself. If you chose to hire an expert, consult your local university—preferably one that houses a department of architecture—and see if any one of its faculty, a class, or an independent study student is interested in helping you. Or you can contact the Environmental Design Research Association (EDRA) and find out the name of a local expert. You can contact EDRA on the World Wide Web at www.telepath.com/edra/home.html or via e-mail at edra@telepath.com.

Should you choose to conduct a short POE on your own, I suggest circulating a set of three simple questions among building users. (1) What do you like best about this building? (2) What do you like least about this building? (3) If you had the chance to redesign this building, what would you do differently? These three questions will generate a lively set of responses. Read them and try to understand how widespread are the various sentiments expressed. If you are hearing the same complaints from several individuals, try to ascertain if in fact you can make any small-scale changes that could address some of these deficiencies. If they are impossible to address, keep them in mind for the next project.

In any case, taking the time to understand the extent to which clients and users are satisfied with your building, like communication skills themselves, is a worthwhile investment. It is an excellent way to earn client satisfaction and repeat business.

Trends in Reprographics, Printing, and Imaging

A Conversation with Jim Maitland

Jim Maitland has worked with the Charrette Corporation, headquartered in Woburn, Massachusetts, for over 20 years, and has been involved in all aspects of the company's reprographics and computing divisions. He earned his BA from Amherst College. Check Charrette's Web site at www.charrette.com for interesting details.

Pressman: *What has changed in the reprographic world in the last several years, and how have those changes influenced architectural design?*

Maitland: So much of the design process is done on the computer that printing computer files is dominating the business. Diazo printing of construction documents is hereby officially obsolete, with the exception of a few old-timers who still draw by hand. Printing technology is not really reprographics.

Today, reproduction is all about output devices and options for printing from computer files.

Pressman: *There are many variables in producing the highest-quality presentation output, ranging from the type of equipment used, the resolution, and most important, perhaps, knowledgeable personnel who operate the equipment. How can an architect ensure the best results?*

Maitland: Plotting is a key issue because so much of that work has gone in-house. Each firm becomes a mini–print shop where those variables you mentioned must be reconciled. Today, over half our business is on-site services. The future wave is printing, and the cost of printing devices has been reduced dramatically, and typically architects want them in their offices. We have determined a way to best deal with this situation. Rather than the architects buying expensive printers, which quickly become obsolete, we basically take our print shop and put it in architects' offices.

This may include a plotter, a fax machine, an engineering copier, black-and-white copiers, color printers—virtually any office equipment. The concept is, rather than invest in these items as overhead costs and capital investment items, we put our equipment in the architect's office—but we still generate an invoice as if the printing was done in our shop. So the reimbursability of the work is still intact, as it always was when architects were sending the work off-site.

Pressman: *You lease the equipment to the offices?*

Maitland: No. We own the equipment. If in 90 days the office wants out of the deal, no problem. We generally offer a three-year contract, which is a similar term to a lease. But it is a nonbinding arrangement. If a piece of equipment turns out to be the wrong thing (for example, it's not appropriate for volume requirements), we replace it. It's very flexible. We grow and shrink with the firm as needed.

Pressman: *If the equipment becomes obsolete within a year, what happens?*

Maitland: We just replace it. What most often happens is that a firm is small and gets a printer which is scaled appropriately to their size, then they get bigger and the plotter or office copier is now too small or too slow for them. So they need to upgrade. Rather than waiting three years on a lease or buyout, we swap that piece of equipment for something more suitable to their current needs. In some cases, we can easily find a home for that smaller piece of equipment with an appropriately sized smaller firm. This business has really transformed.

Pressman: *Any fee associated with this arrangement?*

Maitland: We do it on a per-print basis. We estimate the monthly volume, and then we work out pricing based on that volume. We make sure that at that running rate, we've chosen the correct piece of equipment, which isn't too expensive. We can make a profit, and the firm, in turn, has the right equipment for their office needs. They have the equipment to use, and pass most of the cost on to their clients.

Pressman: *This applies equally to small and large firms?*

Maitland: Not equally. With sole proprietors, the equation doesn't work for us. Two- to three-person offices for on-site services is simply not cost effective. It usually starts at the five- to six-person size. The model for the new office is more technological firepower and fewer people.

Pressman: *What are the typical issues involved in this arrangement?*

Maitland: There are basically three components to the cost of equipment. One, cost of ownership—just to buy the box—this is equally true at home with your home printer. Two, service contract—the cost of keeping and running the equipment. And three, the cost of consumable materials—the papers and inks that go into it.

We cover all of those costs in this program. So what comes out of the machine is just a piece of paper, and that's what we charge for. This is an industry trend.

Our photographic services, for example, were a major part of what people would need for presentation prints. That business is virtually gone.

A facilities management program is a more generic term for on-site services. In the biggest firms, we provide our staff people to operate the equipment.

This model grew out of the law profession, where Xerox, Pitney Bowes, and others developed programs where the law firm didn't want to be dealing with buying copiers and staffing their copy rooms, so they outsourced. Lawyers are similar to architects in terms of getting reimbursed for all the printing costs; it's just that architects are working primarily with large-format documents.

Pressman: *How are construction documents printed for bidding?—And I'll eventually ask how you see that evolving in the future.*

Maitland: The diazo printing process has given way to large-format xerography, and that process has the same degree of productivity as that of a high-speed 8.5 × 11 Xerox machine. One of the industry leaders has a device which is fed by a scanner—digital, wide format, and high speed. It allows you to scan original documents, then go directly to a high-speed print engine that is similar to an office laser printer. It operates very fast with large pages, and prints out right from the scans, or you can save the scan files to a file on a computer, and then print from those scans at a later time. The device is also a plotter. You can send CAD files to it. These types of jobs, however, are too big to do in-house. Presentation components are typically done in-house—construction documents here at Charrette, for example.

Pressman: *Returning to the quality of presentation boards: what questions should an architect ask at the repro shop to maximize the presentation quality?*

Maitland: In general, with photographic subjects, it may be prudent to approach a photo lab. Photo labs have also had to make the transition to digital technology. In general, photo labs have done a better job of staying on top of the technology curve. Many former blueprinters who did some color work in the old days didn't make as sophisticated a transition to the world of high tech as photo labs.

Pressman: *The key is to look to those organizations that have state-of-the-art knowledge and equipment to get the best possible presentation prints.*

Maitland: Certainly, for example, drum-type scanners are generally better quality than flat bed scanners. But equally important is the output device and the RIP. What is the raster image processing—the software—that's going to take that original scan and create the information to print it in such a way that it's the best quality? Those kinds of software tools are what differentiate one printing solution from another.

The scanner and printer don't matter as much as the software capability that's going to take the information from the scanner to the printer. If there's a lesson, it's trying to find time to experiment with different subjects and talk to people, and develop some trust and understanding of what your local repro shops are good at. You might have to go from shop to shop on a project. Then you will be able to use the information you've gathered—the analysis of the quality of work from these different places—to apply to future similar projects.

Pressman: *What is another example of emerging technology related to transfer of drawings?*

Maitland: The project extranet concept. The driving principle is faster communication of ideas. One of the things that we're starting to get involved with now is the project management Web site. An emerging part of architectural practice is the idea that architect, owner, and contractor will all share a Web site—an extranet. Ultimately, the owner of a project will pay a subscription fee of, say, $1000 per month, and there are as many users as the architect, engineer, and contractor want to designate. There are, of course, password protections. It is in its infancy—the whole industry is only a couple of years old.

The fear for a printing company like us is that there would be less need for prints! Electronic files will be shared. The idea is that the contractor, the subs—everybody—can just go look at the drawings online, and perhaps print them out in-house. Extranets also provide a digital "paper" trail that can be very helpful.

One of the possible future services is a Web site where you convince an owner, architect, or contractor to put all the drawings in TIFF file format—not in a CAD file format—on the Web site, and for a fee, authorized people can download those files. So for, say, $20 flat rate per project, it would be possible to download drawings. If you are a subcontractor or manufacturer, simple. Just discard or ignore the drawings that are inapplicable. If you need prints, print them out on your printer, in-house.

Pressman: *Any final thoughts?*

Maitland: Intellectual property rights are an issue. Now, for example, typically architects don't want subs to develop shop drawings from the architect's construction documents.

Pressman: *This seems a bit myopic, and will likely change in the future—it can be viewed as an asset rather than a liability.*

Maitland: Right. So, how information is disseminated on extranets will be an issue. And the quality of drawings is far more consistent now. However, the beauty and detail may not necessarily reflect the content and substance therein! The appearance can be more than the reality simply because of the process.

Architectural Photography

With Steve Rosenthal, Charles Linn, and Norman McGrath

❏ Photographing a completed building, its interiors, and the surroundings is perhaps the final act of a design process. Properly recording the project is essential, as world-renowned architectural photographer Steve Rosenthal elaborates in Supplement 5.3, for marketing, publication, and awards. The client and contractors as well may have specific uses for excellent photographs. The quality of photography—any project documentation—should be consistent with the quality of the design itself.

An artful composition of views contributes to communicating a very specific reality of the design. Certainly, selective framing and the static nature of photographs can depict the most elusive qualities of a project. This requires careful thought by both the architect and the photographer.

The American Society of Media Photographers publishes valuable information on commissioning architectural photographers, including a comprehensive guide to major issues to consider before, during, and after a shoot, together with a membership directory. The society's Web site address is www.asmp.org/publications/pubs/comm.html.

The representation of the building through photographs, then, is central to a firm's portfolio, and has the power to display talent and reveal much about the architect's priorities. Frequently, a photograph is worth a thousand words, or at least the cost of having it done professionally.

Steve Rosenthal

Steve Rosenthal is a critically acclaimed photographer, based in Newton, Massachusetts, specializing in architecture for almost 30 years. Most of his clients are architects and architectural publications. His photographs have been published in all the major architectural journals in the U.S. and abroad. Rosenthal received the American Society of Media Photographers (ASMP) architectural specialty award in 1996, and an AIA honors award in 1984.

❏ Good architectural photography is more than a few seductive images of a building. Architects and the general public are

SUPPLEMENT 5.3

dependent on photography for understanding architecture. Ideally, the role of the photographer is to lead the observer sequentially through a building so that, together with plans, sections, and elevations, the spaces and their interrelationship can be clearly understood.

Why should a building be photographed? Preeminent for most architects are marketing needs. Remember that a potential client will never see firsthand most of the buildings presented to him or her. The architect has the unique opportunity to present the building through photographs as he or she wishes it to be seen, in its best light and under ideal conditions.

Another reason that architects document their work in addition to their own personal needs is for publication in articles, journals, and books. Photographs of a very small gem or a building on a remote site can enjoy a large immediate audience through publication. Fay Jones's Wayfarer Chapel is a good example.

And how can one forget about awards programs? They are competitions, and in order to compete, excellent photographs are essential. Jurors rarely visit the submitted projects, so the photographs literally need to be a stand-in. They need to tell the story, to clearly present the design intent. Sometimes submissions are required to show all exterior elevations and some very specific interior spaces.

Photographing a building is time consuming, expensive, and disruptive to clients. Reshoots can be difficult to arrange, and no architect has complete control over furnishings and building maintenance once the owner is entrenched in the facility. One can see why it is important to hire an experienced photographer who is going to get it right the first time.

The real challenge for the architectural photographer is to be able to do two things at once: to do justice to the design of the building and at the same time to produce an image with a visual integrity of its own. Either one is not that difficult to accomplish, but to do both at the same time requires technical skill, artistry, and an understanding of architecture.

Assessing Architectural Photographs

❏ In Supplement 5.4, Charles Linn, AIA, discusses lighting design in relation to capturing the quality of an interior space on film. Linn explains that there are various tricks to manipulate the photographic representation to align with an architect's editorial predisposition.

Charles Linn

Charles D. Linn, AIA, is a senior editor for Architectural Record *and is the editor of "Record Lighting,"* Record's *quarterly special section on lighting. In addition to writing design features and essays, he occasionally takes photographs for the magazine.*

❏ Many architects spend more time looking at the various design magazines than actually visiting the grand spaces. These magazines do afford an excellent means of taking a monthly field trip to important new and old buildings—even buildings that don't exist any more. But design professionals must learn to be critical of the lighting they observe in architectural photographs, because photographers use multiple exposures, filters, fill light, and other tricks to make their photographs acceptable.

These can significantly alter the way a space looks in a photo, adding shadows and bright spots where they do not appear in real life. Photographic film does not "see" light the way the eyes see it, making it difficult for photographs to render color accurately, especially when multiple types of light sources are used. Fluorescent light looks sickly next to perfectly rendered incandescent light when photographed together. Daylight and electric light are also difficult to photograph side by side.

It takes some study to tell if photographs accurately depict a lighting situation, especially if the observer cannot visit the space personally. But here are some tips:

■ If the ceiling plane is brighter than the floor plane, and there appears to be no source of uplight in the room, the photographer has probably added fill light.

SUPPLEMENT 5.4

- Watch for harsh shadows that don't seem to belong. Why would the shadow of a picture frame appear above the picture unless the light is coming from knee level?

- Watch for bright streaks of light on walls and floors that originate behind sofas, chairs, and potted plants. Sometimes, though seldom, these exist permanently in the interior. More often than not, they are added by the photographer.

- Think about whether the lighting system shown in the room would deliver the sort of light you see. A downlight close to a wall, for example, should project a corresponding scallop of light on the wall. If it is absent, the downlight was probably turned off when the picture was taken. A ceiling full of black holes may mean all of the lights in the room were off when the photograph was taken.

- Multiple sources probably mean that either multiple exposures or filters were used. For example, sometimes rooms with large windows are photographed twice on the same sheet of film. During the day, the exterior scene is exposed. At night, filters are added to the camera lens or placed over the light sources themselves to balance them. Then a second exposure is made.

To a certain extent, there is nothing wrong with photographers manipulating the light in a room to get a picture. Photographs are simulations of reality, and rendering these simulations as accurately as possible is the photographer's art. It is seldom that even the best illumination can be photographed without some manipulation.

But sometimes photographers go beyond simulating the actual lighting and take it upon themselves to create the lighting environment that appears in published photographs. If the designer of the space's lighting has done a poor job, the photographer may have no choice. If designers notice these characteristics in photographs they are studying, it may be as instructive for them to analyze why the lighting had to be supplemented as it is for them to look at projects that required no help from the photographer. The main thing that architects should always remember when looking at photographs is that their eyes should not be believed.

Model Photography for Presentation

❏ Supplement 5.5 is for those architects who want to experiment with photographing models in-house and bolster a presentation. Norman McGrath offers tips on how to accomplish this task most effectively.

Norman McGrath

SUPPLEMENT 5.5

Norman McGrath is a noted architectural photographer based in New York City. His photographs have appeared in numerous publications throughout the world. He is the author of the popular book, Photographing Buildings Inside and Out *(Whitney Library of Design, 1987), which is clearly the definitive source on the subject.*

❏ Do not attempt model photography without a good-quality single-lens reflex (SLR) camera. Even with a reflex camera it's not easy. You should try to get close to your subject, particularly if you wish to simulate the look of a real building. Keep your backgrounds simple. A roll of no-seam paper as a backdrop will

(a)

FIGURE 5.5
(a) Daylight model of a classroom: preliminary. This rough model has the basic geometry and surface reflectances in the space rendered quickly in a study model.

FIGURE 5.5 (Continued)
(b) Daylight model: finished. The finished model is more detailed and shows that you can quite accurately simulate the final design of an interior space.

FIGURE 5.5 (Continued)
(c) Actual classroom. (Photos: Stephen Dent, from student work in an architectural lighting class.)

create a ministudio for your model. Put the model on a table or support so that you can approximate ground-level views.

Shooting outside to take advantage of sunlight can be great, with good, sharp shadows, but watch out for those backgrounds. It is easier to work with reflector spots (or floods) in a room where you can control the light. If you use tungsten or incandescent lights, use a type B film if you're doing slides. With color negative, even a daylight film can be corrected when prints are made. For aerial views, you can tilt the camera down, but for ground-level shots, try and keep it level so your vertical elements will remain vertical. Removable parts of your model may permit you to get in closer with your camera. Your lens, of course, will have to have close-focusing capability. For added depth of field or sharp focus, you will have to stop the aperture of the lens down as much as possible and use a longer exposure, so the camera must be firmly mounted (on a tripod or tabletop stand) and use a cable release. A blue background may suggest sky, but gray may also work. Controlling the lighting of the model as well as the backdrop will create different effects. Don't be discouraged if you don't achieve your objectives the first time.

Design Intelligence and the Art of Persuasion
With James Cramer

❏ In Supplement 5.6, Jim Cramer suggests that excellent negotiating skills can be applied to educating and selling a client on design possibilities. Negotiating skills are essential for conducting business, but can also be used as an integral part of the arsenal of presentation weapons. Directing them for "good" instead of "evil" allows a higher level of understanding and collaboration from the client. Think about that the next time you read a book on management; see how the principles can be used to set a tone for more receptive clients. Cramer echoes Kevin Roche in suggesting that architects have the opportunity and the responsibility to educate their clients, and therefore there can be no such thing as a bad client.

The information delivery process may need to be as creative as the design itself! (See Chapter 2 for information on ascertaining client characteristics—the basis on which to design a presentation for maximum effect.) Obvious but worth repeating to yourself over and over is that presentation is very much a key step in the design process. Great work ends up on the cutting room floor if a client doesn't perceive that it is great.

James P. Cramer

James P. Cramer is the chairman/CEO of the Greenway Group, Inc. management consultants. He is the author of Design Plus Enterprise: Seeking a New Reality in Architecture *(AIA Press, 1994) and is the editor of the* Almanac of Architecture and Design *(Greenway Group, 2000). He can be reached at jcramer@di.net or at 770-209-3770.*

SUPPLEMENT 5.6

Turning Missed Opportunities into Design Intelligence

❑ I recall Ford Foundation Headquarters architect Kevin Roche saying that he had "never met a bad client." His point was that architects have the opportunity and the responsibility to educate their clients. I have never forgotten those words of wisdom.

Today, in our consulting practice, I sometimes hear professional firms saying that they are service practices rather than design practices. Perhaps you too have heard this. These firm principals will go on to say that they are in the business of architecture with the emphasis on serving. The implication is that the best design solutions—the best architecture—happen in elite firms where fees are better or where there is little profit motive.

Smart architects are challenging this point of view. They understand that architecture is both art and business. For example, take Gary Wheeler of Perkins and Will. He talks about good business and good design with his clients at the same time, and is persuasive on both counts. Architecture, he says, should be practiced as a healthy business along with keen design acumen. Design and business are not binary opposites. They are siblings in synergy bringing better planning, better buildings, and better-designed communities.

Mexican architect Ricardo Legorreta was giving a symposium at the National Building Museum in Washington, DC. He said that he feels there is an active threat that uncaring business people without design sense will control future projects, thereby diminishing the architect's role. The question raised by Legorreta could be stated this way: in the new economy, will the architect be the knowledge entrepreneur of influence? Legorreta's answer, and that of Gary Wheeler and Kevin Roche, would be yes—so

FIGURE 5.6
Peter Pfau provided a presentation drawing from his former firm (Holt Hinshaw Pfau Jones Architecture)—a stunning and evocative visual.

long as architects and designers develop their own business savvy. This savvy stresses the negotiation of good design and good business as interwoven.

In private conversations with successful architects, I have learned that they have turned their design goals into facts. They have taken ordinary projects and made them extraordinary. They have turned normal and average projects into pleasant places that foster a sense of community.

It's a missed opportunity when an architect fails to persuade or negotiate for good design. The urban sprawl and "uglification of America" is an issue for architects and designers to think deeply about—and take leadership action on.

Clients tell us over and over again that they invest in architects for both who they are and for what they can do for the client. Expanding the box and raising the bar with your clients truly does unfold new possibilities. Those who integrate the best design solutions with the best of business in ways that are faster, better, and smarter will be those with distinctive competitive advantage. When you serve good design, your practice will soar!

chapter 6

Lifelong Learning

*"I recently saw a videotape of people who
were teaching their babies while they
(the babies) were still in the womb. We will
reach the point, in our lifetimes, where
babies emerge from their mothers fully prepared to
assume entry-level management positions."*

—Dave Barry

Sketches

❏ This chapter has two main objectives. One is to examine the myriad possibilities of professional development focusing on honing design skills. Continuing education is now mandated by a growing number of states to maintain registration, and by the American Institute of Architects (AIA) to continue membership. Notwithstanding minimum requirements in health, safety, and welfare topics, directing those learning units to design is investigated. The second objective of this chapter is to speak specifically to intern architects and advanced students about maximizing design experiences at their career stages, culminating in an illuminating perspective on the Architect Registration Examination (ARE).

Thom Lowther is the director of the AIA's continuing education system, and is articulate about describing the pursuit of high-quality lifelong learning opportunities. (See Supplement 6.1.) I propose that architectural design competitions are one of the most enlightening continuing education strategies because they offer the freedom and luxury to experiment with design thinking. At best, a new commission can be secured; at worst, losing schemes can enhance a firm's marketing portfolio. My conversation with Roger Schluntz, a noted professional advisor for competitions, reveals essential details about participating in this sometimes highly charged architect selection process. Travel is another architectural tradition for learning and growth, the benefits of which are jauntily described by John Cary Jr. and Casius Pealer III, two remarkably talented recent graduates.

Architectural internship is discussed from two perspectives: how the practicing architect can benefit most from utilizing an intern's strengths yet simultaneously be a responsible mentor, and how the intern can maximize the experience in terms of educational value and financial gain. Creating a win-win scenario is the goal. Open letters to advanced students from Helmut Jahn, Hugh Jacobsen, Arthur Erickson, and the late Charles Moore are frankly inspiring to practitioners as well.

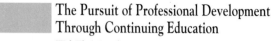

The Pursuit of Professional Development Through Continuing Education

With Thom Lowther

❑ One thing about being a professional: it seems self-evident that seeking continuing education is simply something all practitioners would want to do, because the material covered is inherently interesting and is related to one of your central passions in life. The fact that many states and the AIA are codifying requirements for ongoing education can only be positive. Notwithstanding a few moments of bothersome paperwork, the consequence is that there are now more opportunities than ever to enjoy an increasingly diverse menu from which to choose an appetizing course. Thom Lowther offers a special perspective on the topic, including where to find some of the best educational programs available today.

Thom Lowther

Thom Lowther, EdS, is the director of the American Institute of Architects Continuing Education System. Since arriving at the AIA in 1995, Thom has presented at more than 100 events, including AIA National Conventions, AIA Grassroots, AIA and Construction Specifications Institute (CSI) chapters, architectural and engineering firms, and other related associations throughout the country. Thom is the instructor for such programs as the AIA's "Leadership & Learning: How to Improve Your Firm's Competitive Edge Through Professional Development." In 1998, Thom received the Distinguished Service Award for his efforts in working with AIA components and chapters.

The Pursuit of Lifelong Learning

❑ Regardless of what term you want to call it—continuing education units (CEUs), learning units (LUs), professional development hours (PDHs), or mandatory continuing education (MCE)—it makes no difference. Each state, each profession seems to create its own terms for its own professionals. States are also trying to develop some form of accountability for the professionals within their jurisdictions, and continuing education is one way they have chosen to measure that attempt. Continuing

SUPPLEMENT 6.1

education emphasizes professional learning and enables the architect to keep current, master new knowledge and skills, plan for the future, and responsibly meet the role society entrusts to a professional. In doing so, it has the potential to be one of the primary forces in the improvement and revitalization of professional development throughout the design profession. Programs vary from AIA and CSI chapter meetings, to in-firm lunch programs, to distance education formats, to weekend conferences hosted by manufacturers, universities, nonprofit organizations, and government agencies.

For some architects, the reason for pursuing continuing education is to meet their state licensing requirements for MCE or the AIA Continuing Education System (CES) requirement. The impact during the past five years has been major. There are currently 14 states that have enacted MCE: Alabama, Arkansas, Florida, Iowa, Kansas, Kentucky, Louisiana, Minnesota, North Carolina, Oklahoma, South Dakota, Tennessee, Vermont, and West Virginia. More than 20 other states are at various levels of legislative activity. The average member of the AIA holds between three and four state licenses, which indicates that the odds of holding a license within a state with an MCE requirement are increasing dramatically from what they were five years ago, when just three states had enacted MCE.

The requirements are similar in most states, but they do vary. Alabama, for example, requires 12 hours per year. Florida requires 20 hours every 2 years. Except for Kansas, each of these states requires that 8 to 12 of these hours be in the area described as health, safety, and welfare (HSW). Louisiana and North Carolina have a requirement of 12 hours of HSW per year.

What still confuses many architects is what makes up lifelong learning and how that applies to the profession of architecture.

Training Versus Professional Development

❏ Many architects and other design professionals are perplexed when they are asked the difference between training and professional development. Many architecture firms' training departments are entirely based on some product rep knocking at the door of the firm and offering a meal. If it is a convenient time, this lunch also becomes the firm's training session of the week, month—and in some cases, year. Many firm principals call this their professional development, and it looks something like this: *lunch > LUs/MCE > immediate need (maybe)*.

With the recent attention on the AIA continuing education requirement and state licensing boards requiring MCE, a new scenario is developing within architecture and engineering firms. Training, by definition, is a short-term solution to address a short-term need or problem; professional development is a long-term solution that addresses the needs of the firm and the architects as identified as part of a long-term or strategic plan. A series of planned training sessions should then be applied toward achieving the long-term professional development plan. This means that architects and firms are rethinking their current approach toward continuing education and training. Instead of offering training programs because a product rep or CES provider knocks on the office door with a lunch, the firm's professional development specialist uses the identified needs of the firm as the basis for determining which product rep or CES provider to invite in. Provider programs can still satisfy some of the AIA/CES requirements as well as some of the state's MCE requirements, and many will still provide a free lunch. A firm's professional development program now begins to look more like this: *identified need(s) > LUs/MCE > and maybe even a lunch*. For many, this is a new way of thinking, but a way that can only help the architectural profession grow and be successful. Firms are now putting into place a systematic approach to developing quality educational programming for their architects and engineers to make the best use of time and resources.

Case Study: Reynolds, Smith and Hills (RSH), Inc., Jacksonville, Florida

❑ John Bottaro, senior vice president, was an attendee at the AIA/CES Leadership Summit in 1998. John applied the lessons he learned at the summit to a project in his office. Team members, the project manager, suppliers, and the client discussed what worked and what needed more attention. From this they identified where training might improve the process in the future. John did not stop there, however. Working with other division leaders, RSH, Inc. is now expanding this practice to each of its six divisions. Once all six divisions identify project strengths and weaknesses, the division leaders will pool the information and identify common areas for which they agree training will be a benefit. Further, plans call for expanding the Intern Development Program (IDP) that has been established for the architects using the *IDP Handbook* as a model and drafting a similar handbook for the young engineers. Other plans under development are to integrate the IDP interns and mentors and tie this into job performance evaluations.

As stated in Ernest Boyer and Lee Mitgang's book *Building Community: A New Future for Architecture Education and Practice* (Carnegie Foundation for the Advancement of Teaching, 1996, page 124), "Continuing education for all practitioners can be, as Clemson University architecture dean James Barker has said, 'the best bridge between education and practice we have yet established.' "

Would you run your business without a business plan? How important is a good business plan? Ask any AIA principal, ask any banker, or ask any accountant, and they will tell you it is a must if you want to succeed in business. The AIA has made available to firms an educational business plan titled "Guidelines for an Organization Establishing Quality Programs for Architectural Continuing Education." The CES educational business plan provides a systematic approach to improving educational programming and professional development.

The first step of a five-step plan is based upon the firm's leadership and commitment to offering meaningful continuing education to the architects. This first step includes a strategic development plan that contains action implementation and performance projections. A built-in "ask an architect" phase is suggested. It seems so simple but is too often overlooked.

The second step emphasizes the development of needs assessment and the establishment of learning objectives. It is also important to establish an ongoing educational support system within the firm to ensure continuity.

The third step addresses how the learning activities are designed and delivered based upon the needs of the architects. Considerations of appropriate resources, both technical and human, are important. For AIA members and those architects with state licensing MCE requirements, a structured system should be established that addresses how activities are being recorded and reported.

The fourth step requires a systematic feedback system designed to measure how meaningful the programs offered are to the architect and how effective the delivery of the program is. This step is critical to the long-term improvement process.

Finally, step five addresses those identified needs that are particular to the firm. Various issues should be addressed, such as the long-term impact on job performance for the firm's architects. A systematic approach to offering meaningful continuing education programming takes time and a great deal of effort and commitment on the part of the providers.

The firms that are most successful implement this systematic approach to ensure that programs are meaningful and of consistently high quality. The AIA guidelines help CES providers achieve these goals.

From among the many firms that now provide a structured in-house continuing education program, NBBJ was the 1998 AIA/CES Award for Excellence winner. Quentin Elliott, the principal in charge of NBBJ, states that "The continuing education program at NBBJ is partially responsible for an increase in improved recruitment and firm retention."

Where to Find Quality Continuing Education Programs and Support

❑ For assistance in developing needs assessment, try the AIA Wisconsin Continuing Education Committee. This committee undertook a statewide effort to offer meaningful continuing education to its membership. The committee states: "The purposes of this study were to collect information about architect continuing education activities and opinions of the AIA/CES. This information will be used to respond to the members' needs relevant to their continuing education." To learn more about the subjects, methods, and results, contact Mitchell Spencer, AIA, Chair of the Continuing Education Committee, AIA Wisconsin, University of Wisconsin, School of Industry & Technology, Menomonie, WI 54751. (Phone: 715-232-2416.) Secondary contact is Bill Babcock, Executive Director, Wisconsin Society of Architects. (Phone: 608-257-8477.)

www.e-architect.com >Continuing Ed >CES Programs. AIA/CES providers post their educational activities here on a daily basis. Anyone can sort the more than 1200 program listings by date, location, title, HSW, or even appointment.

Competitions: Learning Opportunities or Exploitation?

❑ Architectural competitions have been likened to a double-edged sword. On one hand, they can provide architects with opportunities, enlighten the public, and advance the design dialogue. On the other, they can exploit architects from financial and intellectual property standpoints. One thing is clear: the stakes can be very high—big money and reputations are often at risk.

Learning Opportunities

❑ Dolf Schnebli, a Swiss architect, views competitions as continuing education because they offer the opportunity to experiment with new technologies and design options. Bruce Kuwabara, principal of the Toronto firm Kuwabara Payne McKenna Blumberg Architects (KPMB), is also emphatic: "Competitions are an important way of expanding our thinking. We see them as part of our body of work." Indeed, architects can push the design envelope in competitions because competitions encourage an open and inventive approach to projects. Even losing schemes can enhance a firm's marketing portfolio, particularly in difficult economic cycles. Moreover, competitions provide a chance for small, evolving firms to have a shot at large-scale commissions.

Roger Schluntz, FAIA, a noted professional advisor for competitions, suggests that one of the biggest beneficiaries of design competitions is the public. The educational consequences of presentations, exhibits, and the media can be extraordinary. Schluntz says, "As a result of the increased awareness of the value of design and heightened expectations, both the profession and public can profit."

Regardless of the outcome, participating in competitions can benefit a firm. New York City-based Kohn Pedersen Fox (KPF) used a competition to pursue its first project in the health care industry, an effort that earned a third-place award. Even though KPF didn't win, the partners were delighted; the experience increased the firm's knowledge of this market and positioned it for similar future projects.

In theory, competitions provide the possibility to secure commissions on pure merit. KPF's London office entered 30 competitions (and won a staggering 17) in its first four years, giving the firm an almost instant reputation and workload. Competitions in Europe tend to be more frequent, shorter in duration, and less costly than those in the States, thus minimizing the risks and increasing the potential return for the architect.

The Downside

❏ Still, all competitions involve some risk for the professional. The biggest problem, according to New River, Arizona–based architect Will Bruder, is politics. Jurors frequently have personal agendas. Bruder cites a competition in which he participated where all five finalists were either former students or employees of jurors. "How can jurors be objective under those circumstances? It's a travesty!" he exclaims.

In the most egregious examples, clients or juries have chosen an architect before the competition begins. Architects have also charged that their ideas have been used even when they did not win. *Architectural Record*, for example, has received numerous complaints from architects who felt that their intellectual property had been appropriated without credit or remuneration.

For architects who don't win, the costs can be substantial. Even if an honorarium is given, it rarely covers all the architect's expenses. Michael Graves, FAIA, deems this "a hideous way to select an architect." Notwithstanding the aforementioned successes of his firm, KPF, Gene Kohn, FAIA, believes it's unfortunate that architects are eager to participate in competitions without a fee. He says these professionals are giving away their most valuable assets: creative ideas.

Because good buildings require the consensus of users and designers, competitions are further criticized because there is no dialogue between client and architect. Hugh Hardy, FAIA, of Hardy Holzman Pfeiffer Associates in New York City, believes the process is inherently flawed. Lacking "proper access to the client," he says, "an architect alone cannot represent all the values required for the best buildings." Roger Schluntz suggests this may not always be the case: "Development of a detailed program for the competition should help distill the issues. After the architect is selected, the dialogue begins anew."

Recommendations

❏ Entering competitions requires vigilance on the architect's part. Critical assessments of selection criteria and jury predisposition are essential to understanding the politics. The financial risks are too high if a firm has no chance to win.

The architect should also understand the competition's rules regarding intellectual property. Typically, the architect owns the "Instruments of Service" and grants the sponsor a nonexclusive license to publish and display submission drawings and models. Once ideas have been published and displayed, however, they can creep into the subconscious, making it difficult, if not impossible, to prove plagiarism. Having an agreement that binds the sponsor and each firm to the competition's schedule, requirements, and honorarium prior to the start of the competition is a must.

The very best competitions result in better designs than the Request for Qualifications (RFQ) process and provide ways for architects to excel based on talent alone. Poorly run competitions, on the other hand, can mire architects in a political muck, which can be costly and unnerving.

The notion of the architectural competition is analogous to a Shakespeare play. In addition to the rarefied layer of design excellence, there's an abundance of subtexts: power struggles, political agendas, and financial issues. Indeed, the Bard might have been "in love" with architectural competitions.

FIGURE 6.1
An example of part of a submission to an "invited" competition for the Green Acre Classroom Facility, Eliot, Maine. (a) Aerial perspective. (b) Computer model superimposed on site photo. (Courtesy of Andy Pressman, Architect/Siegel Design.)

Details of Design Competitions

A Conversation with Roger Schluntz

Roger L. Schluntz, FAIA, is dean and professor at the School of Architecture and Planning at the University of New Mexico. Schluntz has served as professional advisor for a number of national design competitions, including the recently opened Denver Public Library, won by Michael Graves, the Nashville Public Library, and Antoine Predock's award-winning American Heritage Center and art museum for the University of Wyoming.

Andy Pressman: *Do competitions produce better architecture? What about the lack of an ongoing dialogue with clients/stakeholders during the design process—does that result in less responsive or less sensitive designs?*

Roger Schluntz: There is considerable evidence to support the position that a carefully crafted and well-managed design competition can increase the probability of achieving design excellence. Most architects would agree that to accomplish a great building, one needs to have a great client. Development of a good program brief for the competition can help distill essential issues, a process that will involve the client/user group. And it should also be noted that after the architect is selected through a competition, the dialogue begins anew. In the case of many building types, the actual client is the public (or the taxpayer, if you prefer), as well as future generations of users and workers. Significant precedent and understanding exists, for example, for municipal buildings, educational facilities, libraries, and museums. In the normal design process, identification of a client representative can be problematic; having a great one is not all that typical anyway.

Notwithstanding, I have worked with three major public libraries as the professional advisor for design competitions—Denver, Nashville, and Salt Lake City. In each instance, the program and the urban setting provided unique and complex challenges. Following a two-stage competition format that reduced applicants to three or four invited competitors, we were able to integrate executive sessions with each of the design team finalists and the client/user group at critical points during the actual design process. These meetings proved to be very helpful and successful.

Pressman: *What types of design competitions are most commonly used today?*

Schluntz: There is a broad range of design competition categories, and each can be adapted with various characteristics and in differing combinations. "Open" competitions are just that: accessible to all who enter and submit a submission as directed by the competition program. Usually, however, even "open" competitions are restricted in some manner, for example to licensed architects. Entrant eligibility may also be limited to those living or practicing in a specific geographic area or country. Some competitions may require certain combinations of disciplines for the entrant team. Usually there is a fee for entering, and a formal registration deadline.

Open competitions are typically judged without knowledge of the name of the submitter, i.e., anonymously. Awards and prizes are provided for the winner as well as other meritorious solutions. Design competitions can be organized to address a specific building, building typology (e.g., "library of the future," low-cost housing prototypes, teaching and learning environments), a specific technology (e.g., incorporation of a specific product, use of daylighting, strategies for energy efficiency or "green" solutions), or the "highest and best use" for a specific parcel of property or public space. There are competitions for landscape architecture, product design, graphics and signage, and urban design and planning, as well as architecture.

When a competition is not intended to produce or result in a commission for specific built artifact, it is usually referred to as an "idea" competition. These may be academic or theoretical in nature, and are usually intended to increase understanding about a particular issue or problem. The process and resulting publications and exhibitions can be powerful educational strategies, for both the public and a specific interest group. Idea competitions do not result in an actual commission for a project, so the prizes or awards and/or recognition must be substantial to attract serious firms or architects.

Urban design and planning competitions are typically of the "idea" category, even though the winner (or other entrants) may be hired to execute a more definitive scheme or a particular phase of long-term strategy. A civic-oriented group, such as a chapter of the AIA, a governmental agency, a foundation, or a corporate entity typically sponsors open competitions.

Competitions are sometimes invited, and open only to a few selected competitors—usually ranging between three and eight firms. In such instances, the organizing sponsor will normally provide each of the invited competitors a fairly substantial honorarium. A common variation on this type—frequently used by governmental agencies—is a two- and sometimes three-phase process that first invites responses to a published Request for Qualifications (RFQ). From these responses, a limited number will then be selected (and perhaps interviewed) and then invited for the last phase of the selection process, which is the design competition itself. Invited competitions usually conclude with formal presentations by each competitor or team to the jury or selection panel, but in some instances these submissions are also reviewed and judged anonymously without benefit of the presentation.

Architecture design competitions, both open and invited, may also require two distinct design stages. The same jury will review the first-stage entries and select several for the second stage of work or refinement before choosing the winner.

Competitions may be very explicit in the development of the design intent, with many requirements and prescribed drawings and, not infrequently, at least one physical model.

Other competitions are presented as "conceptual," where the submission requirements are far less stringent and often limited to a very few drawings or diagrams along with a concept statement. In these instances, the time frame for the competition may also be much shorter. Because they are less costly to enter, these competitions are more likely to attract the interest of both well-established and very busy architects.

And then there are variations and combinations of most of these classifications. One example is the so-called charrette competition, where invited competitors are asked to work on-site for a very limited amount of time—possibly a few days or a even a week. In such instances the user group/owner and public may also be directly involved in the design process. Following the charrette, a winner may be selected outright, or teams will be given a specified amount of time to work in the conventional competition manner to complete and submit their respective projects.

Today we are also seeing an increasing number of "design-build" competitions, where the competitor is asked to guarantee the delivery of the project as designed for a maximum established price. For large projects, such as the Chicago Public Library, the entrants are invariably developers or construction entities, with the architect (the winner in this case being Thomas Beeby, FAIA) being a part of the builder's team, and not the official competitor. The Portland City Hall, designed by Michael Graves, also resulted from a design-build competition. Unfortunately, too many of these tend to focus far more on building cost than on design, with the estimated cost of the completed proposal the primary if not the sole determining factor in selection of the competition winner.

In any competition, the official rules should clearly state the purpose and the expected final outcome of the process. In the case of real projects, the competition may, quite logically, be intended to determine the design of the building. But some competitions clearly state that the purpose is to determine who will be awarded (or, in the case of public agencies, "recommended") the specific commission, reserving the right to require substantial or complete modifications to the design parti. It is to the advantage of both the competitor and the sponsor, obviously, if the competition results in both the design and the commission.

Pressman: *When the current construction boom ends, will firms likely seek competitions as an integral part of marketing? Is that a good idea? What should firms spend on competitions as a percentage of annual total billings? Is there a publication that lists all open or invited competitions?*

Schluntz: Different firms have different objectives and strategies, but I doubt that some will ever consider design competitions as a basic marketing strategy. It is not unusual, however, for a firm to engage in a competition to bridge a slack time. I suspect that those who consider design to be a critical part of the service they provide will typically consider opportunities that a design competition might provide.

For a small firm that is seeking to move into a different building type or gain access to larger projects, the design competition may provide the primary vehicle for the firm's evolution. This is undoubtedly the case in many European countries, where the use of design competitions for public works is much more widespread.

I know of one fairly large firm—which has had a successful track record with design competitions—that carefully evaluates the cost (risk) of entering relative to its normal marketing costs for an equivalent project. Based in part on this analysis, the firm's executive committee will either decide to engage in the competition or abstain. For small firms, and even some that are well established, unsuccessful competition entries become an essential part of their marketing portfolio.

Competitions magazine, an excellent quarterly published in Louisville, Kentucky, does a good job of announcing competitions through its newsletter and Web site (www.competitions.org). Most serious competitions are also announced in the major design publications and through direct mailings. Competitions for public projects are published as legally required.

Pressman: *Do competitions inherently exploit design firms (even with honoraria)? In terms of the structure of competitions, which types should architects completely avoid, consider, or actively pursue? Should honoraria cover all expenses? What costs do they typically cover?*

Schluntz: Unfortunately, many competitions are exploitive; I urge architects to examine each situation and the competition rules very carefully before committing to engage in one. In a well-run competition, there should be no surprises. There may be other and substantial benefits derivative from a competition entry (e.g., Aalto's intangible "keeping the office staff sharp," marketing, experience gained through the process and research), in addition to winning the commission and/or prizes. In a two-stage invited process, honoraria for invited competitors can help offset some of the direct cost, but seldom all.

The competition advisor should endeavor, in any circumstance, to prescribe final presentation requirements that minimize or limit costs and work to maintain equality among the competitors. Sponsors frequently do not fully comprehend the requirements necessary for the purpose of the final selection, and it is easy for the final submissions (usually models) to run up huge and unnecessary expenses. Direct travel costs also become burdensome; I always try to limit the number of persons from a single competitor that can attend any given meeting or presentation.

Given that a firm can always choose not to enter, I would disagree that competitions are inherently exploitive. But many are, and the potential is there and often the motivation. This is particularly true for many design-build competitions undertaken by the private sector and in those too frequent instances where the sponsor is not committed to commissioning the winner—or worse, when the ownership rights to the final design submissions are vague or unstated.

Pressman: *When do honoria get paid? Is any money paid to competitors up front? Is there a contract with invited firms who are competing?*

Schluntz: In design competitions for public buildings that are supported by public funds, it is extremely unusual for a fee to be paid to the competitors prior to the competition exercise. I think that invited competitions that are organized (usually and unfortunately, in-house) by corporations could easily provide a retainer. A signed agreement between the sponsor and each of the invited firms prior to starting the design competition phase is, in my opinion, an absolute necessity. The agreement should reference the acceptance of the competition rules—its schedule, requirements, and honoraria—and bind each party to specific performance.

Pressman: *Perhaps the selection of jurors is even more important than the selection of a firm. How does that influence the process of producing an excellent building? Or the decision of whether or not a firm should participate? Are there instances where decisions are really made prior to a thorough review of the submissions? And while we're on ethics, how about Eisenman's belief that the only rule for winning competitions is to break the rules? It has worked for him . . .*

Schluntz: If I'm the professional advisor, I can tell you that "breaking the rules" is a risky business, and I think the architects know and appreciate that going into the competition. Because no two competitions or projects are alike it is difficult to generalize, but clearly some lend themselves to inventiveness and risk, while others do not. Part of the due diligence undertaken prior to entering ought to be an assessment of the jury or selection panel, as well as the published selection criteria, which should be clearly articulated in the competition rules. Public and client members of the jury frequently constitute the biggest unknown for the architect.

Pressman: *Historically, competitions have been an effective vehicle for young architects or firms to establish themselves with large-scale projects. Is that still true today?*

Schluntz: Yes, very much so. Although in seeking large projects the odds of success are probably relatively low. Generally, the progression from small projects to large projects goes through a number of steps in the development of a firm. It is not unusual to see collaborative efforts in some invited or limited competitions where talented designers with small organizations work with larger, established firms that are best known for their high level of service to clients.

Pressman: *Who owns the submissions? Does the intellectual property belong to the architect-author, regardless of who wins or places? Can losers then recycle ideas for their real projects to offset their investment? Is that a valid justification for entering, even against poor odds?*

Schluntz: Again, the competition rules ought to explicitly address the questions of ownership of both the submitted materials and the intellectual property. The latter should almost always reside with the architect; the submission drawings and models typically become the property of the sponsor, with the right to publish and display them.

It is not too unusual for an architect to incorporate some aspect of an unsuccessful design entry into a later project, and in some instances we see recurring themes and concepts. But this is also true for projects that were commissioned directly but were not built. There are numerous and well-documented instances of the work of Frank Lloyd Wright, for example, that reappear in projects executed at a much later time.

Pressman: *Competitions in Europe are a more conventional mode of architect selection than in the States. What is the typical structure of those competitions that seem to make participation less painful or costly to firms?*

Schluntz: First, competitions in European countries are normally sanctioned and tend to be effectively regulated by professional societies; coupled with centuries of experience, they tend to be well run. In this country, the AIA cannot now assume this authority because of antitrust legislation and regulations. Decades ago, the AIA would formally approve a proposed design competition. If the competition was not approved, members of the AIA were prohibited from entering. This practice is now considered to be anti-competitive and a restraint of free trade. Second, because competitions are frequently used in most European countries, the number of competitors for a typical project is far fewer than we usually experience in an open competition here. Thus, the odds of prevailing would seem to be significantly higher in Europe. In some instances, competitions will be limited to a select group, e.g., architecture firms of a specified maximum size who have had some previous, and often limited, experience with the specific building type. This strategy provides directed opportunity as well as a smaller number of competitiors.

Pressman: *In the U.S., the federal General Services Administration (GSA) has conducted a few competitions for courthouses and other major public buildings. Has design quality improved? Is that going to start a trend for government projects? And will the private sector then follow?*

Schluntz: The GSA has deployed a broad-ranging strategy for achieving better design, and included in its design excellence program for public buildings are a limited number of design competitions. These competitions have allowed the participation and success of several emerging architects who simply could not have prevailed through the normal competitive RFQ process. Quite a number of years ago, Senator Daniel Patrick Moynihan introduced legislation that would have required design competitions for all major public buildings produced by the U.S. As an advisor to the GSA design excellence program, I believe they have done a good job in increasing the expectation for design quality as well as the realization of better buildings. The competitions that have been employed have achieved their purposes, and I would expect to see more in the future. State and local governmental agencies, in my opinion, ought to look closely at the GSA strategies, procedures, and results.

Pressman: *Rafael Vinoly, Predock, Tschumi, Michael Graves, and Robert Stern all have had great success in winning competitions. What are some of the special strategies that these folks (and some others) employ (i.e., what are the characteristics of successful schemes)? Is it that only signature firms are invited to the prestigious competitions?*

Schluntz: If those you mention have common strategies, I would suggest that it is the following. First, these architects are very selective about which competitions (and competition types) they enter, matching their skills and strengths with the project, the site, and possibly the perceived predisposition of the jury. Second, once the commitment has been made to enter the competition, they approach the task like going to war. Third, they are very careful and intelligent in presenting their respective final submissions. Of course, these are obviously very capable architects and always have talented individuals working with them.

Pressman: *What are some strategies that entrants can use to read between the lines of the standard competition brief to produce optimally responsive designs and increase chances for winning? Is it slick presentation over content?*

Schluntz: Contrary to a few notorious instances, the winning entries for most competitions and for those that I have served as the professional advisor have resulted from a clear and careful response to the program and final presentation requirements, rather than taking the risk of challenging basic presumptions or ignoring major program expectations. This is not to suggest that these successful entries were void of creativity—far from that. But on the other hand, I have seen many otherwise brilliant entries rejected by a single juror because of what was perceived as a fatal flaw of major consequence. Strategies for winning idea competitions could be quite different, however.

If I have any advice for those entering competitions for real projects, it is this: be sure the program is fully and faithfully resolved. And I would be very cautious in using any strategy that would unduly increase the stated project budget. One additional insight I might offer: the building siting and site plan often weigh more in the jury deliberations than the competitors might expect. In my estimation, it has been the brilliance of the plan execution and its relationship with the site, and not the aesthetic intentions, that has provided Michael Graves his remarkable track record with design competitions, for example.

I have learned that most jurors dislike having to resolve confusing (or worse, conflicting) information and presentations. When in doubt, jurors—and particularly those nonprofessionals on the jury—don't want to assume an additional burden of risk for themselves or the sponsor; the whole building undertaking, in its simplest terms, is risky enough! In most instances you will find that the clarity of the submission, usually elegant in nature rather than an example of creative indulgence, plays a role in the winning scheme's success. However, I don't think a great presentation can overcome an inferior design, nor will a great idea always be sustained when conveyed by a weak or inconclusive presentation.

Pressman: *In addition to the advantages and disadvantages of competitions for owners and participants that you have summarized, do you have any concluding observations?*

Schluntz: One of the biggest beneficiaries of design competitions is the public. Through this process, a much broader segment of society and key decision makers is involved; the educational outcomes can be extraordinary. As a result of the public's increased awareness of the value of design and embracing higher expectations, the profession will also profit. In the long term we will have, of course, better design.

Travel

With John Cary Jr. and Casius Pealer III

❏ Travel is an architectural tradition, and for good reason, as eloquently described in Supplement 6.2. During periods when it may not be so easy to find work, traveling is one reliable and fascinating way to keep growing and learning professionally. To get the most out of your travels, study and record the environment. Consider selective advanced preparation to maximize benefit: research plans, photos, and contexts of buildings you anticipate visiting. Slides—and of course, the famous travel sketch—are wonderful ways to record what you see on the road; they are a personal resource that can be treasured and referred to often. And you can bore selected insufferable relatives upon your return as an added perk.

John M. Cary Jr. and Casius H. Pealer III

As past American Institute of Architecture Students (AIAS) national vice presidents, John Cary and Casius Pealer have traveled extensively while living and working for one full year in Washington, DC. They have worked together on a number of initiatives and are the cofounders of ArchVoices, an online resource for interns and young architects. Both have actively pursued cocurricular careers in journalism and are regular contributors to AIA Architect, ACSA News, *and their respective alumni publications. They have also actively participated in the writing and editing of* Crit, *the journal of the AIAS. Pealer earned a bachelor of architecture from Tulane University and is currently serving in the U.S. Peace Corps on St. Vincent Island; Cary earned his BA in architecture from the University of Minnesota and is pursuing a master of architecture from the University of California, Berkeley.*

SUPPLEMENT 6.2

Oh, the Places We Should Go

❏ Travel is critical to the well-rounded education of virtually anyone in any field, especially those within architecture. As an experiential field, architecture employs movement, light and sound, texture and material. Despite our fascination with photographic images, these architectural ingredients simply cannot be fully captured or comprehended unless visited.

Incorporating a variety of jobs in our preprofessional background is arguably as important as travel in diversifying our substantive experience. Accordingly, many faculty members and professionals advise and encourage students to get as much experience working in an architecture firm prior to graduation as possible. Unfortunately, time spent engaged in these summer and part-time jobs takes away from what is often the only time that young people have left to travel and explore other fields and opportunities, before graduating into a rigorous internship and an often more rigorous profession.

Are 21-year-old students, who started a professional degree program at 18, best served by immersing themselves in the traditional practice of architecture? Probably not. The importance of travel is a substantial part of this reasoning, yet the importance of diverse experiences to a mature designer remains the greater goal. Travel requires us to adapt, to be creative, and to understand many things that are often beyond our previous experiences.

Immersing ourselves in another culture—commonly referred to as "study abroad"—often occurs during our formal education, the time when travel is emphasized most. By adapting to a different culture, we encounter many of our own assumptions and prejudices, and thus become better at translating a client's or a community's hopes and dreams into reality. Short trips, complete with visits to museums, natural features, and esoteric architectural works, are often important, but rarely match the lessons from these truly cross-cultural experiences.

Still, the most convenient, yet underutilized, type of travel is local travel. Think about it—we can literally travel on any given afternoon. Unfortunately, many of us get so caught up in our work and family activities that we neglect the beauty and wonder of the cities and places in which we already live. In school, were not field trips some of our favorite activities, regardless of which subject they were focused around? We should do ourselves and our work a big favor by continuing to take field trips, and inviting a friend or colleague while we are at it.

Beyond our own experiences, it is equally important for the public to be engaged and aware of the messages communicated by our cities and those we travel to. Values are inevitably communicated to residents, visitors, and young children by the built environment, either reinforcing or contradicting the stated values of the community. We can talk about the importance of education, for instance,

FIGURE 6.2
Travel sketch. (Courtesy of Kristen James.)

but if the places where we send our children for that education convey a different message, we have to expect our kids to see our real community values in action and to organize their lives around those values.

To bring it back to travel, just as our private homes need a center, or hearth, so do our cities. That center need not be in the center, nor even a single object or plaza. A center is really defined as much by the relationship—both physical and emotional—of the city to that center as by the center itself. In addition to a physical and psychological center, all urban environments have certain orienting devices—towers, monuments, tall buildings, distant mountains, etc.—all of which are centers in their own way in that they allow you to center yourself. Even the expression, "the wrong side of the tracks," indicates orientation, a relationship to something other than oneself. That relationship is a physical and spatial relationship, but one that tells us a significant story.

While orientation is comforting and necessary, comfort is often confused with the absence of discomfort, or more precisely, the absence of any sensation at all. Orientation is necessary only because of the underlying condition of disorientation, not just physically within a city, but emotionally and spiritually in the world itself. While our language implies that orientation is the standard condition and that disorientation is the state of being out of orientation, the reality is, in fact, the opposite: disorientation is our natural state, and so we use both the natural and built environments to orient ourselves within a larger context. Gridded cities are both logically comforting and phenomenally discomforting in the sense just noted, where comfort is simply the absence of sensation. Both planned and naturalistic cities have many positive qualities, and both communicate the positive and negative aspects of those value systems, necessarily shaping the personalities of the people who live in those cities.

So make the most of your lunch hour travels, or look into the AIA's occasional travel programs uniting architects in such meccas as Greece or even Japan. These excursions typically offer some continuing education credit, and with good reason. The Association of Collegiate Schools of Architecture (ACSA) also produces a fine document profiling special programs, namely travel programs, available through its member schools. Many of these schools, and a handful of firms and foundations, even offer travel fellowships.

Above all, remember: travel is the ultimate continuing education program, and as architects we have a responsibility to

FIGURE 6.3
Another terrific travel sketch—the Hagia Sophia in Istanbul—by Robert S. Oliver, excerpted from his book, The Sketch *(Van Nostrand Reinhold, 1979). (Reprinted with permission of Van Nostrand Reinhold.)*

enrich our learning through travel and experiences of the public in their travels.

▬▬▬▬▬▬▬▬▬▬▬▬▬▬▬▬▬▬▬▬

Architectural photographer Norman McGrath offers this tip on developing a personal collection of photographs, a means of recording images from travel experiences:

"To develop a useful reference library of personal images, you must first decide on a convenient format. Thirty-five-millimeter slides are great for projection but are not that easy to view in the hand. You may find that simple, small color prints are easier to refer to and handle. Either way, you should first establish a good filing system, so that you can find a particular photograph when you want to. Some cameras will imprint dates or numbers on the original—preferably optionally. There are times when you may not want this information on a print or slide, but it can be useful.

"Economics will play a major part in determining what equipment you purchase. If you can't afford a 35-mm single-lens reflex (SLR) with removable lenses, you will at the very least need a point-and-shoot camera with a wide-angle lens and 35mm or shorter focal length. This will give you snapshot capability but not much more. The ultimate 35-mm camera would be an SLR with perhaps a wide-angle zoom lens, 24 to 50 or 28 to 70 mm, and, if you're really extravagant, a perspective control (PC) lens (35 or 28 mm), which is what the pros use. For interiors, you will need a tripod for longer exposures. If you are a beginner, you should enroll in a crash course in basic photography. Workshops of a day or so to a week or more are widely available for different levels of expertise—an excellent continuing education venue."

Architectural Internship

❏ *Day one. Building a model out of mat board, using an X-Acto knife. Things going smoothly. After a half hour, realization that the knife penetrated through the cardboard and ruined the custom laminate work surface.*

The tolerance and patience of architectural firms (note the preceding example from my first job) genuinely help the fledgling architect bridge the worlds of school and professional practice. Most architects, as true professionals, take their responsibility of helping, advising, and mentoring interns seriously, and it is of course now mandated by law via the Intern Development Program in most states.

From an employee's perspective, intern architect Tamara Iwaseczko stated, in a New Mexico Board of Examiners newsletter, "If one approaches the intern experience as a time of gestation, as well as a time for fueling one's interests, following one's passions, nurturing the true spirit that brought one to the threshold of this profession, and extending out and sharing the excitement, then the time can be incredibly enriching and can set the tenor for a profound career." In Supplement 6.3, Rob Rosenfeld suggests guidelines that operationalize the sentiment expressed so well by Iwaseczko.

Optimizing Internship Experience for Interns and Employers

With Rob Rosenfeld

❏ Benefits to both the intern and employer are stated in simple terms in a recent IDP publication: "Internship is a two-way street. It requires give and take from both intern and employer in order for it to be an enriching time for both participants." Supplement 6.3 also addresses how interns can get the most out of the time, including educational value, financial benefit, and the intangibles alluded to earlier. Moreover, the discussion includes how employers should treat interns in order to educate interns without losing too much billable time (realizing the long-term investment potential of lower turnover and higher profits); to turn interns into effective team members; to instill a sense of loyalty; and to utilize the interns' strengths effectively. These objectives should be accomplished in the context of the constantly evolving nature of the IDP, the schools, and practice.

SUPPLEMENT 6.3

Robert Rosenfeld

Robert Rosenfeld is the director of Council Record Services at the National Council of Architectural Registration Boards (NCARB) in Washington, DC. From 1980 to 1999, Rosenfeld served as the NCARB's director of student and intern services. He received his architectural registration in 1978. During the past 19 years, he has lectured extensively about the transition from education through internship to practice, and has authored numerous articles and IDP resources. He serves as a mentor to a group of interns in Washington.

❏ Look up the word *intern* in the dictionary and you get two distinctly different definitions. As a noun, interns are "advanced students or graduates, usually in a professional field, gaining supervised practical experience." As a verb, however, to intern means "to confine or impound." For many interns an architectural internship may feel like an internment! And many employers justify this condition by arguing that interns, as new employees, must be limited to the most cost-effective office activities for the firm to meet its bottom line.

These conditions combine to provide less than ideal training environments. And interns must have diversified training to qualify for professional registration. This essay will examine improving the internship process in two ways:

- Providing ideas for interns to get the most out of their internship period
- Giving employers tips to maximize the investment they make in their interns

Internship: Opportunity or Internment?

❏ What distinguishes between a successful and unsuccessful internship experience? According to recent research conducted by Montana State University, six factors significantly affect the quality of one's early professional experience.

1. Have a Game Plan. Few students graduate architectural school with clearly defined professional goals. Since most schools do not require practical experience, far too many graduates begin their careers with little understanding of the realities of architectural practice. Fewer still have given much thought to possible career paths.

A successful career begins with a series of written career goals, including clearly articulated objectives for the internship phase. Objectives are based on several factors: experience/competencies required for professional registration, access to professional development resources, advice given by professionals, personal interests, etc. Experience—both planned and unplanned—continually refines this living document. Goal-oriented interns are better able to assess opportunities within the context of their short- and long-term objectives.

2. Choose an Employer on the Basis of Goals, Not Glitz. Architecture students often feel compelled to work for "signature" firms (e.g., those whose high-profile principals lectured at their school). Working for other firms may be perceived as a step in the wrong direction; however, most recently registered architects rate "quality training" and "the firm's commitment to professional development" as the most significant factors in choosing an employer. These factors are rated higher than compensation, and for good reason—goal-directed interns realize that promotions and greater responsibility are related to competency, not initial salary.

Interns should prepare for job interviews well before graduation. Seeking advice about preparing effective resumes, cover letters, and portfolios, along with acquiring good negotiation skills (after all, an interview is a two-way process), will pay dividends. In addition, interns should carefully research the firms they are considering. What kind of work do they do? What is the office environment like? How committed is the firm to intern development? Interns should explore and compare these and other questions with the personal career goals discussed earlier. Good planning adds immeasurably to long-term job satisfaction.

3. Select a Mentor. Mentorship is a critical component of a quality internship experience. The mentor provides career guidance and serves as an information resource and professional sounding board. Good mentors create opportunities for interns to explore professional options and reflect on connections between the academic and practice worlds. The Montana State study cited "having a mentor" as one of the most significant elements of a positive internship experience.

Interns select their mentors from a variety of sources: their own firms, other firms, their AIA components, or the local architectural school. Some interns have more than one mentor, while others meet as a group with a single mentor. No matter how the intern-mentor relationship is structured, periodic face-to-face meetings are essential. Many mentoring relationships last well beyond initial architectural registration—there is, quite simply, no time limit placed on the need for career advice.

4. Use Continuing Education Resources to Fill Knowledge Gaps. Formal education does not end with graduation from architectural school. Opportunities for interns to acquire comprehensive experience rely in part on the practical knowledge they possess. Why, for example, should a firm involve an intern in writing specifications if the intern does not know what a specification is? Few, if any, firms can afford to pass off remedial education costs to their clients or have sufficient revenues for significant in-house programs.

Successful interns are proactive learners. They use the Intern Development Program's Core Competencies to identify training areas where basic knowledge gaps exist, and they use appropriate continuing education resources to reduce the gaps. These interns understand the relationship between core knowledge and opportunities to attain diversified training. Even more significantly, they begin this process early in their internships.

Continuing education also allows interns to understand emerging practice methods and technological advances. Many interns have noted that their learning curves have actually accelerated since graduation. Architects must know how to efficiently apply innovations to remain competitive in the marketplace. The proactive learning habit must be cultivated during the internship period.

5. Get Involved with Your Profession and Your Community. Another habit worth cultivating is the architect's civic responsibility. Active involvement in one's profession and community helps in four important ways:

■ It aids in developing a sustained commitment to social engagement.

■ It clarifies ways in which architecture benefits the public.

■ It stresses the importance of ethical behavior.

■ It stimulates the creation of new ideas.

Interns must be exposed to different models of effective leadership within the business community. Interns need to understand how groups make decisions that result in architectural solutions—and how architects can influence this decision-making process. Conversely, public leaders will better understand the unique skills architects use to solve problems.

Where does one begin? In a word: volunteer! Join an AIA committee. Get involved with local charity organizations. Pay a visit to the community design center. Attend a meeting of the local planning commission, zoning board, neighborhood association, or historic preservation group. Offer your services to any civic organization. Interns who are active in their communities gain skills and knowledge (and meet people) that will help them throughout their professional careers.

6. Become a Conscientious Time Manager. Architecture is an art and a science. Practically speaking, it's also a business. Most businesses exist to make money (among other, more noble things). No matter what his or her financial goals may be, today's architect must understand the value of time as a company resource. Unfortunately, effective time management skills are rarely taught in architectural schools—in fact, some schools that still espouse the "charrette mentality," and unwittingly teach students to devalue the importance of time. In too many cases graduates carry poor time management (e.g., procrastination) into the real world.

The good news is that anyone can learn effective time management skills. Interns must make this a priority. Without good time management skills, today's inefficient intern will become tomorrow's inefficient architect. Getting the most out of every waking hour (both professionally and personally) requires organization, setting priorities, and the ability to focus energy on the task(s) at hand. Successful interns understand the value of time.

Employers: Maximize Your Investment

❏ When hiring young staff members, how many employers consider them as investments? The answer can often be discerned when reading the firm's mission statement. For example, if the mission statement does not refer to staff development and retention, one may assume that the firm views interns as relatively expendable commodities. Firms that recognize the value of their investment are committed to maximizing their return by providing quality training and encouraging professional development. These firms recognize that today's intern may become tomorrow's project architect, associate, or principal.

Cultivating and retaining high-performance employees makes good business sense. The actual process will vary among firms; however, most follow certain principles.

1. Altering Office Procedures to Accommodate Interns' Training Needs Is Not Necessary. The Intern Development Program was created with the understanding that the firm's production needs are of primary concern. Interns are expected to gain training opportunities—through participation and observing others—as opportunities present themselves. Interns are also expected to fill basic knowledge gaps through continuing education. The firm benefits from these educational activities.

2. Intern Development Is a Two-way Street. If the firm provides training opportunities in relatively nonproductive areas, it can expect interns to "repay" that time after normal working hours. Many firms have established job banks where interns have the option of depositing extra time to be withdrawn as training opportunities arise (check to ensure that such systems meet federal wage and hour laws).

3. Use the Intern's Training Documentation as a Personnel Management and Appraisal Tool. Interns are responsible for accurately documenting time spent in each of the various required training areas. The intern's supervisor periodically (usually every four months) reviews and certifies this training record. The firm is not responsible for preparing any training documentation; however, periodic reviews create opportunities to assess the employee's assignments and job performance, and to develop new office responsibilities.

Successful firms view internship as a developmental process—a period where interns achieve new competencies from a strong foundation of practical knowledge and skills. This process should be monitored to the extent the office can do so. Such a proactive philosophy acknowledges that this period has far more significant goals than serving as a cram course for the registration examination.

Attention paid to intern development serves as an integral component of an in-house staff development program. Firms can measure the return on their investment through the quality and efficiency of work performed, and through their ability to attract and retain qualified employees.

Seeking a Job

❏ There are several tasks in preparing for the pursuit of a job that can occur concurrently: formulating a list and researching firms to contact, creating a cover letter, and determining the content and design of your resume and portfolio. The resume and cover letter present a design opportunity to distinguish yourself both graphically and verbally. (See Supplement 6.4.)

Try to look out for any personal contacts, possible referrals from faculty or colleagues, notices on department bulletin boards in the local university or technical college, names of practicing alumni, and of course classified advertisements. Barring a windfall from one of the preceding sources, contact the local AIA chapter, either in person or online, as a starting point to develop a list of firms to research and approach. Many chapters publish annual directories of all AIA architecture firms in their particular region or state. Typical listings include firm size and specialty, contact persons, principals, examples of projects, and awards—

some even include firm philosophy. This is a great way to narrow down the field and limit the randomness of initial possibilities. Also consult the most recent edition of *ProFile: The Architects Sourcebook*, published by Construction Market Data (a Business Partner of the AIA) at www.cmdg.com/profile. Copies are available at the local AIA chapter for review. *Profile* covers the same sort of firm data nationwide; however, it is limited to firms that have an AIA member as a principal, and therefore it is not entirely comprehensive.

Initial inquiries might include a letter and accompanying resume. Make certain that the letter is tailored to the target firm at least to some degree. You might mention your school experience and the way in which it aligns with the work of the firm. Size might be important to you. For example, "I've always wanted to work in a small firm context so that I would have the opportunity to engage all phases of practice." Or, "I've always wanted to work in a large firm context so that I would have the opportunity to engage projects of significant scale and scope." You get the idea. If you have some compelling attraction to a firm's geographic locale, or to a firm's body of award-winning work, this may translate to a distinctive and valuable bit of information.

Everyone should have an impressive portfolio. Flexibility is the operative word for portfolio format. Develop or select a means of showcasing your work that can (1) evolve as your work improves through the years—you may want to replace old projects with recent work that shows current capabilities or evidence of growth and (2) tailor projects that would be of specific interest to your audience (i.e., for a particular firm or client). A binder or folder that has plug-in or removal capability would be ideal.

Avoid overkill! Do not feel compelled to show every piece of design work that you produced since the first grade! People to whom you will be showing your work will unquestionably have limited time, so edit appropriately.

Aim for a balance of your best design work and production examples. Perhaps include a series of process sketches for a single best project. This provides your prospective employer with a window into how you work. In terms of the more practical, if you

Sketches

have had previous job experience or have taken a course in architectural detailing (or design development), include reproductions of this work. Perhaps it is an entire sheet itself, or single drawings from a larger sheet, translated to your portfolio format. In this way, you leave no doubt about your capabilities.

Consider, during the course of the semester, how you will eventually incorporate studio projects into the portfolio. This may have an impact on selecting your presentation media. Jorge Silvetti, chair and professor of design at Harvard University, has stated: "Students at the graduate level are interested in having a good portfolio so they can get a good job. That means they're not going to try things and be experimental." Do not let the idea of a practical/economical portfolio unduly influence the way in which you approach projects in the studio and diminish the quality of how problems are creatively engaged.

Once again, view the portfolio as a design problem. Conduct research: study the journals themselves for examples of layout strategies. Although you will not have photographs of buildings, you may have photographs of models or perspective renderings. Note the graphic focus, and the relative sizes of the elements: site plans, floor plans, sections, three-dimensional representations, and their relationships. Also note page format—look for how continuity is achieved for each project and for all editorial sections. In your portfolio design, try to match the excellence of the work itself.

When you are eventually called for an interview, refer back to the firm's directory listing, and commit the information to memory. Try to visit one of the typical projects listed. If none are listed, check all indexes in the library (for the architecture journals as well as any trade magazines related to the firm's specialty) to learn about the firm's work. This will help you make a more educated decision and will be quite impressive in your discussions with firm personnel.

Small-firm principals Fred Ordway and George Kousoulas of Bethesda, Maryland–based Ordway-Kousoulas Architects offer some salient comments about interviews. In discussions with prospective employers, make an effort to know what is really behind the standard job descriptions, with an eye toward understanding the range of available positions and their growth potentials. If at first you don't land a job, Ordway and Kousoulas suggest being patient and remaining positive. It may not seem obvious at the time, but a series of interviews provides valuable experience and practice in the ability to present yourself and your work to others. Moreover, you may also have made a professional contact that may prove important at a later date.

Line up potential references. Prepare packages of materials for your faculty or other mentors, including a resume and possibly some selected portfolio inserts. Make sure you obtain first-rate reproductions. Arrange a brief meeting to discuss your plans, leave the package, and request contact information (e-mail, telephone) to complete your resume. Be sure to follow up with news about job outcome (good or bad) to all references. This is not only the correct protocol but common sense—your reference undoubtedly spent time on your behalf and deserves to be kept informed.

Norman Rosenfeld

SUPPLEMENT 6.4

Norman Rosenfeld, FAIA, is the founding principal of Norman Rosenfeld Architects, a New York City–based architectural firm since 1969 specializing in programming, planning, and design for health care, education, and commercial projects. Rosenfeld has lectured widely and taught hospital planning and design courses for graduate students and architects.

❏ The decision by a firm principal as to which young architect to hire is frequently more visceral than quantifiable. We're looking for the bright-eyed and energetic next generation. Grade point average is a superficial indicator but not a clincher, nor is an advanced degree. Degrees from certain schools may offer better promise, but school reputations are often cyclical. Broad interests, a good hand, computer literacy, an inquisitive mind, a poised personality, professional potential, and the right fit for the office all count.

The Resume

❏ Of course, the resume is an important calling card—presentation counts! A resume gives you the opportunity to show your computer skills, your graphic sensitivity, your good design sense, and that you consider it important to present yourself well and professionally. Poorly presented resumes will be left aside for the third- or fourth-round review, if that ever happens. After all, everyone knows you can and often do tell a book by its cover; at least, you may buy it and begin to read it before you put it down. You do want the reader to read on.

The content and style of resumes are important. How an intern applicant presents his or her minimal experience will indicate a certain initiative and imagination—not dissimilar to architects who submit their credentials for a new project for which they may have no special qualifications. Clients and potential employers may look past slim experience if other things present well. Often, personal recommendations from respected colleagues, or staff, are the best door opener. Getting the interview is what you want!

The Interview

❑ First impressions count! Show up on time. Dress generally to match the office's style. Some minor quirky statement may be useful to impress. I often annotate a resume during an interview with lots of facts and impressions, but also may note the interviewee's unique eyeglass frames or tie as a future memory trigger. You may think you are unique, but all those bright faces do sometimes blur.

Always have an extra copy of your resume. Resumes have a way of getting buried in other papers, preventing easy recall and causing me some embarrassment while rummaging. Help me with a fresh copy gently proffered. The resume undoubtedly contained something of interest—that's why you were invited to the interview. Be prepared to answer questions about school, job experience, and other skills if you are light on architectural office experience. CAD skills are obviously essential to prospective employers. CAD proficiency is a modern-day substitute for tracers who did the routine drafting. Skills in other computer applications are valuable in the graphics, presentation, and marketing efforts of an office.

The Portfolio

❏ Presentation counts! One assumes that the substance and content of intern architects is limited to schoolwork. Graphic quality, organization of project material, as an adjunct to the interviewee's discussion of the material, will demonstrate a sense of design and an ability to express verbally unique aspects of the development thought process or project presented. I often silently review the portfolio, but will concurrently ask several searching questions to determine if the interviewee understood what was drawn, and has an agile mind and verbal presence to respond to questions from left field. These attributes can turn adversity into success and then point my questions in another more fruitful direction.

Closing the Hire

❏ I enjoy interviews that are a two-way street. After I have reviewed the portfolio and asked my questions, I welcome the interviewee who poses questions to me. Not about fringe benefits or office vacation policy, but unanswered professional questions—perhaps about what the office does or how it does it. While I try to cover this ground during my introductory discussion, I encourage questions that will give me insight into what interests the interviewee and how his or her mind and spirit work. It may be questions on our built work—which I will likely have shown those who have lasted through my early questioning—or it may be how the office is organized and staff assigned—finishing with what employment opportunity is available. The outcome of this exchange may be that I sense that the interviewee has great potential and could be a valuable addition to our staff. I may then mentally create a new job position on the spot as I am talking. It has truly happened.

Salary is best left to the end and is usually the least difficult hurdle to address—except when you choose to interview with those firms who believe their experience opportunity is so valuable that it is a privilege to work there, at minimal or no salary. You know who they are. Everyone else knows what a hiring wage is, or should be, with some relationship to your level of contribution. The commitment to hire is rarely done at the first interview, but the sense to hire is usually established. I may have other interviews scheduled, partners to meet with, and scheduling to consider, but positive messages can be given and a time frame for decision committed to. A follow-up short letter from the interviewee, again as we do with new client prospects, is a nice touch and a good reminder that you are interested.

In the Trenches

❏ Once you have the job, the message is to be a good soldier. The whole point is to learn about professional practice; get exposed to as many diverse tasks as possible. In contrast to the old army wisdom, volunteer for everything!

A general student concern is whether the tasks assigned will be boring. The fear is that while school studio focuses on design and is incredibly stimulating, an entry-level experience will require nothing but getting coffee and doing everyone else's most unpleasant leftovers. To some extent that is true; however, make the most out of whatever opportunity is presented. You *are* qualified to do some design-related work, and firm principals know this. For example, you may be asked to develop a tile layout for a toilet room. Adopt the attitude that these relatively mundane tasks can be transformed into intriguing design challenges (which is true). It is precisely this attitude that ultimately produces better results, and ostensibly, satisfaction. What kind of interesting floor/wall pattern can be developed? Can you propose a small band of color tile? Can you propose using a couple of different sizes of tile? Can you use a few tiles along the wall to create an interesting accent or mosaic? Can you develop elegant connection details? Actors say, "There are no small parts, only small actors." The same applies to architectural projects: the designer has the power to make the most seemingly insignificant projects into something very special that has an impact. That's

FIGURE 6.4

This is an example from my practice of a "mundane" kitchen renovation in Chicago that was budgeted at $8000 (construction cost, not architectural fee). We went through the process of programming and analyses, and even built a study model. It was a satisfying experience for both client and architect, and what we didn't receive in fees, we more than made up with publication in Popular Science *and* The Washington Post. *This is not to suggest we don't want larger scale projects—it's just to demonstrate that an attitude of service for clients who present with seemingly everyday projects can be quite rewarding. (Courtesy of Andy Pressman.)*

why, in my own practice, I rarely turn down small-scale projects that have practically no budget (see Figs. 6.4 and 6.5). In fact, I *want* these types of projects! I actively seek them out (begging can be a very effective marketing strategy). You'd be amazed at the gratefulness of clients, not to mention enormous publicity that can result from attentiveness to a small problem, and a clever and sensitive response. Another benefit is that it keeps the architect in touch with reality—dealing with some of the most basic issues of daily life. When you are relegated to bathroom details as an intern, or when you become a star architect and have your own practice, remember this point.

FIGURE 6.5
Another "ordinary" project for which the thought of hiring an architect would not even occur to most people. Back rooms like this can offer architects challenges involving lighting, space planning, ceiling forms, color, and casework. This one in Princeton, New Jersey, functions as playroom and occasional guest suite with bathroom. Total construction cost including new bathroom: $15,000. (Courtesy of Andy Pressman.)

A First Job

With Michael Sobczak

❏ Supplement 6.5, written by a talented intern architect, characterizes some of the issues in starting out. There is great diversity not only within a specific job, but within the profession itself. Also expressed is the theme that the design of buildings does not constitute a singular effort—typically, many people contribute within the firm, in addition to outside consultants.

Michael Sobczak

Intern architect Michael Sobczak worked throughout his undergraduate studies and was a teaching assistant in the design studio during his graduate studies at the University of Wisconsin-Milwaukee. He has been honored with scholarships, and his designs have been recognized by the Wisconsin Society of Architects.

School and Practice—A Balancing Act

❏ In the field of architecture, as in most professions, there is a great difference between school and practice. Training in school or studio focuses on the development of conceptual and critical thinking skills. Designs are too often executed in this ideal setting with no budgets, clients, or thorough attention to the practical issues, such as technology. And, in school, one student typically orchestrates every aspect of a project.

Unlike in the school studio, in the real world a design is the product of many people, not a single author. These people may include planners, project managers, architects, draftspeople, consultant engineers, interior designers, and field supervisors. To many new interns, this division of the job is a very new idea and the seemingly small role that each may play can be a shock. The notion of teamwork is relatively new! Many interns spend numerous hours laying out room elevations, doing door schedules, and making drafting changes on construction documents. Although the school and practice experiences may be quite different, they are, nonetheless, both parts of what an architect is about; a certain complementary balance exists between the

SUPPLEMENT 6.5

acquisition of basic skills in the ideal studio and how those skills are tempered and applied in professional practice.

The intern architect should approach his or her first job with open eyes and a willingness to learn new things. During an internship you will learn about construction techniques and drawings, shop drawings, construction administration, budget, programming, client presentation, and marketing. The intern should observe the process in the office and develop a feel for where he or she would like to specialize (i.e., as project manager, field supervisor, or designer). Do not neglect to communicate your preferences to management. If you happen to be in school while simultaneously holding down a part-time job, you can also focus on aspects of your curriculum that will support the attainment of your goals.

The intern should take responsibility for his or her professional development by letting principals know his or her aspirations. Take professional development classes and attend seminars. This professional take-charge attitude will help develop your strengths and will be appreciated by employers.

An intern should view school as a place to learn design in its purest form, and practice as a place to make it reality. Architects are constantly compromising between the ideals they aspire to and the realities of practice. This dichotomy not only characterizes practice but leads to creative solutions. Finally, an intern must be patient with the apparently slow progress in learning the skills inherent in the practice of architecture. These new skills will combine with and balance the idealism of the school to produce an effective and efficient architect.

Open Letters to Advanced Students
By Helmut Jahn, Hugh Jacobson, Arthur Erickson, and Charles Moore

❑ Several of the most prominent practitioners and educators in North America agreed to speak to student readers. This distinguished group was chosen to respond to the more general aspects of design in an academic context. Surprisingly, the messages are universal, and have applicability to professionals as well. In open letters, the following three questions were addressed:

- What values do you feel students should consciously strive to incorporate and practice?
- What should students know or do, or what preparation might they undertake, to minimize the anxieties of starting out?
- What advice/message would you offer beginning students to support successful performance in the design studio?

Helmut Jahn

❏ With respect to values, perseverance, integrity, and consistency would rank among the highest, given the status of the time in which we live. Perseverance is obvious. Integrity, because difficult times create difficult situations. Consistency in work, in attitude, and in approach. To me it is obvious that there is no difference between the personal values one has and the architecture one produces; both have the same qualities.

Anxiety was present for me when I started out, and it will be present for all others as well; it can't be eliminated but it certainly can be controlled. Self-confidence and a positive plan of action for achieving your goals will go a long way toward minimizing anxiety. Doubt and a lack of self-confidence not only fuel anxieties but produce a negative image that may exist even after early anxieties have subsided.

With respect to work in the design studio, I feel the choice of the terminology *design studio* itself sends the wrong message to the student. The student's goals should be to be the best all-around architect, not the best in design or any one aspect of architecture. In the beginning, the student should want to learn everything. His or her top priority should be his or her work. His or her

Regards,

Helmut Jahn

approach should be one of total flexibility. The student should do any task given with the same level of enthusiasm and effort. Each task has a learning curve, but the payback is experience.

What I especially appreciate about Helmut Jahn's comments is the point he makes about work in general as a priority, in contrast to a singular or premature focus on a specialty. Particularly at an introductory level, one is not striving to be a designer, a historian, or a technologist. Rather, the goal is to work hard at absorbing and integrating as many facets of architecture as possible. Whatever specialty interest a student eventually develops will be best served by the most comprehensive background.

Hugh Jacobsen

❏ Our profession is one of many facets. I do not believe that every professional is capable of design, nor should he/she try to practice accordingly. Because I do believe that design is the most important facet, I will address your question with design in mind. Those few students who are encouraged by their training to understand the full meaning of architecture and design should endeavor to practice as principals. Design is personal and private and from a committee it comes not.

When starting out, the student or the beginning professional should never try to be original. It will be hard enough to learn how to build and keep a building dry inside without taking on Frank Gehry. It is far more important to be good. Architecture is an old person's profession. Try to contribute.

To perform successfully in the design studio, the student should:

- Listen and ask questions.
- Read and reread history. You can *never* know enough!
- Know that there are no solutions, only approaches. Work hard to understand the problem and what it means, simplify, and try to solve it. Then try again.

I hope the above helps ~
— Hugh Newell Jacobsen

Hugh Jacobsen's feeling that not everybody is destined for design seems an important and natural extension of Helmut Jahn's comments. I don't think it can be overstated that the studio is a place in which all manner of specialists are born. Whether in lighting, programming, marketing, computer applications—whatever the area—the studio provides the medium from which interests and properly informed choice grows.

Jacobsen's deemphasis of originality and solutions as goals in themselves is also noteworthy. It is implicit that tenacity and approach will lead to an innovative and effective solution.

Arthur Erickson

❏ A student needs to have nourished an aesthetic sensibility. If he doesn't have it, he cannot develop it. It cannot be learned. If it is there, he can nourish, refine, expand it infinitely. Since architecture is a visual art, it is his visual sensitivity that must prevail over all other abilities. If that sensitivity exists, he can transfer it from one visual art to another—from the two-dimensional to the three-dimensional, the sculptural to the spatial. If he has an ability in any visual art, he is well ahead. He must only recognize and become practiced in the basic elements of architecture—space, structure, and place. I emphasize place because architecture is not conceived in a vacuum, but always for a place, and that place is inevitably part of its composition. If the student is familiar with any art form, he will recognize that at a certain point, the artist is no longer the creator but the midwife of a creature that from that point on takes over to determine itself on the basis of the compositional rules that it was given in the first place.

Nor can the student ever be satisfied fully with his work, but must be anxious to go on exploring to satisfy his curiosity with the next challenge. He needs an endless curiosity, sense of wonderment, and love of craft. The greatest teacher is actual experience of architecture and art through personal contact with it in the widest possible context—the world itself—as well as nature in its endless creative response to challenge and delight in being. The student has to learn to distrust the intellect, letting it serve rather than lead the creative quest. Design is instinctual and must be felt by the inner perceptual sense and not thought out, for the mind can never be trusted in itself, only when it follows the conviction of the senses. Perception is the key.

Cultivate the eyes by looking—the senses by feeling through exposure to the arts—not through magazines or film unless the film is an artwork in itself—but through exposure to the real thing. The student needs to remove himself somehow from the artifice of the mercantile world and expose himself to other world cultures in their vivid interpretation of the issues of existence. Only then can he begin to see himself as part of a culture that wrestles with the same issues and needs his contribution to give value and meaning to those issues.

Don't give up. Struggle even if you don't seem to be getting anywhere. Often only when you are completely frustrated does a solution come. No one who creates finds it easy unless what he's doing is only superficial inventiveness. It is often necessary to get away from a challenge that you are struggling with to see it in a new light: look at it upside down, backward in a mirror, between your legs, standing on your head; or immerse yourself in something else enlightening and inspiring before coming back to it. Remember, it is not easy for anyone who is any good.

Yours sincerely,

Arthur Erickson

Arthur Erickson persuasively advocates active exploration of, and immersion in, the cultural and perceptual realms of human experience. Instinctual talent for design is a blessing, but it must be cultivated. Even then, as Erickson points out, creativity is not easy.

Erickson also wants us to prize other golden rules: persistence is important, as is the habit of developing alternative ways of looking at a problem. Erickson's final caveat is worth repeating: "Remember, it is not easy for anyone who is any good."

Charles Moore

❏ Students should strive toward an awareness of their own dignity and the dignity and worth of the inhabitants of their buildings.

To minimize the anxieties of starting out, students should have confidence in the place they come from and the values they cherish. They do not have to be remodeled in another image to be architects.

To perform successfully in the design studio, relax. Remember that the things you're designing are meant to be useful and to give the inhabitants of your designs the confidence to make their own lives fuller. You are designing a support system, not a hair shirt.

Sincerely,

Charles W. Moore, FAIA

The late Charles Moore's message is timeless and deceptively simple but contains a rather profound dual reminder. First, each of us has a distinctive worldview with particular priorities and tastes, and maintaining a strong sense of what we prize somehow complements and motivates us. Second, we serve others who are likely to have equally distinctive and different worldviews. If we are doing our jobs well, we will incorporate our personal priorities with an understanding of others' and—the architecture we then produce for them is more likely to be successful.

The Architect Registration Examination
With Stephen Schreiber

❏ The following outline and description of the Architect Registration Examination (ARE) in some ways parallels the pragmatic topics in this book, which can serve as an effective review. Even though the exam doesn't test for poetics, magic, and passion, these elements need to be informed by a basic knowledge of the architect's codified responsibilities to the public that ensure the well-being of building inhabitants. This knowledge must be so ingrained in a design process that it is like breathing. And it does have an impact on form making.

Of particular note to exam candidates are Steve Schreiber's preparation tips, listed in Supplement 6.6. I would underscore the value of all four of his recommendations for passing the exam on the first attempt.

Stephen Schreiber

Stephen Schreiber, AIA, is the director of the School of Architecture and Community Design at the University of South Florida in Tampa. His design work and articles on urban design have been published in Architecture *and numerous other journals. Schreiber has won awards for his teaching and for his competition work. He is past vice-chair of the New Mexico Board of Examiners, and coordinator of one of the ARE graphic subcommittees.*

The licensing of architects is one of the means by which registration boards in the United States and Canada safeguard the public health, safety, and welfare. A person must demonstrate that he or she is qualified to offer architectural services by meeting the "three-legged stool" requirements of each board—education, experience, and examination. Perhaps the most consistent and the most daunting of these three legs is the licensing exam.

In the early twentieth century—when most registration laws were passed in the United States—examinations were written and scored by individual registration boards. Groups of states began to organize to address problems of uniformity in examina-

SUPPLEMENT 6.6

tions. These efforts led to the Architect Registration Examination (ARE), developed by the National Council of Architectural Registration Boards. The exam was adopted by every state licensing board by 1983. Generally, applicants can take the exam only after completing an accredited degree program in architecture and a three-year internship.

The Architect Registration Examination is designed to determine whether applicants for architectural licensure possess sufficient knowledge, skills, and abilities to provide professional services while protecting the health, safety, and welfare of the general public. Each of the nine divisions of the ARE is designed to test for minimum competency in a specific area that is important to the protection of the public.

The design of the test and the content of each division are determined through scientific studies of the current profession of architecture. These task analyses identify minimum competencies required of licensed architects to provide various critical services. The exam is written and pretested by dozens of architects, consulting engineers, and code officials. Exam writing committees for sections of the exam meet several times a year to write and revise and approve questions and vignettes.

Prior to computerization, the ARE was a grueling 34-hour rite of passage. Nearly three days of seven multiple-choice sections were followed by a day and a half of graphic sections, including the infamous 12-hour building design problem. The exam was administered only once or twice a year. It was common to see hundreds of candidates at a time sitting for the exam in some large cities.

In 1997, a new computer exam was launched. Candidates can now take divisions of the exam in any order, six days a week, at testing centers throughout North America. The exam format emphasizes the judgmental aspects of the practice of architecture. It is designed to test candidates' abilities to apply technical, theoretical, and practical knowledge to issues of a professional nature.

The ARE consists of six multiple-choice divisions (Pre-Design, General Structures, Lateral Forces, Mechanical/Electrical Systems, Materials and Methods, Construction Documents and Services) and three graphic divisions (Site Planning, Building Planning, and Building Technology).

The Pre-Design division focuses on environmental analysis, architectural programming, and architectural practice, including:

- Evaluation of existing structures
- Impact of sociological influences on site selection and land use
- Effect of physiographic and climatic conditions on land use
- Ability to develop construction cost estimates and budgets
- Development of design objectives and constraints for a project
- Effect of human behavior, history, and theory on the built environment
- Interpretation of land surveys and legal restrictions
- Principles of practice, including office management
- Consultant coordination

The General Structures division covers structural systems and long span design, including:

- Basic structural analysis and design
- Selection of appropriate structural components and systems
- Calculation of loads on buildings
- Incorporation of building code requirements
- Identification and selection of various structural connections
- Analysis of soil reports

The Lateral Forces division concentrates on effects of lateral forces on the design of buildings, including:

- General concepts of lateral loads
- Identification and calculation of wind loads and seismic loads
- Incorporation of code requirements
- Requirements for nonstructured building components related to lateral forces

The Mechanical/Electrical Systems division addresses mechanical, plumbing, electrical, and acoustical systems (and their incorporation into building design), including:

- Incorporation of code requirements
- Evaluation, selection, design, and incorporation of appropriate plumbing, HVAC, electrical, and sound control systems
- Determination of heating and cooling loads
- Selection of building envelope elements
- Evaluation of costs of mechanical and electrical systems

The Materials and Methods division addresses the evaluation and selection of materials and methods of installation and the development of building details, including:

- Evaluation of site conditions
- Incorporation of environmental and cultural issues
- Identification of and ability to detail concrete, masonry, wood, structural metal, and miscellaneous metal construction
- Analysis, selection, and ability to detail moisture and thermal protection systems, door and window systems, finish materials, specialties, and conveying systems
- Evaluation of costs of systems
- Incorporation of code requirements

The Construction Documents and Services division covers the conduct of architectural practice, including:

- Preparation and review of working drawings and specifications
- Coordination of contract documents
- Preparation of bidding instruments
- Evaluation of substitutions and preparation of cost estimates
- Interpretation of general conditions
- Review of standard agreements
- Observation of the progress of work and material testing
- Preparation and review of documents for change orders, progress payments, and project closeout

The Site Planning division focuses on the relationship between site use and environment; the consideration of topography, vegetation, climate geography, and law on site develop-

Sketches

ment; and the synthesis of programmatic and environmental requirements. Six vignettes test the candidate's understanding of specific areas:

- *Site design*—general site planning principles
- *Site zoning*—cross-sectional building area limitations imposed by zoning and other setback requirements
- *Site parking*—requirements and limitations that influence the design of parking areas and driveways
- *Site analysis*—requirements and limitations that influence subdivisions of land and delineation of building limit areas
- *Site section*—influence of site design requirements on sections
- *Site grading*—understanding of requirements affecting topographic changes

The Building Planning division covers the synthesis of programmatic and environmental issues into coherent designs through the process of schematic design. Three vignettes test the candidate's understanding of specific areas:

- *Block diagram*—development of a diagrammatic floor plan from a bubble diagram
- *Interior layout*—principles of design and accessibility that govern interior space planning
- *Schematic design*—understanding of the planning process involved in the schematic design phase

The Building Technology division also concentrates on the synthesis of programmatic and environmental issues into coherent designs at the design development level. The six vignettes test the candidate's understanding of specific areas:

- *Building section*—impact of structural, mechanical, and lighting components on the vertical form of buildings
- *Structural layout*—basic structural framing concepts through development of a framing plan for a simple building
- *Accessibility/ramp*—accessibility requirements related to ramp and stair design

- *Mechanical/electrical plan*—integration of mechanical, lighting, and ceiling systems with structural and other building components
- *Stair design*—the three-dimensional nature of stair design and code issues
- *Roof plan*—basic concepts related to roof design through the development of a roof plan for a small structure

Computer scoring engines have been developed to objectively assess each candidate's solutions based on conformance to the specific programmatic requirements of each vignette. The vignettes are not strictly pass or fail. The scoring engines evaluate an extensive list of tasks and features before determining the final score for a vignette. This model compensates for weakness in some areas when strengths in others are demonstrated. The individual scores on the vignettes are then combined and result in a determination of the final score for the division.

Preparation for the practice-based ARE generally requires a formal education and practical internship. Although it is difficult to cram for the exam, candidates can prepare for the ARE in numerous ways:

1. Understand Exam Content and Format. ARE guidelines explain the content of the nine divisions of the ARE and include a listing of reference material for each division. A free practice program for the graphic divisions is available complete with tutorial and sample vignettes. These materials describe the content of each division of the exam in detail, and explain how the computer interface works. They are both available for downloading at www.ncarb.com. Private organizations and individuals also publish handbooks on the exam.

2. Identify Content Areas in Which Knowledge and Skills Might Need Improvement. Very few interns excel in all of the wide range of areas of competency expected of contemporary architects. Since the exam sections can be taken in any order, it is wise to start the divisions in the candidate's areas of strength—to become familiar with the test centers, exam process, and to build self-esteem!

3. Locate Resources to Help Improve in Areas of Weakness. Several organizations sell workbooks that can help candidates improve knowledge and skills in specific areas such as structures, plumbing, mechanical systems, predesign, etc. NCARB literature identifies bibliographies of reference books and textbooks for each division. Read these! Also, many universities, local AIA chapters, large firms, locally organized groups, and other organizations run seminars and study groups on ARE-related topics. However, since the exam is practice based, the best source of information should be the office. Weak in lateral forces? Ask the firm's structural consultant. Need to brush up on materials and methods? Volunteer to write a specification.

4. Learn to Use the Computer. While the ARE graphics program is designed to be used by candidates with varying levels of computer experience, it helps to be familiar with the principles and concepts of digital drafting and design, particularly the layering and fundamental drafting tools. In fact, the ARE software is an excellent introduction to CAD, for those few interns with no computer experience.

The future will witness numerous changes to the ARE, particularly as divisions change in response to new practice analyses. The examination process has continually evolved, and will continue to adapt to the ever changing practice of architecture.

Illustrations

❏ Following are images of the Pierce House in New Mexico, designed by Stephen Schreiber Architect in 1999–2000, to illustrate the practice-based principles of the Architect Registration Examination.

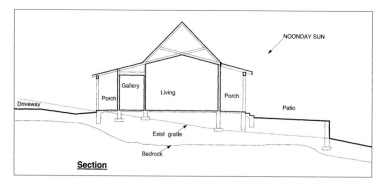

FIGURE 6.6
In the Site Section vignette of the Site Planning division, the candidate is given a program and an existing cross section. The candidate manipulates the site profile and places three elements to achieve stated objectives—drainage, accessibility, maximum height, protection from elements, etc.

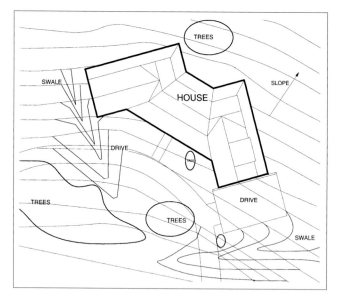

FIGURE 6.7
In the Site Grading vignette of the Site Planning division, the candidate is given a program and an existing cross section. The candidate modifies the contours to divert water around defined objects while leaving other areas undisturbed.

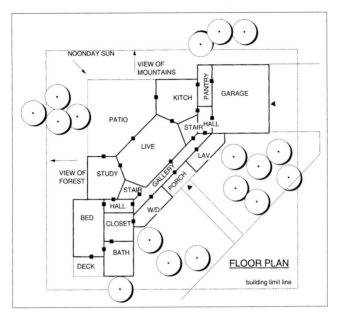

FIGURE 6.8
In the Block Diagram vignette of the Building Planning division, the candidate arranges spaces on a site plan in response to a bubble diagram and program. The candidate must also indicate key direct access points between spaces.

References

Brown, Andrea (ed.). *Preparing for the Architect Registration Exam*. Washington, DC: NCARB, 1997.

National Council of Architectural Registration Boards. *The History of NCARB* (NCARB circular). Washington, DC: NCARB, 1996.

National Council of Architectural Registration Boards. *The Architect Registration Exam* (NCARB circular). Washington, DC: NCARB, 1997.

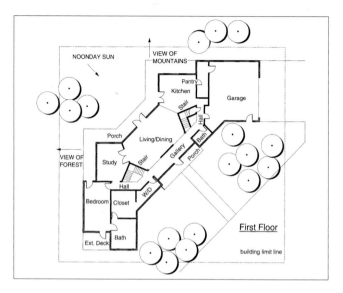

FIGURE 6.9
In the Schematic Design vignette of the Building Planning division, the candidate is required to produce a schematic design for a two-story building that responds to a program, code, and site plan.

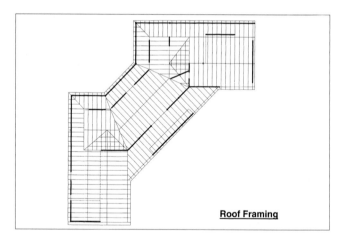

FIGURE 6.10
In the Structural Layout vignette of the Building Technology division, the candidate completes a roof framing plan (with joists, beams, columns, and bearing walls) for a given floor plan and program.

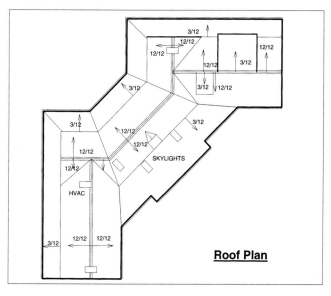

Roof Plan

FIGURE 6.11
In the Roof Plan vignette of the Building Technology division, the candidate completes a roof plan (indicating slopes, directions, elevations, and accessories) for a given base plan.

Solomon, Nancy. "The New Registration Exam," *Architecture*, January:130–133, 1997.

Architecture Licensing Seminars Web site, www.als.com. NCARB Web site, www.ncarb.org.

Thanks to Steve Nutt, Assistant Director of NCARB, for his input and review of this article.

Sketches

chapter 7

The Future:
A Manifesto

"There is no room now for the dilettante, the weakling, for the shirker, or the coward."
—Sir Winston S. Churchill

Sketches

❏ Business-centered, service-centered, and design-centered firm cultures: these are not mutually exclusive, but rather mutually supportive. They are all necessary components. Each, by itself, is insufficient to conduct a successful (profit-making, client-pleasing, culturally significant) architectural practice, now and in the future.

This book has focused mainly on the culturally significant: excellent design. This decision has been motivated by empirical knowledge. Just look around at the ubiquitous, less-than-thrilling architectural outcomes throughout the U.S. Reasons for this condition are probably multifarious and complicated. Bad design notwithstanding, however, this aspect of practice—creating wonderful buildings—is arguably the profession's reason for being. In many cases, it is elusive or not perceived to be highly valued by practitioners and/or clients.

The objective in this last chapter in particular, and the entire book in general, is to promote an awareness of the value of excellent design, and how to operationalize the creation of its inherent value.

My conversation with Thom Mayne of Morphosis, which immediately follows, perhaps best crystallizes the pressing issues and questions, and profiles one individual's very personal and idiosyncratic approach to being a professional architect concerned with all three of the cultures mentioned in the introductory paragraph. Mayne's passion, of course, is design, but not to the exclusion of the other factors.

Thomas Fisher and I separately discuss the seemingly mundane but potentially huge topic of awards programs and what role they should play in expanding knowledge, educating the public, and encouraging advancement of the profession in multiple dimensions. Marginalization of the profession is another major area of concern in this manifesto. It is absolutely crucial that architecture become more relevant to broad segments of society and address major social and economic problems. I discuss how architects can significantly influence policy and contribute to the public good. My interview with the king of activists, Michael Pyatok, inspires by example. Marilys Nepomechie implores architects to be aware of the enduring value of preservation efforts when viewed in a critical manner. She illustrates her thinking with a poignant case study from her practice.

Gregory Palermo sets the stage for an enlightening discourse on ethics and the practice of architecture (also the title of a new book he coauthored with Barry Wasserman and Patrick Sullivan). Christopher Alexander, in his own manifesto of 1991, stated, "The architectural profession is not only suffering from a theory that fails to solve massive problems it ought to solve, it has maintained itself in a way that must frankly be admitted to be ugly in spirit. It has abandoned its role as a moral force."

The chapter and the book end with a summary manifesto: a top 10 list of principles to aspire to in creating architectural designs for the next hundred years.

Getting at Design

A Conversation with Thom Mayne

Andy Pressman: *This book, as you know, is focused on elevating the quality of preliminary designs. What could you say, in general terms, to help raise the bar? What are some critical strategies that, for example, you use to achieve both beautiful architecture and happy clients in a context of fairly low budgets?*

Thom Mayne: There are several ways of approaching the question. First, the work arises from a long continuum of research and exploration that comes out of one's life and career experience to date. Raising the bar, as you suggest, has to do with one's ability to produce architecture that is a natural consequence of that experience. Excellent architecture, as opposed to excellent engineering or excellence in business, requires that the research and investigation be integral with one's development over time.

An architecture of quality does not exist absent an intense interest and commitment to formal qualities, pragmatic issues, environmental questions, tectonics, and so on, which are quite separate from issues of program and budget.

Pressman: *I'd like to underscore a point here. You're suggesting transcending the specific project perspective?*

Mayne: Exactly. The specific projects become part of a gestalt—a broader agenda that has to do with our ability to produce architecture of value. It is, of course, one of the struggles related to highly contingent, individual, specific, idiosyncratic projects that are trying to fit within a coherent set of ideas. There is always a struggle or tension to deal with the more generalized approach, theory, idea structure, or conceptualization versus the specific demands of the project, the pragmatics of program and budget. This is probably the central struggle of any architect, especially when starting out. Somehow, you must figure out how to hold to your agenda since that is so clearly the place where architecture is located. It is not located in program and budget; it is in fact located within that conceptual territory. And this is really the difference between architecture and building.

Bringing to bear something outside the pragmatic engenders architecture. This is the central point of our discussion . . . it is completely within the domain of the creative process of the architect or group of architects.

On a more specific level, there could be multiple answers. I would challenge the normative client-centered strategy . . . the one that dictates that our highest priority is to please the client (whatever that means). In our office we expend an enormous amount of effort and time in solving the pragmatic issues that are brought to us by the client. There is no limit to the energy we'll dedicate to solving these issues . . . this is simply a given that applies tectonically, to the construction assemblies, mechanical and structural systems, and economic realities related to budget. With these solved, there is rarely a discussion or an expectation that would impinge on issues of ideology or concept. These design issues are less negotiable because they've developed out of a culture and over a long period of time to frame the conceptualization and meaning of the work. This is what we're hired to do.

Pressman: *Is this reactionary to the mediocrity that surrounds us, or is it just fundamental to your design process?*

Mayne: It's not reactionary, although I do find the level of architecture to be fairly abysmal these days. It's equivalent to what's happened in television. It is sad . . . the idea of feeding the consumer what a corporation thinks they want . . . This approach ends up pandering to the lowest levels of taste and culture . . . the public itself even begins to complain. Finally, of course, the issue is artistic. One doesn't ask the public what they want in other artistic areas—literature, music, film, etc. It would be preposterous to begin asking our artists to be anything other than visionary. Whether it's through writing, music, painted or sculpted media, or architecture, it takes a certain talent and sensitivity that is unique to some people and not to others. Not complicated! Why would you possibly want someone to dictate the color or style of a building? Frightening.

Pressman: *Architects shouldn't be asking those questions.*

Mayne: Absolutely! You shouldn't ask questions when you couldn't tolerate the answers! You want to position yourself to ask only those questions that are related to an agreed-upon agenda—part of a collective territory that exists between you and the client. This is one of the most important tasks to establish early on with a client: an agenda wherein their input and your questions comprise the basis of a meaningful discussion. That is, that their participation is real, useful, and vital to the collective endeavor that involves solving the pragmatics: program, budget, certain site ideas, any number of idiosyncratic situations that crop up in the complexities of architecture. At this level, I would say, without any doubt, that every building we've produced is a product of the collective effort that emerges between ourselves, our client, and our builder. It is impossible to do otherwise. Buildings, again on this pragmatic level, are collective enterprises, and you must be able to negotiate in this territory while still holding firm to a vision.

Pressman: *Would you say that there is, then, in your process, a dichotomy: one, a collective endeavor and two, your personal agenda?*

Mayne: Yes; however the *auteur* in film is perhaps the best analogy. The architect is similar to a director in cinema in that his or her responsibility is the general thrust and conceptual focus of a work. Subsequently, tasks become more specialized. As with film directors, there are vast differences in approaches, from hands on everything to controlled chaos. In most cases, and for myself, being an architect is like being a director. I am the generator of a direction, but that direction is open to any number of interpretations by the project team, including the client, the consultants, and the engineers. We've presumably been hired by a client who is educated and is making an informed decision about the vision they are after. We're asking questions and searching for creative solutions relative to the mechanics, structure, and end use of the building. The process involves the client, looking for different interpretations of program use, human activity, and so on. We are all exploring, not simply accepting what's given at face value.

Pressman: *So what best characterizes your process?*

Mayne: We are very question/answer oriented. Ours is a classically heuristic approach in which we attend to a process to arrive at a solution rather than to begin from an a priori position. Many people think architects are solution oriented. The discussion we're having is actually about exploring a problem and articulating questions, which becomes the focus of our design investigations. The viability of the methodology is based on the question-posing process, which is an inclusive process designed to elicit creativity rather than to inhibit it.

At some point most architects, after having worked for many years, have become cognizant of where they locate ideas. How that occurs over a long period of time and how they become renewed is the challenge. Finally, one exhausts a particular idea structure—and the question becomes how to renew the sources. I think that inclusiveness of team members is a tremendous tool that allows us to continually challenge the stasis of a particular position.

Pressman: *What seems to be elusive to many practitioners and is partly responsible for contributing to the mediocrity surrounding us is defining what that evolving, overarching value is—the conceptual territory that you were referring to earlier.*

Mayne: One of the ways architecture has changed in the last 30 years, since I was a student, is that it has become predominately market driven. This has been destructive to the field on many levels, not the least being that it has changed the perception of architecture from an art to a service. Architecture used to operate like medicine in some regards. It operated in a framework that was somewhat autonomous from the market economy—it operated on its own terms. Now that this model has disappeared for medicine and for architecture, it is time for a new model. I am, of course, advocating the model of filmmaking, as we discussed earlier.

Pressman: *Well, it has kind of sucked the professionalism out of doing architecture.*

Mayne: Right. Again maybe like television, the paradox is that you get a group of people who are now "focused on client needs" and who are producing work that is not very interesting. This is strange.

On the other hand, Thom Mayne and Morphosis will be criticized by the market-driven architect for being egocentric, or arguments will be made that the client will not get what they need because the work is being driven in terms of a particular architectural language that may or may not suit the client's needs. This is all just marketing, positioning, competition. But it is degrading the profession . . . it's taking us away from what we need to do, which is to lead rather than lag in a cultural sense. The biggest problem with market-driven architecture is that it calls upon people to make assumptions about what the client's needs actually are. Budgets, ratios, conversations about resale value, all impact the architect in the direction of making more conservative choices in their design solutions. The client is often misread and underestimated. The culture at large and the profession in particular are the losers in this scenario. The client gets a relatively highly rated TV show (maybe); they could have gotten an Academy-Award-winning film.

I'm actually not pessimistic. I don't think society is as blind or ignorant or uninterested as they (the market-driven architects) think it is. Clients and end users are treated with a kind of contempt. I look at the output and say that it is insulting to the culture in which we live, it lowers the bar in your terminology.

I believe in the opposite position. One of my roles as an architect is to be an educator. And I would feel the same if I was a writer or in the theater or cinema. Any endeavor that includes an interpretive medium has the chance to be elevated through a pedagogical or didactic engagement. Maybe I'm overly optimistic, but I still believe that architecture has some sort of therapeutic mission . . . It has the power to elevate cultural self-esteem. That power should be utilized.

Pressman: *Give me a recent example from your practice.*

Mayne: We are doing some schools right now. They are wonderful projects because they offer possibilities of working with a program that has the potential to influence people when they're still quite young. Our schools are public schools, built on extremely tight budgets. The approach in California, for the last 20 years, has been to warehouse students in portable trailers or bungalows, assuming that a roof over their heads is all that is necessary to create an educational environment. I couldn't disagree more. I may be a lone voice in this, but I consider the didactic possibilities inherent in architecture to be a gold mine of opportunity. I want students in the schools we design to grow up inspired to be architects or designers or intelligent consumers of design (among other things). The buildings we build should inspire their questions. . . . Why is the site used as it is, why are the buildings designed as they are? A meaningful discourse can occur with very young children that will serve them well later in their lives. Then there are the esteem issues. Children should be educated in buildings that reveal an underlying respect for the educational process they are experiencing and for them as human beings. To accomplish this, we assume an optimistic attitude toward our client. We may actually overestimate the client sometimes; we may make them reach! If I were going to make a mistake, I'd rather overreach than underreach.

Pressman: *Take that school example. How is your agenda as an artist applied in that project?*

Mayne: The Diamond Ranch High School in Pomona rather typifies what I mean by expanding the discourse of architecture. Herbert Muschamp hit the nail on the head in a review of the building when he said that you look around at the buildings and think, "poverty made this." This is a reference to the ridiculously low budgets our state allocates to public school buildings, which is a direct reflection of our attitudes toward our youth and toward our future.

My position, upon receiving the commission, was ambivalent. Upon examination of the budget I could have said, quite rightfully, "Can't be done." I could have taken a pass, let a formulaic school architect do his or her thing on the site, and saved myself some headaches. But this is not what I'm interested in doing, never have been. High budgets can tie your hands in more complicated ways than low budgets. With the very low budget we were given, I had to find a way to still produce an architecture that would transcend the reality of this poverty of imagination that we find in our public school system today. The campus needed, above all, to be transcendent of all of this as it sought to make connections to its site and to its function and to ignore any and all preconceived ideas of what a high school for teenagers should look like. We built for people, not for kids. And the reaction from the end users, kids and teachers, has been phenomenal. They are aware that they are being educated in a very unique place. Their senses are on alert, they ask questions, they are stimulated. They are beginning to learn something about architecture. This was not in the agenda of the school district, but it was in mine.

Pressman: *How do you preserve design quality on large-scale projects—when dealing with multiheaded clients, committees, and so on?*

Mayne: Like anything: you commit yourself to it, you fight for it, and you attempt to articulate it. There must be a discourse about finding a collective agreement on the meaning of what we're trying to accomplish. Sometimes it can be argued within traditional rational terms, and other times it takes a certain amount of suspension of disbelief and trust on the client's part. Trust between the architect and client is crucial, particularly when dealing with subjective matters. It is the fundamental basis for the relationship . . . absent trust there will likely be a very unsatisfying experience. Developing trust doesn't come automatically; it comes over time and must be worked for and earned. With the more rationalized aspects of the work, such as program, budget methodology, questioning, listening, incorporating the client's agenda, etc., there is an opportunity to prove yourself to earn the client's trust. At the end of our early meetings I want to hear the client say, "You heard me." After they rattle off a couple of hundred independent bits of data and information, we show them at the next meeting that we can incorporate a large amount of what they want in our scheme. It's the beginning of a relationship where someone knows we're listening to them—simple as that—we're all trying to solve the same problem.

Then, at some point I expect a different kind of involvement from the client. It is not a passive, one-way relationship that I am interested in (in contrast to the market-driven architecture that exists solely to please the client). I am most satisfied when my clients are fully engaged at a fairly high level. This is what is required to produce a truly valuable work. When both parties finally come to realize that they have each other's best interests in mind as they sit down to resolve problems . . . then the best work results.

Pressman: *That refers back to your comment that many architects, whether consciously or not, view clients as fools.*

Mayne: We've got great clients. Most of them are eager to be engaged. People want to be part of the work and it's up to us to establish the terms. Doctors and lawyers establish the terms with their clients. . . . Okay, maybe we're not dealing with life and death here (maybe), but in many cases, on larger projects, there are major consequences to every decision. Whether it's about program or budget or timing, it's up to us as architects to establish clarity of dialogue. It's important to be able to articulate the ideas clearly so that when clients are asked to make choices, they can make them intelligently.

Pressman: *And once you've nailed their agenda, their functional, budget issues, and all of that, that gives you an opportunity to then engage in the higher-level discourse—it enables the trust that facilitates the dialogue after they're convinced you can deal with their problems. And then you can elevate the dialogue.*

Mayne: Absolutely.

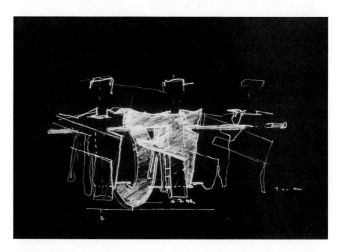

FIGURE 7.1
Sequence of three process images of the school in Pomona. (Courtesy of Thom Mayne.)

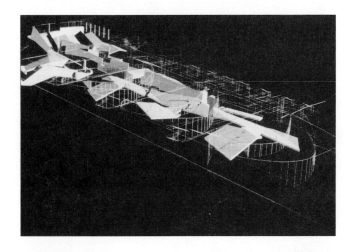

FIGURE 7.1   (Continued)

Awards Programs: "You Like Me! You Really Like Me!"

❏ How many times have you been in the shower and rehearsed your acceptance speech for that big design award?

"I'd like to thank my colleagues, our staff, who worked tirelessly behind the scenes for no money (even though I signed the AIA interns-get-paid-a-lot disclaimer), my clients, who made it all possible, my wife, Meg, who is my collaborator and shining star, and of course my puppy, Sparky, who put up with endless newspaper hits on the snout."

Thomas Fisher, Dean at the University of Minnesota, has had extensive experience managing awards programs and as a juror. Is it all a big game? I asked. Tom acknowledged that juries give awards to their friends and former employees, and likewise, entrants have been known to fool juries into believing they've followed the rules when they haven't. One stunning example of chutzpah and narcissism occurred several years ago when Robert Stern, while chair of a national American Institute of Architects (AIA) book awards jury, gave his own book an award. Is it who you are, who you know, and not the work itself that is being judged?

If You Don't Schmooze, Do You Lose?

❏ Not always, according to Fisher. There are people with integrity, honesty, and courage who prevail. Politics and passion, however, infiltrate this process as much as any human endeavor. So, notwithstanding the intrinsic satisfaction of knowing you did a bang-up job, what constructive actions can be taken by (1) entrants, (2) jurors, and (3) policy makers?

1. *Entrants* must be honest and follow the rules. If the program requires that you have a client, you can't use your sister-in-law to play the role and answer the phone. Fisher says this has happened more than a few times.
2. *Jurors* must excuse themselves if they have a connection with an entrant, i.e., friend, former student, mentor, or date

from last night. How is it possible to remain objective even if you just know that Andy's project is a brilliant work of genius, and should be on top of the pile? Jurors must not attempt to influence the other jurors if such a connection exists, even if they themselves don't vote on the project. What type of connection should make it necessary to bow out? As in any ethical dilemma, there are shades of gray. Moreover, it is important to emphasize anonymity. How do you accomplish that with signature buildings? No one can disguise a Frank Gehry building, for example—although beware of knock-offs. The "riding on the coattails" phenomenon is alive and well. In the 1980s, when Michael Graves was very popular, *Progressive Architecture* and other programs would receive submissions with exactly the same drawing style on yellow tracing paper.

3. *Policy makers* administering the awards program should set forth basic rules of conduct from the start. (Forget about selection criteria—how they should be different for different building types, and so on—that's what Thomas Fisher will address in Supplement 7.1.) There must be an enforcer—Clint Eastwood, or someone like him—to observe and ensure that rules are followed. Less-than-scrupulous people will take advantage of casual rules and no surveillance.

Fisher recounts one instance during the *P/A* Awards when, despite best efforts to select a philosophically and geographically diverse jury, the jurors greeted each other as comrades-in-arms: "We'll have to give one to Frank, one to Peter, and of course Eric." It was as if they were parceling out the honors to their buddies. There was no conflict of interest—they weren't directly benefiting from it—but, as Tom says, it felt too much like a club.

Fisher concluded my interview by beginning to touch on selection criteria. He feels that there should be a much larger critique of awards programs, involving the design of the jury process. Questions about what is included or excluded must be asked. Fisher argues for a greater variety of awards programs, formatted in fundamentally different ways to better serve the profession. This would honor a range of accomplishments and add to the knowledge base of architecture—from the traditional aesthetic, form-oriented jury to those that are exclusively about functional or technical innovations. Tom graciously agreed to elaborate on these major proposals for change in Supplement 7.1.

Ideally, from my generalist stance, none of the categories should be mutually exclusive; functional innovations could be expressed beautifully. Tom says that's a key issue—we want to believe that all this stuff is integrated. In many cases, however, a functional innovation is not strong formally. Maybe the fact is that you can't or shouldn't be good at everything when pushing the envelope. If form is always honored first, Tom continues, we're potentially excluding many other significant projects from the recognition process. This contributes to the marginalization of the profession (yet again, a topic for another supplement, later in this chapter) by shortchanging the perception of what we offer.

Okay, Tom has salient points. Psychology 101 informs us that people, dogs, and architects want to be stroked. Many architects covet recognition, and go to great lengths to get awards for their work. Call it a marketing plan (if you're cynical), insecurity (if you're neurotic), notoriety (if you're narcissistic), noble (if you want to share knowledge to advance the profession), or whatever; many of us naturally seek some sort of validation from peers.

Thomas Fisher

Thomas Fisher is a professor and dean at the College of Architecture and Landscape Architecture at the University of Minnesota, currently the co-editor of Architectural Research Quarterly, *and formerly the editorial director of* Progressive Architecture *magazine.*

What's Missing in Architectural Awards

❏ Few professions award their members as frequently as architecture. And few professions give awards programs as much play in their journals as our field. The two major architectural magazines in the U.S., for example, both devote one issue a year to awards—one for unbuilt and the other for built work—and many of the regional architectural magazines annually publish the awards given by the state chapters of the American Institute of Architects.

This system of awards and publication seems to benefit everyone. The architectural firms that receive awards, of course, get recognition from colleagues, attention from the press, and an honor that can help attract clients and employees. The magazines that publish these awards, in turn, get a lot of editorial material at little cost, since the firms submitting provide the photographs and much of the text. At the same time, the awards issues often prove popular among professional readers eager to see who among their competitors is doing what. Finally, the professional associations that sponsor many awards programs get a chance to fete their members and get publicity in the process.

Criticizing this aspect of the architectural culture thus seems like bad form, like party crashing. But as we pat ourselves on the back in the ballroom, other professions have begun to walk out the side door with the family silver, and we had better pay some attention to that if there is to be much left for us to do after we have handed out all the awards. What have we overlooked amidst all of these awards? Despite all the benefits of honoring each other and publicizing the results, how does doing so blind us to other ways of thinking about ourselves and what we do?

To answer those questions, we need some historical context. The architectural culture has diverse roots, but one of the oldest and strongest grows out of the educational system established by the French bureaucracy in the nineteenth century and institutionalized at the École des Beaux Arts in Paris. Brought to the United States by the founders of some of the early architecture schools here, that system, among other things, put a premium on awarding work. Students would compete for awards as part of their studio work. The most coveted of these awards, the Prix de Rome, gave students a five-year state-supported pension to study in that ancient capitol. The winning of that prize and other top awards at the École also helped ensure one's career in the French bureaucracy, designing the most important public buildings. While some North American architecture schools have carried on this tradition, most of the awarding has now switched to the profession for reasons very different from those of the École.

Awards have become, for architects, the major form of peer review. Unlike most other professions, which have many peer-reviewed journals that evaluate the work of both academics and practitioners and represent the collective body of knowledge in the field, architecture suffers from a lack of research, a dearth of peer-reviewed journals, and even an uncertainty about what constitutes the knowledge base of the profession. As a result, we have difficulty demonstrating the value of what we do apart from the awards granted by our peers. Awards do address the concerns of clients who seek third-party endorsement of a firm they want to commission. Awards also meet the needs within the profession of spotting new talent, identifying new ideas, and changing old assumptions. But awards programs and their publication fail us in important ways, in part because of the way the evaluation and presentation of the work occur.

Awards and publications have certain traits in common. Most awards programs consist of collecting binders or boards, categorizing them, often by building type, and bringing in a group of jurors to judge them. Most awards programs insist that projects be anonymous, although frequently the jurors know the work or can guess its origin. And in most programs, the judging happens rapidly, with jurors having just minutes to see the work and to decide whether to keep it in for discussion in later rounds, so the clarity of the ideas and accessibility of the presentation counts for a lot. Some juries try to decide on criteria before the judging begins, and some organizations running awards programs try to ensure that issues other than aesthetics get considered in the process, but most juries end up basing their decisions on what they see, with little time to read or consider other nonvisual aspects of a project.

The publishing decisions made by editors parallel this process. Here, the work arrives in a steady stream rather than all at once according to some deadline. The editors review projects in much greater depth than most awards juries have time for. And nothing remains anonymous; editors want and need to know who did what, since that becomes part of the story to tell. Still, the review process at most of the magazines differs little from that of awards. Editors need enough material to understand a project without becoming buried in text or photographs; they move quickly past work that holds no interest to spend more time debating those projects that merit discussion; and they decide, ultimately, based on their judgment of what looks like good work and what will appeal to readers. The review process among editors and jurors alike also fosters a certain conformity. Whatever differences exist among those judging the work, they need to reach a consensus in order to get on with things, which adds an element of peer pressure to the peer review.

This can work in an architect's favor, but it definitely does not work in the favor of the profession. It is no coincidence that professions better compensated than ours—such as medicine and law—also have a much more rigorous process of peer review, in which referees review work anonymously and separately and write their opinions without knowing what other referees have written, thus greatly reducing peer pressure. While our form of collective refereeing has its roots in the jury system, it tends to skew decisions in certain directions and exclude whole areas of professional activity.

The judgment of architecture based solely on plans, elevations, sections, and photos is efficient and very effective in evaluating form and functional issues, but this encourages those evaluating the work to overlook other innovations in, say, the relationship with the client, the participation of the community, the process of the design, the organization of the practice, the selection of materials, the delivery of the construction, the management of the facility, and so on. Awards juries do not have the time, or often the inclination, to deal with such matters, and while

Sketches

magazines do, these nonvisual issues tend to get relegated to the front or back of the publication, among the ads and far from the visual feature articles. It's no mystery why clients think our profession doesn't care about much other than form. We demonstrate that in what we award and how we publish time and time again.

Architecture schools have begun to change the way they evaluate student work. Instead of presenting once to a collective jury, students now have one-on-one conversations with individual jurors who move from project to project, giving students practice in presenting and defending their ideas in front of a diverse audience and allowing jurors to focus to a greater degree on their area of interest and expertise. Publications, too, have altered their evaluation procedures. At *Progressive Architecture*, we went from judging work based almost solely on photos and plans to having editors present story ideas at our weekly meetings, with the architecture as illustration. That helped diversify the type and focus of articles, and led to feature articles on practice and technology issues as well as on design. The journal I currently co-edit, *Architectural Research Quarterly*, takes this further, with articles in each issue on a full range of architectural activity—from history, theory, and design to technology, practice, and computation—with peer reviewers rendering independent opinions on anonymous articles.

The time has come to make similar changes to the awards process. The profession needs to find ways to recognize a greater range of innovation and to enable more independent judgments by jurors. One option would be to adopt the traditional peer review process, with jurors reviewing work independently and rendering their judgment based on their particular expertise. Another option would be to have more specialized awards programs, with the appropriate juries focusing just on technical or organizational or intellectual advances. Either way, we need to expand the scope of what we recognize if we are to expand our knowledge base, our range of services, and our perceived value by clients and the general public alike. If not, other fields, more ready to address these issues, will continue to walk off with the family silver—those parts of our profession that are ours to lose.

Marginalization: Not Just a Formatting Problem

Architects Can Influence Policy and Contribute to the Public Good

❑ Many architects share aspirations to improve communities and the environment and to address basic social problems through design. This drive toward civic activism is not only laudable, but essential if practitioners are to enhance the public's perception of architecture and make the field more relevant to broad segments of society.

Activist Strategies

❑ There is growing evidence that architects are skillfully forging alliances in the realms of politics, policy, and education. And there appears to be an increasing awareness of what architects can offer in the civic arena. Local planning and zoning boards, and other profession-related groups—such as the National Trust for Historic Preservation, Main Street, Habitat for Humanity, the Congress for New Urbanism, and AIA chapters, for example—need volunteers or board members. In these roles, architects can be innovative and persuasive in proposing and implementing bold initiatives, and they can testify at hearings on pressing community issues. In a general sense, the skills architects practice virtually every day make them especially effective in public service: a capacity for synthetic vision, problem solving, and group facilitation.

Nonprofit community development corporations, such as the United South Broadway Corporation in Albuquerque, often require advice from architect-volunteers or board members. Architects bring value to such groups because they can specifically guide an A/E selection process, represent the organization's interests in neighborhood planning and economic development, help assess prospective sites, and advise on proposed project feasibility.

Identify Appropriate Organizations

❑ It is critical to approach prominent members of the community to learn where help is needed most. Attending city council meetings is a great way to see who is active in town and to gain insight into the disposition of council members and the mayor. Ask them about becoming an advisor or board member. Moreover, there might be an opportunity to sit on city policy committees. Consider writing an op-ed piece for the newspaper, communicating directly with government representatives, or even running for office.

Community design centers, located throughout the country, typically provide planning, programming, building survey and evaluation, cost estimates, and design services to nonprofit community groups. They are supported by a network of volunteer designers from professional societies and universities. (The Association for Community Design publishes a directory of these centers.) Regional or local foundations also present opportunities for applying specialized architectural expertise. Cornerstones Foundation in New Mexico, for example, is well known nationally for its excellent community-based church restoration program.

Pro bono work can provide enormous benefit to society. "Clients" who might not otherwise be able to afford architectural services—and who really need them for code compliance or other facility improvements—include religious institutions, child care centers, and homeless shelters. This type of work can take many forms, but should be executed with the same reasonable standard of care as any other architectural project. Outline services in writing so all parties are aware of specific objectives.

There are worthy local projects to which architects can offer their special skills and energy. DiGeronimo, PA, architects in Paramus, New Jersey, allots 7 to 14 percent of gross receipts to charities as pro bono service. For example, the firm renovated a halfway house for babies afflicted with AIDS. The house was upgraded (walls, heating system) to comply with code. The architects developed and filed documents with the building department and stayed with the project through construction.

While the motivation to pursue publicly minded work is fundamentally noble, there are secondary pragmatic benefits. Greater exposure and contacts are natural consequences and may produce leads for future work involving the community and important social agendas.

Case Studies

❏ Bruce Fowle, FAIA, of Fox & Fowle Architects in New York City, refutes the Rodney Dangerfield dictum that architects "don't get no respect." Fowle implores architects to "speak about community issues." Contrary to what architects believe, Fowle says the public respects them and wants to hear what they have to say.

Speak out he does, especially regarding zoning initiatives. Fowle is currently involved on an AIA task force that is assessing a proposal to simplify New York City "bulk" zoning regulations. His primary concern is the impact of these restrictions on the quality of architecture in the city. Fowle says, "There's nothing more important than ensuring that zoning regulations are not unduly restrictive and that they allow the culture of the city to survive. Due to zoning constraints on tall, thin towers, you can't even design an Empire State Building anymore!" He believes that if architects are not in the trenches, then developers and bureaucrats will make myopic decisions without considering long-term implications or the public interest. If Fowle and his committee had not been so vocal, an architectural perspective would not be a respected part of the dialogue. Fowle orchestrates a successful system of checks and balances in one of the largest and most politically complex cities in the world.

Architect Michael Pyatok, FAIA, based in Oakland, California, is another brand of activist. He has called on architects to take leadership positions on affordable housing, urban planning policy, environmental sustainability, historic preservation, and design guidelines. Pyatok became active in his local AIA chapter; he held public forums and sponsored talks about the housing crisis. That led to membership in the National AIA Affordable Housing Task Force, which promoted housing-related projects at various chapters. Pyatok observes, "Talented designers have power they haven't begun to tap. They have an automatic platform since they are credible. They can use that platform to advocate important causes at the same time they're making awesome buildings."

Supplementing Fowle's and Pyatok's large-scale approach, Albuquerque architect Mark Childs, AIA, believes architects can use their skills to raise children's awareness of the built environment. He volunteers to work with elementary school teachers to develop and present urban design workshops in the classroom. One urban design game he conducted with second-graders was an original idea he devised for the incremental development of a town. They were enthralled: "Why'd you put your gas station next to my house?" They stayed through recess to play design.

Yet another example of activist effort is illustrated by New York City architect Richard Dattner, FAIA. Dattner is a master at engaging the political process. He "demarginalizes" his practice by selecting commissions that align with his socially responsible principles. For example, Riverbank State Park in West Harlem was built on the roof of a sewage treatment plant in a neighborhood opposed to the plant's construction.

Eight years of political maneuvering included extensive design sessions with neighborhood residents and elected officials. The intent was to demonstrate that high-quality design and programming of recreational facilities would provide a genuine community amenity and neutralize the plant's location, thereby avoiding the NIMBY ("not in my backyard") issue. A constant threat of loss of funding from federal, state, and city agencies prompted the state to require a value engineering analysis.

Dattner responded with creative design solutions that preserved the project's original spirit while reducing costs. His overarching responsibility and determination to contribute to the public good resulted in one of the most frequently used parks in the state.

Architects design projects of all types, but they can also strive to become model citizen-professionals. By wisely embracing social responsibility and political process, they can positively influence the public domain in ways that extend their talent and goodwill beyond buildings. This, of course, has the side effect of enhancing public recognition of the full scope of the profession. In light of societal problems and challenges, it seems especially timely for more of us to consider emulating these examples and becoming agents of progress and indispensable resources in our communities.

Getting Wired

A Conversation with Michael Pyatok

Oakland, California–based Michael Pyatok, FAIA, is an award-winning designer of multifamily housing for nonprofit and for-profit developers nationwide, and a professor at the University of Washington. He holds degrees from Pratt and Harvard, and is a coauthor of Good Neighbors: Affordable Family Housing *(McGraw-Hill, 1997).*

Andy Pressman: *Marginalization is the topic, and I want to get your thoughts on how noble-thinking architects—and I know there are many out there—who have design talent and who are involved with everyday sorts of projects can help raise the profession out of the margins. What can these folks do to really make a difference and become relevant?*

Mike Pyatok: The motivation should come first and foremost from the person's concerns about what they see as not happening properly out there in the world. Either from the point of view of social justice or environmental sanity, whatever the cause may be, the person has to be motivated from somewhere deep inside to want to take action, step out of the mold, be willing to speak up, and begin to join organizations, boards, or committees—whether they be at a neighborhood, city, county, or national level. They need to join efforts to help carry out what they feel deeply about, and must be changed.

They can't be doing it because they want to promote their careers, or because they want to promote the image of architects and improve the standing of architects in the community. They have to be genuinely emotionally charged up on some issue that becomes a cause in their life, beyond just making beautiful buildings. While that's a good cause in and of itself, one must also pursue that simultaneously with thinking about the implications of who they are really serving.

Consider asking questions such as, "Is what I'm doing further destroying the environment or am I actually setting an example?" Just being motivated by doing good design is simply not enough! There have to be social and environmental questions posed by the designer to come to honest terms with what they are doing.

If they find an unsatisfactory response, such as, "Maybe by continually doing this kind of work, I'm not helping many people who need my help, or by helping the people I am, I'm just helping them get richer or more powerful, or in fact hurting others," then they may begin to take action. Sometimes that may mean you don't abandon what you're doing, because people have to make a living, but you accept certain compromises in dealing with the system.

On the other hand, you can begin to make some choices to steer away from certain kinds of projects and client types and begin to work hard toward some that may be closer to achieving those principles you're emotionally charged up about. There are two ways to accomplish this. One, continue to pursue what you're doing by day even if it's out of whack with your principles, but guide it closer to your principles. Two, concurrently, with your free or volunteer time, plug into those organizations, efforts, and movements that are much more directly aligned with achieving in practice those principles that you hold dear.

A number of things happen as a result of this second track. You meet lots of people; you get more informed about the principles you believe in and how you can take action on them. You are, in a sense, simultaneously matching your pursuit of social and environmental principles with the reality that if and when you ever get the opportunity to practice on your own, the only way you're going to be able to do that is to be connected to a very broad network of people. Some of these people may be in positions where they will need to hire architects to implement whatever projects they're pursuing either through their organizations or on their own. So, what it comes down to is that there are ways of unintentionally, in a kind of Machiavellian way, using social causes to build your own career. That aspect of building your own career is secondary—it happens anyway, just by actively pursuing your beliefs and connecting with people. You build more and more rings of folks around you whom you know to be associated with these causes. If you engage hundreds of people—even if you only connect with 10 percent, they may be in positions where they are controlling the investment of monies in the creation of projects that may need architects.

Another recommendation to young graduates is to recognize that they're still highly vulnerable and malleable in their beliefs and career direction tendencies. They are in their midtwenties and they really need about another five or six years of continual exposure to challenging ideas to strengthen their own beliefs. That's not easy to do when they have to face eight hours a day of the nitty-gritty work of architecture. You can't always have the opportunity to step back and think those heavy thoughts. That's why during that period of around 25 to the early thirties, before you have kids, the way to strengthen all those beliefs is to make sure that you're *carefully* using your volunteer time. Your out-of-office time is the realm in which these other belief systems and attitudes will get their opportunity to be nourished and grow. That opportunity in an office setting is rare. That's not to say the office is not good; there's just a whole ton of technical knowledge that needs to be acquired that could never have been acquired in school. And these first five years in the office are critical.

How should these efforts be complemented so that we don't turn into drones or focus on design as an end in itself? Engage in those outside volunteer activities in any kind of environmental or social justice movement. Keep those juices flowing to balance the very essential experience of working in an office to develop technical skills as an architect.

Pressman: *How would you be convincing to those practitioners who have a very narrow definition of design, who think they're great at it, and have been conditioned to believe that through the heroic model in school, and then reinforced by local*

AIA awards? How do you broaden that definition to include application of creative impulses to social causes that can be viewed as design problems in and of themselves? How can enormous talent be directed to the public good, and be satisfying to those who undertake it?

Pyatok: It's interesting to see the choices of work to engage. There are those that include high-end custom homes, shopping centers, and office buildings—that's the sort of mainstream backbone of the system as it is. And the question is: do you put yourself in an environment where that's all that's going on, or an environment where some of that's going on because the firm recognizes that you have to do that for bread and butter, but they're also engaged in other activities? They're pushing the envelope by being be more environmentally sensitive, or by getting involved in public service work—being hired by cities or counties that are struggling with growth management, planning policies, and urban design guidelines, and these broader public service–oriented types of commissions. You seek out firms that seem to strike a balance between those two. Some firms seem to survive solely on the latter kinds of projects.

There is so much planning and urban design work that has to be accomplished today in small- and medium-sized towns, suburban communities, and major cities. To me, this is important public service work. You have to be careful because often that work is commissioned by central redevelopment agencies, and their belief systems are that people with more buying power and the opportunity to own are the more valuable residents of any community. So some of these public agencies have a tendency to cater to their wishes, and tend to ignore the needs of those who have less buying power. Nonetheless, that doesn't mean we avoid those kinds of problems. That's the kind of forum within which those kinds of issues can be debated. You can't debate those issues if you're doing shopping centers, office buildings, and custom residences.

If you are engaged in urban design, planning policy, or growth management, or whatever kind of feasibility studies for the redevelopment of old areas of cities or development of new areas of cities or towns—those are publicly funded commissions. While you may not totally agree with the goals of the agencies that may be funding them, they expect, to some extent at least, some discussion about the full impact of what it is they're attempting to do. Then it is appropriate to raise the concerns that we may have about social and economic justice or environmental sensibilities. They are supposedly representing all the public good by commissioning these kinds of studies and projects. So that's a whole avenue of work that can be pursued.

As a young professional matures, during the first five years—reflecting on my own experience—as much as I thought I knew what I was doing, I also realized I didn't know what the hell was going on! You're naturally hesitant to speak out: your views are not shaped enough and you haven't had enough experience to bolster your confidence. So in those first five, six to eight years, you're still incubating both as a technician and as a carrier of ideas. As you reach the early thirties, and you begin to spread your wings a bit more, then it is possible that you find yourself, both in your volunteer and work worlds, being turned to for your opinions. People begin to believe that you should have something to say by now because you're beginning to have some "stuff" under your belt.

My recommendation to those who are just starting out: be patient! These first seven to eight years represent a long gestation period before you have the capabilities. I usually say that it's not until you're 40 that you should consider yourself a junior professional, and that all the time before that you really were apprenticing. Then by the time you are 50, you kind of know what you're talking about, and by the time you're 60, you're really humming along—it's like breathing. Then you've got about 10 more years, and you die! So we have a short period where we're really at our peak.

Pressman: *What about the more extreme and immediate strategies of getting things done?*

Pyatok: There are certainly more activist organizations out there dealing with environmental issues that are prone to getting involved with protest. That's a different kind of animal than an organization dealing with the same issues but attempting, on a daily basis, to try to implement policy to make the change. So there's the advocacy groups and the implementation. The implementation groups tend to be a bit more moderate because they have to do business with the system both in terms of getting money and spending it properly. So their actions to get projects implemented will be a bit calmer than those who are more activist, advocate types.

I've done both. When I was younger, I was in the former type; I was the activist advocate who was willing to come before a microphone at a council or county meeting, or at any kind of rally or protest and speak my mind. That takes a constant state of emotional charge. As I gradually moved from that into positions as a board member, my life overlapped both of these realms. I began to realize that the way I had to behave, think, function, and speak as an advocate had to gradually be tempered and modified in dealing with the day-to-day realities of projects.

So, you begin to transform, you still have sympathies and support for those who are on the front line doing the shouting and advocacy work; they need to be there. But then as a board member, you have to temper your attitude a bit. You don't want to bring that organization grief, anxiety, or a bad name because one of its board members is considered a bad boy. So you play both roles and gradually transform from one into the other. I think both stages are important in any young professional's life: keep your juices flowing when you're younger and say what you really feel. And then, as you get more skilled in implementation, you learn to be diplomatic in how you say things. You might still be saying what you feel, but you say it in a way that is more digestible by the person you're saying it to—without alienating everyone around you. In the end, you have to get something accomplished, and you need the help of people who don't always agree with you.

Pressman: *Do you find that your background as a skilled architect lends more credibility to what you say?*

Pyatok: Absolutely. An outspoken architect on whatever set of issues will never be listened to with much credibility either by his or her peers or by the general public unless that person has demonstrated over and over again extraordinarily good design work. You've got to be several notches above the norm. In the end, whether we like it or not, that's how we are judged. How well did we get to implement our ideas and how well did the final product stand out above and beyond what is typically done for that building type or project? While one can be engaged in all of these other paraprofessional or metaprofessional activities, the person can never lose sight of the absolutely critical nature of being as good a designer as you can possibly be.

Pressman: *This is the argument that is so central—that I've been looking for—this is something I can discuss with architects who are exclusively focused on "elite" design.*

Pyatok: I can't begin to tell you the importance of the quality of design work that comes out of my office—it gets a level of respect that allows me, then, to speak. Maybe 25 to 30 times a year, I get invited to universities, conferences, or some kind of public forum where I get a pulpit. While I'm showing my work, I'm also talking about—before, during, or after—a whole bunch of other ideas that this audience has to come to grips with that are in some way tangentially related to the work. They deal with social, economic, and environmental issues. I would not get to that position of gaining access to those forums if I hadn't been producing what the profession and others outside the profession consider excellent design work.

Just recently we had our annual office retreat. I gave a little talk to our staff of about 18. I underscored the importance of producing the best work we can. I can't tell you how significant it is to the tenants who live there, the neighborhoods who get the benefit of, and feel good about it, and the nonprofits who can point to it as part of their track record, which makes it easier for them to get into new neighborhoods in the future. Finally, one point that is often misunderstood, and that the staff doesn't see, is the catapult that the work has provided for me to get to positions where I can speak out on all these policy issues that shape the work that we do. I would never get to these positions if the quality of work at the project level were not at the high level we strive to reach.

A Case Study by Michael Pyatok: The Power of Design

❏ I responded to a request for proposal (RFP) from the City of Oakland. The city had four surplus properties in the downtown area—all fairly large, in prominent locations. The city was looking for private developers to develop housing and mixed-use projects. My first take on it was: "Well, most of our work is affordable housing for nonprofits." On the other hand, they were such prominent and important sites, if they got screwed up we'd all feel terrible about it. So I felt obligated, as a designer, and as a resident of the city, to put my best effort forward to make sure that a good project was submitted on at least two of the sites.

I entered on two of the sites. I contacted a developer friend with whom I had never done any work but who knew my work because he would attend awards ceremonies for various housing projects each year on the West Coast that gave awards to both for-profit and nonprofit housing. Then he'd see me winning awards for nonprofit affordable housing and was always surprised to see the quality of the buildings, and realized he couldn't see any difference between them and the market-rate condo development that he does—at least superficially from the outside.

So, he agreed to be the developer, and I would do the design work for these two sites. Another motive of mine for doing these projects was that the mayor and his staff were totally unsympathetic to the concerns of those who felt that not enough affordable housing was being built in the downtown, and the only interest was being shown toward bringing in higher-end folks. I'd written him several letters with no response. I felt, if I win the competition for a couple of these major sites, they'll see me in a different light, and they'll listen to me more, or at least I'll have frequent access to them while doing these projects. Every time I get together with them, I can raise this issue about needing more affordable housing, and they should feel the obligation to provide that.

That is exactly what happened. Our team won; there were about a dozen entries for each of the sites, and ours was considered by far the best design. The city staff and the mayor were thrilled. The night that the council approved our team for the exclusive right to negotiate with the city for these sites, I walked over to the mayor's chief person for this program and said, "Okay, now you owe me one." He said, "What? What do you mean?" I said, "We've brought the city a good developer from San Francisco, we've brought great designs, the mayor is happy, you're going to get more people living in downtown with higher incomes—now you have to spend a day with me touring affordable housing projects in Oakland as a demonstration." I wanted to prove to them that these things are high-quality places, well-managed, and the people who live there are good people, most of whom are working hard to improve their lives and community.

I had to help get rid of the stereotypes these people had about who lives in affordable housing. So he smiled and said, "Okay, it's a deal." And he came with me and the head of the advocacy group for affordable housing in town; we spent four or five hours touring about a half dozen projects and meeting some of the management staff and residents, and it turned him around. He said that he'd never seen anything like this before, and that he would talk to the mayor and bring him on the same tour.

I trace the success of that advocacy effort and changing the opinion of those critical power brokers back to my ability to design. I used it as leverage, as a way of getting my foot in the door. They now had to take me more seriously because I was as good as or better than others in a realm that they respected. They did not have respect for who's doing what in affordable housing. But they had respect for who's doing what in the higher-end market-rate housing. That's the power of design.

Preservation: A Cultural Legacy Under Architectural Stewardship

With Marilys Nepomechie

❑ Supplement 7.2 provides yet another wake-up call: this concerns the value and meaning of preservation and the role architects can play in contributing to the culture of historically significant structures and communities. Architects can indeed be positive forces in confronting the trend toward homogenization of neighborhoods, with their deeper understanding of indigenous conditions and their impact on design.

Marilys Nepomechie

Marilys R. Nepomechie, AIA, NCARB, is assistant professor of architecture at Florida International University and an architect in private practice in Coconut Grove, Florida. Her projects have won numerous design awards and have been exhibited and published both nationally and internationally. The events recounted in this supplement are the inspiration for a current research/publication project documenting and analyzing the vanishing architecture of turn-of-the-century African American neighborhoods in the post-Reconstruction South. (© Marilys R. Nepomechie.)

❑ Initially a movement formed to protect the history of the privileged few, preservation in the U.S. has evolved to include the histories of the varied (and often disenfranchised) ethnic, racial, and immigrant groups that have struggled to make a life in America. Although the necessity of financing the enterprise often ties it to gentrification, preservation, as it is understood today, is ultimately not an issue of aesthetic judgment passed upon a romanticized and commodified past. Rather, it is an interest in the stewardship of a diverse cultural heritage as it is expressed in the physical form of a given place. This is not an easy agenda to either accept or promote—particularly in the face of the painful histori-

SUPPLEMENT 7.2

cal legacies that preservation's new, broader constituency must include. Indeed, the issues and consequences surrounding the prospect of preservation in such cases are highly complex and finely nuanced. My own eyes were opened to some of these issues, as a result of an extraordinary experience with the design of an affordable infill house submitted in response to a competition brief seeking contextual residential proposals for a historic African American Florida neighborhood of the mid-1800s.

In the spring of 1992, the city of Delray Beach and its Community Redevelopment Agency (CRA) sponsored a national competition to design affordable infill houses for scattered vacant lots throughout the turn-of-the-century African American neighborhood of Mount Olive. One of many "Colored Towns" whose labor supported the agricultural and tourist economies of the Florida Gold Coast from its earliest development through the middle of the twentieth century, Mount Olive is still inhabited by the descendants of many of its founding families. In varying stages of disrepair, its homes comprise the fabric of an imperiled place—an historic neighborhood losing its upwardly mobile population to the more affluent suburbs. (See Fig. 7.3.)

FIGURE 7.3
Typical existing "cracker" vernacular bungalow, Mount Olive, Delray Beach, Florida. (Courtesy of Marilys R. Nepomechie, architect.)

Part of a program to provide well-designed, affordable single-family houses for residents with annual incomes ranging from $17,000 to $25,000, the competition was intended to assemble a portfolio of houses for an area with some 300 scattered empty lots. Potential residents, prequalified by the CRA and state lending agencies, would be free to choose new, 1,250-square-foot, $40,000 homes from among the winning designs for construction in their historic neighborhood. The competition brief sought a contextual response. My firm's own entry was a hybrid of two vernacular housing types common across the southeastern United States: the shotgun house, in evidence throughout Mount Olive, and the Charleston, South Carolina, side porch house, brought to south Florida from a region with similar climate and history and original home to many of the neighborhood's original residents. Finding merit in its dignified approach to filling missing teeth in the fabric of a historic neighborhood, the competition jury awarded our small house a first prize. (See Fig. 7.4.)

The cold reception that met this announcement took sponsors and judges of the competition (not to mention ourselves) completely by surprise. Although prospective African American residents of Mount Olive acknowledged that ours was an ideal tropical residence, sensitive to and respectful of their historic neighborhood, they insisted that its relation to the shotgun house tied it too directly to the history of slavery in America. Indeed, enslaved or indentured African Americans constructed some of the earliest examples of the shotgun house in this country in order to lodge the slave labor force of large plantations in the Antebellum South. In the Reconstruction aftermath of the Civil War, legions of newly emancipated slaves carried their building traditions with them throughout the South, accommodating and transforming the typologies from rural agriworker housing to the urban fabric structures of places like Mount Olive, which became the settings for their new lives.

Long before it played a role in the slave history of the American South, however, the shotgun house thrived as a West African (Yoruba) residential prototype. In "The Shotgun House: An African Architectural Legacy" (Vlach, 1986), historian John Vlach writes that the shotgun house was first brought to the New World in the 1700s by means of the West Indian slave trade, taking

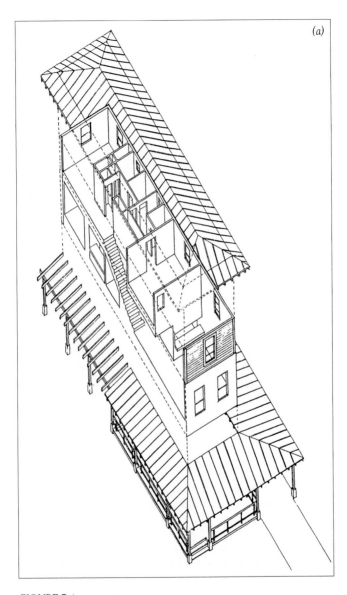

FIGURE 7.4
(a) Exploded axonometric drawing of the competition proposal for a hybrid shotgun–side porch house, Mount Olive. (Courtesy of Marilys R. Nepomechie, architect.)

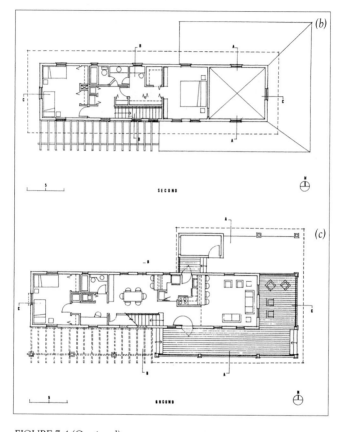

FIGURE 7.4 (Continued)
(b, c) Floor plans of the competition proposal for a hybrid shotgun–side porch house, Mount Olive. (Courtesy of Marilys R. Nepomechie, architect.)

hold in the Caribbean and finding its way to the U.S. through New Orleans and other cities on the Gulf of Mexico. An expression of African cultural heritage maintained in the face of extraordinary strife, today the shotgun house is widely regarded as a significant contribution to the American built landscape. Nevertheless, in the eyes of Mount Olive residents, the erection of any house with a perceptible lineage to a slave past would serve only to stigmatize and marginalize them further. They refused to commission any building with a resemblance to the quarters of their slave forbears and voiced a preference for seeing all the existing examples of those typologies destroyed. Some eight years after the competition, although our project has gone on to win design awards from the AIA, to be both published and exhibited nationally and internationally, and even to be solicited by the developers of such upscale neotraditional Florida towns as Seaside, our small house remains unbuilt in a place where it has deep historic significance, and where it represents a direct extension of local building traditions.

Predictably, the reluctance of Mount Olive residents to build contextually has placed the physical integrity of the neighborhood in real jeopardy, as missing teeth in its fabric are filled with examples of contemporary middle-class tract housing and, gradually, existing vernacular houses are demolished and replaced with more of the same. Similarly, and without fanfare, countless African American neighborhoods throughout the post-Reconstruction South are disappearing. With them, a built legacy of the African experience in the New World is also disappearing, ironically destroyed not by developers bent on demolition for profit, but, more alarmingly—and infinitely more poignantly—by African American residents who see in these neighborhoods stigmatizing reminders of a Jim Crow past. Not only do these neighborhoods comprise some of the largest repositories of wood-frame vernacular architecture in the urban South, but they constitute a large percentage of the surviving examples of turn-of-the-century mid-density urban planning in and around the former Confederacy. Their destruction—that of the only remaining physical record of the African American experience in the southeastern United States at the end of the nineteenth and beginning of the twentieth centuries—becomes the destruction of a material culture of exile for a group whose coerced presence in the New World never paralleled the search for opportunity, freedom, or adventure that characterized the early years of colonization for white European immigrants to North and South America. The eradication of these neighborhoods—either through a physical dismantling or through the gentrification that often accompanies historic preservation— begs the question of whose history deserves (or desires) a place in the collective memory of the New World. (See Fig. 7.5.)

FIGURE 7.5
Typical new construction, Mount Olive. (Courtesy of Marilys R. Nepomechie, architect.)

In what Thomas Fisher, writing as editor-in-chief of *Progressive Architecture*, called "a post-Romantic era of professional practice" (Fisher, 1994), the Mount Olive case study raises important questions. Not only do these probe the ambivalent social role of preservation, but they direct self-reflexive inquiries about the design stance of the profession: as architects, where does our responsibility lie when our professional and social mandates appear to be mutually exclusive? In the context of an (admittedly flawed) competitive process such as the one we entered, in which the jury and the intended inhabitants of its product turned out to have vastly different agendas, is it ever really possible to reconcile disparate aspirations and physical form?

Amos Rapoport has written eloquently on the definition of the house as a cultural phenomenon, explaining that in primitive and vernacular cultures, no single factor determines its form. In *House, Form and Culture* (Rapoport, 1969), he notes that contrary to popular belief, indigenous cultures often build "irrationally"—against the dictates of climate, site conditions, and even of available technology—in favor of expressing religious beliefs, prestige, status. Rapoport explains that "what finally decides the form of a dwelling is the vision that people have of the ideal life." Similarly, in "The House as Symbol of the Self" (Cooper Marcus, 1974), Clare Cooper Marcus argues that the house is our most intimate and universal means of self-expression. She concludes that architects will only serve their clients well when they respond to their clients' concepts of themselves. Yet neither Cooper Marcus, thinking at the scale of the individual, nor Rapoport, at the scale of the community, addresses the fundamentally fluid character of self-definition: with the passage of time, self-definition invariably changes. Neither author acknowledges that the spaces that once described our highest aspirations might, as we change, also require change. Nor do they confront the very real physical costs of disregarding the complexities implied in that fluidity. Invariably, places like Mount Olive are destroyed, either by the external forces of redevelopment and gentrification or by the internal need of residents for self-redefinition. Unfortunately, such communities seldom consider themselves—nor do others consider them—as meriting the attention that will ensure their archival survival in the face of nearly certain physical extinction. As a result, all evidence of the early presence of an entire group of persons in the New World disappears.

Unchecked, its residents' dismissal of the value of their own built history will inevitably lead to the destruction of Mount Olive. And with full respect for their reasoning and wishes, we acknowledge frankly that we may have been mistaken, that our original design proposal may not have been the best or most appropriate response here. Nevertheless we remain, perhaps unreasonably—and certainly uncomfortably—reluctant to concede that the corollary destruction of neighborhoods like Mount Olive should take place. We continue to hope (although not to insist) that their residents might be somehow persuaded that these places are well worth saving. Our own current response to the Delray experience has been to embark on a far more humble project of documentation. Through archival and current drawings and photographs of a series of such neighborhoods in the American Southeast, we—working with the support of their community leadership—hope to produce a physical record of the existence of these places before they completely disappear. We hold out the possibility that both the process and the product of that endeavor will work as tools of persuasion. As architects who perceive their professional responsibility to include stewardship of the built environment—not as a means to freeze places and persons in time but as a way to retain evidence of a rich cultural legacy—we hope that our work will encourage others to preserve, enhance, and transform—but not destroy.

References

Cooper Marcus, Clare. "The House as Symbol of the Self." In Lang, Jon, *Designing for Human Behavior: Architecture and the Behavioral Sciences* (pp. 130–148). Stroudsburg, PA: Dowden, Hutchinson and Ross, 1974.

Fisher, Thomas. "Escape from Style." *Progressive Architecture*, September:59–63, 100, 1994.

Rapoport, Amos. *House, Form and Culture* (p. 47). Foundations of Cultural Geography Series. Englewood Cliffs, NJ: Prentice Hall, 1969.

Vlach, John Michael. "The Shotgun House: An African Architectural Legacy." In *Common Places: Readings in American Vernacular Architecture* (pp. 58–78). Athens, GA: University of Georgia Press, 1986.

Meditations on Quality: Considerations for Designing
With Gregory Palermo

❏ Gregory Palermo's contribution on ethics (Supplement 7.3) is a powerful and important monograph more than it is an essay or sidebar that one would expect in a handbook. No cutesy graphics here. It is simply so good and valuable that it had to become part of this last chapter.

One of the most difficult challenges for any profession is the discussion of ethics. Writing about them, teaching them, and even applying them to practice are also extraordinarily challenging. Palermo's work is transcendent; in rather concise yet dense form, he makes the subject both theoretically and clinically available. His erudite discussion builds to a final statement on what he calls "The Architect's Virtue." This operationalizes the discussion and crystallizes its relevance for practice. Palermo's contribution is a tour de force.

Gregory Palermo

Gregory S. Palermo, FAIA, is associate professor and associate chair for undergraduate studies in the Department of Architecture of the College of Design at Iowa State University in Ames, Iowa. He is a coauthor of Ethics and the Practice of Architecture *(Wiley, 2000). (© 2000, Gregory S. Palermo.) [The "five lenses" presented later in this essay in much condensed form, is the original work of Gregory Palermo and is included in Wasserman, B., Sullivan, P., and Palermo, G.* Ethics and the Practice of Architecture *New York: Wiley, 2000, pp. 80–91.]*

SUPPLEMENT 7-3

❏ Architecture is:

- ■ About people and places
- ■ Meeting utilitarian needs
- ■ Inescapable art
- ■ The design of space
- ■ Structures that make space
- ■ Free thought and ideas
- ■ History and cultural heritage

—Student definitions from the first day of class in "An Introduction to Architecture," January 11, 2000

Part I: Embedded Ethics

❏ Many seemingly everyday events in architectural practices are ethical in their import: business and marketing choices (deciding on what projects to undertake, with whom to work, the values of each, etc.); design deliberations and critiques (function, aesthetics, concepts); budgets (durability of architecture, value for expenditure); client and contractor interactions (honoring contracts, fairness, trust, and advising); contracts (equitable conditions, value for service, mutual respect, and duties); public presentations (who has the right to know and be advised about projects); and staff development and recognition. Embedded within these events are ethical questions. Duties to self, the client, the general public, and the discipline itself can clearly be traced. They are ethical, and demand ethics. It is in the particular questions, in particular circumstances, that architecture's ethics are shaped. When we pull the threads on one of these everyday concerns, what unravels are the deepest questions and premises of the discipline.

Architecture's Essentially Ethical Condition. Architecture in its broadest sense can be conceptualized as the practice of thinking about, designing, and constructing humankind's places of habitation. Those places include buildings, urban and rural landscapes, and interiors. They utilize natural and economic resources, shelter us from the elements, frame spaces for various uses, and symbolize our institutions. The practice of architecture includes immersion into all facets of the discipline, from history and theory, tectonics, and design to the social-political-professional-craft process of bringing built form about. Five ethical precepts are here proposed through which to examine the essentially ethical nature of architecture.

1. Purposefulness. Architecture is grounded in human intention and purpose. It is therefore subject, as are other human affairs, to judgment with respect to its intentions and outcomes: who and what purposes are served by those intentions, how well those intentions are met. These are not only practical or utilitarian judgments, but also ethical ones. For example, intentions and purposes may be beneficial or good (a day care center) or harmful or evil (a genocide machine). A project may serve an economically disadvantaged community (a community-based sweat equity housing project), or it may contribute to suburban sprawl (an urban fringe strip mall). Projects may serve the interests of despots, dictators, military juntas, or democracies; they may serve the interests of powerful individuals against the public interest; and they may displace or marginalize the weak or the discriminated-against (ghettos still exist). Ethical judgment needs to be reached in evaluating the intentions and purposes of architectural projects. Beyond origination intents and purposes, judgment of how well those are met through proposed architectural solutions is another measure of relative merit or goodness of the built result—goodness, in this sense, being the ethical virtue of the work: how well it satisfies its intended purposes.

2. *Material production.* Architecture is a material production.[1] The built inhabited landscape tends to be large and demands many resources for its accomplishment. Once built, even examples of ephemeral, portable architecture such as teepees or yurts have a physical and enduring presence, even if only for a short period of time at any one place. Material production uses natural resources either held or needed in common. Those resources may be used well or wastefully (more than one society has made itself extinct due to desertification of its locale). With the growth in global population and standard of living expectations, sustainable practices of resource use and settlement patterns are almost an ethical imperative.

Constructions may be built well to safely endure winds, rain, earthquakes, and gravity, or they may be constructed poorly, endangering our lives. Ethical (and legal) obligations with regard to the craft and constructional integrity of what is built have a long history. For example, the penalty in Hammurabi's seventeenth century BCE Code, Section 229, for building collapse killing someone was for the builder to be killed; Section 232 requires the builder to rebuild and replace property losses due to faulty construction.[2] When designing and building, an ethical duty is incurred with respect to resources utilized and sustainable conceptions of life, and with respect to personal physical safety.

3. *Aesthetic virtue.* The third precept is that of aesthetics: architecture's relationship to art, its being an art, and its relationship to the philosophy of art and aesthetics, the beautiful and the sublime, and human flourishing. This may be the most debated issue of ethics in architecture, because for many it is the self-aware artfulness of architecture, the desire to make beautiful buildings, that differentiates architecture from mere building, as

Sketches

Nikolaus Pevsner does: "The term architecture applies only to buildings designed with a view to aesthetic appeal."[3] While we disagree with Pevsner's narrow definition of architecture, in its role of giving form, appearance, image and meaning to societal expectations, aspirations, or needs, architecture's aesthetic virtue in the ethical sense is critical to its social contribution to the quality of life.

Architecture, being a material production, results in things, artifacts. One might say that by its very existence and inhabitation—by its duration, even if brief—that a building's practical intents have been met. What differentiates buildings—architecture—as what differentiates other artifactual productions, then, is not the level of service but their aesthetic character, their beauty, aesthetics being supportive of and/or essential to human well-being and/or a discrete presentation of reality or being (depending upon the philosophical position being taken).

In all cases, aesthetics and beauty matter, either as art per se or as a beneficial contribution to happiness or flourishing. The constructions of many cultures—those that are self-consciously aware of the search for beauty, such as contemporary American society, and others, such as indigenous societies, where design values are intrinsic to everyday life—possess aesthetic depth. Thus, a building's aesthetic embodiment is a part of its virtue, its ethical value.

As briefly sketched here, a building's ethical perfection is interdependent upon purpose, material production, and aesthetic quality. This is expressly not the language or the meaning of Vitruvius' utility-firmness-beauty triad. Utility is only one measure of ethical purpose, firmness only one of material production, and beauty in the classic Western sense only one aspect of aesthetic quality.

4. Architecture's rhetoric and ideologies. A fourth lens of ethical consideration is that from within architecture's rhetoric and ideologies. I will use a few examples of design-driven ideologies to illustrate this perspective.

As early as Horatio Greenough in the 1840s, observers in America were calling for a "true American architecture," one that would cast off Europe's formal iconic precedents and that would emerge from American climate, functional necessities (the settlement of America, its commerce and the construction of its institutions), and expression.[4] These themes are later taken up and find manifestation through Louis Sullivan and Frank Lloyd Wright, whose work bridging the nineteenth and twentieth centuries stands in contradistinction to the impact of the 1893 Chicago Exposition, which was still looking to the European Beaux Arts for formal sources.

The Modern Movement's intentions in the first half of the twentieth century were profoundly ethical: to make an architecture of the modern era, to utilize technology of its time, to discard the historical styles and academic architecture, and to address social projects such as worker housing. When combined, these strategies were to sweep aside capitalist bourgeois class restrictions and to make a more egalitarian society, using architecture as a vehicle to give it form and expression. Whatever its naivete viewed in hindsight, this was an ethical stance. Even though after the Museum of Modern Art exhibition of 1931 the aesthetic of modernism was usurped as an object of connoisseurship and adopted by the modern corporation (exactly opposite its original objectives), many of its intentions continue to have ethical merit.[5]

Another ideology with ethical force is that of sustainable design—designing in resource-conserving ways and with materials and methods that slow the degradation of resources so that future generations will have a world to inhabit. This is now a growing force in the direction taken by contemporary architecture.

In the Greenough, Wright, Sullivan, Modern Movement, and environmental sustainability ideologies, interlocking intentions, social-political-economic-cultural threads, and formal strategies to support them are proposed as the premises for a "true architecture:" architecture with an explicit intent to make the world better through design—an ethical architecture. Other conceptual positions, relying upon the relationship of architecture to power, social elites, and controlling mores, and upon architecture's potency to construct order (while simultaneously excluding "others"), frame additional aspects of the ethical in architecture that are linked to rhetoric and ideology.[6]

In addition to ethics that arise from design ideologies, there are ethics that may arise from process ideologies—such as the philosophy that architecture is a problem-solving process, or that public architecture ought to be the result of public participatory design processes, each of which implies methods and means that have an ethical import.

Design and process rhetoric and ideologies, which speak to architecture's purposes, aesthetics, and methodologies, define the discipline and profession. Understanding those definitions and acting from them is another basic framework for considering architecture's ethics.

5. *Praxis.* Praxis is defined as "Practical application or exercise of a branch of learning."[7] The term is used here to highlight the total array of practices that making architecture requires, and to break the implied business or professional limitations often associated with practice. Praxis focuses us on thoughtful action arising from the knowledge of a discipline. In addition to its being the built landscape, architecture is a practice, or a collection of practices—an art. The architectural practitioner is obliged to master knowledge of the discipline: its history and theory; its technological foundations; its order of beauty and formal conception; methods of problem statement, speculation, and design conception; its impact on human well-being and capacity to satisfy of intended purposes; its representational and symbolizing capacity; and its processes of concept origination, decision making, client consultation, and construction processes. To do otherwise is to not practice architecture well—to practice without virtue. *Virtue* is here used in the sense that contemporary philosopher Alasdair MacIntyre has recaptured from Aristotle: that of the virtuous practice of a discipline, which defines its content, quality, and ends and which therefore can be judged regarding its ethical merit.[8] This applies to both the activities of practicing and the resultant works of practice.

As noted at the beginning of Part I, many seemingly everyday events in architectural practices are ethical in their import.

Summary Proposition: The making of architecture is an ethical event; the architecture made is constructed ethics!

Part II: Could Be, Ought to Be, and the Architect's Virtue

❏ Architecture (shaping the landscape we inhabit) is fundamentally a projection about a future state of affairs: what could
be. The origination of architectural projects lies in a specific person, a committee, a board of directors, or a community of persons
dreaming and conjecturing about the future: if I (we) were to
build a new place (a church, an office building, a genetics
research laboratory, a school, etc.) then life would be better
(worship would be more meaningful and inspired; the work and
laboratory environment would be more commodious and supportive of productivity; learning would be enriched, etc.). We do
not undertake architectural ventures to lower the quality of life.
Making architecture, thereby positively influencing the quality
of life, is about creating that beneficial situation toward which
humanity strives—what ethicists refer to as the good. And architectural practice is a futures-oriented process—designing and
making decisions regarding the particular way that future state of
affairs ought to be. The shift from what could be to what ought
to be is an ethical shift.

By common definition, an architect is a person who possesses
the skills and knowledge, and who practices the art and science
of building design, including landscapes within which buildings
occur and the spaces within buildings. What are the attributes of
the knowledge, skills, and practicing capabilities that comprise
the definition of the architect's virtue—that is, the qualities of
excellence without which one cannot be an architect? These
themes are explored in the following sections.

1. What could be. Architecture arises when we decide to
change the environment we inhabit to suit some intention of
ours. *Environment* is used here rather than *buildings* or *architecture*
to encompass a range of scales from the rural and urban landscapes to the room and the furnishing and outfitting of rooms.
We dream or make careful conjectures of what it is we desire.
This occurs not only through the names we give to types of
places and their functions (school, factory, prison, power plant),
but also through our feelings (to give visible formal expression to
our civic institutions, to satisfy our need for more beautiful

places). Architectural intentions emerge in particular social, political, and economic circumstances. They are never value free; they are always then value laden.

Clients express these qualities of what could be in many ways. It is rare that someone building a home does not have a sheaf of clippings and color photos of "places they like," or have visited, that "are like" what they want—but not exactly, of course—they want something fresh and new, theirs. The program is not the square footage and the list of spaces but rather the spirit of what they understand "new" and "desired" to be. For institutional and corporate clients, we visit precedent projects. Same thing: what is out there is like what we aspire to, but is a departure point for us, not an end point.

One client presented me and the project team with a one-page program for a $135 million project. At the bottom it said, "Design the hotel with this idea in mind: when you return on your next visit, the doorman will remember your name." Another client, a private college with a 170-year-old central quadrangle bounded by red brick and limestone buildings, wanted to build a computer/satellite/distance education media center on the last open site framing the boundary of the quadrangle. One of the trustees asked: "You are not going to put some steel, concrete, and glass building in there, are you? We don't want you to copy the existing buildings, but we don't want you to affront them either." These are value statements about the quality of what a place could be; the spirit and character that ought to infuse design proposals. Designing the form of those proposals is the task of architecture.

The ethical center of architecture is this: architecture does not belong to the architect. Architecture is about distilling the essence of what could be in the client's terms, however broadly *client* may be defined. It is the essential act of discerning architecture's purpose in a given circumstance. Such listening and understanding is more than a programming and design skill; it is more than good business practice; it is an ethical mandate. Without it, architecture is an abstract formal exercise in search of a reason for being.

2. What ought to be. When conjecture about the environment moves to action to bring about a desired end, a shift happens.

Intentions are defined more formally in terms of spaces and needs, desires and value expectations are more clearly articulated, budgets are developed, site locations and contexts are defined, etc.: the architectural project is defined. The architect's contribution is this: explorations, analyses, inventions, and creation of specific design proposals that address the issues at hand. Form and image are made specific; how a place ought to be is definitively proposed. Utilitarian objectives are resolved; structural, environmental conditioning, and construction assemblies are designed; appearance beauty and image are determined; all of this is subject to economic resource allocation. Out of an infinitude of possibilities, a singular proposal—or at most a limited number of proposals—is shaped. The architect's invention redefines what could be as what ought to be. It becomes, in Karsten Harries' terms, "construction of ethos."[9]

No amount of design value discussion about accommodation of heterogeneous readings, alternative generative models of architectural space and form, or virtual possibilities changes the fact that the architectural proposition is ultimately, if only for a short time, fixed. It is what it is. In any design proposal, there are a particular set of relationships between landscape and building form, exterior form and interior space, the room and the object, image and meaning: these are physically, visually, and experientially particular. They are how it ought to be—the *it* being the place and the manner of inhabitation to be inseparably constructed. The architect has made an ethical determination of the best way to change the environment to support the better way of life that was the originating position of the project.

Two fundamental aspects of what ought to be in proposing and realizing architecture are its material realization and the experiential result.

2a. Material realization of what ought to be. Envisioned environmental changes—the architectural design—are realized through tectonics: construction methods and assemblies. Particular materials and technologies, possessing particular visual, sensual, durability, constructive, and economic qualities that extend a design concept into reality, are selected and specified. Architectural fabrications tend to be large, using many material and energy resources, some renewable, some reusable, and some not renewable or reusable. Fundamental to design configuration is the manner in which environmental forces that demand energy control, such as heat, humidity, and cold, impact the interior of a structure—because such energy forces require that countervailing energy resources be expended to ameliorate them for comfortable human occupancy. A building, normally considered a design invention, a spatial and decorative work, or a construction of inert material, is also an ecological construction.

The ethical content of material production has several aspects beyond fire safety and structural integrity: durability to withstand weathering and use, life expectancy, sustainability, labor contribution, and so on.

2b. Experiential result. In the end, architecture is not ideas about architecture, its generative models and methods, or the events of its origination and construction. It is not its representations of itself: it is not graphics, computer visualizations, or models. It is itself. It is a phenomenon to be experienced[10]—not only visually (the Western eye is powerful in its shaping of experience), but in time and motion, and via scent and sounds and heat and tactility. Our mental/poetic interpretation of the direct experience of a particular architectural work may sense that work's origination, may ascribe an imagined history to it, or may evoke realizations or remembrances in us, and we may judge and resonate to its aesthetic character from our perspective. It will be inhabited and judged for its capacity to support our lives. Solitariness, communal social gatherings, the rituals of social institutions, the rituals and habits of everyday life—they all take place somewhere: the places, the architectural frameworks of our experience.

The ethical challenge is this: no design decision—e.g., relation to context, form and space, functional resolution, aesthetic quality, material fabrication—is neutral. The architect needs to understand the experiential implications of design proposals. They are all culturally connected; they are all consequential for the present-day life and into the future. In Winston Churchill's terms: "We shape our buildings, and afterwards, they shape us!"[11]

3. The architect's virtue. The architect's virtue is this: the capacity to design ethical landscapes.

We can normatively describe the stuff that an architect needs to master. Architectural practice in our time will of necessity be framed in the terms of our time. Mastering these requisites is a condition of the architect's virtue. Without them, the architect does not possess the capacity to design ethical landscapes.

- Exploring architectural history and precedent to date
- Developing and maintaining a knowledge base of architectural theories and ideas
- Continuing to develop effective methods of design and invention
- Rethinking the cultural heritage of the West and its position in a compressed, diverse "e-world"
- Mastering a respect for, and basic understanding of, the material and productive technologies through which architecture is realized
- Utilizing emerging technologies
- Nurturing greater understanding of global sustainability and addressing sustainability through design decisions, and understanding site ecology
- Understanding contemporary conditions of practice and professionalism; developing the capability to conduct design processes that engage the public, government officials, contractors and craftspeople, clients, and other designers
- Fostering collaborative and interdisciplinary approaches to addressing environmental design questions
- Searching for forms of these times and those of the near future rather than seeking comfort in nostalgia
- Developing a capacity to invent architectural space and form

We add to this all sorts of specialized knowledge, such as that of contracts, design media, and the specifics of contemporary construction systems, the policies and techniques of historic preservation, how to calculate beam sizes and heating loads, the capacity to be a continuous learner, etc. This core knowledge of the architectural discipline supports the gift of talent, as well as personal initiative and the passion to pursue excellence.

These are beginning points. The specific relevance of many of them will fade in the future, with new aspects taking over. The larger ambition of continuous self-motivated learning about architecture, and recognizing the manifestly rich and ethical role that architecture plays in life, is what will prevail.

However, this knowledge in the abstract has limited merit. One remains, as Vitruvius points out in Book I of the *Ten Books of Architecture*, "chasing the shadow, not the substance of architecture." Two fundamental ethical challenges for the architect are described here: the discernment of what could be (conceptions of what would be good), and the generation and realization of design solutions for what ought to be (determination of what is right in order to bring about that good). Only when core knowledge of the discipline is refined and applied to the inherently ethical dimensions of architecture is the architect's virtue realized.

Epilogue

❏ This brief essay does not identify specific ethical problems or tasks such as how to be fair to contractors, how to guard the client's financial interest during construction, how to assure accessible buildings, determine how safe is safe enough, etc. Nor does it judge one type of building purpose—say, day care centers—compared to another—prisons. Nor does it explain traditional ethics—the search for the good, the right, and the just, in its classic teleological and deontological forms. What has been attempted is a general model defining the enduring episodes of architectural work that have ethical dimensions inherently within them. Nor is it an end point, providing discrete answers about architectural ethics. The reader is challenged to consider his or her own design efforts in light of the proposition here that architecture is an intrinsically ethical discipline—recognizing that those ethics are under construction.

Notes

1. Stating that architecture is material production does not deny the critical power of architectural thought and speculation. It is only that such speculation in drawing, text, modeling, film, and

other media and virtual reality simulation is architectural—of architecture—and a stimulation to imagination, but it is not architecture.

2. Hammurabi, King of Babylonia, *The Hammurabi Code and the Sinaitic Legislation* (trans. Chilperic Edwards, 1904). Reprint, Port Washington, NY/London: Kennikat Press, 1971.

3. Pevsner, Nikolaus. *An Outline of European Architecture* (7th ed., p. 15). Harmondsworth, UK: Penguin Books, 1963. Pevsner's words resound through history and resonate with many: "A bicycle shed is a building; Lincoln Cathedral is a piece of architecture. Nearly everything that encloses space on a scale sufficient for human beings to move in is a building; the term architecture applies only to buildings designed with a view to aesthetic appeal."

4. Greenough, Horatio. *Form and Function: Remarks on Art, Design and Architecture* (Small, Harold A., ed.; introduction by Erle Loran). Berkeley, CA: University of California Press, 1947 and 1966.

5. Robert Twombly addresses this in *Power and Style: A Critique of Twentieth-Century Architecture in the United States* (pp. 52–88; New York: Hill and Wang, 1996). The MOMA exhibition publication coined the phrase *International Style* and applied it to the Modern architecture that had emerged in Europe between 1918 and 1930. Colin Rowe explores Modernism's program and style in *The Architecture of Good Intentions: Towards A Possible Retrospect* (New York/London: Academy Editions, 1994).

6. Joining Ulrich Conrads' *Classic Programs and Manifestoes on 20th-Century Architecture* (trans. Michael Bullock, Cambridge, MA: MIT Press, 1970) are four new compendiums of short texts that provide fertile ground for initial exploration of architecture's moral intents through its ideologies and rhetoric: Ockman, Joan (ed.). *Architecture Culture 1943–1968: A Documentary Anthology* (A Columbia Book of Architecture; New York: Rizzoli, 1993, [with the collaboration of E. Eigen]); Nesbitt, Kate (ed.). *Theorizing a New Agenda for Architecture: An Anthology of Architectural Theory 1965–1995* (New York: Princeton Architectural Press, 1996); Stein, Jay, and Spreckelmeyer, Kent (eds.). *Classic Readings in Architecture* (New York: WCB/McGraw Hill, 1999); and Hays,

K. Michael, (ed.). *Architecture Theory Since 1968* (A Columbia Book of Architecture; Cambridge, MA: MIT Press, 1998).

7. *American Heritage Dictionary of the English Language*. Boston: Houghton Mifflin, 1992.

8. MacIntyre, Alasdair. *After Virtue* (2d ed.) London: Duckworth, 1984. [Particularly Chapter 14, "The Nature of Virtues."]

9. Harries, Karsten. *The Ethical Function of Architecture* (p. 4). Cambridge, MA: MIT Press, 1997.

10. Benedict Spinoza pursues an intriguing exploration of the necessity of the direct perception and experience of the essence of a thing in its reality, rather than the idea or representation of it, in his short essay *On the Improvement of the Understanding* (1677).

11. Churchill, Winston. *Winston Churchill: His Complete Speeches, 1897–1963* (8 vols.). James, Robert Rhodes (ed.). New York and London: Chelsea House and R. R. Bowker, 1974. [House of Commons speech, 28 October, 1943, p. 6869.]

Sketches

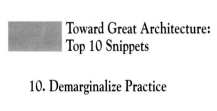

Toward Great Architecture:
Top 10 Snippets

10. Demarginalize Practice

❏ Creative and activist application of design talent and knowledge can help architects influence policy and contribute to the public good. Addressing basic social and environmental problems will make the field more relevant to broad segments of society.

9. Celebrate Context and Stakeholders

❏ As cited by David Lewis, the late Jules Gregory implored architects to "hear the nuances, so that every new building would be a graft spliced into the heart of a living city . . . and be accountable not only in technical terms, but socially, economically, and culturally." We need to widen our focus from buildings to places in order to be optimally sensitive and responsive to clients, users, and the cultural landscape.

8. Seek Economy of Means

❏ Derive the most from our precious resources. This is especially salient for environmental sustainability issues. This notion also has application to meaningful and beautiful form making in which components are configured and assembled to create a rational and artful whole.

7. Employ Digital Technology to Enhance Design

❏ Take full advantage of the computer alone and in concert with other media to fully investigate design possibilities. This constantly evolving and powerful tool creates new potentials for innovation and synthesis of fresh ideas and their implementation.

6. Cultivate Passion for Construction and Engineering

❏ The architectural design process is meaningless and myopic if it is not truly and completely informed by construction and engineering processes. John Brittingham makes the analogy that details can be seen as words composing a sentence. As the selection of words and styles gives meaning to a sentence, the selection of details and their manifestation gives character to the architecture of buildings.

5. Communicate Effectively with Clients, Colleagues, and the Public

❏ The information delivery process may need to be as creative as the design itself. Communication skill is very much a part of the design process. Excellent work ends up on the cutting room floor if clients or the public do not perceive it as excellent. Moreover, significant discussions with the client and collaborators are invaluable in eliciting information that helps define the problem and provide cues to solve it. New York clothing retailer Sy Sims' advertising sound bite, "An educated consumer is our best customer," eerily applies to architecture. Architects have a pedagogical responsibility to broaden clients' perspectives about the built environment.

4. Inform Time Management with Overarching Priorities

❏ It is crucial to think about the relevance of what one does, and its implications for prioritizing time. Another way of voicing this goal is captured in the following quote from noted Austrian psychiatrist Alfred Adler, in his discussion of the importance of striving for superiority. Adler said, "The impetus from minus to plus is never-ending. The urge from below to above never ceases. Whatever premises all of our philosophers and psychologists dream of—self-preservation, pleasure principle, equalization—

all of these are but vague representations, attempts to express the great upward drive." The point here, of course, is that the overarching goal to do something of real significance and meaning should be wedded to the way we use our time, to achieve the noble ends.

3. Pursue Lifelong Learning

❏ It would seem self-evident that seeking continuing education is simply something all practitioners would want to do, because it's inherently interesting material related to one of their central passions in life. Consider design competitions as one of the most enlightening continuing education strategies because they offer the freedom and luxury to experiment with and hone design thinking. The experience can then be applied to "everyday" projects to elevate the quality of their designs.

2. Promote an Ethical Stance

❏ The basic mission of a professional is to provide a service that is value laden. Unlike the artist, who creates beauty and emotion, and unlike the scientist, who discovers and explains, the architect also has to do good. It is not easy to do good in a complex world. Gregory Palermo suggests that "the making of architecture is an ethical event; the architecture made is constructed ethics!" Refer to his supplement (Supplement 7.3) for a transcendent discussion on this topic.

1. Raise the Bar

❏ Because it is so easy to whine about the mediocrity surrounding us, we need to be especially conscientious about allocating energy toward creative and activist methods of raising the level of meaning and content in architectural design. Thom Mayne suggests that excellent architecture is a consequence of one's life and career experience; that project research and investigation become integral with one's development over time. Mayne says, "Bringing to bear something outside the pragmatic engenders architecture. . . . An architecture of quality does not exist absent an intense interest and commitment to formal qualities, pragmatic issues, environmental questions, tectonics and so on, which are quite separate from issues of program and budget."

general references

Allen, Edward, and Iano, Joseph. *Architect's Studio Companion: Rules of Thumb for Preliminary Design*, 2d ed. New York: Wiley, 1995.

Brookes, Alan, and Grech, Chris. *The Building Envelope and Connections*. Oxford, UK: Architectural Press, 1996.

Brown, G.Z. *Sun, Wind, and Light: Architectural Design Strategies*. New York: Wiley, 1985. [Illustrations by V. Cartwright.]

Cherry, Edith. *Programming for Design: From Theory to Practice*. New York: Wiley, 1999.

Childs, Mark. *Parking Spaces: A Design, Implementation, and Use Manual for Architects, Planners, and Engineers*. New York: McGraw-Hill, 1999.

Cullen, Gordon. *The Concise Townscape*. New York: Van Nostrand Reinhold, 1961. [Reprinted 1990.]

Frampton, Kenneth (ed.). *Technology, Place and Architecture: The Jerusalem Seminar in Architecture*. New York: Rizzoli, 1998.

Goldman, Glenn. *Architectural Graphics: Traditional and Digital Communication*. Upper Saddle River, NJ: Prentice Hall, 1997.

Jones, Tom, Pettus, William, and Pyatok, Michael. *Good Neighbors: Affordable Family Housing*. New York: McGraw-Hill, 1995.

Lam, William M.C. *Perception and Lighting as Form-givers for Architecture*. New York: Van Nostrand Reinhold, 1977. [Reprinted 1992.]

Laseau, Paul. *Graphic Thinking for Architects and Designers*, 2d ed. New York: Van Nostrand Reinhold, 1989.

Lynch, Kevin, and Hack, Gary. *Site Planning*, 3d ed. Cambridge, MA: MIT Press, 1984.

Moore, Fuller. *Environmental Control Systems: Heating, Cooling, Lighting*. New York: McGraw-Hill, 1993.

Simonds, John. *Landscape Architecture: A Manual of Site Planning and Design*, 3d ed. New York: McGraw-Hill, 1998.

Stein, Benjamin, and Reynolds, John S. *Mechanical and Electrical Equipment for Buildings*, 9th ed. New York: Wiley, 2000.

Wasserman, Barry, Sullivan, Patrick, and Palermo, Gregory. *Ethics and the Practice of Architecture*. New York: Wiley, 2000.

Yatt, Barry. *Cracking the Codes: An Architect's Guide to Building Regulations*. New York: Wiley, 1998.

about the author

❑ Andy Pressman, NCARB, AIA, is associate professor and director of the Architecture Program at the University of New Mexico, and leads his own architectural firm based in Albuquerque. His work has been featured in over 20 professional, scholarly, and professional publications, including *Architectural Record*, *Architecture*, and *The Washington Post*. He has written five books on architecture, and holds a master's degree from the Harvard University Graduate School of Design.

Cover photo © Steve Rosenthal of New England Residence designed by Andy Pressman, AIA Architect.